THE WALL STREET JOURNAL ON ACCOUNTING

Lee Berton
Jonathan B. Schiff

Dow Jones-Irwin
Homewood, Illinois   60430

Sponsoring editor: Jim Childs
Project editor: Waivah Clement
Production manager: Irene H. Sotiroff
Jacket design: Mike Finkelman
Compositor: Compset, Inc.
Typeface: 11/13 Century Schoolbook
Printer: R. R. Donnelley & Sons Company

Library of Congress Cataloging-in-Publication Data

Berton, Lee.
   The Wall Street Journal on Accounting / Lee Berton, Jonathan B.
Schiff.
      p.   cm.
   ISBN 1-55623-225-X
   1. Accounting—United States.   2. Accounting—Standards—United
States.   3. Finance, Public—United States—Accounting.   I. Schiff,
Jonathan B.   II. Title.
HF5616.U5B47   1990
657—dc20   89–36247
                                                               CIP

Printed in the United States of America

1 2 3 4 5 6 7 8 9 0 DO 6 5 4 3 2 1 0 9

INTRODUCTION

This book should be useful for accountants and non-accountants alike, and for others who want to know more about the complexities of accounting but find the subject too technical, too dull or seemingly irrelevant. Because these articles were written for *The Wall Street Journal*'s vast audience of 2 million readers, they attempt to demystify accounting.

The articles also try to show the enormous impact of accounting on people's livelihoods, their retirement benefits and the nation's business and economic climate. Few people except accountants seem to know the far-reaching effects of accounting rules under which business, government and nonprofit entities operate. If the public could grasp the influence of accounting on people's lives, I am sure they would be vastly surprised.

As former editor of a major magazine for accountants—The *Journal of Accountancy*—I have often been asked why I cannot be more sympathetic to them. Covering the accounting profession as a writer for *The Wall Street Journal* is similar to a political reporter's mission in the nation's capital. Thus, I'm obliged to write about the warts as well as the wows.

The reader may ask why accountants are so often criticized for failing to warn the public of impending financial disasters. The answer may be that, like ancient messengers, they are the targets of people who rely on their message. Columbia University scholar Jacques Barzun said it more than a decade ago: Public expectations are a lot higher of society's professionals than they used to be. And the mystique that had been built around all professions, including accounting, is rapidly disappearing.

Accountants bridle at being used as the "deep pocket" for collapsed companies whose investors look for villains with pots of cash to insure these investors against their own mistakes. Accountants must remember that in the early 1930s, they asked the government for the job of watchdog for the public over many of the nation's business affairs. Accountants, after all, audit the books of public companies. They audit the financial reports of government units. They help business set up systems to keep companies and nonprofit organizations whole. They tell us whether it was worth putting our money or efforts into certain enterprises.

This book examines how accountants themselves sharply criticize their own standard-setters, how accountants are attempting to police their own profession thus preventing government intervention and how accountants try to market their services without eroding their integrity, which is, after all, the hallmark of their profession.

The public often clamors for better financial disclosure and for increased help in figuring out the growing intricacies of tax law. Accountants are supposed to be the first line of defense against financial ignorance. And big questions are often raised as to whether they do their job well, or even do it at all.

This book looks into the elaborate rule-making mechanisms and rules with which accountants must grapple. And it tends to show that accounting isn't a science or even an art. Judging from the criticisms leveled at accountants, maybe accounting is pursuing a will o' the wisp that can never be captured: a perfect financial reporting system that tells us everything we would like to know.

Accounting academics are fond of telling the tale of the balloonist who landed in a field and asked the first passerby where he was. "You're in a basket in a field," the passerby replied.

"You must be an accountant," the balloonist said. "Your information is perfectly accurate but it's of absolutely no help."

"And you," retorted the accountant, "are typical of all balloonists. You're in a craft over which you have no control. And you want me to tell you where you're going."

As you will see from this book, accountants play an important role in tax reform, industry and investment strategies, detecting fraud and informing business and the public about the costs of resources and benefits and how to preserve them. Despite providing such needed services, accountants rarely win medals. And their standard-setters often are the object of brickbats from within and outside the profession.

There is no question that society needs accountants. But as far back as the time of ancient Egypt, the Roman emperors blamed accountants for hard times in the Empire. So it should be no surprise that when the accounting profession's main rule-making body—The Financial Accounting Standards Board— was formed in 1973, it should be called "a minnow in a pool of sharks." One major accounting firm has called the FASB's pension ruling, forcing some companies to put bigger liabilities on their balance sheets, "a turkey."

As this book will show, the FASB has amazingly survived, and its rules affect the lives of everyone. Its rules can alter our retirement benefits, pay, bonuses and other work incentives. The FASB also can affect the capital-raising process and the machinery of Wall Street by issuing rules on the cost of issuing certain securities and by deciding whether certain borrowings can be kept off the balance sheet.

This book details some of the key issues the FASB will be facing in the future:

Should U.S. companies reserve for future medical and insurance benefits paid to retirees? These costs aren't deductible from taxable income and could hit corporate profits with the impact of a falling giant redwood tree.

How should savings and loan associations value the new and riskier business deals that volatile interest rates have forced them to initiate?

Should the value of stock options be deducted from profits, making such options less attractive for start-up companies trying to woo executives from long-established giants of industry?

Victor H. Brown, an FASB member and former chief financial officer for the Firestone Tire & Rubber Co., conceded that while financial reporting is basically good and fair and only blemished now and then by fraud or lack of disclosure, an expectations gap continues with the public and legislators. "There is always a tension—a gap—between what is expected and what can be delivered," Mr. Brown said in an interview with my co-author Jonathan Schiff. "While I don't see the gap disappearing, I think that efforts to narrow it have been, and are, constructive."

Besides chronicling changes in that gap, this book attempts to take the reader through a recent history of the accounting world. It is a journey filled with potholes, turns in the road, nightmares—ending in a touch of humor to ease the tension.

Lee Berton

CONTENTS

PART 1

THE NEW WORLD OF ACCOUNTING

CHAPTER 1

WHO'S WHO IN
ACCOUNTING TODAY

Knowing the backgrounds of the key players in the accounting community can help in understanding this complex profession and its impact on business. The field of accounting is attracting talented, strong and capable individuals into its top ranks. This trend will continue as more of our top business students come into accounting and related fields. Once the province of "trade school" education, accounting today is a business discipline that has strengthened its image within the academic halls, as well as in the corporate boardrooms.

FASB Appoints D. R. Beresford
As Its Chairman

By Lee Berton

September 18, 1986

Dennis R. Beresford, a partner of Cleveland-based Ernst & Whinney, has been appointed chairman of the Financial Accounting Standards Board, the chief rule-making body for accounting.

Mr. Beresford, 47 years old, succeeds Donald J. Kirk, 53, who has been chairman since 1978. Mr. Kirk was eligible for reappointment, under FASB bylaws. Mr. Beresford was appointed to a five-year term, effective January 1.

He joined Ernst & Whinney, the third-biggest U.S. accounting firm, in 1961 in the Los Angeles office, and was made a partner in 1972 and national director of accounting standards in 1976.

Mr. Beresford has been an activist member of the FASB's 15-member emerging issues task force since its inception in July 1984. The task force attempts to deal with pressing accounting problems, and its members often push the Stamford, Connecticut-based FASB for action in disputed areas.

Accounting profession observers say that Mr. Beresford will likely urge the FASB to be more timely in setting standards. Critics score the FASB's lengthy due process procedures in rule-making. They note that in such areas as inflation and taxes the FASB didn't get rules drafted until after the economic conditions that led to the rules had changed.

Mr. Beresford "has top practical and technical experience for the job and will seek to expedite standards for accounting problems so the rules aren't too little and too late," said Douglas R. Carmichael, an accounting professor at the City University of New York's Baruch College.

Thornton O'glove, publisher of the *Quality of Earnings Report,* a monthly for institutional investors, says Mr. Beresford is a "household name in accounting who is certainly on top of every major accounting issue."

In an interview, Mr. Beresford said he will press the FASB to "continue its open lines of communications" between standard-setters and federal regulators. If Congress or the public worry that accounting standards "aren't working well enough, these are matters that the FASB should address," he added.

FASB's Beresford Wants Rules Set Faster

New Chief Faces Major Accounting Issues

By Lee Berton

February 6, 1987

STAMFORD, Conn.—When Dennis R. Beresford speaks about accounting for income taxes, stock options and retirement benefits, business had better listen.

The 48-year-old Mr. Beresford has just taken over as chairman of the Financial Accounting Standards Board, the chief rule-making body for accountants.

After the nine-year chairmanship of Donald E. Kirk, 54, who just retired, Mr. Beresford begins a five-year term on the standards-setting body during a critical time for U.S. business.

"The accounting issues faced by American corporations over the next three years will have major impacts on profits and borrowing positions," says Joseph Sciarrino, a vice president and technical director of the Financial Executives Institute, an organization of 13,000 corporate financial officers.

"Our members will be watching every move the FASB makes because the upcoming accounting issues can affect financial health as much as heavy competition and poor economy," Mr. Sciarrino adds.

Thus, Mr. Beresford, former national director of accounting standards for Cleveland-based Ernst & Whinney, will be directing the FASB during one of the board's most crucial junctures.

What the 14-year-old board decides could be a major factor

in spurring economic well-being or malaise for corporations and the nation, financial executives and economists say.

As a former member of a major FASB advisory body, the emerging issues task force, Mr. Beresford was outspoken on accounting issues important to business and the time it takes to implement changes. Last year he openly chided the board for not moving quickly enough on the issue of accounting for deferred income taxes, which would affect the profit of most U.S. companies this year.

Speeding Decision-Making

As chairman, Mr. Beresford is more anxious to speed the FASB's decision-making than to completely change the board's operating procedures. "I would like to see the time trimmed between adding a project to our agenda and issuing the first proposal," he says, noting that some projects currently take two to three years to reach the point where a draft proposal is published.

Some critics of the board, however, say that Mr. Beresford is far from being radical on accounting issues and will be far more conservative than several other candidates who weren't selected for his job.

Mr. Beresford, who likes to play golf and read detective stories for relaxation, fits the image of a conservative, wearing pin-striped suits tailored to fit his 6-foot-5, 185-pound frame.

His predecessor, Mr. Kirk, has guided the FASB through the controversial waters of accounting for currency translation, inflation and pensions. But Mr. Beresford may encounter even greater storms ahead. Facing the seven-member board are such thorny issues as accounting for:

Income Taxes. U.S. companies have built up vast credits on their balance sheets for deferred income taxes they have yet to pay. The FASB must decide whether to pare such longtime credits because of new lower tax rates, a move that would result in sharply boosted corporate profits for 1987.

At the same time, the FASB may take a big bite into profits by forcing the same companies to set up balance sheet reserves for unrepatriated foreign earnings or earnings of unconsolidated U.S. subsidiaries. "It would be a big hit that most multinational companies won't like," says James J. Leisenring, the FASB's research director.

Mr. Beresford says the FASB is scheduled to decide this issue in the third quarter after public hearings. "We're moving quickly to expedite this issue because of its importance," he says. Tentatively, the FASB staff has decided to back off on the reserve for unrepatriated foreign earnings, he adds. "This would make a lot of multinationals happy," Mr. Beresford says.

Stock Compensation.   The value of stock options granted by companies to employees isn't currently deducted from profits. The FASB has proposed that companies granting such options take a charge against earnings, and many start-up and high-tech companies have complained that this change would hurt them because they have limited funds.

The FASB is scheduled to issue a final rule next year, but may delay it if the clamor grows too loud. "The big problem for the FASB staff is to determine fair values within a reasonable degree," says Mr. Beresford. "But we are aware of business concerns. Our mission is to reflect economic consequences, not cause them."

Retirement Benefits.   Controversial accounting rules on pension costs issued late in 1985 raised the hackles of many financial executives at companies with underfunded pension plans. That's because the rules forced the companies to sharply boost debt on their balance sheets.

Now the FASB is considering assessing a liability in advance for post-employment health and insurance benefits—a much more explosive issue than pension costs for two reasons. One is that while companies fund pension costs in advance, other benefits generally are recorded only when they're paid. The other is that total liabilities for such benefits would be billions of dollars bigger than for pension benefits.

The FASB will hold hearings and issue a proposed rule next year. "This could be one of the most controversial issues the board will deal with," Mr. Beresford says. "Accruing such costs could be relevant since some bankrupt companies have tried to stop such benefits. But others would argue that disclosure of the liability is sufficient since legal obligations to pay such benefits are open to question."

Consolidating Results

The standards-setting body has other issues on its plate over the next few years that are sure also to bring gray hairs to corporate financial executives, accountants say. For example, how the FASB decides whether to consolidate results of majority-owned subsidiaries or joint ventures could load a lot more debt on the balance sheets of many U.S. companies. Those most likely to be affected are companies with finance subsidiaries, or corporations in heavy industries such as energy, autos, steel and construction.

The FASB plans to issue late this year a final rule on whether to consolidate results of all majority-owned subsidiaries. Currently, most U.S. companies don't consolidate the results of such subsidiaries, particularly if the unit is in the financing business.

"As to joint ventures, we have seen instances where three public companies in a joint venture all report their interests and obligations to the venture differently," says Mr. Beresford. "For the sake of consistency alone, aside from off-balance sheet financing issues, we will have to tackle this question over the next few years."

Other Issues

Other issues for the FASB over the next two years involve disclosure and measurement of liabilities connected with new financial instruments, how insurance companies should report earnings and obligations from certain insurance products, and accounting by utilities to recover construction costs on big projects approved by regulators.

"Each of these issues will raise hues and cries among the corporate community," concedes the FASB's research director Mr. Leisenring.

'Cheap Shots'

The FASB's former chairman, Mr. Kirk, who came to the board from Price Waterhouse, says he doesn't want to offer Mr. Beresford any advice. But Mr. Kirk notes that on occasion business-men unhappy with the board's action try to take "cheap shots" at the FASB or to use "strong-arm" tactics. He says such tactics include flooding the staff with a stream of form letters denounc-ing the board but containing little substance.

"We only got the difficult issues," says Mr. Kirk, who is cur-rently teaching financial reporting at Columbia University's Graduate School of Business in New York.

Mr. Beresford will be paid well for the pressure he will en-counter from business, the banking and Wall Street community. His annual salary is $300,000 and fairly comparable to what he earned at Ernst & Whinney, the third biggest U.S. accounting firm. Other FASB board members earn $240,000 a year.

Though Once Bitten, Abernathy Isn't Shy

By Lee Berton

May 15, 1987

NEW YORK—John D. Abernathy, chairman of Seidman & Seid-man, the accounting firm, shudders when he remembers the early 1970s.

In 1972 Seidman acquired Wolfson Weiner & Co., a small Los Angeles-based accounting firm whose principal client was Equity Funding Corp. of America. Equity Funding collapsed a year later after fraud was uncovered involving management and Wolfson Weiner.

"It was the toughest period of my professional career," re-calls Mr. Abernathy, who was named Seidman's director of ac-counting and auditing in 1973, the year the scandal broke. "It was difficult to obtain new business for several years after that."

A Wolfson Weiner partner served three months in prison for helping Equity Funding management cover up $2 billion in non-existent life insurance policies. Investors, trusts, pension funds and endowments lost many millions of dollars in the fraud.

Rapid Growth

But the 50-year-old Mr. Abernathy, who was named Seidman's chief executive two years ago, didn't let the Wolfson Weiner debacle sour him on mergers. Since mid-1985 Seidman has acquired 16 local accounting firms, boosting its revenue and becoming the 11th-largest firm in the United States, up two notches. Revenue is expected to spurt 30% for the fiscal year ending June 30 to $145 million, after a 30% gain the year before, he estimates. Seidman has 283 partners in 46 offices.

Still, aware of how a faulty merger can muddy an accounting firm's reputation, Mr. Abernathy says he learned a lesson from the Equity Funding incident. "If you acquire another accounting firm, you'd better be sure it has a solid quality-control system," he says. "Since Wolfson Weiner, we're a lot more careful."

Nevertheless, he adds, Seidman has "begun to accelerate our pace for acquiring other CPA firms."

Mr. Abernathy receives much of the credit for Seidman's growth. "He has woken up a formerly sleepy accounting firm and helped erase the Equity Funding scandal," says Arthur Bowman, editor of an Atlanta-based accounting newsletter.

Maintaining Standards

But not everyone in the industry applauds Mr. Abernathy's penchant for acquisitions. "We don't want mergers for the sake of growth alone," says Charles Kaiser, managing partner of Houston-based Pannell Kerr Forster, the 13th-biggest firm. Mr. Kaiser says he is happy with Pannell Kerr's 15% annual growth rate, fueled mostly by new business, although the firm has made four acquisitions in the past year and a half. "It's difficult to absorb a lot of mergers at any one time and retain high standards," he adds.

Mergers among accounting firms have become a way of life in the 1980s as competition heated up for a pool of audit clients that has been diminishing because of the corporate merger boom.

Mr. Abernathy says it is possible to grow through mergers and still retain quality; about half of Seidman's current revenue growth stems from mergers. Before making an acquisition now,

Seidman sends teams of partners to check quality-review procedures and work-papers.

"I was very impressed with Seidman's thoroughness," says Ernest Davies, a partner in the former Leopold & Linowes in Washington, D.C., which Seidman acquired in September. Now a Seidman partner, he recalls that Seidman sent audit and tax partners to check on selected work-papers for two days last August. "They asked a lot of technical questions indicating they have high standards."

Mr. Davies says Mr. Abernathy went out of his way to make sure former Leopold & Linowes personnel retained their esprit de corps. "After the merger, he sent us all a personal letter saying that if any uncertainties arose, we should feel free to phone him personally. I didn't, but knowing I had the option gave me a feeling of security."

Carol Raimondo, a former partner in Brigante, Suarez & Raimondo, Torrance, Calif., and now a Seidman partner, recalls that Mr. Abernathy invited her firm's four partners to Seidman's annual meeting in Dallas weeks before the firm was acquired last November. "He made us feel we weren't the flea being swallowed by the elephant," she says.

New Frontiers

While considered "low-key" and conservative by colleagues, Mr. Abernathy says that increased competition among accounting firms makes it necessary to push out to new business frontiers. "We've got to develop more profitable services," he says.

As a result, he is steering Seidman into uncharted waters, such as helping clients obtain financing, assessing clients' business risks and appraising businesses for tax purposes.

Also, in an unusual move for an accounting firm, Seidman has registered a personal financial-services arm as an investment adviser with the Securites and Exchange Commission. The business, which offers investment monitoring, estate planning and life insurance analysis, has five offices in five cities, and will expand to 10 or 12 offices by September.

A soft-spoken, second-generation accountant, Mr. Abernathy is considered a "people person" by employees, a colleague says. When Seidman's New York staff moved to a new office recently, the lean, 6-foot-2-inch executive helped some staff members pack and lift cardboard boxes.

Mr. Abernathy likes to work out business tensions on the golf course; he plays in the low-80s to mid-80s. He takes a lesson from the sport. "Equity Funding is well behind us now and the future is bright," he says. "As on the golf green, you can't replay a previous hole, but have to learn from your mistakes."

Wyatt Quits FASB; Some Cite His Views

By Lee Berton

August 4, 1987

NEW YORK—Arthur R. Wyatt has resigned from the seven-member Financial Accounting Standards Board in a move that some accountants say reflects Mr. Wyatt's frustration over the growing role of businessmen in accounting rule-making.

Mr. Wyatt, 59 years old, was scheduled to end his first five-year term on the FASB—the chief rule-making body for accountants—at the end of 1989. But accountants close to the FASB said that Mr. Wyatt decided to leave earlier because of his disappointment over the direction in which the FASB has been headed.

While Mr. Wyatt, a former partner of Arthur Andersen & Co., a major accounting firm, wouldn't comment on specific reasons for his leaving the FASB, accountants who know him said that he has been upset about being passed over for chairman and is currently discouraged by what he considered the FASB's slow pace and toning down of certain accounting rules. Mr. Wyatt was one of three candidates for FASB chairman late last year, but wasn't picked because his views are so strong on standard-setting, accountants said.

"The FASB is meeting the needs of businessmen, rather than the needs of users," said John C. Burton, dean of Columbia

University's Graduate School of Business. Mr. Burton, who was chief accountant of the Securities and Exchange Commission from 1972 to 1976, added that the FASB is losing "its best member as far as the public interest goes."

Asked about his plans, Mr. Wyatt said he is considering several job possibilities in teaching and at accounting firms and will take some time "to look around." His resignation is effective as soon as a successor is appointed, but not later than the end of this year.

"Obviously certain things here (at the FASB) led me to want to do something else, but I'm not going to be disruptive about this," Mr. Wyatt said.

Earlier this year at a public FASB meeting, Mr. Wyatt criticized the FASB for failing to move quickly enough to set accounting rules that would stop businesses from orchestrating sales and leasebacks of assets to keep debt off the balance sheet. He also has urged the board to move more quickly on its project to require companies to consolidate in their financial statements the results of all majority-owned subsidiaries. The latter rule would boost debt shown on a company's balance sheet.

Pressure on FASB Denied

Businessmen deny they are pressuring the FASB to give them more leeway with accounting principles or to move more slowly in rule-making. "Business is only expressing the view that the benefits derived from accounting rule-setting should exceed the costs," said Eugene H. Flegm, an assistant controller at General Motors Corp. and author of a 1984 book that strongly criticized the FASB. "We don't consider this undue pressure, but our right to express our opinion," he said.

However, Columbia's Mr. Burton noted that almost 30% of the FASB's $11 million operating budget for 1986 was paid by contributions from more than 2,100 companies; public accounting firms contributed only 23%, he said. He pointed out that the FASB, acting under pressure from business organizations, late in 1985 appointed a second business representative to the seven-member board. The other members are from public accounting firms, government and academia.

Another Business Representative
Critics of the FASB also have noted that the Financial Accounting Foundation, which funds the FASB and appoints its members, last year said it planned to add another business representative to its 16-member board of trustees. This would balance the five foundation trustees from public accounting firms with five representatives from business and banking by the end of the year. The other trustees are from government, Wall Street and academia.

Mr. Wyatt, a former member of the accounting faculty at the University of Illinois at Champaign-Urbana, has been earning $240,000 a year as an FASB member. Duane Kullberg, managing partner of Arthur Andersen, where Mr. Wyatt was a partner before joining the FASB, said that "when Art left us we recognized that he had strong opinions regarding accounting and gave him a standing offer to come back if things don't work out."

Touche Ross, Setting Precedent, Names a Lawyer to Top International Position

By Lee Berton

September 1, 1987

NEW YORK—Touche Ross International named Richard H. Murray, a 50-year-old lawyer, as its executive director. It is the first time a major accounting firm has named a lawyer to its top international post.

Some leading accountants said the choice of Mr. Murray indicates how pervasive liability problems have become for accountants world-wide. "Picking Rick recognizes that law is now a major business problem for major CPA firms," said John C. Burton, former chief accountant for the Securities and Exchange Commission and currently dean of Columbia University's Graduate School of Business.

Major U.S. accounting firms have paid out more than $300 million in legal settlements and judgments since 1980 in professional malpractice cases.

New York-based Touche Ross International consists of 54 affiliated accounting firms with 490 offices and 30,000 employees in 89 countries. Its largest member firm is Touche Ross & Co., the eighth biggest U.S. accounting firm.

Edward A. Kangas, chairman of Touche Ross International's executive committee and managing partner of Touche Ross & Co., conceded that naming a lawyer head of Touche's international operations is "an unusual move." He said that a few Touche Ross partners asked why a lawyer, rather than an accountant, was picked.

"Mr. Murray is more a leader than a lawyer and has been very active in helping the many Touche Ross International member firms handle their insurance and risk management problems," Mr. Kangas said. "As global financial markets demand more standardized accounting principles and auditing approaches, we feel Rick is the right man for the top job."

Highly Regarded Expert

Mr. Murray, who has been Touche Ross & Co.'s general counsel since 1974, is considered one of the top legal experts on accountants' liability and audit risk. Two years ago, he was a main force in organizing a captive offshore liability insurance company for the eight biggest U.S. accounting firms. A captive insurance company is one that is owned by the insured firms, which also provide the funds to cover any claims. Mr. Murray also has been chairman of the insurance unit, Professional Asset Indemnity Ltd., which writes excess liability coverage for the Big Eight.

In discussing his selection to the post, Mr. Murray said, "It wasn't because of the liability problem but because of my years-long involvement with the firm's administration."

With Mr. Murray as general counsel, Touche Ross & Co. has been able to limit its payments for court judgments and out-of-court settlements in malpractice suits to about $6 million since 1980—among the lowest payments of the Big Eight.

Intense Pursuit of Goals

Accountants at Touche say that Mr. Murray is intense and single-minded when trying to implement a new business strategy. "Rick doesn't try to muscle anyone, but he simply wears them down with his ability to work day and night to accomplish new strategies," says Mr. Kangas.

A graduate of Harvard University and Harvard Law School, Mr. Murray was successively a partner in two Midwest law firms before joining Touche Ross in 1974.

Mr. Murray will become executive director of Touche Ross International today, succeeding two men who share the job, John F. Keydel in New York and Douglas R.P. Baker in London. Mr. Kangas said Messrs. Keydel and Baker plan to retire as Touche partners within the next three years.

As executive director, Mr. Murray will be responsible for coordination of business and strategic planning as well as maintaining adherence to professional standards of the 54 member firms.

Mr. Murray is considered articulate and rarely loses his poise, even when provoked, colleagues say. At a recent meeting of Touche Ross partners, a British journalist insulted lawyers, joking that they were considered to replace white mice in laboratory experiments but were rejected because "people can't get as attached" to lawyers as they do to mice. Mr. Murray smiled and retorted: "Only a journalist would follow white mice and lawyers around."

In the fiscal year ended yesterday, Touche Ross International's world-wide revenues rose 30% to about $1.5 billion, Mr. Kangas estimated. Touche Ross & Co.'s U.S. revenues, which are included in the world-wide figure, rose 14% to about $650 million. Touche Ross has 2,600 partners world-wide, including 829 in the United States.

Weinbach Named to Andersen's No. 2 Job

By Lee Berton

September 16, 1987

NEW YORK—Lawrence A. Weinbach was appointed to the newly created position of chief operating officer world-wide of Arthur Andersen & Co., one of the biggest international accounting firms.

Mr. Weinbach, 47 years old, is former chairman of the board of partners of Chicago-based Andersen world-wide and former managing partner of the firm's New York office.

Mr. Weinbach is known as a tough boss who pushes partners to work long hours. "Our people are going to have to work harder to develop new business and provide greater resources for our clients," Mr. Weinbach says.

Andersen will need a "hard driver to get their partners' adrenalin flowing to meet the stiffer competition for business among the major accounting firms," says James. C. Emersen, publisher of the *Big Eight Review,* a Bellevue, Washington-based monthly newsletter for accountants. "Such internal growth can replace the technique of merger for growth, which is creating new and formidable rivals to Andersen for U.S. and world-wide business."

Last April, Peat Marwick, then the second-biggest U.S. accounting firm, acquired KMG Main Hurdman, the ninth-largest, and eclipsed Andersen as the biggest firm world-wide. Andersen and Peat are tied for the biggest U.S. firm, based on annual revenue.

'Morale Builder'

Mr. Weinbach as New York managing partner since 1980 has shown he can manage one of the most competitive U.S. offices. "New York area partners are tough, independent thinkers and not easy to manage, but Larry expects as much of himself as he does others," says an Andersen partner. "He's a good business and morale builder." Mr. Weinbach works as many as 60 or 70 hours a week, colleagues say.

Duane R. Kullberg, 54, was elected to a third four-year term as Andersen's managing partner and chief executive officer. Mr. Weinbach, in his new position, will remain in New York and report to Mr. Kullberg, who heads the firm.

Mr. Weinbach's father, a Waterbury, Connecticut, furniture-store owner, died when Mr. Weinbach was 12, and the son earned his way through the University of Pennsylvania's Wharton School on a work-scholarship program. "In high school, I worked as a part-time teller in a bank," he recalls. "It was rare in school for me to have an extra penny in my pocket."

Accountants say that with increased competition, it is fitting that Mr. Weinbach should be picked to head Andersen's operations because he will keep a close eye on the dollar. Andersen's operations are being reorganized into three regions worldwide and into five regions in the United States. Mr. Weinbach says the reorganization will permit Andersen "to marshal more resources regionally for big jobs in audits, tax and consulting work."

Developing Computer Systems
For example, Mr. Weinbach says Andersen plans to organize teams of as many as 100 professionals to handle "systems work for multinational clients, securities firms and governments." Andersen is developing about a dozen new computer systems for tracking trading positions and exposures for securities firms in London and Tokyo, he says.

"We plan to hire 7,500 more personnel world-wide over the next year which is 15% to 20% more than we hired a year ago in such areas as consulting for telecommunications, manufacturing and the capital markets," Mr. Weinbach says. "In the past, our hiring needs have risen only up to 10% annually."

As part of his new job, Mr. Weinbach will be responsible for the profits of 226 offices with 2,100 partners of Andersen world-wide. In the United States, Andersen has 80 offices and 1,250 partners. Mr. Weinbach estimated that in the fiscal year ended July 31, Andersen's world-wide revenue rose more than 20% to

$2.3 billion, and U.S. revenue rose more than 10% to about $1.5 billion.

"We're going to really have to stay on the stick to keep up our 20% growth internationally as this business becomes more competitive and specialized," Mr. Weinbach says. "My success or failure will depend on how well we do that."

In the United States, Andersen's biggest audit clients include ITT Corp., Texaco Inc., Salomon Brothers Inc. and Merck & Co. But in Europe, Peat Marwick—by acquiring KMG's operations in the Netherlands, Britain, West Germany and France—has vaulted over other major accounting firms including Andersen to become the biggest accounting firm in Europe.

"There's no doubt that Peat is now our toughest rival in Europe, and we don't have a lot on our plate there," Mr. Weinbach says. "But don't count us out, because we plan to put more emphasis on our European business in the future."

Andersen's Lawrence Weinbach Picked to Head Firm Amid Its Restructuring

By Lee Berton

March 23, 1989

NEW YORK—Lawrence A. Weinbach was nominated to be chief executive officer of Arthur Andersen & Co., the biggest U.S. accounting firm, which recently has been rocked by defections of consulting partners.

Mr. Weinbach, the firm's 49-year-old chief operating officer, is assured of election to the post, as he will be the only candidate on the ballot when Andersen's 2,200 partners vote next month, the firm said.

Mr. Weinbach will succeed Duane R. Kullberg, 56, who resigned in January to help expedite a restructuring of the firm. Mr. Kullberg, who had been named chief executive in 1980, was completing a third term ending in 1991 when he abruptly de-

cided to quit amid friction between consulting and other partners. Andersen said Mr. Kullberg will become a senior partner
and "help implement the restructuring."

The announcement of a successor came sooner than expected. "This pick was fast and early," said James Emersen, publisher of the *Big Eight Review,* a monthly newsletter for accounting firms. "It had to be, because the firm has been in limbo for
several months and needs a new leader, a new team in place and
to get on with its business."

At a news conference, Mr. Weinbach said that after the early
1990s, consulting may account for more than 50% of Andersen's
revenue, which is expected to top $3 billion this year. Consulting
now contributes about 40%.

As to how he plans to stop further defections of consultants
from Andersen, Mr. Weinbach said the recent reorganization
boosted compensation for high-revenue producers such as consultants and increased participation of consultants in the firm's
organization. In recent months, about 35 consulting staff members, including seven partners, have left Andersen.

"You can't mandate within an organization that people must
remain," Mr. Weinbach said. "People stay because they want to,
but we've created ways to solve our compensation problems and
to get sufficient representation of consulting, audit and tax partners, and geographic units in separate Andersen business
units." Mr. Weinbach said that six of the 12 members of the committee that nominated him are consultants.

Andersen has sued a group of consultants that left the firm,
which also has the biggest U.S. consulting organization. The suit
seeks to stop the defendants from acquiring or using trade se-
crets belonging to Andersen and from continuing to raid Andersen's personnel. The group has countersued, claiming that Andersen is violating antitrust laws by trying to put these
consultants out of business.

Accounting observers said Mr. Weinbach, who has been Andersen's operating chief since late 1987, will have many tough
problems to solve in his new post. Mr. Weinbach "will have to
balance the relatively slower growth of Andersen's audit and tax
practice with the explosive expansion of consulting, and keep
both sides happy," said Arthur Bowman, editor of a monthly

newsletter for accountants that is published under his name in Atlanta.

Mr. Bowman said that if "dissension continues among top partners at Andersen, it will filter down through the ranks and hurt the firm."

Andersen recently set up separate units for consulting, auditing and taxes. Consulting partners defecting from Andersen and other major accounting firms had complained that they hadn't been adequately compensated for bringing in bigger chunks of the profits in recent years.

Mr. Weinbach joined the audit staff of Andersen in New York in 1961, following his graduation from the University of Pennsylvania's Wharton School. He was elected a partner in 1970, and in 1983 became managing partner of the New York office and area managing partner for metropolitan New York.

He is known as a tough boss who pushed partners to work long hours. His father, a Waterbury, Connecticut, furniture dealer, died when Mr. Weinbach was 12. Mr. Weinbach went through Wharton on a work-scholarship program.

Departing SEC Accountant Who Favors Full Disclosure Is in Lead for FASB Post

By Lee Berton and Bruce Ingersoll

September 25, 1987

Clarence Sampson, chief accountant of the Securities and Exchange Commission and the most powerful member of his profession for more than a decade, will retire next year and is the leading candidate to join the Financial Accounting Standards Board.

Mr. Ingersoll is a staff reporter of THE WALL STREET JOURNAL.

Accountants say his appointment would strengthen the resistance of the FASB, the chief rule-making body for the profession, to pressure from corporations who have been pushing the FASB to reflect more closely the comments of business in its rulings.

At the FASB, Mr. Sampson would "represent the views of users of financial statements and will help the board remain more independent of pressures from the business community to ease accounting rules," said John C. Burton, the former chief accountant of the SEC and dean of Columbia University's graduate school of business.

Mr. Sampson, who is 58 years old and will have 30 years of government service under his belt by mid-November, won't confirm the possible appointment publicly. But he has privately told a few colleagues that he is interested in the FASB job.

Duane Kullberg, chairman of the selection committee of the Financial Accounting Foundation, which will pick a new FASB member by the end of next month, confirmed that Mr. Sampson is one of four candidates. "Until the actual selection, I can't say more than that," Mr. Kullberg said. Sources close to the foundation say Mr. Sampson is the leading candidate.

Full Disclosure Advocate
Mr. Sampson was appointed the SEC's acting chief accountant in September 1976, succeeding Mr. Burton, and was named as chief accountant in October 1978. He is known as a strong advocate of full disclosure for users of annual reports, and he has been adamant at meetings of FASB task forces in pushing FASB decisions toward more conservative and uniform accounting treatments of financial data.

"Clarence obviously knows the subject of accounting and has established a credible record as chief SEC accountant," Mr. Kullberg said.

An imposing presence at accounting profession meetings, Mr. Sampson has been known to influence the fate of rule-making initiatives with a mere nod of his head. Mr. Sampson is 6 feet 4 inches tall and always wears a bow tie, making him seem taller, say colleagues. During John Shad's five-year reign as chairman of the SEC, Mr. Sampson played an important role in the agency's campaign against financial fraud and accounting irregularities.

If Mr. Sampson is appointed to the FASB job, his salary would jump from $77,500 to $240,000 a year. Even if he isn't selected for the FASB job, he said he will retire sometime next year from the SEC. He has put in 28 years at the agency, but because of two years of military service, he will pass the 30-year mark Nov. 17, making him eligible for early retirement.

Representing Government

The spot Mr. Sampson would fill on the seven-member FASB is being vacated by David Mosso, 61, a former U.S. Treasury Department official who must retire from the FASB after two five-year terms. Mr. Mosso has been filling the seat representing government on the board, and the Financial Accounting Foundation is seeking another government official for the spot.

Last week, the foundation picked James J. Leisenring, 47, as a member succeeding Arthur R. Wyatt, 59, who resigned earlier this year because of his belief that the FASB was influenced too much by business.

Mr. Leisenring, the FASB's director of research for the past five years, is also considered a strong advocate for users of financial reports and is known to resent pressure from business to have more of an influence on the board.

Last year both Mr. Wyatt and Mr. Leisenring were passed over by the foundation, which funds and selects members for the FASB, as candidates to head the FASB in favor of Dennis Beresford, a former Ernst & Whinney partner who is considered more moderate in his views.

The SEC already is planning to fill a key accountant vacancy. Robert Sack, 53, left as chief accountant of the SEC's enforcement division at the beginning of this month to become a lecturer at the Darden School of Business Administration of the University of Virginia in Charlottesville. Mr. Sack has worked on many of the SEC's major accounting cases over the past three years.

The changing of the guard at the SEC would be complete if Howard P. Hodges Jr., chief accountant of the agency's corporation finance division, decides to take early retirement.

Price Waterhouse Picks Shaun O'Malley as Chairman, Surprising Many Partners

By Lee Berton

November 30, 1987

NEW YORK—Shaun F. O'Malley, 52 years old, has been named chairman and senior partner of Price Waterhouse, the fifth-biggest U.S. accounting firm, effective July 1.

His selection to a five-year term by Price's 18-partner nominating committee comes as a surprise to many Price partners because Mr. O'Malley, who has been partner in charge of the firm's Philadelphia office since 1980, wasn't considered a front-runner for the job.

A leading contender was Dominic A. Tarantino, Price's vice chairman, taxes, along with three other top Price partners. "There isn't any front-runner until the smoke comes up," said the 55-year-old Mr. Tarantino. "It would have been a great honor to be picked, but I think the selection was excellent and support it in every way."

Mr. O'Malley's reputation as a hard driver stressing client service, and his closeness to Joseph E. Connor, the 56-year-old current Price chairman who has held the job for a decade, may have been big factors in his selection, say some Price partners.

In mid-1988, Mr. Connor becomes chairman of Price Waterhouse World Firm, the umbrella organization that includes Price's chief U.S. firm. In four years, Mr. Connor will reach the firm's mandatory retirement age of 60, so he didn't seek re-election for the top U.S. post.

International Organizations

Accounting firms' international organizations, such as Price Waterhouse World Firm, advise affiliated firms in each country on business strategies and professional standards. Of Price Waterhouse World Firm's $1.75 billion in revenue for the year ended June 30, the U.S. firm contributed $848 million.

In the United States, Price has long been considered the Tiffany of the Big Eight firms because of its major share of audits of big U.S. companies. But problems have been cropping up over the past few years.

Last year, for example, it lost Bankers Trust Co. as an audit client to Arthur Young & Co. and lost several other major clients because of mergers. And a $6.5 million consulting job for the New Jersey Division of Motor Vehicles turned out a disaster; motor vehicle registrations were held up and mishandled, and Price had to pay $3 million of its own money to correct the problems.

But Price has made a strong comeback this year with new clients, and Mr. O'Malley doesn't seem daunted by the competitive pressures facing accounting firms.

"We're going to focus hard on getting the right people for the right jobs for our clients, which could mean creating new partners," he says. "Also, I want to make sure Price fires up new global initiatives to meet tougher competition overseas by moving key people around more quickly than the current chain of command permits."

Price has long had among the least number of partners per professionals of the major firms, and Mr. O'Malley concedes it could be a problem beefing up the current number. Price has 810 partners in 112 U.S. offices.

Price recently boosted entry-level pay for top accounting graduates 20% to 35% but eliminated overtime pay, which has been a long tradition for starting accountants, particularly during the busy tax season. The move hasn't yet been matched by other big accounting firms, which nonetheless say they'll remain competitive and that without overtime, the boost isn't as big as it seems.

Mr. O'Malley concedes that the increase for entry-level accountants will cost Price's partners $15,000 a year, but says it's worth it.

"Even those of us who supported the move aren't happy about taking money out of our own pockets," Mr. O'Malley adds. "But we have a trusteeship to hand to the next generation running this firm a better share so that they make a longer term commitment to public accounting."

Long Hours

A Philadelphia native and one of eight children, Mr. O'Malley began his freshman year at the University of Pennsylvania in 1952 as an English major, with hopes of one day becoming a journalist or author. But his father, an attorney, died of a heart attack in 1955, and the younger O'Malley, along with three other brothers, decided to switch to business to help support the family.

As a manager, Mr. O'Malley concedes he pushes subordinates to work long and hard hours if necessary. "But as a boss, I pick my spots to be tough," he adds. "I also like to let professionals show how good they can be on their own."

Mr. O'Malley says he doesn't plan any big changes at Price, but will look at all department budgets and initiatives with a fresh eye to keep costs down.

Both Mr. O'Malley and Mr. Connor say that a big challenge facing accounting firms over the coming decade will be the need for more specialization in auditing, tax and consulting. And both believe that audits will have to be strengthened to spot more fraud.

"The profession needs more credibility," says Mr. O'Malley. "We can't simply issue clean opinions on client companies that go under a few months later. We're going to have to be tougher with our audits."

Mr. O'Malley joined Price in 1959, became an audit partner in 1970, and in 1984 was elected to the firm's policy board—a prerequisite for selection as chairman.

Price's U.S. partners will begin voting on the firm's top post within a week with Mr. O'Malley's name the only one on the ballot. His election, therefore, is a formality.

SEC's Coulson Is Appointed Top Accountant

Agency Aide Vows to Seek Tougher Enforcement of Auditing Standards

By Lee Berton

January 8, 1988

Edmund Coulson, the 42-year-old deputy chief accountant of the Securities and Exchange Commission, was named the agency's chief accountant, a post that oversees many crucial financial decisions by U.S. businesses.

While Mr. Coulson has been considered less of an activist than some other candidates for the job, he emphasized in an interview that he will work hard for increased disclosure of financial data.

Mr. Coulson said, for example, that he will push the SEC toward stronger enforcement of improved accounting and auditing procedures and standards. "Steps must be taken to improve the quality of overall audit practice before the commission," he said.

In the past year, Mr. Coulson helped develop SEC proposals that would require accounting firms to undergo mandatory peer review and tell more about why they left or were dismissed from the audit of a public company.

'Early-Warning Device for Fraud'
"Disclosure about changes of an auditor—which sometimes show auditor-shopping by a company—are an important early-warning device for financial fraud, and I am going to work hard to get this proposal, and the peer review proposal, approved and implemented," he said. He said he expects the SEC to vote on the proposal in March after considering public comment.

Mr. Coulson said he considers the SEC "a law enforcement agency with its full resources devoted to full and fair disclosure."

He added: "We want to address key issues such as . . . implementing the recent recommendations" of a panel on corporate fraud. The accounting profession recently suggested tightening auditing standards to spot more management fraud—a recommendation that is being resisted by some corporations. The fraud panel, representing five accounting and business organizations, in October also urged strengthening the roles of audit committees of corporate boards and internal auditors at companies.

Mr. Coulson was one of five candidates for the job. He probably gained the edge on the others because of his long and intimate knowledge of the SEC. He has been deputy chief accountant to the former chief accountant, A. Clarence Sampson, 58 years old, for the past five years.

Mr. Coulson joined the SEC in 1975 after working for a regional accounting firm following his graduation from the University of Maryland in 1970. Mr. Sampson retired last December after a decade as chief accountant to join the Stamford, Connecticut-based Financial Accounting Standards Board, the chief rule-making body of accountants.

Backing Away from Activism?

Some accountants and legislators—including U.S. Rep. John Dingell (D., Mich.), who heads a House subcommittee scrutinizing accountants—still worry that Mr. Coulson will be too low-profile in enforcing improved financial disclosure. Mr. Dingell had backed Frederick Wolf, currently assistant controller general at the General Accounting Office, for the job, contending that he was more of an activist than the other candidates.

"I hope the SEC isn't signaling a backing-away from an activist stand, and that it will be more forceful in accounting matters," said John Burton, a former SEC chief accountant who is now chief accountant of Columbia University's business school.

But many financial executives said he will be more of an activist in his new job. "He'll be fair, but tough, and his own man," says Gaylen Larson, group vice president, finance, of Chicago-based Household International Inc. Mr. Larson is chairman of the Financial Executives Institute's corporate-reporting committee.

Bluey Must Hold Peers to Strict Account

By Lee Berton

April 19, 1988

Theodore F. Bluey just got one of his profession's toughest jobs: As the government's chief accounting enforcer, he stands to earn enemies, make less money and garner small glory.

As chief accountant of the Securities and Exchange Commission's enforcement division, Mr. Bluey will judge his peers, deciding whom to punish for dressing up financial results or fooling investors.

A former partner at high-powered Deloitte, Haskins & Sells, he says with an accountant's directness why he took the job: "public service and the excitement of knowing I can make a contribution." And he explains with an accountant's prudence why he was able to take the job—whose $71,000 annual salary is far less than the $200,000 a year that most Big Eight partners earn: "I'm not a high liver and a portion of the college education for my two children is already provided for."

Asserts Howard Hodges, chief accountant of the SEC's corporate finance division: "It's one of the hardest and most important jobs in the SEC and could be very depressing and contentious. But it gives credibility to the other SEC divisions because without deterrents, filers of financial statements might continue to see what they could get away with."

The 40-year-old Mr. Bluey works with 13 accountants and 148 lawyers in the division, which can enjoin companies and accounting firms either on its own or through the courts from continuing financial fraud. Traditionally, it preferred to put offenders on the straight and narrow quietly in administrative actions. But in recent years, it began slapping companies and certified public accounting firms with public sanctions under securities laws.

"This isn't the kind of job that I'd want anyone to say I took it easy on offenders," says Mr. Bluey, who was Deloitte's accounting and auditing coordinator for the Washington-Baltimore-Richmond area. Mr. Bluey, who reports to SEC enforcement chief Gary Lynch, says he will particularly watch for accounting violations in pumping up sales, cost deferral and new types of financial instruments.

Businessmen are concerned about who holds the job because of the effect on how they sell equity or debt. "The chief accountant of the SEC's enforcement division is the watchdog who looks over our shoulder and can turn back our securities registrations, proxies or financial statements if the accounting isn't properly applied or disclosure is incomplete," says Robert Orben, vice president and controller of Cummings Engine Co., Columbus, Indiana, and a member of the Financial Executives Institute's corporate reporting panel.

Under Mr. Bluey's two predecessors, enforcement actions were taken against such companies as AM International Inc., American Express Co., Baldwin-United Corp., Burroughs Corp., Charter Financial Corp. and Continental Illinois Corp. Division actions forced Financial Corp. of America to take big write-downs on securities and U.S. Surgical Co. to lower inventory values, reducing profit.

"When holding this job, you cannot worry about making enemies among companies and accounting firms," says John C. Burton, an accounting professor at Columbia University and a former SEC chief accountant.

Mr. Bluey concedes he will face "many difficult calls in the months ahead on accounting issues, particularly with the recent new accounting standards on pensions, consolidation, cash flow and deferred taxes." Accountants point out that although standard setters issue rules, there is often much leeway for applying principles either to boost or depress profit or hide debt off the balance sheet.

Mr. Bluey's job is difficult because accounting investigations, unlike insider-trading cases, can drag on and draw little fanfare. "Such investigations are extensive, tedious and time-consuming," observes Edmund Coulson, the SEC's chief accountant. "Those with complex accounting questions can take up to two years."

Mr. Bluey says he wants to focus on important cases. "I don't plan to bring a lot of little actions," he says. "I'd rather concentrate on meaningful topics of substance."

Mr. Bluey joined Deloitte in 1969 after graduating from Franklin & Marshall College in Lancaster, Pennsylvania, with a bachelor of arts and business administration focusing on accounting. In his new SEC job, he succeeds Robert Sack, who left last August after three years for a college teaching position.

He says he won't be shackled by former ties to Deloitte: "While I'll step aside and let other enforcement division people handle cases of my former firms or with accountants I've worked with (which is standard for the job), I will go out after the Big Eight as well as the smaller firms if the case requires it."

CHAPTER 2

TREADWAY COMMISSION

The effects of the Report of the National Commission on Fraudulent Financial Reporting ("Treadway" Report), issued in October of 1987, have yet to be fully realized. This industry response to outside pressure, specifically from Congressmen Wyden and Dingell, has caused corporate America to reevaluate the existing system of internal controls and related internal management and oversight issues, particularly those involving the activities of the corporate audit committee. The recommendations of the Treadway Commission are far-reaching and are not only addressed to business, accountants, and educators but also to the Securities and Exchange Commission, given its role in protecting the public interest.

As time passes, we will see if Congress will act to impose new regulations on the accounting and auditing establishment and on the corporate financial management establishment (as it threatened over a decade ago at the prompting of Congressman Moss and Senator Metcalf), or if they will be satisfied with the current environment of self-regulation. The Report of the National Commission on Fraudulent Financial Reporting is an element of this self-regulatory mechanism.

Corporate Fraud Will Be Studied by Special Panel

By Bruce Ingersoll and Lee Berton

June 28, 1985

WASHINGTON—Four major accounting and business groups announced a special commission to examine the causes of corporate fraud and develop possible remedies.

The National Commission on Management Fraud will conduct an 18-month inquiry into the apparent surge in white-collar crime that is "eroding public confidence in American business," said James Treadway, Jr., chairman of the panel. "We won't have any sacred cows," the former Securities and Exchange Commission member vowed yesterday at a news conference here.

The six-member panel will scrutinize the traditional procedures of corporate accountability, the enforcement policies of regulators, and accounting and auditing practices, Mr. Treadway said. It will examine whether the Reagan administration's emphasis on deregulation has led corporate officials to believe they can get away with improprieties.

The commission will seek ways to improve the detection and prevention of fraud, said Ray J. Groves, chairman of the American Institute of Certified Public Accountants, the panel's main sponsor. It will focus on breakdowns in auditing, the falsifying of financial reports and the types of "corporate culture" that encourage improprieties, he said.

The announcement was met with considerable skepticism. Abraham Briloff, an accounting professor at Baruch College, New York, expressed concern that the commission "will simply be an apology for white-collar crime that tends to rationalize the status quo."

Others questioned what the panel could achieve. Lee Seidler, a Bear, Stearns & Co. general partner, said it will "do noth-

Mr. Ingersoll is a staff reporter of THE WALL STREET JOURNAL.

ing but take up a lot of time" and reinforce the public's exaggerated perception of rising corporate crime. "There just isn't that much more of it now than before," Mr. Seidler said.

"I can't stop them from judging the study in advance," Mr. Treadway said. "But if our report is any good, we will step on toes."

The panel has a $1 million budget. Its staff, comprising a director and at least three researchers, will prepare a report for distribution to Congress, regulatory agencies, accounting firms and businesses.

The other members are Donald H. Trautlein, chairman of Bethlehem Steel Corp.; William S. Kanaga, chairman of Arthur Young & Co.; Hugh L. Marsh, chief internal auditor for Aluminum Co. of America; Thomas I. Storrs, former chairman of North Carolina National Bank Corp.; and William M. Batten, former New York Stock Exchange chairman.

The commission is being financed by the Financial Executives Institute, the American Accounting Association and the Institute of Internal Auditors, as well as the AICPA. The National Association of Accountants said it is supporting the idea of the commission and is studying whether to help finance it in the future.

Name of Group to Study
Fraud Splits Accountants

Group Faults 'Management' in Title of Special Panel Picked by CPA Institute

By Lee Berton

July 12, 1985

NEW YORK—A dispute has erupted between two accounting organizations over whether management or outside auditors are responsible for uncovering corporate fraud.

Two weeks ago, the American Institute of Certified Public Accountants announced a special commission, the National Commission on Management Fraud, to examine the causes of corporate fraud and develop possible remedies. More than 220,000 CPAs, most of them with independent CPA firms, belong to the institute.

Irritated by the special panel's name, the National Association of Accountants has issued a strong statement saying it won't lend financial support to the commission. The association includes 90,000 management accountants, most of whom work for companies.

"We think a national commission to investigate 'management fraud' might be better named, and more concerned with auditor inadequacy since it is advanced by and financed by the AICPA," said Herbert C. Knortz, the NAA's president. Mr. Knortz is executive vice president and comptroller of ITT Corp.

Philip Chenok, president of the institute, said in response to the association's statement that "the issuance of defective financial statements is a shared responsibility of all those involved in the financial reporting process."

Mr. Chenok said the study will take 12 to 18 months and cost about $1 million. The six-member panel is chaired by James Treadway, Jr., a former member of the Securities and Exchange Commission.

Officials of the association said that the institute had asked other organizations sponsoring the commission for contributions but that the association has declined to contribute. Mr. Chenok said a figure of $50,000 had been discussed but hadn't been settled on.

Other sponsoring organizations are the Financial Executives Institute, the American Accounting Association and the Institute of Internal Auditors.

Mr. Chenok said, "Before announcing the commission, we held discussions with all groups involved, including the NAA, and believed we had their support."

Panel Is to Urge More SEC Clout to Battle Fraud

By Lee Berton

October 22, 1986

NEW YORK—A special commission on corporate fraud will recommend that federal regulators be empowered to impose sanctions on corporate officers in financial fraud cases, the panel's chairman said.

Under current securities laws, the Securities and Exchange Commission can prohibit accounting firms accused of permitting improper financial disclosure from practicing before the agency. And the agency can ask for an injunction barring corporate officials from repeating an offense.

Speaking before an accountants' group in Kansas City, Missouri, James C. Treadway, Jr., the commission chairman, said that managers who cause financial fraud should "be regularly considered" by the SEC in enforcement proceedings to be barred from corporate office.

Opposition Expected

Mr. Treadway was an SEC commissioner from 1982 to 1985.

The recommendation is sure to encounter opposition from many major corporations, which prefer to avoid any adverse publicity about corporate fraud and inadequate disclosure. "The companies we work for prefer to keep corporate discipline involving financial fraud under wraps," said the partner at a major accounting firm.

Because it has been busy with insider trading cases and has a limited budget, the SEC itself isn't particularly eager to broaden its powers against corporate officers involved in financial fraud or inadequate financial disclosure.

While the SEC can initiate a civil action against corporate officials, it doesn't have the power to initiate criminal actions. Some critics of the SEC and the accounting profession have urged Congress to pass legislation giving the SEC such clout.

"We have brought more civil injunctive actions against corporate officers and accounting firms in recent years than previous administrations," said John Shad, SEC chairman. During fiscal 1986, ended September 30, Mr. Shad noted, the SEC initiated disciplinary action against 15 accounting firms and 33 corporate officers, directors, and employees in financial fraud cases.

'Cost-Effective' Sanctions

"Before recommending increased penalties for corporate fraud, the commission should examine the extent of the problems and whether increased sanctions are cost-effective," Mr. Shad said.

Asserting that charges of widespread corporate fraud are exaggerated, Mr. Shad said that "alleged audit failures are only a fraction of 1% of total audits."

John C. Burton, dean of Columbia University's graduate school of business and former chief accountant of the SEC, disagrees. "If anything," says Mr. Burton, "the SEC should be given the power to prosecute offenders in corporate fraud cases instead of having to refer criminal cases to the Justice Department. There just aren't enough scalps on its belt to discourage corporate fraud, which remains a major problem."

The National Commission on Fraudulent Financial Reporting, which Mr. Treadway heads, was formed in mid-1985 by four major accounting and business groups to develop possible remedies to corporate fraud. Mr. Treadway said its final report, expected late next year after a period for comment, also will recommend stiffer auditing standards for business and a new member for the public on a professional accounting body that sets auditing standards.

Panel to Recommend Stiffer Penalties, More Audit Safeguards to Fight Fraud

By Lee Berton

April 27, 1987

NEW YORK—A special panel on corporate fraud will recommend stronger penalties against officers involved in fraud, further disclosures in some aspects of financial reporting and more public participation in setting auditing standards.

The National Commission on Fraudulent Financial Reporting, formed 18 months ago by five major accounting and business groups, is expected to issue its 170-page report today.

The report has already drawn criticism from some who say the recommendations don't go far enough to penalize financial fraud.

James C. Treadway, Jr., commission chairman, admitted the panel's recommendations have drawn "static from some parties." But he said he expects most of the suggestions will be widely accepted in business and accounting circles.

"We may not satisfy all congressional critics of business, but we think that most corporations and major accounting firms will recognize the need for these changes," added Mr. Treadway, a former Securities and Exchange Commission member who has just been named general counsel of PaineWebber Inc., a securities firm.

More Power to SEC

In one of the most sweeping changes, the panel urges that the SEC be given more power by Congress to impose fines, bring cease and desist proceedings, and bar or suspend violators from serving as corporate officers or directors.

Current securities law allows the SEC to seek only a court injunction to bar corporate officials from repeating an offense.

John C. Burton, dean of Columbia University's graduate school of business and former chief accountant of the SEC, criticized the panel for "not going far enough. The panel should have urged that the SEC should be given the power to bring criminal charges on its own against individuals involved in financial fraud."

Under current law, the SEC can refer criminal cases to various federal attorneys, and the report suggests only that with SEC assistance, "criminal prosecution for fraudulent financial reporting should be made a higher priority."

Streamlining Auditing Board

Another controversial panel recommendation calls for streamlining and adding more public members to an auditing standard-setting body. Currently, a 21-member auditing standards board, with two or three members who aren't in public accounting practice, set such rules.

The board is an arm of the American Institute of Certified Public Accountants, the major membership body for CPAs in the United States and a sponsor of the fraud panel.

The panel recommends that the auditing standards board be reorganized into an eight to 12-member body with half its members "persons who are knowledgeable about auditing but not engaged in public accounting."

J. Michael Cook, chairman of the CPA institute, said he had "reservations" about sharply reducing the board's size.

"It will never fly," said Mr. Cook, who also is chairman of Deloitte, Haskins & Sells, an accounting firm. "A much smaller board with less public accounting expertise wouldn't have sufficient resources to set proper standards."

Nevertheless, Mr. Cook said he endorses the rest of the panel's report.

"It puts a broad focus on fraudulent financial reporting by asking for stronger corporate governance and education standards, and stiffer enforcement penalties in business against fraud," he said. "In the past, too much focus for fraud was placed on the public accounting profession."

The report also recommends that companies that change auditors or shift accounting principles disclose more about any disagreements with outside auditors. It urges that audit committees of corporate boards be given more clout in accounting, auditing and disclosure areas, and that outside auditors become more involved with quarterly financial statements.

It also recommends that all public accounting firms be peer-reviewed—a requirement currently being weighed by the SEC. And it urges accountants to upgrade the quality of their reports through required reviews by a second partner, and use of reviews that analyze industry financial ratios to spot business problems.

"Implementing our recommendations would increase the cost of an audit, but it would be well worth it," said Mr. Treadway.

After a 60-day comment period, the panel's final report will be issued, about October 1.

Besides the CPA institute, the panel's other sponsors are the American Accounting Association, the Financial Executives Institute, the Institute of Internal Auditors and the National Association of Accountants.

Internal Auditors' Role in Disclosing Misdeeds Will Be Examined by Panel

By Lee Berton

July 10, 1987

A House subcommittee investigating the accounting profession will begin pressing the internal auditors of U.S. companies to uncover more corporate fraud and improprieties.

The Oversight and Investigations Subcommittee, chaired by John D. Dingell (D., Mich.), since early 1986 has been criticizing the outside auditors of major companies for failing to blow the whistle on companies that fail to disclose business problems.

Now the subcommittee, which resumes hearings today, will turn its spotlight on the internal auditors of U.S. companies and why they may not have enough clout within their organizations to stop fraud, waste and other business problems.

'Muffled' Voices of Auditors
"There's little evidence that internal auditors that work for the major corporations are raising enough red flags to the audit

committees of company boards to stop such improprieties," asserts Rep. Ron Wyden (D., Ore.), a subcommittee member. "If the voice of the internal auditor who works with the outside independent auditors is muffled, no wonder investors and the public aren't protected."

"Internal auditors need stronger lines of communication to the audit committees," says Ronald L. Bell, chairman of the Institute of Internal Auditors, which has 30,000 members. Mr. Bell, a director of audit for General Motors Corp., estimates that only half of the public companies traded on the New York Stock Exchange give their internal auditing staffs enough clout. "For all public companies, that portion would likely drop to a third," he says.

As evidence of the failure of internal auditors to stop corporate misbehaving, the subcommittee will cite examples of defense contractors accused of improperly inflating contract costs. The Pratt & Whitney division of Hartford, Connecticut-based United Technologies Corp., for example, in the early 1980s overcharged the government "thousands of dollars" by adding to contracts the costs of strolling minstrels and for health club dues for wives of executives, according to the subcommittee's staff.

A spokesman for Pratt & Whitney says that the company "complied with government regulations and policies at that time." Since then, he noted that following a 44-month investigation of Pratt & Whitney, federal law enforcement officials declined to prosecute the company last August. He declined to comment on specific charges.

Questions about TRW

Earlier this year the subcommittee asked the General Accounting Office to see whether internal auditors have installed proper checking systems at TRW Inc., a Cleveland-based defense contractor, to stop overcharging of the government. Subcommittee staff members say that TRW from 1979 to 1984 inflated research and development costs and padded work schedules on contracts for airplane and engine parts.

A TRW spokesman says that the company told government authorities about these improprieties and offered repayment. The overcharges are "still being settled," he adds.

The House subcommittee also will note that overcharges in

1983 by St. Louis-based General Dynamics Corp. included charges to government contracts for kenneling a company executive's dog, for company executives' country club dues and to take the children of executives on a ski trip to Aspen, Colorado.

A General Dynamics spokesman says that the company "has drastically revised the way we do business" since these improprieties were uncovered. "We've installed new procedures for contract compliance, time-card reporting and ethics and have strengthened our internal controls," the spokesman adds.

The subcommittee also will maintain that the supersecret or "black programs" of defense contractors such as Lockheed Corp., Calabasas, California, aren't subjected to sufficient auditing oversight by internal or outside auditors.

A Lockheed spokesman says that under current contract rules the government agency ordering these programs specifies how many internal and outside auditors have "security clearance" to look at program details. "Those are the rules and Mr. Dingell apparently wants to change them," the spokesman declares.

Members of the special panel on corporate fraud testifying before the subcommittee today will represent five organizations. They are the Institute of Internal Auditors, the American Institute of Certified Public Accountants, the American Accounting Association, the Financial Executives Institute and the National Association of Accountants.

One of the scheduled witnesses at a later hearing, the internal auditors institute's Mr. Bell, insists that most internal auditors are "properly doing their job." But, he adds, there's no question that management should provide their companies' auditing with more personnel and computer resources. "Internal auditors should be leaders of keeping companies' internal controls sound," he says.

Panel Urges SEC Be Given Power to Bar Corporate Officers Involved in Fraud

By Lee Berton

October 2, 1987

NEW YORK—A special panel on corporate fraud urged that the Securities and Exchange Commission be given the power to bar corporate officials involved in fraud from holding corporate office.

The National Commission on Fraudulent Financial Reporting, in its final report, said the SEC should be given statutory authority to temporarily suspend or permanently bar corporate officers and directors from official posts in a public company if they are involved with fraudulent financial reporting. Fraudulent action would be determined by the courts and law enforcement or SEC investigations.

The SEC currently has the power to suspend or permanently bar officers and employees in the securities industry and can also act against public accountants. But the SEC rarely has been able to take such action against officials in public companies, and only with the official's consent, because the SEC lacks statutory authority in this area.

James C. Treadway, Jr., chairman of the fraud commission and a former SEC commissioner, said that surveys taken by the commission show "The public is as upset with fraudulent financial reporting as it is with insider trading." In an interview, he added, "Stronger deterrents are needed within corporations to prevent fraudulent financial reporting."

The fraud commission was organized in 1985 by five accounting and business organizations following a rising tide of lawsuits alleging financial fraud against accounting firms and public companies. U.S. Rep. Ronald Wyden (D., Ore.), a member of a House oversight subcommittee that has been investigating financial fraud, said he is considering introducing legislation to implement the fraud commission's recommendations.

In its final report, the panel backed off its earlier recommendations that the audit committee of a corporate board be given approval power in two key areas.

One recommendation would have given the audit committee approval power over a company's quarterly financial results. The other would have given the committee the right to approve in advance the amount of consulting work done by the company's outside auditor.

The final report recommends only that the audit committee "oversee" or "review" management's decisions in these two areas. Rep. Wyden said the commission should have stayed with its original stronger recommendations.

In an interview, Mr. Treadway said, "We didn't back away from the audit committee monitoring independence in an oversight capacity. But many in business and accounting said it would be impractical for the company to get advance approval of each and every consulting engagement by its outside auditors, regardless of how small."

The fraud commission also recommended that companies be required to disclose all their accounting discussions with the previous auditor after the companies change auditors. And it urged that outside auditors review quarterly financial results prior to their issuance, rather than afterward, as is the current practice.

The Financial Executives Institute, which represents corporate financial officers, opposes forcing companies to disclose all accounting matters with previous accountants after changing auditors. "Disclosing everything the company has discussed with the previous auditor is overkill," said Burton E. Broome, a member of the institute's committee on corporate reporting.

CHAPTER 3

REGULATION OF
ACCOUNTANTS

Professional accounting is a self-regulated industry in the United States. Self-regulation involves response to criticism, adjustment to the pressures of the times that are precipitated by a perception of an increase in fraudulent activity, and resolving potential conflict of interest within the accounting profession. The following articles summarize the rigor with which accounting professionals examine themselves and search their souls in order to improve their practices and the public's perception of their profession. The articles also describe the pressures put on the profession to continually pursue excellence, both in appearance and in reality.

Rep. Dingell to Take Aim at Accountants, SEC in Hearings on Profession's Role as Watchdog

By Lee Berton and Bruce Ingersoll

February 19, 1985

WASHINGTON—For Rep. John Dingell, a fowler of some repute, the bird-hunting season is over. But the nation's certified public accountants aren't convinced that Mr. Dingell has put away his guns.

Mr. Ingersoll is a staff reporter of THE WALL STREET JOURNAL.

The accounting profession is on the defensive these days. The managing partners of so-called Big Eight accounting firms, in particular, are feeling besieged by critics. More and more shareholders of companies in bankruptcy-law proceedings are suing accounting firms for malpractice; federal regulators are investigating the role of auditors in a dismaying number of bank failures, and there are antitrust grumblings about the Big Eight's growing dominance of the profession.

In fact, 1985 may turn into open season on accountants and auditors. For the first time in eight years, Congress is investigating just how well the profession has performed as a public watchdog and independent umpire in the realm of banking and business. Tomorrow Rep. Dingell will open a series of seven or eight hearings that could run into the fall.

Top officials at the Securities and Exchange Commission are as anxious about the proceedings as the accountants are. Mr. Dingell intends to scrutinize the SEC's oversight of the accounting profession and examine the mixed results of letting accountants regulate themselves. While Mr. Dingell insists he is embarking on the hearings without any preconceptions, he acknowledges, "There's a strong possibility that the SEC hasn't used its power to assure that the best generally accepted accounting principles have been applied."

Dingell Is a Power Broker

As chairman of both the House Energy and Commerce Committee and its subcommittee on oversight and investigations, the 6-foot-3 Democrat from Michigan is a political "big foot," one of Capitol Hill's power brokers.

The hearings are likely to generate a lot more adverse publicity for the Big Eight firms that have been involved in major auditing failures. They may also lead to significant regulatory initiatives or, conceivably, legislation that would stiffen corporate-disclosure and financial-reporting requirements, not only for all public companies but for the accounting firms themselves.

The oversight subcommittee's goal is "to see how the accounting profession is functioning as a part of the federal regulatory system," says Mr. Dingell. If improperly audited financial statements and other "bad data" are being filed with the SEC and the banking agencies, he says, the system breaks down and investors and bank depositors suffer. But he adds, "We don't have any roster of hobgoblins, devils and monsters that we're trying to exorcise."

Despite this protestation, Chairman Dingell does seem to be on a hunt. "You're talking to a quail shooter," he says. "I always use good dogs, and I never go into a field where I don't think there are quail." He hopes to flush out a controversial covey of issues with such questions as:

• Are outside auditors really independent of their corporate clients? "If CPA firms are doing consulting work for the same companies whose books they're supposed to audit, how can they be completely objective?" Mr. Dingell wonders.
• Do federal regulators and the investing public know enough about the financial might and influence of the Big Eight? Perhaps accounting firms should be required to file with the SEC the same type of annual 10-K reports as their clients, setting forth their financial results and detailing their operations, Mr. Dingell says.
• Are auditors giving the public enough advance warning about the deteriorating finances of banks and other companies? In recent years, Rep. Dingell says, the level of "busted audits" has been "too high and too spectacular."
• Shouldn't investors be told more about how audit failures occur and how much they are costing accounting firms in confidential out-of-court settlements? "We should know whether it's fraud or slipshod accounting that was the problem," Mr. Dingell asserts.

Some Are Fretting Privately

The American Institute of Certified Public Accountants says it "welcomes" the chance to update Congress on the profession's progress and expresses an eagerness to improve the performance of auditors in preventing and detecting fraud. But privately, top accounting executives fret that the hearings will only trigger more lawsuits by shareholders in failed or troubled companies or depositors in closed or merged financial institutions.

They deny that their firms' management-consulting business detracts from their independent role as outside auditors. "There's a lot of useful synergy developed between auditing and consulting," says Duane Kullberg, managing partner of Chicago-based Arthur Andersen & Co., the biggest of the Big Eight, based on 1983 revenue. "Through auditing, we can do a better job in helping our clients know what they need in the computer markets."

Peter Scanlon, chairman of Coopers & Lybrand, the No. 3 firm, adds, "CPA firms feel they are in the best position to help their clients set up management-control systems with computers." Any curbs on consulting would keep top people from going into auditing, he warns.

As for an auditor's independence, that's "a matter of professional integrity which you can't legislate," contends William Gladstone, managing partner of New York-based Arthur Young & Co., the No. 6 firm.

Auditors Seen as More Cautious
The rash of malpractice suits has made auditors a lot more cautious, says Larry Horner, chairman of New York-based Peat, Marwick, Mitchell & Co., the second biggest firm. "CPAs are beginning to feel like doctors who perform a lot more tests because they don't want to get sued but the patients may not be helped."

SEC officials insist that the agency hasn't neglected its oversight role. The SEC brought 18 accounting cases last year, compared with 11 in 1983 and three in 1982, in efforts to crack down on "cooked books" and improper "shopping" for favorable auditor's opinions. The officials also note that the audit-failure rate among 10,000 SEC-regulated companies is less than 1%.

What the agency and the accounting profession are dreading is a long series of "horror stories." But Rep. Dingell promises: "We're going to run a fair hearing. You're talking to John Dingell, not Joe McCarthy."

House Democrats Question SEC's Role in Guarding against Audit Failures

By Bruce Ingersoll

March 7, 1985

WASHINGTON—House Democrats fought to a verbal standoff with Securities and Exchange Commission officials over whether the agency has failed to guard against accounting irregularities and audit failures.

Rep. John Dingell, chairman of the Energy and Commerce Subcommittee on Oversight and Investigations, and other panel members repeatedly challenged the effectiveness of the accounting profession's self-regulating system under the SEC's auspices. Rep. Ronald Wyden (D., Ore.) twice warned SEC Chairman John Shad that the agency was "inviting" Congress to "step in and write a whole new set of rules."

It was clear from the questioning of Mr. Shad and other witnesses at yesterday's hearing that the panel already has concluded that the SEC has deferred too much to the Public Oversight Board and other self-regulating organizations. But in one testy exchange, Mr. Shad countered, "We have not set aside our obligations to the public; we're doing a hell of a job of meeting our responsibilities." In another flareup, he asserted, "We're coming down with hobnailed boots on audit failures."

An audit failure occurs when an independent auditor approves the financial statements of a company that shortly thereafter goes bankrupt or develops major financial problems. Mr. Shad testified that the rate of alleged audit failures among more than 10,000 publicly held companies that report to the SEC is less than 1%. He said the agency isn't lax in prosecuting those responsible for such breakdowns.

Mr. Shad said that in the past three fiscal years the SEC's enforcement division has filed more financial disclosure cases than in any comparable period in 25 years. It brought 33 such cases against companies last year, a 34% increase over 1983. In addition, he said, the agency filed 18 cases against accountants and auditors, an increase of 64% over 1983.

The hearing was the second in a series of eight planned by the subcommittee, which is examining the SEC's oversight of the accounting profession.

Mr. Dingell (D., Mich.) and other panel members expressed deep concern about several "spectacular" cases of audit failure, including those related to the 1982 collapse of Drysdale Government Securities and the 1983 collapse of Baldwin-United Corp. Mr. Wyden pointed out that Ernst & Whinney, one of the Big Eight accounting firms, was "essentially a three-time loser," having been involved in alleged audit failures at Franklin National Bank, United American Bank and Continental Illinois Bank.

Reached by phone, an Ernst & Whinney spokesman said that "most professional services firms have clients that are not financially successful in the long run. It does not follow that either the regulatory authorities or the independent auditors can prevent such failures."

Mr. Dingell told Mr. Shad that he didn't know "whether we ought to have serenity of mind because there are only a few audit failures or whether we ought to be scared to death because they're so big."

In defending the self-regulation approach, Mr. Shad said, "The present systems of checks and balances in the accounting profession are the most pervasive in any profession, but they aren't perfect. He conceded it's impossible to eliminate "human errors and defalcations."

Mr. Wyden derided the Public Oversight Board as the "Private Oversight Board" and argued that the idea of the accounting profession regulating itself is inherently flawed. "This is an industry where the same people write the (financial accounting) rules, interpret the rules . . . and enforce the rules," he said.

He also accused the SEC of dealing harshly with small accounting firms and lightly with major firms.

Mr. Shad denied there was any double standard of enforcement. He said the most egregious violations tend to occur at small firms because they often lack internal quality controls and expertise in securities law.

The SEC chairman also disagreed with the notion that accounting firms face a potential conflict of interest if they provide management advice to a corporation and audit its books. "I think they can advise the client and still not infringe in any way on their independence as auditors," he said.

Price Waterhouse Is Urging Formation of Group to Regulate Accounting Firms

By Lee Berton

November 20, 1985

NEW YORK—In a move that already has met with industry opposition, Price Waterhouse is urging creation of a self-regulatory body for the accounting profession under the oversight of the Securities and Exchange Commission.

The recommendation is part of a three-point plan by the nation's fifth-largest accounting firm to help stem the profession's liability and credibility crisis.

The suggestion has drawn a cool reception from other major firms, which strongly support leaving self-regulation in the private sector. "I don't think that business in this country needs another regulatory body to control its destiny," said Ray Groves, chairman of Cleveland-based Ernst & Whinney, the third-biggest U.S. accounting firm. "Price's suggestion (for the new regulatory body) doesn't make sense and sounds a bit naive."

Price Waterhouse, which is expected to formally announce its program soon, has been circulating draft copies among accountants and the SEC in recent days.

Joseph E. Connor, the 54-year-old chairman and senior partner of Price Waterhouse, said in an interview yesterday that the firm also will suggest strengthening the audit process to improve fraud detection at client companies, and will urge federal legislation to limit the liability of outside auditors in lawsuits stemming from financial collapses of companies.

"Major lawsuits against major CPA firms world-wide now aggregate $2 billion" in requested damages, he said. "The economic viability of the profession hangs on whether we can bring some sanity to the liability process." Mr. Connor added that the claims are about four times larger than the total capital of major accounting firms, which he estimated at $500 million.

Mr. Connor's suggestions for stiffer audits and a cap on liability have more support among other accounting firms than the one for a self-regulatory body. But the firms say that similar efforts are already being considered by industry trade and standard-setting bodies.

The auditing standards board of the American Institute of Certified Public Accountants, the profession's trade group, has been considering ways to increase auditors' responsibility for detection of fraud. And the institute earlier this month appointed a committee to study how to limit firms liability exposure through new legal approaches or state and federal legislation.

"Price Waterhouse's suggestion for more public regulation is troubling, and his (Mr. Connor's) other recommendations seem duplicative of the institute's current efforts," said Philip B. Chenok, president of the institute, which has more than 230,000 members.

However, support for the proposed self-regulatory body was expressed by Rep. John Dingell (D., Mich.), who chairs a House subcommittee that has been holding hearings on the accounting profession since February. "The reliability and integrity of the accounting profession could certainly benefit" from the proposed body, Mr. Dingell said yesterday.

"But it would require vigorous involvement" on the SEC's part, he added.

A. Clarence Sampson, the SEC's chief accountant, said the SEC has seen an early version of Price Waterhouse's recommendations, "but we can't comment until the final version is issued." Liability exposure for accountants is an "extremely important" issue, and "we"ll be interested in the reaction of others to the Price Waterhouse proposal," he added.

Seven years ago the institute initiated a new division for

public accounting firms that requires peer review every three years and has a five-member public oversight board. Mr. Connor said his oversight body would include the current board's five members plus about 10 others from public accounting.

"The SEC would provide oversight for the self-regulatory effort but wouldn't be able to pierce the wall of client confidentiality," he said. Sanctions for bad audits would include suspension or a ban from practice before the SEC, he added. The new regulatory body would require amending securities law passed in the 1930s.

Mr. Connor argued that current self-regulatory efforts of the profession and peer reviews are seen as "too secret" and too mild by the public and Congress.

Price Waterhouse, which audits 102 of the 500 biggest U.S. public companies, has a long tradition of breaking with the accounting profession on issues. In the mid-1970s, John Biegler, the firm's former chief executive, recommended that accounting firms issue a detailed financial report similar to annual 10-K reports issued by public companies. The suggestion generated a storm of protest from other accounting firms and wasn't adopted.

Earlier this year, Rep. Dingell required the 16 biggest U.S. accounting firms to file such a detailed report with his subcommittee.

Close Accounting's Confidence Gap

By Joseph E. Connor

December 3, 1985

A Gallup Poll last month showed that the public has a low level of confidence in business, despite a generally healthy economy. Possible explanations for this include the recent spectacular failures of businesses and financial institutions—100 bank failures

---

Mr. Connor is chairman and senior partner of Price Waterhouse & Co.

so far this year; headline-making cases of business fraud; "cooked books"; "cute accounting," and a flurry of congressional inquiries.

I am not indulging in finger-pointing. The accounting profession may not be on Gallup's list as a separate entity, but it is there in spirit right along with the rest, because every failure, every fraud, every instance of accounting gimmickry and every inquiry have produced the same refrain: "Where were the auditors?"

The House Subcommittee on Oversight and Investigation and other congressional panels are asking this question regularly, in a prolonged examination of the accounting profession.

Even without percentages in a poll, the public perception is that the accounting profession has fallen short of its responsibilities as the "public's watchdog." And the public may well be asking, "If we can't have faith in those who are supposed to ensure the integrity of the financial information that drives business, how can we have faith in business?"

Fraudulence Should Be Disclosed

The public's expectations, not congressional inquiries, are the real challenge facing the accounting profession. These expectations fall into three categories:

• *Expectations that the auditor should uncover and disclose fraudulent financial reporting.* Current auditing standards imply that the responsibility to search for fraud resulting in misleading financial statements is a byproduct of the main responsibility to examine and report on the financial statements taken as a whole.

But the Securities and Exchange Commission, the courts, many members of senior management and audit committees, and members of Congress believe that prevention of fraudulent financial reporting is one of the auditor's *primary* responsibilities.

• *Expectations that the auditor will warn the public of impending business failure.* Demands for an "early-warning system" have seldom been so forceful. The public does not understand how firms can fail almost immediately after receiving clean audit opinions. Invariably, business failures in such circumstances are characterized as audit failures.

• *Expectations that the profession's peer-review process will prevent substandard audit performance and mete out swift punishment if it occurs.* Under the process created in 1978, accounting firms voluntarily undergo a periodic quality-control review by another firm. Critics view this process as too secretive and self-contained, and too reluctant to exact penalties—"hang out scalps." Admittedly, with some logic, they do not understand how firms now accused of failed audit performance could have received clean bills of health from peer reviews.

> *I am not advocating direct SEC regulation of accountants. I instead envision a self-regulatory organization similar to the National Association of Securities Dealers.*

Equally as daunting as the expectation gap is the fact that the profession confronts the problem in an atmosphere of litigation run rampant. Like many other disciplines, accounting firms are victims of a breakdown in the civil liability system. Deteriorating standards governing both access to the courts and the determination of liability encourage many to seek and often obtain unprecedented monetary rewards.

How should the accounting profession respond to the dual challenge of credibility and an out-of-control liability system?

Whenever any individual or group is criticized, the natural response is to become defensive and point to what is being done right.

The accounting profession can do that. In fact, it should do that. The public needs to know what's right about the accounting profession, and it is entitled to a realistic explanation of the auditor's role. It needs to know, for example, that a business failure does not mean there has been an audit failure, and that out of 50,000 audits of public companies in five years, there have been only a few more than 100 cases against auditors of those companies alleging audit failures.

But, in keeping with its public mission, the profession has the obligation not to stop there. It must shoot for zero audit failure, although it is unattainable. And, it must make a searching and thorough examination to see where there is need for improvement.

I believe the profession should consider an integrated three-part response to the challenges confronting it.

• *Expand audit responsibility.* The accounting profession should clearly acknowledge that the auditor has the responsibility to search for material conditions leading to fraudulent financial reporting through the application of professional standards designed to reduce the risk that such conditions will go undetected.

To accomplish this, the auditor would be required to review and evaluate the company's system of management controls, including those elements of the system that bear on the company's financial condition, as opposed to financial position. That's an important distinction. The auditor currently deals with financial *position*—the traditional snapshot of a company's resources at a given point in time. Financial *condition* covers expectations and the financial impact of the company's operating environment.

In addition, the auditor would be required to identify symptoms in a company's business environment that indicate a higher risk of an intentional (i.e., fraudulent) misstatement of the financial statements. If such symptoms are present, the auditor would be required to consider performing certain substantive audit procedures.

This dual-purpose proposal is designed to narrow the expectations gap and to place auditors in a better position to respond, to the extent circumstances so warrant, to the public's cries for an early-warning system.

• *Enhance self-regulation.* The profession's present peer-review program should be converted to an appropriately tailored self-regulatory organization under the Securities Exchange Act of 1934.

This means governmentally supervised self-regulation, *not* direct regulation by the SEC. I envision an entity similar to the National Association of Securities Dealers.

What significant changes would the SRO [self-regulatory organization] make in peer review and quality control?

First, as opposed to the present voluntary approach, participation in the SRO would be mandatory for all accounting firms or sole practitioners auditing public companies. In order to retain their membership in the SRO, and thus the right to practice before the SEC, firms would have to comply with a number of quality-control requirements, including continuing education and independence standards, as well as the requirement for periodic peer reviews.

Second, public participation in the peer-review process would be increased in two ways. Members representing the public interest would be appointed to the SRO's governing board, which would have rule-making and disciplinary powers over the peer-review process. And the SEC would act as a forum for review of board disciplinary decisions.

Fairness for Both Parties

Let me emphasize that the SRO must be structured to ensure the maintenance of the confidentiality of individual audit engagements to preclude the access of the SEC or any other government agency to specific client information. This would preserve the current arrangement with the SEC and is fundamental to my support of the SRO concept.

• *Seek equity in civil liability.* I certainly do not contend that those injured by substandard audit performance should be denied the rightful application of legal remedies. I do contend that fairness demands equity for the defendant as well as the plaintiff.

To this end, the profession should develop a plan of priority options to provide liability relief. The plan's objective would be to effect a more equitable approach to the determination of liability.

Confidence in business and confidence in the accounting

profession are inseparable. The profession's primary role is to help sustain confidence in our business and economic system by ensuring the integrity of financial information. When the public's faith in our effectiveness in carrying out that role wanes, so does faith in the system itself.

The pressing need is for action—prompt, decisive action—whether on my proposals or on effective alternatives. The profession must demonstrate once more that it can shoulder the heavy obligation the Supreme Court has called "fidelity to the public trust."

Self-Regulation by Accountants Divides Industry

By Lee Berton

June 20, 1986

Self-regulation is dividing the accounting profession.

The controversy centers on whether accounting firms should be forced to submit to "peer review"—under which one firm judges another firm's quality controls. There's also a debate about whether the reviews do any good.

The outcome of the debate—and the debate itself—could affect the self-regulatory efforts of other professions. The American Bar Association, for example, considered peer review several years ago but discarded the idea because of problems of client confidentiality and possible client conflicts. "These arguments among accountants would certainly discourage the association from considering firm-on-firm peer review again," says Richard Collins, director of public affairs for the ABA.

Pressure from Congress

Accountants are under growing pressure from Congress and federal regulatory bodies to stiffen self-discipline as a way to reduce audit failures. (In an audit failure, a company suffers severe business problems soon after receiving a clean opinion on its financial statement from its outside auditors.) In testimony before a House subcommittee investigating the accounting profession, U.S. Comptroller General Charles A. Bowsher yesterday criticized the profession's self-regulatory effort for being too secretive and for lacking toughness in discipline.

But the outside criticism pales in comparison with the internal dissension.

Much of the debate involves advertisements put out by the more than 240,000-member American Institute of Certified Public Accountants, the leading professional accounting group, which has formed a self-regulatory division.

The ads, appearing in publications directed at bankers, attorneys and businessmen, stress that accounting firms in the self-regulatory division are reviewed every three years by peer firms or others. The ads offer a directory of division members, an obvious effort to spur clients to hire accounting firms that have undergone peer review.

'Good Housekeeping Seal'

Such less-than-subtle pressure riles some accountants. "Less than 1,500 of the institute's 30,000 (member firms) belong to (the regulatory division)," says Eli Mason, former chairman of the National Conference of CPA Practitioners, an organization of more than 1,100 small and medium-sized accounting firms. "So what right does the institute have in spending membership dues to tell potential client companies and their business advisers that division membership confers the 'good housekeeping seal of approval'?"

John Abernathy, a top official of the institute's self-regulatory division, says that the advertising "wasn't intended to be elitist but to educate the public about what the division does." Mr. Abernathy, chairman and chief executive partner of Seidman & Seidman, notes that his firm is now undergoing its third peer review by Arthur Young & Co. since 1978.

"The reviews have given our firm a sense of discipline and helped improve our quality control," says Mr. Abernathy. And Wayne Collins, director of accounting and auditing for Seidman & Seidman, notes that the firm has stiffened its evaluation of managers and supervisors. "We now look more closely at relationships with clients and (managers and supervisors') management ability, rather than just technical expertise," Mr. Collins says.

Meanwhile, a public oversight board linked to the division has urged all accounting firms that audit public companies to join the division. And seven of the eight biggest accounting firms recently urged the Securities and Exchange Commission to require firms that audit SEC registrants to join the division.

Voluntary Review Urged
Those efforts, too, annoy accountants, particularly at the smaller firms. Irwin Pomerantz, chairman of the National Conference of CPA Practitioners and managing partner of Irwin Pomerantz & Associates, a Los Angeles accounting firm, believes that membership in the self-regulatory division should be voluntary or the division should be eliminated. He says that the leaders of his group have even discussed quitting the institute unless it becomes more responsive to its demands. The conference's firms have about 10,000 accountants.

"There's no evidence that peer reviews . . . have reduced audit failure," says Mr. Pomerantz. "Stronger punishment for accountants that do substandard work would be more effective."

Moreover, he says, "the bigger accounting firms, which are the main culprits in audit failures, are using the division to promote their business. They're hoping that like small ants, we'll disappear."

CPA Self-Regulation: Contradiction in Terms

By Lee Berton

August 19, 1986

Can self-regulation of the accounting profession prevent financial fraud?

The spotlight has been thrown on this issue by Congress

and federal regulators, as they question the efforts of accountants to keep their own house in order.

"The accounting profession's self-regulatory system operates in secrecy and has not disciplined a single firm involved in well-known audit failures," asserts John Dingell (D., Mich.), chairman of a House subcommittee that has been investigating the accounting profession since February 1985. (In an audit failure, a company encounters major business problems or declares bankruptcy soon after receiving a clean audit opinion.)

Major accounting firms see a different purpose for self-regulation. "The entire process is not intended to be punitive but preventative," maintains Peter R. Scanlon, chairman of Coopers & Lybrand, the fourth-largest U.S. accounting firm. "I'm not for hanging people from a lamppost," he says. "It's destructive."

Nine years ago the accounting profession began a self-regulatory effort that included peer reviews every three years of accounting firms by other CPA firms or groups of accountants. Two years later a disciplinary arm, the Special Investigations Committee, was added to the self-regulatory unit of the American Institute of Certified Public Accountants, which today has 240,000 members.

Deaf Ears

In a peer review, outside accountants examine whether an accounting firm's quality-control system is working and whether its accounting and auditing work is performed in compliance with professional standards. The Special Investigations Committee, which has nine experienced auditors, investigates alleged audit failures to see if they result from personnel problems, systems failures or inadequacy in professional standards. The committee may recommend increased partner review of audits, reassignments of personnel, more stringent standards or greater discipline by other ethics bodies.

Critics of the effort say that because the Special Investigations Committee works behind closed doors and the names and offenses of miscreants are withheld from the public, its efforts fall upon the deaf ears of other accountants and fail to prevent the mounting numbers of audit failures, particularly of financial institutions. Federal regulators predict almost a twofold increase in bank failures this year from the 90 in 1985. Five years ago, only 10 banks failed—an annual number that had continued for a decade.

"Self-regulation of accountants cannot work without scalps of offenders who fail to adhere to professional standards hanging on the belts of the regulators," asserts John C. Burton, a former chief accountant of the Securities and Exchange Commission. Mr. Burton is dean of Columbia University's Graduate School of Business.

"The entire process is not intended to be punitive but preventative," maintains Peter R. Scanlon, of Coopers & Lybrand. "I'm not for hanging people from a lamppost."

Until recently, the SEC had been hesitant in putting more pressure on the accounting profession to tell the public more about the firms it has been investigating for possible violations of professional standards. But under pressure from the subcommittee of the House Commerce Committee chaired by Rep. Dingell, the SEC has given the accountants a six-month deadline to improve disclosure of their disciplinary efforts.

The Special Investigations Committee holds that it would prefer to work in secret because it feels it receives more cooperation from the firms whose operations it's scrutinizing. Robert Mautz, a member of the Public Oversight Board, which oversees the committee, points out that the committee has no subpoena powers.

"The committee doesn't want to feed ammunition to the litigant bar," says Mr. Mautz. In recent years, malfeasance suits against accounting firms have increased to the point where insurance has become very expensive and, for smaller accounting firms, difficult to obtain.

But critics note that the self-regulatory program of the New York Stock Exchange has been expelling members and publishing their names since the early 1970s. "While we have had no subpoena powers, we weren't limited by the prohibition against self-incrimination that protects defendants in the courts," says Robert M. Bishop, who ran the Big Board's self-regulatory efforts from 1973 until he retired two months ago.

Member firms, he says, "cannot refuse to give the Big Board information about themselves." Expulsions and suspensions have doubled to more than 100 each year from 50 a decade ago.

A recent report issued by the accountants' Special Investigations Committee is instructive as to how far its disciplinary actions have gone. Of 128 cases it has closed since its inception in late 1979, only eight were referred to the institute's professional ethics division with a recommendation for further investigation. The institute can expel miscreant members and urge state regulators to remove their licenses to practice. Seventeen firms were forced to take corrective action. In four of these cases, personnel and responsibilities were reassigned.

The report doesn't indicate that any individuals were dismissed by the accounting firms. Nor does it cite any firms by name that have been disciplined by the institute. But an institute publication notes that Nemiroff, Cosmas, Titus & Colchamiro, a small Secaucus, New Jersey, accounting firm, had been expelled from the institute's self-regulatory division for failing to cooperate with peer-review procedures.

Robert S. Nemiroff, a partner in the firm, which has eight employees, including two partners, says it was expelled from the self-regulatory program because it couldn't adhere to the peer reviewers' suggestions. "They wanted us during audits to have numerous reviews by other partners," he says. "Our firm is too small and isn't capable of that."

Mr. Nemiroff is angry that his firm has been the target of a practice-upgrading effort that he feels should be aimed at bigger CPA firms. "Since the early 1940s, we've never had one malpractice suit filed against us," he says. "I don't think this [self-regulatory] procedure will stop financial fraud or audit failures. It's simply preventing small firms like ours from competing with big firms."

As a result of being expelled from the self-regulatory program, the firm has had to drop its one public client, which shifted to a Big Eight firm.

Discipline of the big accounting firms has apparently been mild. Mr. Mautz says that pressure from the SEC may eventually force the self-regulatory unit to tell the big accounting firms "they have no choice but to disclose more about their disciplinary efforts."

Mr. Bishop admits that some Big Board member firms felt its self-regulatory program "helped gather information for the other side in litigation." But even if the charges have merit, he says, "you can't stop the disciplinary process nor should you hide it." In truth, he says, litigation helps "develop information for self-discipline because there are usually so many depositions being taken."

Mr. Mautz insists that self-regulatory programs only supplement government regulation and legal action. "Remedial measures over time can eliminate more mistakes and irregularities than punishment," he says. "Most failures to adhere to professional standards are the result of ignorance and carelessness and can be corrected by new procedures and retraining. But there is no regulatory program that can correct evil completely. And not all things that appear to be evil are evil."

In testimony last year before the House subcommittee chaired by Rep. Dingell, John Shad, SEC chairman, said the Special Investigations Committee looks into accusations of alleged audit failures and tries to "upgrade the quality of audits" after companies have had such failures. "There are many, many allegations that aren't even proven," he added. "Some are proved to be baseless."

But Rep. Ron Wyden (D., Ore.), a subcommittee member, accused the SEC of "endorsing a system that ensures that the public gets no information whatsoever."

'Doubts Aren't Assuaged'

Mr. Burton, the former chief SEC accountant, says: "Self-regulation so far doesn't appear to be working and these doubts aren't assuaged by its performance." He says he "isn't terribly impressed by the efforts of the committee when one looks at the magnitude of the misdeeds."

Unless the accounting profession "is ready to take stronger action than patting its colleagues who fail to meet professional standards on the wrist, its self-regulatory efforts won't be very effective," declares Mr. Burton.

The public reports issued by the Special Investigations Committee seem to support Mr. Burton's allegations. Now that a six-month deadline has been set to improve disclosure and performance of the profession's self-regulatory efforts, we must wait and see. But like Mr. Burton, many observers remain skeptical that enough doors will be open and enough scalps will be taken. The concept of self-regulation may itself be oxymoronic.

SEC to Rule Soon on
Peer Reviews for Accountants

By Lee Berton

January 8, 1987

NEW YORK—The Securities and Exchange Commission within a month will decide whether to make peer reviews mandatory for accounting firms that audit public companies. Such companies must register with the SEC.

A. Clarence Sampson, the SEC's chief accountant, wouldn't disclose whether the SEC staff will recommend that the agency require such reviews. But SEC officials have indicated that the staff favors mandatory peer reviews.

Under peer review, outside parties check whether an accounting firm's work follows certain standards, and whether it has high quality-control standards.

While accounting firms have been undergoing voluntary peer review since 1977, a number of firms have dropped out of the voluntary program, partly because of the expense. And some firms resented pressure from the American Institute of Certified Public Accountants to undergo peer review every three years.

Some 1,671 accounting firms are members of the institute's self-regulatory program for auditors of SEC registrants. The SEC estimates that an additional 800 accounting firms who audit SEC registrants haven't joined the institute's self-regulatory program. In mid-1981 membership in the institute's self-regulatory arm was a record 2,205.

Meanwhile, the National Conference of CPA Practitioners, a rival organization to the institute, has begun to organize its own peer review program to compete with the institute's program. The conference has 1,250 accounting firm members with total personnel of 10,000. The institute has 240,000 members.

The conference has opposed efforts of the institute to make institute membership for firm partners dependent on membership in the institute's self-regulatory program. Institute members will vote on such a requirement later this month.

Eli Mason, former conference chairman, says adoption of its peer review program could attract members away from the larger institute. Accountants from some smaller firms believe the institute is dominated by the Big Eight accounting firms.

The institute isn't happy that a rival self-regulatory program is being considered by the conference. "Before any organization sets up on a parallel (peer review) program, it ought to explore in great depth why it isn't joining ours," says Thomas Kelley, an institute vice president.

He adds that peer reviews cost from $500,000 to $1 million for the biggest accounting firms and could cost as much as $4,000 for a small accounting firm with 10 CPA employees.

SEC Proposes Mandatory Peer Reviews of Accounting Firms of Public Companies

By Cynthia S. Grisdela

March 27, 1987

WASHINGTON—The Securities and Exchange Commission voted to seek public comment on a proposal to require a mandatory peer review every three years for accounting firms that audit publicly traded companies.

Currently, many accounting firms undergo voluntary peer reviews through membership in the SEC Practice Section of the American Institute of Certified Public Accountants. These accountants audit about 84% of all publicly held companies registered with the SEC, the agency said. Other accounting firms are peer-reviewed by associations of firms.

Under the proposed rule changes, accounting firms would have the option of having the peer review conducted through an existing peer review organization, such as the institute's program, or having the review supervised by the SEC. In a peer review, one auditing firm or a team of accountants examines another auditing firm's quality-control system and its accounting and auditing practice.

Addressing Antitrust Worries

Having the option of a review supervised by the SEC addresses complaints by some in the accounting profession that mandatory peer review would require them to join the institute, raising antitrust concerns. All reviews would have to be conducted in accordance with standards established by the commission.

Under the proposal, accounting firms that don't submit to peer review would be barred from auditing publicly traded companies. And if an accounting firm failed to correct weaknesses in procedures after a peer review, the proposed rule changes

---

Ms. Grisdela was a staff reporter of THE WALL STREET JOURNAL.

would allow the SEC, after an administrative hearing, to disqualify the firm from certifying financial statements for companies registered with the SEC.

A. Clarence Sampson, the SEC's chief accountant, said peer review won't stop all audit failures, but it will "deal very well" with accounting firms whose procedures aren't adequate enough to do a good audit.

'Cannon to a Fly'

Although the vote to seek comment on this issue for 90 days was unanimous, Commissioner Joseph Grundfest compared mandatory peer review to "taking a cannon to a fly." At his suggestion, the commission agreed to seek comment on whether simply disclosing in the financial statements if the auditing firm had been reviewed would provide adequate investor protection.

Under the proposals, an accounting firm that became subject to the rule because it obtains a new public client or an existing client goes public would be allowed 18 months to obtain its initial peer review. During the grace period, however, all of the firm's audits of public companies would have to be reviewed by an accounting firm that had a peer review within the last three years.

The SEC estimates the cost of complying with the rule change would total about $2,250,000 over three years for the 500 firms that currently don't undergo voluntary reviews.

CPA Group Sued over Bid to Require Membership in a Self-Regulatory Unit

By Lee Berton

March 31, 1987

NEW YORK—Four members of the American Institute of Certified Public Accountants sued the organization in state court here to prevent it from making membership in a self-regulatory unit mandatory for its members with publicly traded clients.

New York Supreme Court Judge Edward Lehner issued a temporary injunction barring the institute from declaring the outcome of two votes on the mandatory membership issue pending a court hearing Friday.

The institute is seeking membership approval for a plan that would require accounting firms with any publicly traded clients to join its self-regulatory unit for firms that practice before the Securities and Exchange Commission. Membership in the SEC practice unit is currently voluntary.

The lawsuit centers on the manner in which the institute is balloting its 250,000 members. But institute officials say that the dispute really concerns opposition to mandatory membership in the SEC practice unit.

Rift between Firms

The four plaintiffs are also members of the National Conference of CPA Practitioners, a group with 1,100 CPA firms that has been pressing the institute to pay more attention to small and medium-sized CPA firms. Thus, the suit indicates that a long-standing rift in the profession between big and smaller CPA firms may be widening, industry observers say.

The plaintiffs are Philip Goldstein, managing partner of Shapiro, Fleischmann & Co., a Miami-based firm; Eli Mason, managing partner of Mason & Co.; Ralph Rehmet, a partner of Mahoney Cohen & Co.; and Stanley Sachs, a partner of Weinick & Sanders. The latter three firms are New York–based.

The institute first mailed ballots last January permitting members to register their votes anonymously. The plaintiffs say that when the ballots received showed only about 60% approval, less than the two-thirds vote required, the institute sent out a second ballot that wasn't anonymous and didn't include material giving both sides of the issue as the first ballot did. This second ballot, the suit says, violated the institute's "lawful procedures" and was "arbitrary and capricious."

Donald Schneeman, the institute's general counsel, said the organization didn't have time to send a "secret ballot" in its second mailing and was rushing because of pressure from federal regulators and the institute's ruling council to increase membership in the self-regulatory unit. Under institute bylaws, a ballot of the members must be completed within two months of an initial vote mailing.

SEC's Proposal
The SEC has just proposed mandatory peer review for CPA firms with publicly traded clients. The institute's ruling council last October approved sending the ballot and recommended an affirmative vote.

Mr. Goldstein, one of the plaintiffs, said it's unfair for the institute to make membership in the SEC practice unit mandatory for CPA firms with publicly traded clients. If his own firm didn't join, he said, "all eight partners in the firm would lose institute membership entailing group-liability and life insurance, which are otherwise difficult to obtain for such low cost."

More than 1,600 accounting firms are members of the SEC practice unit. The unit's public oversight board, a body that critiques the unit's effectiveness in self-regulation, has recommended that more accounting firms join to give the SEC practice unit more credence. In 1981, the unit had a record 2,205 accounting firms as members, but the cost of peer reviews required every three years by the unit caused some firms to resign.

Earlier this year, the National Conference of CPA Practitioners set up its own peer-review program for its members and others to rival the one that has been run by the institute since 1977.

CPAs Defeat Plan on Self-Regulation in Narrow Vote

By Lee Berton

April 10, 1987

NEW YORK—Accountants narrowly defeated a proposal requiring mandatory membership in a self-regulatory program.

In a ballot by the American Institute of Certified Public Accountants, 61% of the 130,000 members who voted backed the measure. The proposal was defeated, however, because it required a two-thirds majority to be enacted. The institute, the profession's major membership organization, has 248,000 members.

Under the institute's voluntary self-regulatory program, which continues, participating members' auditing proficiency is reviewed by other accounting firms or groups of accountants every three years.

Some accountants interpreted the vote as a victory for small firms. They added that it reflects a continuing rift between big and small firms over which organizations should oversee self-regulation and conduct reviews. Bigger firms favor the voluntary program, set up in 1977. Smaller firms, feeling that the institute is dominated by large firms, want self-regulation to be done by groups outside the institute.

J. Michael Cook, institute chairman, said that in view of the vote, the institute will strongly support a similar proposal by the Securities and Exchange Commission for mandatory peer review.

"I would have preferred for our proposal to have been adopted first, but recognize that the SEC approach will in substance achieve the same objective," said Mr. Cook, who also is chairman of Deloitte, Haskins & Sells, a major accounting firm.

The SEC is expected to vote on the proposal in the second half of the year.

Four institute members sued the organization in a state court here over the way the vote was conducted, but the suit has been dropped because of the outcome of the vote.

Eli Mason, one of the plaintiffs, said the proposal's defeat is a "signal to the institute that it needs to reform the old-boy system in which it is run by bigger accounting firms."

SEC to Propose Forcing Firms to Disclose Auditor-Shopping for Optimum Opinions

By Lee Berton

June 23, 1987

The Securities and Exchange Commission is expected to propose today a controversial rule that would force public companies that are changing auditors to disclose when and why they have "shopped" for favorable accounting opinions.

In the past, the SEC has dealt with opinion-shopping by challenging auditors' opinions of specific companies that have changed auditors. The proposed rule would require all companies changing auditors to disclose every difference of opinion with its auditors over the past two years. The SEC is expected to make a final decision on the rule later this year, after a three-month period for public comment.

Financial executives at major companies generally are opposed to such added disclosure. "It would serve no useful purpose and in many instances would inhibit my discussions with normally helpful accounting firms other than our auditors," said Burton Broome, vice president and controller of San Francisco-based Transamerica Corp.

Mr. Broome, who also is chairman of a Financial Executive Institute subcommittee that deals with the SEC, added that if the SEC approves the proposal, it "may force financial executives to ask advice from other (publicly held) corporations rather than from the accounting profession."

"Trying to find the best application of accounting standards isn't opinion-shopping," asserted Herbert D. Ihle, senior vice president of Minneapolis-based Pillsbury Co. "The SEC is trying to fix something that isn't broken. The proposal is disclosure-overkill." Mr. Ihle also is a member of the institute's SEC subcommittee.

More Auditor Switches

Edmund Coulson, the SEC's deputy chief accountant, said an unusually large number of companies has switched auditors in recent years. The Public Accounting Report, an Atlanta news-letter, noted recently that last year there were 737 auditor changes by public companies, up 36% from 1985.

"While only about 5% of these result from disagreements, we feel that the public perception of such auditor changes requires more disclosure," Mr. Coulson said.

In the past, the SEC has sternly warned corporations and accounting firms about "the dangers inherent in opinion-shopping." Such conduct "erodes the public's belief in the integrity of both the financial markets and the independent audit function," the SEC has said.

The current proposal would require a public company changing auditors to disclose any significant accounting issues it discussed with the new auditors or any other auditing firm over the past two years. It also would widen the definition of "difference of opinion" between a company and its auditors that must be disclosed.

The proposal is less stringent than one urged recently by the National Commission on Fraudulent Financial Reporting, which conducted a two-year study of financial fraud under the sponsorship of five accounting and financial executives' organizations. The commission, headed by James Treadway, a former SEC commissioner, last month recommended that companies disclose differences of opinions with outside auditors over the past three years, rather than over two years, as the SEC has suggested.

Some businessmen have complained that forcing companies that change auditors to disclose every discussion with accounting firms over opinions could raise too many red flags and confuse investors.

Tougher Rules Called For

But some accountants believe the SEC should be even tougher on disclosure about company-auditor relationships. "What the SEC did was a modest step in the right direction, but much more could and should be done," said John C. Burton, former chief accountant of the SEC.

Mr. Burton, dean of Columbia University's Graduate School of Business, said the SEC should require all companies to disclose the nature of all fees for auditing, tax work and consulting paid to outside accounting firms. "The relationship between a company and its auditors should be an open one to the public, and this could help prevent the kind of auditor abuses we've seen in recent years," he added.

In recent years, court suits against accounting firms charging negligence and lack of independence have increased as many companies encountered major business problems after clean audits.

In the past four years the SEC has filed administrative proceedings against three thrifts for switching auditors after disagreements over accounting principles with previous auditors. The thrifts are Southeastern Savings & Loan Co., Charlotte, North Carolina; Scottish Savings & Loan Association Inc., Greensboro, North Carolina; and Broadview Financial Corp., Cleveland. The thrifts agreed to accept accounting treatments mandated by the SEC.

The SEC said that Southeastern and Scottish spread one year's trading losses over 12 years instead of taking them all at once, as was required. When the institutions' accountants objected, the thrifts hired new auditors, the SEC added. Broadview fired its auditors over a difference of opinion on a real estate transaction, according to the SEC.

Accountant Kaiser Changes His Mind, Leads Push for Required Peer Review

By Lee Berton

December 14, 1987

For years, Charles Kaiser, Jr., was adamantly opposed to any self-regulatory program for accountants. A decade ago, he insisted before a congressional committee that a subsequently adopted voluntary program wasn't needed.

These days, the accounting profession is considering whether to make that program mandatory. And one of the proposal's biggest boosters is Mr. Kaiser, the 53-year-old managing partner of Los Angeles-based Pannell Kerr Forster, the 14th-biggest U.S. accounting firm.

Mr. Kaiser has not only changed his mind, he is singing the praises of the measure to the 255,000 members of its sponsor, the American Institute of Certified Public Accountants.

Mr. Kaiser heads an eight-member institute committee that is backing the proposal and spending $1 million to promote it. He has been crisscrossing the nation to persuade members to vote for it. Although accountants are usually low-key, Mr. Kaiser has mounted a high-profile campaign that includes audio and video cassettes, imprinted baseball caps and giant campaign buttons. The push has raised the ire of some institute members.

Under the institute's current voluntary self-regulatory program, accounting firms can elect to have their audit procedures reviewed every three years by other firms or groups of accountants to make sure the audits are done properly. If the new proposal is approved by two-thirds of those who vote, it would make such a peer review a mandatory requirement of membership in the institute, the most prestigious professional organization of accountants.

Institute members are currently casting ballots by mail, and the final count will be in by mid-January. The new program also would make continuing professional education mandatory and require five years of college education for accountants by the year 2000.

'Forced on Us From the Top'

What made Mr. Kaiser shift his opinion on the self-regulatory program? "The first one 10 years ago was put in place by the institute's leadership without consulting the entire membership," he says. "It was forced upon us from the top down."

Since then, he notes, the institute has fine-tuned the program "so that it works for all the members, and we're now asking all the members to vote on making it more effective. Working from the bottom up is a much better way to do things."

Not everyone agrees with Mr. Kaiser. "It's appalling that the institute is spending so much money to try to cram some of these controversial programs down the throats of some members, who don't practice as accountants," says Lee Seidler, an institute member who is a managing director of Bear Stearns Cos., a major securities firm.

Mr. Seidler, a former accounting professor at New York University graduate school of business, is particularly opposed to continuing professional education, or CPE, for institute members who work for industry and government. "Most CPE courses are so bizarre anyway and are hardly worth the effort of attending," he says.

Some members from small firms feel the institute is controlled by the big accounting firms, which can better afford the cost of peer review. They say Mr. Kaiser changed his original convictions because he wanted to join the establishment.

One dissident group, the National Conference of CPA Practitioners, which has 1,350 small accounting firms as members, recently ran a newspaper ad nationwide opposing the proposal.

The proposal is "caused by the failure of the AICPA to convince the vast majority of medium-sized and local firms to join" the voluntary self-regulatory effort, the ad says.

Heading Off the Government

Mr. Kaiser concedes the institute proposals are controversial. But he believes that the accounting profession must upgrade its image on its own without government urging or it will lose the confidence of the public and be subject to more government regulation.

"Peer review is costing my firm $180,000 (every three years), but it's worth it because it has helped us upgrade our quality-control procedures, and as a result we're obtaining more audit clients," says Mr. Kaiser. Pannell Kerr, with 147 partners and 40 offices, has annual revenue of about $100 million.

"In the past, I was a skeptic, but I've changed my mind because I can now see how important self-regulation is," says Mr. Kaiser. "The profession now has its fate in its own hands, and I'd hate to see it drop the ball because there are some perennial critics among us who haven't kept up with the times."

Considered an iconoclast, Mr. Kaiser has a keen sense of humor and works hard to dispel the image of dullness traditionally assigned to accountants. He put a picture of King Kong and a ghoulish cartoon by Charles Addams on the covers of his firm's promotional brochures.

"I admit to being a bit of pixie now and then," he says.

Accountants Vote Required Program of Self-Regulation

By Lee Berton

January 14, 1988

NEW YORK—The accounting profession approved a program of mandatory self-regulation under which accountants will be required to review the quality of each other's work.

Despite bitter opposition from some small accounting firms, the members of the American Institute of Certified Public Accountants voted to require that all the institute's members undergo a "quality review" once every three years.

Under the institute's new program, accounting firms' audit procedures will be scrutinized by other firms or groups of accountants to make sure audits are done properly. The AICPA is the leading membership body for U.S. accountants.

Of the institute's 264,000 members, about 183,500 voted, and 76% of those voting—more than the required two-thirds—approved the quality-review measure. Such peer reviews have been voluntary for accountants in the past decade.

Lawsuit by Some Members

The program was opposed by some members of the AICPA, who had filed a suit in New York state Supreme Court seeking to block the institute from tallying the votes on its membership referendum. The court this week declined to grant a temporary restraining order but scheduled a hearing for this morning on whether the voting procedures were proper.

The suit was filed by five AICPA members who also belong to the National Conference of CPA Practitioners, which has

1,350 small accounting firms as members. Last year the conference ran a nationwide newspaper ad opposing the peer-review
proposal.

Edmund Coulson, the recently named chief accountant of
the Securities and Exchange Commission, praised the new program, calling it "a positive initiative for quality practice." But he
said the SEC will also continue to press for its own peer review
measure. In essence, the SEC contends that accountants who
aren't institute members should also be subject to mandatory
peer review.

Voluntary Participation

The SEC has been disappointed by the small number of firms
that have joined the AICPA's longstanding program of voluntary
self-regulation. Only 2,000 of 34,000 firms participated in the
voluntary program.

Some legislators previously recommended that the government take a stronger hand in regulating accountants unless the
accountants cleaned their own house. John C. Burton, dean of
Columbia University's graduate business school, says approval
of the mandatory program will "reduce the likelihood of more
government regulation."

Institute members also approved changes requiring continuing professional education for all members, and a fifth year of
education for members who join starting in the year 2000. And
they let accounting firms engage in other occupations that don't
involve conflicts of interest.

"This vote means accountants are recognizing that the public interest requires us to keep our house in order," said A. Marvin Strait, a Colorado Springs accountant who is the institute's
chairman.

CHAPTER 4

THE MARKETING OF ACCOUNTING FIRMS' SERVICES

The marketing of accounting firms' services has changed dramatically. Traditionally, accounting firms have primarily marketed accounting and tax services to companies and to individuals in a very low-key manner. The last decade has witnessed a tremendous growth in management consulting activities for leading accounting firms. These activities have not only become the major source of revenue for many firms, but also represent the most profitable segment of their operations. This increased diversification is not unlike the increased diversification of products and services offered by financial services companies.

As consumers of these products, readers of this volume would do well to sharpen their understanding of the recent dynamics that have effected this diversification of services. Also, the more aggressive marketing approach from the traditionally staid and conservative accounting firms is changing the way outside accounting and consulting services are purchased and managed.

Accounting Ethics Rules Are Studied for Anti-Competitive Impact by FTC

By Lee Berton

February 21, 1986

NEW YORK—The Federal Trade Commission is trying to find out whether the accounting profession's ethics rules are inhibiting accountants' ability to compete with management consultants.

According to accountants questioned by the FTC, the investigation focuses in part on rules that ban accountants from taking commissions and contingency fees from clients. The FTC also is looking at rules that make it difficult for accountants to make business forecasts for clients, and require firms to bear the names of individuals. Management consultants, who can give their firms colorful corporate names, aren't bound by such limitations.

The profession's rules, for example, prevent an accountant from taking a commission for advising a client to buy specific computer hardware, or taking an audit or consulting job if the final fee is based on the benefit derived by the client.

Over the past year the FTC has been quietly gathering thousands of documents from the American Institute of Certified Public Accountants, a trade group that sets the profession's standards.

While the FTC yesterday declined to confirm or deny existence of the investigation, Donald Schneeman, the AICPA's general counsel, said the institute has forwarded 16,000 pages of documents since last March and plans to send 25,000 more pages soon. "We are cooperating fully and hope that the FTC investigation is near a conclusion," Mr. Schneeman said.

In Philadelphia, Jerome W. Rosenberg, managing partner of Laventhol & Horwath, the 10th-biggest U.S. accounting firm, said FTC investigators will be meeting with partners of the firm over the next week or so. "We understand the investigation concerns whether ethics rules banning contingent fees, and so on, stifle competition," Mr. Rosenberg said.

The debate over whether accounting firms should be able to charge clients for extra services or on a performance basis has split the accounting profession. Big firms structure fees to include consulting advice. Some middle-sized firms would like to end the bans on commissions and contingency fees.

But smaller firms oppose ending the bans because they feel the bigger firms would gain a marketing advantage. "The FTC is trying to convert accounting into a marketplace where we sell like purveyors of toothpaste and breakfast food," says Eli Mason, founder of the National Conference of CPA Practitioners, a group of 1,100 small firms.

In the spring of 1984, the 250-member governing council of the 230,000-member AICPA by a narrow margin opposed ending the contingency-fee ban. The issue was referred to an AICPA committee, which is studying whether a number of rules require change.

In the late 1970s, the FTC investigated the AICPA for two years to see if certain of its rules hindered competition within the profession. Among other things, it scrutinized a prohibition against accountants licensing their services, as well as the tough national certified public accountant examination. "No FTC actions resulted," the AICPA's Mr. Schneeman recalled yesterday.

Accountants Group Votes to Keep Ban on Contingent Fees

By Lee Berton

October 20, 1986

NEW YORK—The major professional body for U.S. accountants voted by a narrow margin to continue its long-standing ban on working on a contingency-fee basis—as attorneys are permitted to do—despite pressure from federal regulators to drop the ban.

Under their current ethics rules, accountants generally are prohibited from providing services with the fee contingent upon benefits or profits they get for their clients. Their current fees are based on hourly rates.

But the Justice Department and the Federal Trade Commission over the past few years have insisted that the ban by accountants against contingent fees is a violation of the antitrust laws and decreases competition.

In recent months, the FTC has been increasing the pressure on the American Institute of Certified Public Accountants, which has 240,000 members, to eliminate the ban. Institute officials say that the regulators have told them to expect a lawsuit if members don't eliminate the ban.

Over the weekend, members of the institute's ruling council, meeting in Kansas City, Missouri, voted 98-97 to continue the contingency ban. The ban was upheld in two council votes in 1984.

The latest institute proposal would have permitted accounting firms to take contingent fees for consulting and tax work only, but it would have prohibited the firms from doing audits for clients that pay them on a contingency basis for other work.

"Even though the vote was so close this time, we feel the mood of most institute members is to continue the ban," said J. Michael Cook, the institute's newly elected chairman. "Most of our members feel contingencies erode professional standards and create conflicts of interest."

Advocates of the ban say that accounting firms doing audits might be more likely to favor projects or business systems for which they have provided advice on a contingency basis. Institute officials say the council was asked to consider eliminating the ban because of pressure from regulators and the fear of litigation against the ban.

In other action, the council approved asking members to vote on a proposal that would require accounting firms whose partners are institute members to be members of a self-regulatory effort involving public clients. The council urged members to support the new requirement.

Many small accounting firms have opposed the mandatory membership requirement because they believe that the self-regulatory effort benefits only the big accounting firms, which are often targets of huge lawsuits over allegedly faulty audits. But the institute has supported mandatory membership in its self-regulatory effort because it believes that the effort improves audit quality for the entire profession.

Accounting Group Will Fight Efforts by FTC to Lift Ban on Contingent Fees

By Lee Berton

July 28, 1987

NEW YORK—The major professional body for U.S. accountants said it will resist efforts by the Federal Trade Commission to eliminate the group's long-standing ban on contingent fees.

This marks the first time in a decade that the American Institute of Certified Public Accountants has rebuffed federal regulators' requests to abolish what regulators feel are anti-competitive practices of accountants.

Since 1977, the institute—under pressure from federal regulators on antitrust grounds—has eliminated bans against advertising, competitive bidding and uninvited solicitation of clients. Regulators also are trying to upset state rules or laws retaining such bans.

After a two-year investigation involving subpoenaing 18,000 documents of the institute, the Federal Trade Commission recently asked the institute to eliminate its ban on contingent fees for work that doesn't involve audits, the institute said. "We're not going to go along this time, but will let the courts decide," said Donald J. Schneeman, the institute's general counsel.

Under the institute's current ethics rules, accountants generally are prohibited from providing services with the fee contingent upon benefits or profits they get for their clients. Accountants' fees are currently based on hourly rates.

"Now we're prepared to fight to keep the government off our backs," Mr. Schneeman added. "Many of our 250,000 members feel that increased competition has only eroded professional standards for independence and hurt their professional image."

Officials of the FTC publicly declined to comment on the investigation of the institute involving the contingent-fee ban. But privately they expressed surprise that the accountants, group is now throwing down the gauntlet on contingent fees after yielding for a decade to government pressure for increased competition.

"There's no question this will cost both the institute and the government money involving hearings and legal fees over the next two years," said Mr. Schneeman. But he noted that some institute members have said that they would be willing to put up funds to fight the current FTC effort.

He noted that five years ago, the National Society of Professional Engineers spent $1.2 million unsuccessfully defending in court its ban against contingent fees. "The engineers lost in the U.S. Supreme Court, but unlike engineers, accountants have a responsibility to the public when they audit their client companies. Many of our members feel that the ban against contingent fees helps accountants remain independent and objective."

In an FTC private antitrust investigation of a professional group, if an organization being investigated declines to follow the FTC staff's order, the organization can appeal to an administrative law judge and the full commission. If those appeals fail, the organization can turn to the courts, starting with a U.S. court of appeals.

The institute said it will suspend enforcement of its ban against contingent fees "until a final resolution (of the matter) can be obtained, a period that could take longer than two years." Mr. Schneeman said that complaints during the period against CPA firms that violate the ban will be processed by the institute when the matter is resolved, if the courts support the ban.

If an institute member violates any ban in the institute's code of ethics, his membership in the institute can be suspended. This is considered a "black mark" that few CPA firms concerned about their reputation would want, Mr. Schneeman said.

A Battle Cry for America's Accountants

By Lee Berton

September 23, 1987

NEW YORK—Accountants usually like to keep a low profile, especially with the government. But two of the profession's leaders—A. Marvin Strait and J. Michael Cook—say now they're ready to fight.

Mr. Strait succeeded Mr. Cook this week as chairman of the 255,000-member American Institute of Certified Public Accountants, although Mr. Cook will continue to work actively in institute affairs. Both are preparing to battle with the Federal Trade Commission over FTC assertions that the accounting profession is stifling competition within its own ranks and denying clients access to certain services.

FTC officials concede privately that they're shocked that America's accountants may be digging in this time. Since 1977, the institute has yielded without resistance to FTC prodding to allow accountants to advertise, bid competitively and solicit clients uninvited.

"At first we thought the fight wasn't worth it since the FTC has been so successful in eliminating other ethics rules," says Mr. Cook. But last year by a narrow vote and twice in 1984 the institute's ruling council voted to continue its ban on contingent fees.

"Now we're prepared to take a stand," Mr. Cook says.

Earlier this year, the FTC asked the institute to drop its long-standing ban on contingent fees. Under the ban, accountants cannot charge fees contingent on the benefits or profits they get for clients, as can lawyers and other consultants. Instead, accountants charge a flat hourly fee. The FTC also wants accountants to be able to take commissions, incorporate their firms and use names other than their personal names in a firm's title. The institute currently bans these practices.

Mr. Strait, who runs a Colorado Springs, Colorado, firm with only five partners, and Mr. Cook, who heads the nation's seventh-largest accounting firm, are adamant that such steps would erode an accountant's independence, no matter what the size of the firm. They believe they have overwhelming support from their colleagues.

Mr. Strait, the 53-year-old executive partner of Strait, Kushinsky & Co., says: "Accountants can't be compared with architects, engineers and doctors because we do audits for a third party—the public—and thus have to be purer."

Adds Mr. Cook, 45, chairman of New York–based Deloitte, Haskins & Sells: "When we audit a client company's books, independence is the keystone to our integrity." Mr. Cook, who notes that his firm has such big audit clients as General Motors Corp. and Procter & Gamble Co., says that "if our fees depend on what benefits we can obtain for our clients, we can hardly be the public's watchdog."

While the biggest accounting firms support the institute's position, there are some smaller local firms that would remove any restraints on getting business because they believe the profession is clinging to dated anti-competitive practices. But most seem to believe that turning accountants into "jazzy salesmen who would do anything to make a buck," as a partner of one local firm says, would damage the profession's independence and integrity.

While the FTC won't comment publicly on its differences with the institute, the agency, in a letter to state accounting regulators last June, said it wanted the ban dropped to "permit increased competition" and to "benefit consumers by permitting accountants to provide services that consumers want." The ban, the FTC said, "may harm consumers by restraining price competition among accountants."

Mr. Cook and Mr. Strait concede that the FTC didn't expect the institute, the leading membership organization for accountants, to resist. "First of all, the battle will be long and expensive," says Mr. Strait, who plans to cross the country with a stand-up-and-fight message to certified public accountants during the next year. "We're not turning back," he says. Institute officials estimate that legal fees for the battle will be at least $1 million.

In its opposition to the FTC, the institute plans to seek a hearing before an administrative law judge and, if it loses that round, to appeal to the full commission. If those steps fail, the institute says it will turn to a federal appeals court.

Mr. Strait has been active in institute business since 1967 and believes he can convince institute members in small local firms that fighting to retain the contingent-fee ban is right.

Mr. Cook joined Deloitte in 1964, became a partner in 1974, and last year became chairman and chief executive officer. Deloitte has annual revenue of $700 million.

Mr. Strait opened a Colorado Springs office in 1973. When that firm merged with Coopers & Lybrand, a major firm, in 1977, he decided to stay with a small firm. "I felt that with a local firm, I could make my own decisions," he says.

"When I'm in the boondocks on institute business, local CPAs often ask me, 'What do you institute guys in your ivory tower in New York really know about our small-town problems?'" Mr. Strait says. "I remind them that I started practice in Lamar, Colorado, where I was the only accountant for 6,500 residents in a five-county area."

Accounting Group to Consider Dropping Ban on Contingency Fees and Commissions

By Lee Berton

August 25, 1988

NEW YORK—Accountants are close to accepting certain fees and commissions they long have shunned as inviting conflicts of interest.

Next Tuesday in Chicago, the ruling council of the 272,000-member American Institute of Certified Public Accountants—under regulatory pressure to become more competitive—will vote in a closed session on whether to drop bans against such compensation.

Under a proposed compromise between the institute and the Federal Trade Commission, the bans would be lifted, with one major exception. They still would apply in situations involving clients where accounting firms perform audits, do financial reviews and compile data.

Steering Business

Several types of fees are at issue. First are the commissions that accountants might get for steering business to a client; accountants, for instance, could earn money from sellers of computer equipment, if a client took the accountant's advice and bought the equipment. Then there are contingency fees, which would give accountants a percentage of savings they achieve for a client by devising such things as a cost-cutting plan, or for assisting in a merger or acquisition.

In a letter last year to the National Association of State Boards of Accountancy, the FTC said allowing contingency fees could lower the cost and raise the quality of accounting services by linking CPAs' fees to the results of a job rather than the time put into it. In the same letter, the FTC said allowing commissions would give consumers an option of "one-stop shopping for financial-planning services," thereby letting accountants be more competitive with rivals in other fields.

Under current ethics rules of the institute, the industry's principal professional group, accountants can only charge hourly fees for such advice and cannot accept any contingency fees or commissions. Contingency fees and commissions may be much bigger than hourly fees, but an accountant runs the risk of working for nothing if, for example, a client doesn't follow his advice.

But for many accountants, the major problem with fees and commissions is that they are fertile ground for conflicts of interest because they could lead an accountant to give biased advice just to get a bigger fee. Accepting such fees could change accounting to a cutthroat business from a profession with a reputation for objectivity, advocates of the ban say.

"Permitting contingency fees and commissions will only make us unprofessional and create a lot of problems for our clients," says Edwin Kliegman, managing partner of Marcum & Kliegman, a small Hicksville, New York, accounting firm.

But some accountants say dropping the bans would benefit clients by allowing accountants to compete with other consultants who are under no such restrictions.

> *'Permitting contingent fees and commissions will only make us unprofessional and create a lot of problems for our clients,' says one accountant.*

H. D. Vest, an Irving, Texas, accountant who has threatened to sue the institute if it doesn't drop the bans, says eliminating the restrictions "will permit CPAs to provide broad-based financial services to their clients at lower prices." Mr. Vest, who began offering clients financial-planning services in 1979, has been the object of an institute investigation over ethics violations since 1985. Mr. Vest says he has been accepting contingency fees and commissions for several years from clients of his financial-services company, which offers insurance and brokerage services in addition to limited accounting services.

"The institute restriction on commissions places us at a competitive disadvantage compared with other financial planners," Mr. Vest says.

While the FTC won't comment publicly on its two-year investigation of the institute's ethics rules, institute officials say the group has been negotiating with the agency almost as long over the bans on contingency fees and commissions. At first the FTC wanted the contingency fee and commission bans dropped for all work performed by accountants, but in recent months the agency has been more willing to compromise, institute officials say.

That's apparently because the institute late last year vowed to fight the FTC in court and pointed out that the bans were supported by its ruling council in four votes since 1984. But since then, some members of the institute who accept contingency fees and commissions in violation of its ethics ban have threatened to sue the group on antitrust grounds.

Willkie, Farr & Gallagher, the institute's outside counsel, has advised the institute that in the current legal climate of open competition, the bans probably wouldn't be upheld in court. So last week the institute's 20-member board voted, without a public announcement, to advise the 259-member ruling council to accept a consent decree from the FTC dropping the bans for non-audit clients.

'Emotional Issue'

"It's a very emotional issue with our members, but at this point we feel it would be very difficult in an antitrust sense to sustain total bans against all contingency fees and commissions," says Donald Schneeman, the institute's general counsel. "We expect the council debate to be lively but have every expectation" that it will accept the board's recommendation, he adds.

If the institute accepts the consent decree, an FTC agreement to drop its investigation would be subject to public comment and review by the full commission. Jeffrey I. Zuckerman, director of the FTC's bureau of competition, declines to comment on specifics of the consent decree. But he notes that the FTC doesn't have jurisdiction over state laws that can ban business practices of accountants. "We're hopeful that if the institute drops its bans, the state boards of accountancy or legislatures will get the message," Mr. Zuckerman says.

Nation's Accountants Vote to End Bans against Certain Fees and Commissions

By Lee Berton

August 31, 1988

NEW YORK—The nation's accountants approved dropping long-time bans against accepting certain fees and commissions.

By a vote of 191 to 5, the ruling council of the American Institute of Certified Public Accountants, meeting in Chicago, agreed to permit the institute's 272,000 members to accept contingency fees from clients, and commissions from suppliers recommended to clients by accountants. Accountants had long opposed such arrangements as possible conflicts of interest.

By dropping the bans on contingency fees, accountants can

now be paid a percentage of savings or profits the accountants help a client achieve. Under previous professional rules accountants could only charge hourly fees for such advice.

One Major Exception
Under a compromise with the Federal Trade Commission, which began an antitrust investigation of the bans a few years ago, there would still be one major exception. The bans would remain in force for clients where accounting firms perform audits, do financial reviews, compile data, and examine predictions of financial positions, operating results and future cash flows.

A. Marvin Strait, the institute's chairman, said the exception "leaves untouched our ability to adopt reasonable rules (involving clients) for whom we do work that will be relied on by third parties." He added: "We continue to believe that the accounting profession is different from other professions against whom the FTC has taken action. Our requirements of independence and objectivity are crucial to continued public confidence in our work."

Disclosure Rules
Under the agreement, accountants would be required to disclose to clients that the accountants have accepted fees from others for products or services referred to the clients.

The compromise with the FTC also requires the institute to drop bans against advertising that had forbidden self-laudatory statements or testimonials by clients. In the late 1970s, under pressure from the FTC, the institute dropped an outright ban against all advertising by its members.

The FTC for at least a decade has been pressing professionals, including accountants, attorneys, physicians and dentists, to get rid of professional ethics bans that the FTC feels are anti-competitive.

The FTC at first had wanted the institute bans to be dropped for all work performed by accountants. But after the institute council voted four times since 1984 to keep the bans, the federal agency in recent months was willing to compromise. Several institute members recently threatened to sue the institute if the bans weren't lifted. The institute's outside counsel advised that the bans couldn't be upheld in the current legal climate of open competition for the professions.

The latest institute agreement with the FTC staff is subject to public comment over a two-month period and review by the full commission.

CHAPTER 5

THE CHANGING ROLE OF THE INDEPENDENT ACCOUNTANT

Once considered a safe profession, accounting is now laden with pitfalls, "dangerous liaisons," and high-profile risks. The growing consulting services, lucrative tax practices and accounting and audit services now offered by accounting firms have increased exposure for the public accountants who work in today's litigious business environment. As a result of these changes, accountants need to change and adjust to their new roles. Only those professionals with flexibility and breadth can hope to compete effectively in this increasingly competitive market. The following articles describe some of the forces that have changed the accountant's role and the risks in his or her service to industry.

Price Waterhouse Head Recommends Expanded Audits

By Lee Berton

June 4, 1986

WASHINGTON—The chairman of a major accounting firm urged the Securities and Exchange Commission to require the auditing of certain data in the annual report outside the financial statement.

The change, recommended by Joseph E. Connor, head of Price Waterhouse, would significantly broaden the outside audit at a time when most big accounting firms would prefer that it be restricted. Mr. Connor specifically said he favors broadening the audit so that it includes the annual report section labeled "management discussion and analysis."

This section usually contains predictions about the company or information on loss of market share or new competitive factors facing the company. Auditors generally prefer to avoid signing their names to such "soft data" because they fear suits by investors, creditors or suppliers if the predictions prove incorrect.

Mr. Connor's suggestion drew sharp opposition from other accounting profession officials at a SEC-sponsored panel, and noncommittal responses from SEC officials, who said they would study it. But several panel members who supported it asserted that more comprehensive audits or financial data could serve as "early warnings" of coming business problems.

John C. Burton, former SEC chief accountant, said he supports Mr. Connor's suggestion. Mr. Burton said the SEC could check on the accuracy of the predictions in later years. Mr. Burton is dean of Columbia University's Graduate School of Business in New York.

J. Michael Cook, chairman of Deloitte, Haskins & Sells, a major accounting firm, said he opposes Mr. Connor's suggestion because extending the audit to company predictions or discussion of problems would involve auditors in major management decisions. Such broadening of accountants' duties is "neither desirable nor appropriate," he said.

Mr. Connor's recommendation highlights a major split in the accounting profession between Price Waterhouse and the seven other major accounting firms, collectively known as the Big Eight. Mr. Cook's rebuttal to Mr. Connor's proposal also added a touch of irony because Price Waterhouse and Deloitte, Haskins & Sells in 1984 began talks for a possible merger, which was later aborted.

Besides heading Deloitte, Mr. Cook also is chairman-elect of the American Institute of Certified Public Accountants, which has more than 230,000 members. The institute recently received a report of the seven other Big Eight firms, excluding Price Waterhouse, suggesting stricter audits but not extending the audit to other data in the annual report as Mr. Connor, who heads Price Waterhouse, recommends.

This so-called "Big Seven" report also urges the SEC to require all accounting firms that audit SEC registrants to join a self-regulatory unit of the institute. Currently, only 400 of 1,000 accounting firms with SEC clients are members of the unit, which has mandatory peer reviews every three years.

Several panel members criticized the self-regulatory efforts of the institute as being too mild and secret. But Philip Chenok, institute president, noted that one New Jersey accounting firm had been expelled from the self-regulatory unit for failing to comply with its peer-review standards.

SEC to Oppose Bill that Forces Auditors to Report Possible Fraud by Their Clients

By Cynthia S. Grisdela

June 20, 1986

WASHINGTON—The Securities and Exchange Commission plans to oppose a House bill that would force independent auditors of publicly held companies to report possible fraud by their clients.

In an unusual, hastily called meeting, the commissioners and staff members debated proposed testimony on the matter that SEC Chairman John Shad is scheduled to deliver Monday to a House subcommittee investigating the accounting profession. The commissioners urged Mr. Shad to strongly oppose the bill.

The commissioners all expressed "grave reservations" about provisions of the bill that would require auditors to report known or suspected fraud to securities regulators and other law enforcement agencies. They said they worried about making fundamental changes in auditors' relationships with clients and regulators.

The bill, said commissioner Aulana Peters, would "turn in-

Ms. Grisdela was a staff reporter of THE WALL STREET JOURNAL.

dependent professionals into state-regulated examiners," similar to those in the insurance and banking industries. She also questioned whether the independent auditor "is the right person to focus on this problem of fraud detection."

Early Warning System

The House bill was introduced last month by Rep. Ronald Wyden (D., Ore.) to help provide "an early warning system." It came in response to a number of widely publicized financial failures in recent years.

Rep. Wyden, a member of the House Energy and Commerce Committee's oversight and investigations subcommittee, said, "If the public cannot depend on the SEC and the auditing profession to detect fraud, then it will be left to Congress to crack the whip." He said that at the Monday hearings he will suggest that the SEC be given the power to inspect auditors the way the regulatory agency inspects broker-dealers.

Half the bank failures in the United States are a direct result of management fraud, Rep. Wyden said. "It isn't a responsible action for the SEC and the auditors to bury their heads like ostriches . . . (while) the public perceives management fraud as continuing."

Currently, auditors are required only to tell management about any fraud they suspect or discover in the course of examining a company's financial records. If management doesn't respond or take appropriate action, the auditor may resign.

To protect whistle-blowing auditors, the Wyden bill would forbid lawsuits against them by clients or others who might allege breach of confidential relationships or damages to reputation.

The SEC stressed that it believes detection of fraud is primarily the responsibility of management rather than the outside auditor's. The SEC long has supported the self-regulatory efforts of accountants. But the accounting profession itself is divided on the effectiveness of such self-regulatory efforts.

Rising Costs Seen

The SEC staff said the Wyden bill is likely to boost substantially the cost to publicly held companies for yearly audits required by securities regulations. Chairman Shad said the additional costs probably would have to be borne by public companies and their shareholders, who are "the very people we're trying to help." The bill, he added, also would increase the agency's workload.

In addition, it would represent "quite an extraordinary imposition of auditors into a position they might not be qualified to handle," because they aren't lawyers, Mr. Shad said. He added that companies have a vested interest in maintaining adequate internal control systems.

Several commissioners said they were troubled that the Wyden bill implies that auditors must find and report every instance of fraud, regardless of the cost, rather than concentrate on impropriety that would have a material effect on a company's financial position.

The need for legislation, the agency said, should be reassessed after studies are completed by the Auditing Standards Board of the American Institute of Certified Public Accountants, the profession's trade group, and the National Commission on Fraudulent Financial Reporting. Commissioner Joseph Grundfest warned in particular against cutting off debate prematurely, although he shared the other commissioners' skepticism about the Wyden bill.

The commission also opposed parts of a Price Waterhouse proposal to set up a self-regulatory organization for accountants under the SEC's oversight.

Although the agency hasn't reached a conclusion on the need for such an organization, the commissioners unanimously agreed that they couldn't support an accounting self-regulatory organization like the one proposed by the big accounting firm.

Under the Price Waterhouse plan, a "Chinese Wall" would be established between the organization and the commission to maintain the confidentiality of audit clients. It would mean, among other things, that the self-regulatory organization [SRO] wouldn't turn over results of its investigations to the SEC.

Commissioner Peters said that "the inherent contradiction of the Chinese Wall would in essence isolate the SRO from the SEC," contrary to the relationship the commission has with other self-regulatory bodies.

Rewriting the Rules: Jerry Sullivan Leads Effort to Increase Auditors' Responsibility

By Lee Berton

December 17, 1986

NEW YORK—Jerry D. Sullivan, director of audit policy for Big Eight accounting firm Coopers & Lybrand, is an ardent jogger and amateur sports-car racer.

But the race he finds himself in now may be the most challenging of his career.

As chairman of the powerful auditing standards board of the American Institute of Certified Public Accountants, Mr. Sullivan heads a task force that is writing the most comprehensive changes in auditing rules in almost 40 years. The proposals, which were presented to the board yesterday, are a response to the growing number of critics who want tougher corporate audits and who blame auditors for failing to signal coming business disasters.

While Mr. Sullivan doesn't believe that auditors have done as poor a job as their critics say, he admits that in the current rapidly changing economic and competitive climate, "auditors could have been more skeptical." If the standards board adopts Mr. Sullivan's proposals, such skepticism will be integrated into the annual audits of most companies in the United States.

Looking under Rocks

The rules "will force the auditor to look under almost every rock," he says.

Time, however, is running out. If audit standards aren't sharpened by next year, Congress has threatened to intervene in an industry that has been allowed to set its own policies for half a century. The 53-year-old Mr. Sullivan, who has been working on the project for 15 months, says that at the end of a three-month public hearing next July, the board will have just a few months to completely revise the rules.

Auditing is a highly technical discipline that involves such complex procedures as statistical sampling of inventories, estimating the risks of business decisions and checking controls to ensure that funds or goods aren't leaking from a company.

But many investors, as well as federal regulators, financial analysts and members of Congress, argue that auditors aren't doing enough. "Why do we need auditors if all they do is issue clean opinions on companies that later go sour?" asks Michael Barrett, chief counsel for a House subcommittee that has been investigating the role of accountants in business failures.

Mr. Sullivan says that auditors are needed because they can require public companies to tell more negative news than they would like to. And while he admits that auditors should have been doing a better job of finding fraud, "the responsibilities aren't as simple as fixing a broken race car," he says. "In audits, there's a lot of room for disagreement."

The new rules, Mr. Sullivan explains, would help narrow such disagreements. "We're trying to fathom not only company condition, which was the usual audit job, but company position" as well, he says. "Where does the company stand with its competitors? Can it survive for another year? Is management turnover high?"

The biggest change in the proposals would expand an auditor's report to provide for "reasonable assurance" that financial statements aren't "materially misstated because of fraud or error." Such a strong statement is considerably riskier for auditors; currently, satisfactory reports state only that the financial position of the company is "fairly presented in conformity with generally accepted accounting principles on a consistent basis."

Mr. Sullivan also wants audits to be extended beyond the traditional financial statement to a section of the annual report in which the company sometimes predicts whether it can continue in existence for another year. The section is known as the management discussion and analysis.

In the past, auditors have generally shunned auditing such forecasts because if they agree the company won't go out of business and it does, investors and creditors would likely sue the auditors. "But with more U.S. industries such as autos, banks and oil experiencing problems," Mr. Sullivan says, "public expectations have grown that auditors should raise more red flags over 'going concern' questions such as potential bankruptcy. Like our clients, we're going to have to learn how to live with increased risk."

The proposed overhaul would also require auditors to inform the audit committee of a company's board of directors if management is "shopping around" for an auditor that is more amenable to the company's treatment of financial results. (The committee can ask the full board to act on such problems.) And the new rules would focus on several previously neglected "risk" factors. These include whether a company is dominated by a single individual, whether its attitude toward financial reports is "over-aggressive," whether management turnover during an audit is high and whether there is undue emphasis on meeting earnings projections.

"Being aware of such risk factors is now implicit but not spelled out in auditing standards," Mr. Sullivan says. "If adopted, the new standards would require the auditor to do it—no ifs, ands or buts." Auditors would have several options in such cases, such as resigning, qualifying the audit or informing the company's audit committee of their concerns.

If audit standards aren't sharpened some time next year, U.S. Rep. Ron Wyden threatens to reintroduce new legislation to force auditors to develop stricter standards. "The accounting profession is making a lot of promises, but they've been ducking their duties for a long time," the Oregon Democrat says.

Audit Fees
At the opposite pole, financial executives of major companies worry that rising pressure from Congress may prompt unnecessary changes from the auditing standards board. "Audit fees are high enough already," says Burton E. Broome, a vice president and controller of Transamerica Corp., San Francisco. "We don't mind raising fees if there is value added, but I don't see it in the new audit proposals."

Mr. Sullivan recognizes that the board "must tread a fine line between the urgings of Congress and the concerns of business." The board tried to toughen audit standards seven years ago but failed, largely because it seemed unwilling to make auditors responsible for spotting management fraud on their own.

A Chicago native with a master's degree in accounting from George Washington University, Mr. Sullivan has spent his entire 28-year business career with Coopers & Lybrand, the fourth-biggest U.S. accounting firm. Three years ago, he became chairman of the 21-member auditing standards board and has now spent thousands of hours directing the task force that is framing the new proposals.

"It's been a long hard road and may be getting longer the next few months," says Mr. Sullivan. "I don't mind the race, because the goal is worth the effort."

Consulting for Audit Clients: A Conflict of Interest?

By Lee Berton

July 8, 1987

As big certified public accounting firms' revenues from management consulting skyrocket, more critics are asking whether accountants can objectively audit business decisions they help make. Also, management-consulting firms that do consulting only are fretting that the auditors gain an unfair competitive advantage by recommending their own services to clients.

This two-pronged attack on the ethics of the accounting profession is gaining momentum, and the criticism is being carefully monitored by congressional staffs that caution the CPA firms to avoid any conflicts of interest between auditing and consulting.

"There's a serious question as to whether accounting firms should do any consulting work for audit clients," asserts Michael Barrett, chief counsel for a House subcommittee that will resume hearings Friday on whether accountants properly protect the public. "There's too much potential danger that the auditor will be less critical of business decisions with which he's involved."

In its defense, the accounting profession maintains that it erects a Chinese Wall between its auditing and consulting arms so that auditors can objectively judge a client's decisions. And big accounting firms note that other CPA firms do the audit work for between 60% and 90% of their consulting clients. But that leaves 10% to 40% of their audit clients as consulting customers, and some competitors maintain the credibility gap is widening over whether the accountants can keep consulting and auditing separate.

In addition, "the consulting arms of the Big Eight are growing like gangbusters," says James H. Kennedy, publisher of Consultants News, a Fitzwilliam, New Hampshire–based monthly newsletter on the industry. "If present trends continue, it won't be long before they're the top five among U.S. management consultants."

Indeed, five of the top 10 management-consulting firms in the United States today already are Big Eight accounting firms. Arthur Andersen & Co., one of the biggest, is in first place; Peat Marwick is fifth; and Price Waterhouse, Ernst & Whinney and Coopers & Lybrand are eighth, ninth and 10th, respectively, according to Consultants News.

With the auditing side of the business remaining static or growing less rapidly as a result of corporate client mergers, consulting has gained allure. "Consulting now averages 21% of the total fees or chargeable hours of the biggest U.S. accounting firms compared with only 12% a decade ago," observes Mr. Kennedy.

Ettore Barbatalli, chairman of the Milwaukee-based Valuation Research Corp., which does asset valuation for corporate clients, says that five years ago his firm was losing practically no clients to big CPA firms. "Now we're losing up to four clients a month," he says. "I'm getting very upset because it's a conflict of interest for the auditor to tell his clients that his CPA firm is the most qualified for a consulting job."

Criticism also has mounted against CPA firms for moving into specific areas of consulting that previously were thought to border on conflict of interest with the auditing side of the busi-

Accountants as Consultants

	Consulting Revenue[1] (in millions)	Consulting As a % of Total U.S. Practice[2]	Share of Consulting Revenue from Audit Clients
Arthur Andersen & Co.	$433	31%	36%
Peat Marwick	205	19	35
Ernst & Whinney	185	20	20
Coopers & Lybrand	170	19	39
Price Waterhouse	150	20	21
Touche Ross & Co.	128	20	22
Arthur Young & Co.	118	15	25
Laventhol & Horwath	95	30	12
Deloitte, Haskins & Sells	71	12	33[3]

[1]For fiscal '86 years
[2]In annual fees or chargeable hours
[3]Figure supplied by Deloitte, Haskins & Sells

Source: *Consultants News.*

ness. For example, Peat Marwick recently bought a major share of a public-relations firm. Arthur Andersen has become a major competitor in the asset-appraisal business. And Deloitte, Haskins & Sells and Touche Ross & Co., major accounting firms, are putting heavier emphasis on consulting for investment bankers in corporate mergers, reorganizations and bankruptcies.

According to a survey done last year of 1,000 businessmen, financial analysts, bankers, attorneys and academics, some 50% or more see the growing number of consulting services done by CPAs as impairing an auditor's objectivity. The survey—done by the Public Oversight Board, which scrutinizes the self-regulatory arm of the American Institute of Certified Public Accountants, the nation's leading CPA membership group—lists such services as valuing assets acquired in a merger and implementing and developing strategic planning for clients as causing potential conflicts of interest for CPA firms. And practically all the major CPA firms are boosting their efforts in these areas.

For their part, CPA firms say that the experience they gain as auditors makes them better consultants for their clients. And they assert that most of the criticism against their consulting gains is "sour grapes" by consulting firms losing business to accounting firms.

"The public's concern should be on making auditors more useful for investors, not on our consulting gains," says Duane Kullberg, managing partner of Arthur Andersen. "Such criticism of our management consulting is a red herring," he maintains. He notes that auditing standard-setters are working "right now" to tighten auditing standards and help raise "more red flags" for investors to spot management fraud and deception.

But Mr. Kullberg concedes that the rapid growth of consulting by CPA firms does create a "conflict-of-interest appearance problem" for the accounting profession. "There's enough of a thread there for our competitors in consulting to make the argument" that CPA firms lack independence, he says, adding: "But those who complain about unfair competition are really complaining about competition."

No doubt some of the accountants' worst critics have axes to grind. But the accounting profession should still be careful of where its management-consulting business is headed. When it moves over the line of giving advice to making the actual business deals and directing business strategy for audit clients, it may encounter the ire of congressional watchdogs.

And the watchdogs may force the big CPA firms to spin off their consulting businesses or to reorganize them so that consulting is done more at arm's length. Such action isn't currently being considered by Congress, but one big audit scandal involving a consulting client could bring it about.

Some holes are beginning to appear in the wall between auditing and consulting at some major accounting firms. The wall could use some shoring up.

Legal Time Bomb: Big Accounting Firms Risk Costly Lawsuits by Reassuring Lenders—Turning into a 'Deep Pocket'?

Their 'Solvency Letters' Say Company Can Pay Debt; No Court Cases So Far

By Lee Berton

January 14, 1988

NEW YORK—Big accounting firms have quietly been planting legal time bombs that could blow up in their faces.

Despite the reluctance of many of their own partners, they have been writing "solvency letters." Though not an audit, such letters reassure lenders that a company loading up with debt is solvent and probably will remain so in the near future.

Amid all the talk about the next recession, solvency letters help corporate borrowers. Even companies deep in hock—such as those doing leveraged buy-outs, mergers and restructurings—find that with the letters they can arrange loans.

But the accounting firms writing solvency letters may be plunging into more legal risk than they can afford.

"The solvency letter could be the trapdoor to liability through which many major accounting firms fall," warns Dan Goldwasser, an attorney and consultant to the New York State Society of Certified Public Accountants.

Increasing Numbers

Over the past two years, solvency letters have been requested in increasing numbers by lenders seeking assurance that certain borrowers caught up in the merger and acquisition craze of the 1980s won't be undermined by the added debt. Major accounting firms have provided the little-known service for fees ranging up to $500,000 a letter.

The firms can use the money. As corporate mergers pare their lists of audit clients, they are under pressure to find new sources of income from consulting and other operations. With solvency letters so new, none of the firms have been sued for writing one—so far. But the firms admit that they are at risk.

"If a leveraged buy-out runs into trouble, there is no question that accounting firms that provide these letters may wind up as a 'deep pocket' in a later lawsuit," says Stephen Key, an official at Arthur Young & Co., a major accounting firm. Many accounting firms have been sued, when, following a clean audit, the company that got it faltered because of inept or fraudulent management.

Undisclosed to Public
However, unlike audit letters in client companies' annual reports, solvency letters usually aren't disclosed to the public. The lender files them away to help it fight any suit filed against it or others involved in the transaction linked to the loan. The lender would use the letters in court to try to show that it had been prudent in seeking outside expert advice—from an accounting firm—on whether the borrower could remain afloat despite the additional debt.

A suit might be filed by unsecured creditors left out in the cold during a bankruptcy proceeding. A bank losing such a suit could then sue the accounting firm, claiming the solvency letter gave the bank a bum steer, liability lawyers say.

Most public accounting firms are reluctant to discuss solvency letters. The accounting profession itself hasn't spelled out the risks, and accountants' clients don't want the letters revealed. Not one major accounting firm interviewed for this article would talk about specific transactions involving solvency letters, although some discussed them in general. Examples cited here were extracted from court papers, proxy statements and other sources.

Reluctant Letter Writer
A spokesman for Cleveland-based Ernst & Whinney declines comment on solvency letters, but a partner who requested anonymity says the big accounting firm has written several dozen of them. "We're not enthusiastic about doing this work, but the banks have been pressing our clients for them," the partner says.

The letters, says Richard Murray, executive director of Touche Ross International, are "risky because they involve future events that can change very quickly in the current stock-market environment."

The firm's U.S. affiliate, Touche Ross & Co., found that out after issuing a solvency letter to Southland Corp. Following the October 19 stock-market crash, Southland had trouble arranging long-term debt to pay off short-term loans from big commercial and investment banks. The Dallas-based convenience-store chain had used the loans to buy back its stock and go private. Southland's investment bankers had to sweeten the deal with stock-purchase warrants before it could raise the money.

Refusing to write a solvency letter can threaten an accounting firm's client relationships. In November 1986, Touche Ross declined to provide a letter to Allied Stores Corp., an audit client. The letter was requested by Citicorp and Manufacturers Hanover Trust Co., which headed a bank group lending more than $2 billion to Campeau Corp. The Toronto-based real-estate concern wanted the money to complete a takeover of Allied with the help of First Boston Corp., the investment bank.

The letter was needed quickly; taxes on the deal could have risen $200 million unless the takeover was completed before January 1, 1987. Late in November 1986, the agreement hit a snag. Declining a fee close to $500,000, Touche Ross refused to write a letter; it considered the deal too risky. So First Boston, which helped underwrite $1.15 billion in junk bonds and preferred stock in the takeover, gave the banks its own solvency letter for a $1 million fee.

Was this a conflict of interest? First Boston says no. "We knew the credit [situation] as well as anyone at that point and felt comfortable with it," a First Boston spokesman says.

Client Defections Threatened

Some accountants say some corporate audit clients threaten to change auditors if an accounting firm refuses to write solvency letters. After Touche refused Allied, it lost the Allied account to Peat Marwick, Campeau's auditor. First Boston officials say that the switch was expected because acquired companies often change to the parent's auditor and that Touche refused the letter because it already knew it would lose Allied. "Why take the risk with the solvency letter if you're not going to keep the client?" a First Boston official asks. Touche Ross declines comment.

More banks are seeking solvency letters because more creditors of companies in bankruptcy proceedings have been threatening to sue them for allegedly pushing the companies into insolvency.

"By lending for reckless deals, some lenders are helping the borrowers drown themselves," asserts Dean Dickie, an attorney specializing in bankruptcy law. "When the body comes to shore, previous shareholders and the banks get their pound of flesh, but the unsecured creditors wind up with less than the bones."

These unsecured creditors, many of them vendors and suppliers, are contending that banks are fraudulently acquiring borrowers' assets as security for loans. Most solvency letters, Mr. Dickie argues, are "bought for high prices to give legitimacy to suspect transactions."

Mr. Dickie is a partner of Phelan, Pope & John, a law firm that sued in federal district court in Chicago last September on behalf of hundreds of unsecured creditors of Wieboldt Stores Inc., a Chicago-based department-store chain. The defendants include lenders and former owners of Wieboldt, which did a $38 million leveraged buy-out in late 1985 and filed for protection under the bankruptcy laws in late 1986.

The suit charges that the retailer took on too much debt in the buy-out, and Mr. Dickie says Laventhol & Horwath, a big Philadelphia-based accounting firm, wrote a solvency letter "to assuage the lenders." Mr. Dickie calls the latter a "sham and not worth the paper it's written on."

Laventhol & Horwath, which isn't a defendant in the suit, sent a solvency letter in late 1985 to General Electric Credit Corp., which lent Wieboldt more than $20 million. In the letter, the accounting firm says that based on a projection of Wieboldt's financial results from December 1, 1985, through January 1987, it didn't believe that the $107 million by which Wieboldt's assets exceeded its liabilities in December 1985 would change "materially" in the future. "Generally, an excess of current assets over current liabilities indicates an entity is presently able to pay its debts as they come due," the letter says.

The letter concedes that the accounting firm's procedures weren't as thorough as a regular audit and that perhaps financial surprises could crop up. It also says it makes "no representation regarding the sufficiency of the procedures" it was asked to do by the lenders.

Early Defaults Noted
But Mr. Dickie says Wieboldt's financial statements showed that as early as November 1985, "the fair salable value of its assets was exceeded by its liabilities" because its assets weren't liquid or easily sold. The suit notes that in October 1985, Wieboldt couldn't pay $12 million of its debts and was in default on other loans.

Sheldon Holtzman, a partner in Laventhol & Horwath's Chicago office, says the firm is confident that it issued the letter based on "agreed-upon" procedures with Wieboldt and the lenders. "We feel we did what was asked of us," he declares. He declines to comment on Mr. Dickie's charges, except to note that Laventhol hasn't been sued. However, Mr. Holtzman says some accounting firms may avoid issuing solvency letters because "any time you do anything outside the safety net of audits, you extend the possibilities of your liability exposure."

GE Credit says it relied on Laventhol's letter in lending to Wieboldt. A defendant in the case, the General Electric Co. unit is negotiating a settlement with the creditors. Whatever the terms, says John Costello, an attorney for GE Credit, "we will retain the right to sue Laventhol . . . if we find the letter was inadequate and the suit costs us a lot of money."

Even some lenders asking for solvency letters admit that although the letters help close risky transactions, they predict little. "The fact that a company is solvent at one moment can give you cold comfort a few months later when it falls apart," says the head of a major securities firm's leveraged buy-out lending unit. He adds:

"I'm very skeptical about solvency letters, but bankers I work with want them. Frankly, I think such letters are useless and will wind up getting accountants that write them in big trouble."

CPAs May Soon Have to Report Fraud Earlier

By Lee Berton and Daniel Akst

January 22, 1988

If you owned stock in a company whose outside auditor quit because management fraud was suspected, wouldn't you want to know right away?

Too bad. Under current securities rules, it could take six weeks before shareholders are told why an auditor left. This disclosure gap—which cost lenders and shareholders millions in the collapse of ZZZZ Best Co. last summer—is prompting legislators and regulators to move toward mandating faster notification.

"Crooks aren't going to tell on themselves," says an attorney for the House Energy and Commerce Committee's Oversight and Investigations Subcommittee. "We keep being told by accountants that the current reporting system on auditor changes is adequate, but we think investors need an earlier warning."

Hearings on Fraud

Next Wednesday, the subcommittee will reopen hearings on the role of accountants in disclosing suspected management fraud. Its focus will be the stunning downfall of ZZZZ Best—which Barry J. Minkow, 21 years old, had built from a tiny carpet-cleaning concern into a fire-damage and water-damage refurbisher valued at more than $200 million.

Last July, the Reseda, California, company collapsed in what federal officials say was one of the biggest securities frauds on the West Coast in more than a decade. Authorities charge that ZZZZ Best's big damage-restoration contracts were bogus, that revenue and profits were inflated, and that its Securities and Exchange Commission filings were rife with lies.

Earlier this week, Mr. Minkow and 10 others pleaded not

Mr. Akst is a staff reporter of THE WALL STREET JOURNAL.

guilty in federal court in Los Angeles to charges of racketeering, money laundering and fraud in connection with the company's collapse. A 12th defendant is in custody in Texas on an unrelated narcotics charge and hasn't yet pleaded.

Where were the auditors during all the alleged skulduggery? Well, Ernst & Whinney quit as ZZZZ Best's auditor June 2, suspecting that one of the company's major contracts was nonexistent. Under current rules, however, the auditor didn't have to tell the SEC of its suspicions until mid-July.

The ZZZZ Best case is "the most recent and most vivid proof that the present system for independent auditors reporting financial fraud doesn't work," says subcommittee Chairman John D. Dingell (D., Mich.). Between the auditor's resignation and the disclosure of the suspected fraud, the stock price plummeted and the company got new loans, he says.

Companies have 15 days to notify the SEC of a change of auditors and to explain why. Using the maximum time, ZZZZ Best didn't file until June 17—and when it did file, it said it hadn't any major disagreements with the Cleveland-based accounting firm "on accounting principles or practices, financial statement disclosure, or auditing scope or procedure."

Ernst & Whinney then waited its maximum allotted time— an additional 30 days—before informing the SEC of its suspicions. By then it was July 16, eight days after ZZZZ Best filed for protection from creditors under Chapter 11 of the federal Bankruptcy Code. The company's assets were subsequently liquidated—and investors took a bath.

The accounting firm says it resigned before completing its audit, and that it alerted the company's board of the suspected fraud.

Tighter SEC Rules

Edmund Coulson, the SEC's new chief accountant, says the agency is "looking for ways to enhance the timeliness of these filings to alert investors and the SEC to potential problems." In March, the SEC will vote on a proposal that would require accounting firms to make a preliminary report—possibly within five business days—on why they quit as a company's outside auditor, Mr. Coulson says.

Lawyers who specialize in shareholder suits against accounting firms, however, say that no matter how tough the rules, outside auditors are unlikely to adequately watch out for investors' interests.

The auditors are "generally the handmaidens of their client companies, who want them to put holy water on their cooked books," says Melvyn Weiss, a partner of Milberg Weiss Bershad Specthrie & Lerach. The New York firm has filed a class action against ZZZZ Best's management, Ernst & Whinney and others, alleging fraud and malpractice and seeking damages for shareholders.

Accounting Board Clears Rules Ordering Auditors to Watch for Corporate Fraud

By Karen Slater

February 10, 1988

NEW YORK—The accounting profession, which has been criticized for failing to detect corporate fraud, instructed its members to watch for such illegal activity during audits.

Critics of current auditing practices, including some congressmen, said the new standards don't go far enough. "There is real progress . . . but we still aren't there yet," said Rep. Ron Wyden (D., Ore.).

The new rules, adopted by the Auditing Standards Board of the American Institute of Certified Public Accountants, for the first time specifically charge auditors to look for fraud. The rules, which generally become effective next January 1, mean an auditor must "design the audit to provide reasonable assurance of detecting errors and irregularities that are material," said Dan M. Guy, vice president for auditing at the institute.

Ms. Slater is a staff reporter of THE WALL STREET JOURNAL.

Possible misdeeds then would be brought to the attention of the audited company's board.

The new provisions on fraud are part of the most sweeping redesign ever of the auditing standards, which were introduced in 1939. Among other changes, accountants now are specifically required to evaluate whether there is substantial doubt about the company's ability to continue as "a going concern." Such doubt, when it exists, would have to be disclosed.

In the past, Mr. Guy said, the auditor only addressed the going-concern issue if he or she had suspicions the company might fail to survive.

In another change that will be visible in thousands of corporate annual reports next year, the Auditing Standards Board also altered the language of the auditor's opinion. To clear up what the institute says are widespread misunderstandings, the auditor's report will specify that the financial statements are the representation of management, not the auditors.

But, addressing the fraud issue, the opinion will go on to say that the audit was performed "to obtain reasonable assurance about whether the financial statements are free from material misstatements."

Some critics, including Rep. Wyden, believe auditors need to report their suspicions or findings of corporate fraud to the Securities and Exchange Commission or law enforcement officials. Telling the company's board "doesn't do anything" if directors are involved in the fraud, said a staff member of the House Energy and Commerce Committee's oversight and investigations subcommittee. That body last month held hearings on auditor performance that focused on the fraud-linked collapse of ZZZZ Best Co. last summer.

In another matter, the institute's Auditing Standards Board reviewed a proposed interpretation that would prohibit accountants from the lucrative practice of giving so-called solvency letters to banks and other lenders. These letters assure lenders that a company loading up with debt is solvent and probably will remain so in the near future. Mr. Guy said the interpretation will become effective in the next few months, upon publication in an accounting journal.

Accountants Group Bans the Sending of Solvency Letters

By Lee Berton

February 26, 1988

NEW YORK—A major accounting standards group ruled that big accounting firms can no longer write so-called solvency letters.

The ban, effective immediately, was enacted yesterday by the auditing standards division of the American Institute of Certified Public Accountants, which has 264,000 members.

In solvency letters, accountants privately assure lenders that a company loading up on debt is solvent and likely to remain so in the near future. Lenders involved in leveraged buyouts and recapitalizations have requested such letters in increasing numbers in the past three years.

A front-page article in *The Wall Street Journal* last month discussed concerns that writing such letters could broaden accountants' liability exposure in times of volatile markets.

The letters were barred because they involve "legal concepts subject to legal definition and varying interpretation not clearly defined in an accounting sense," the division said. It also banned accounting firms from providing other assurances related to clients' solvency, adequacy of capital and ability to pay debts.

Some accountants believe that the solvency-letter ban could put a crimp on marginal buy-outs, mergers and recapitalizations. "When financial strength is thin, without a solvency letter the impetus may be to restructure the deal or to stop it altogether," said Jerry Sullivan, a partner for Coopers & Lybrand, a major accounting firm based here. He is chairman of the accounting institute's auditing standards board, which sets auditing rules.

By some estimates, the 14-largest accounting firms made as much as $100 million in revenues from solvency letters between early 1986 and the end of last year.

The ban comes at a bad time for accounting firms, which face increasing competition as the number of major clients dwindles through mergers and buy-outs. "Solvency letters have been a high margin business for major accounting firms," said Lee Seidler, a CPA and senior managing director of Bear, Stearns & Co., a New York investment firm. "There's no question that other consulting firms and investment bankers will move into the writing of such letters."

Rule to Curb Firms' 'Opinion Shopping' among Auditors Wins SEC Approval

By Thomas E. Ricks and Lee Berton

April 8, 1988

The Securities and Exchange Commission approved a rule that is aimed at corporate "opinion shopping" and significantly increases the information that public companies must disclose about disputes with their auditors.

But the new rule dropped a proposal that would have required a company that has changed auditors to disclose all of its discussions with accountants in the two years before the change. As adopted, the rule will require a company to file with the SEC statements only about disagreements with its former auditors and discussions with its new auditors in the previous two years.

The commission also proposed for public comment a rule shortening the period in which companies have to disclose a change in auditors or a resignation by a director. The period would be trimmed to five calendar days from 15.

Effects of New Rule
The proposed rule also would shorten the period in which a company's discharged auditors must give the company a letter stating whether they agree with the company's version of why the

---

Mr. Ricks and Mr. Berton are staff reporters of THE WALL STREET JOURNAL.

change was made, and to explain any disagreement. This period would shrink to 10 days from 30.

Currently, a company is required to tell the SEC when it changes auditors and to say if there had been a disagreement with the former auditors. Edmund Coulson, the SEC's chief accountant, told the commission that the new rule both expands and clarifies the definition of the kinds of accounting disputes companies must disclose.

Under the rule, which will probably take effect in about five weeks, a company must tell the SEC whether an auditor resigned or was fired, whether points of disagreement were discussed with the company's board, and whether its management imposed limitations on the new auditors' communication with the old ones.

The provision designed most directly to discourage "shopping" for favorable auditors' opinions requires a company to say what accounting issues it discussed with its new auditors in the two years before hiring them.

The SEC has warned in the past that opinion shopping erodes public confidence in the integrity of the financial markets and of independent auditors.

"It's actually quite an expansion," Mr. Coulson later said of the new rule.

Initial Proposal

Mr. Coulson also listed the kinds of events that the SEC will consider "reportable" under the new rule. One such instance, he said, would occur when an auditor comes to distrust a concern's management and the information it provides, and resigns or is fired. Another would be a situation in which an allegation requiring an investigation is made, and the auditor is changed. Furthermore, he said, an auditor could conduct such an investigation, conclude that management must alter its financial statements, and then be let go.

But the SEC backed down from its initial, more stringent proposal, which would have required companies changing auditors to disclose every discussion with auditors on accounting rules. Corporate executives argued that such broad disclosure would have a "chilling effect" on useful discussions with auditors other than a company's current outside accountants.

Financial executives welcomed the SEC's deletion of the broader disclosure requirement. "With the new complex accounting rules, it often helps to talk to more than one accounting firm as to how a rule fits in with the tax code," said Galen Larsen, group vice president and controller of Chicago-based Household International Inc., and chairman of the Financial Executive Institute's committee on corporate reporting.

Arthur Young Sues Two Partners, Alleging a Defection Scheme at Consulting Office

By Lee Berton

May 27, 1988

NEW YORK—Arthur Young & Co. filed suit in a state trial court here alleging that two partners in Chicago planned to leave the accounting firm and take part of its Midwest consulting practice with them.

Reached in Chicago, the partners, Albert Beedie, Jr., and Joyce Bennis, denied the allegations and said they had been "fired" by Arthur Young earlier this week for "baseless and incorrect reasons."

The alleged defection of consultants from Arthur Young, the sixth-largest U.S. accounting firm, follows a similar incident at Chicago-based Arthur Andersen & Co., the nation's largest accounting firm. Last week Andersen relieved of his duties the partner who heads the company's domestic consulting operation, claiming he planned to leave Andersen with some of its consulting business. Andersen's consulting business is the largest in the United States.

Accounting profession observers say that these splits between consulting partners and the leadership of major accounting firms underscore the more rapid growth and possibly greater profitability of consulting compared with accounting, auditing and tax operations of the major accounting firms.

At Arthur Young, consulting is expected to account for 17%

of total revenue in the year ending September 30, up from 15% or $110 million, of total revenue the previous year, said William Gladstone, Arthur Young's chairman. Arthur Young is the 12th-biggest U.S. consulting firm, Mr. Gladstone said.

Arthur Young's suit in the state Supreme Court of New York County alleges that Mr. Beedie and Ms. Bennis breached contractual obligations to the firm by violating bans on soliciting other employees and possibly clients to begin a new business separate from Arthur Young.

Mr. Beedie said that prior to being asked to leave, he was looking "at various alternatives" to his job "in the best interests of the firm, its clients and its people." He declined to be more specific.

Ms. Bennis said she had previously planned to resign from Arthur Young and was "waiting for an appropriate opportunity" when she was told to leave.

Arthur Young's partnership agreement permits top managers of the firm to terminate the employment of partners if they breach its terms, Mr. Gladstone said. On the other hand, Andersen said its partnership agreement requires two-thirds of its partners to approve removing the former head of its U.S. consulting practice as a partner.

Mr. Gladstone said that three other partners and other employees in the Midwest consulting practice had resigned earlier this week after learning of the firm's investigation into breaches in employment contracts. He said letters were being sent to them, "alleging removal for cause." He estimated that the firm's Midwest consulting practice, involving installation of big computer systems for companies in the consumer products, general manufacturing and defense businesses, amounted to about $25 million.

Cutting the Pie:
Accounting Firms Face a Deepening
Division over Consultants' Pay

As Revenues in Advice Field Outrun Rises in Auditing, Partners Start to Defect—Latest Arthur Andersen Flap

By Lee Berton

July 26, 1988

As the heads of major accounting firms held a periodic get-together at Arthur Andersen & Co.'s Chicago headquarters last month, the sound of moving furniture rumbled from the floor above. "That must be the consultants," someone quipped.

There was polite laughter, but the accountants weren't just joking. Big accounting firms, which have long been happy marriages of accountants and management consultants, may be headed for the divorce courts. As consulting revenues soar, more and more consultants, miffed that their compensation isn't rising fast enough to suit them, are leaving accounting firms and taking business with them.

The feuds could affect thousands of businesses that rely on accounting firms for more than just audits and tax returns—for such things as market research and management training and for advice on factory layouts, product distribution and installation of data-communications systems. As consultants leave to go it alone, the increased competition could drive down fees for clients.

Risks for Clients
But the defections also could be disruptive for clients. "It's disconcerting, to say the least," to have a consultant quit before finishing a job, says James Phillips, the director of management information services for a Bally Manufacturing Corp. unit that suffered just such an experience. "Before hiring an accounting firm for a consulting job, I'd check carefully to see the firm

isn't having internal problems with its consulting partners," he cautions.

Such a firm may be hard to find nowadays. Arthur Andersen's top U.S. consulting partner was recently relieved of his duties for allegedly plotting to defect with its huge consulting practice. And Arthur Young & Co. fired five of its Midwest consulting partners and sued to stop them from luring away consulting business and key consulting personnel.

But such incidents are mild tremors compared to a coming earthquake for the two professions, some accountants and consultants predict. Behind the scenes are bitter, Byzantine battles more evocative of a John Le Carre novel than of such staid professions. Groups of consultants from several major firms are meeting secretly to plot defections. In some instances, management is learning of these meetings through well-placed moles. Ringleaders are summarily fired. Job recruiters are secretly trying to lure away consultants.

Big Money at Stake

The stakes are huge. World-wide consulting revenues of Arthur Andersen alone last year were $838 million—almost equal to the total annual revenues of both McKinsey & Co. and Booz, Allen & Hamilton, two of the best-known independent consultants. Consulting revenues of 11 major accounting firms in 1987 reached $2 billion, about two-thirds of the U.S. total.

The stakes are growing rapidly. At major accounting firms, consulting revenues are ballooning at an average 30% annual rate, about double the growth of auditing and tax work. Some contracts are big: Arthur Andersen recently won a $12 million Social Security Administration contract to install a nationwide administrative and financial-records system.

As the stakes grow, consulting partners of accounting firms are more likely to rebel. That's true even though consultants are generally at the high end of the pay scale at the firms, where the average annual compensation for all partners ranges from $180,000 to $225,000.

"If the balance of power remains with the accountants and a disparity continues between revenues consultants bring in and what they earn, you're going to see more unrest, discontent

Should the Consultants and Auditors Be Divorced?

Some critics aren't surprised at the recent strains at major accounting firms because they have long believed that consulting and auditing, like oil and water, don't mix.

That's because accounting firms serving as outside auditors are supposed to judge objectively whether their client companies are making proper business decisions. But auditors are likely to be less critical of decisions in which they themselves have been deeply involved, critics say.

Some consultants and legislators call this a potential conflict of interest. And some independent consulting firms complain that consultants at accounting firms gain an unfair competitive advantage by pushing their services to clients that their firms may also audit.

In response, accounting firms call the problem of a seeming conflict of interest a red herring. They contend that the experienced gained as auditors makes them better consultants and that criticism of their gains in the consulting field comes simply from competitors irked by their own loss of business.

and departures of the consultants," says Gresham Brebach, the Andersen partner relieved of his job. He denies he was trying to sabotage Andersen's consulting business; he says he was seeking a bigger voice for the consultants there.

Albert Beedie, Jr., a former partner in Arthur Young's Midwest consulting practice, says accounting-firm consultants "are tired of feeling like second-class citizens because most of us aren't certified public accountants." Mr. Beedie, one of the five fired partners, recently offered Arthur Young $50 million for the Midwest practice. The firm calls the offer "preposterous" in light of his alleged disloyalty.

With consulting growing so sharply, some consulting partners want to boost their compensation faster. They want to avoid sharing such accounting-firm overhead as litigation costs arising from faulty audits. And they want to switch to a business structure where they alone control spending for growth and share more in the rewards of an expanding enterprise.

"The way we look at it, we just don't have a lot to lose leaving our accounting firm and setting up a separate business," says a consulting partner at another major accounting firm who requests anonymity. "In a partnership, which is how all accounting firms are set up, consultants alone can't decide on acquisitions and product development and can't sell their shares to the public at higher prices as we can get for our own business."

Such rocketing rewards, and frustration at failing to get the firm's top position, led to the departure of Victor E. Millar, Andersen's top consulting partner, to Saatchi & Saatchi PLC in late 1986. The London-based advertising giant is paying Mr. Millar $1 million a year to build a consulting business, especially in information-systems consulting, which some expect to grow into a $100-billion-a-year market.

So far, Mr. Millar has arranged Saatchi's purchase of eight small and medium-sized consulting firms. But he hasn't hit the jackpot he was hired to hit: a major acquisition. He even offered to buy all of Andersen's consulting practice for Saatchi but was quickly turned down. Nonetheless, Saatchi, for the first time last year, became one of the top 10 U.S. consultants, with $267 million in consulting revenue.

Mr. Millar, standing next to a tall antique schoolmaster's desk in his Washington, D.C., office, says, "I've had inquiries from dozens of consulting partners from other firms to join us, and half of them are with the Big Eight" accounting firms. "They seek equity and governance . . . more of a hand in running the business than they now have."

Looking Abroad

Some accounting firms, recognizing the growing schism, are trying to soothe consultants. Ernst & Whinney is beefing up its overseas consulting practice and giving consultants a growing share of the earnings pie, indicates Clinton A. Alston, who until this month headed domestic information-systems consulting for the Cleveland-based firm.

Says Mr. Alston, who is transferring to London with about 10 of the firm's consulting personnel: "We want to leverage our rapidly expanding consulting practice world-wide and let our consulting partners share in the rewards. Information-systems consulting revenues are exploding, with 40% annual growth, compared with only 17% to 18% for total firm revenues."

Consulting Practices of the Biggest Accounting Firms

Firm	1987 World-Wide Consulting Revenues[1] (in millions)	Percentage of Total World-Wide Revenues	Number of Consulting Professionals
Arthur Andersen	$838	36%	9,639
Peat Marwick	438	13	4,700
Coopers & Lybrand	381	18	4,712
Ernst & Whinney	374	21	3,255
Price Waterhouse	345	20	4,300
Touche Ross	248	17	2,142
Deloitte, Haskins & Sells	209	14	2,271
Arthur Young	204	12	2,443
Laventhol & Horwath[2]	136	25	1,100
Pannell Kerr Forster	62	26	540
Grant Thornton	60	9	675

[1]In millions of dollars of management consulting revenues only, less reimbursed expenses.
[2]Name of international organization is Horwath & Horwath.

Sources: *Consultants News*, Fitzwilliam, N.H. and *Bowman's Accounting Report*, Atlanta, Ga.

Arthur Andersen is using its 866-room training center, in a woodsy locale along the Fox River in St. Charles, Illinois, to keep its ranks loyal. Because Andersen leans so heavily on consulting, at least 60% of the visitors to St. Charles have been consulting personnel. But some say that favoring consulting personnel with the center and its many perks, which include a full range of athletic facilities, could backfire.

"Being coddled can produce elitists among the consultants rather than loyal employees," says a recent visitor from outside the firm. "Andersen has obviously carved out a unique niche in consulting, and now greed among its consulting partners is taking over."

Building Loyalty?

Duane Kullberg, Andersen's managing partner, disagrees. He says the training center "promotes employee loyalty and camaraderie and builds teamwork because we do train across firm divisions." He adds: "Consulting is a hot business right now, and so consultants [in accounting firms] are getting a lot of attractive offers from the outside. But in the long run, many will come back because of the flexibility and resources we provide. They may run their own shops their own way, but they will find they'll have to make more compromises" with regard to the resources available to them.

Some defections are being encouraged by people outside the firms. In June 1987, an executive recruiter from Dallas, Stephen J. Page, held a secret meeting at a La Guardia Airport club in New York with consulting partners from Andersen, Peat Marwick, Price Waterhouse, Coopers & Lybrand and Deloitte, Haskins & Sells. He says he was trying to form a huge new consulting firm and arranged the meeting by sending "personal and confidential" letters to 50 accounting-firm partners. In the letters, he said he would help them "to fully attain their professional goals and to double or triple their current earnings."

But bad luck and a dash of intrigue sabotaged the meeting. One letter reached an Andersen partner who had the same name as another partner who might have been amenable to Mr. Page's offer. The recipient gave the letter to Mr. Kullberg, Andersen's managing partner, who then distributed it to the heads of all Big Eight firms. "This blew our participation, and we immediately ran for cover," says one partner who attended the meeting.

A Mole at Work

And last April, a dissident group at Arthur Andersen was betrayed by a management mole. Andersen's Mr. Brebach called a secret two-day meeting of 11 Andersen partners at Manhattan's posh 21 Club. While they sipped cocktails, the partners consulted three attorneys about the wisdom of opposing a management proposal aimed at discouraging defectors. The proposal was to amend the firm's partnership agreement so that people who resigned couldn't solicit clients or invite other Andersen people to join them.

"We wanted to stop this proposal before it split the firm down the middle," Mr. Brebach says. They did. The proposal was voted down.

But one of the 11 later told Mr. Kullberg about the 21 Club meeting. Mr. Kullberg acted quickly. A few days later, he and Larry Weinbach, Andersen's chief operating partner, confronted Mr. Brebach in his New York office and relieved him of his duties. "I'll be leaving soon, most likely to set up my own operations in consulting," Mr. Brebach says. He probably will take some Andersen partners with him but denies rumors it will be as many as 50.

More recently, five Arthur Young partners led by Mr. Beedie began considering leaving the firm to start their own consulting business. Late in May, William Gladstone, Arthur Young's chairman, fired them and sued them in a New York state court to enjoin them from luring away the firm's clients or more personnel.

Mr. Beedie, whose group has founded a Chicago-based consulting firm called Technology Solutions Co., says he already has 35 employees. His group has just countersued Arthur Young for $14 million, contending that the accounting firm is illegally trying "to destroy our professional reputations and to unlawfully intimidate prospective clients and capital sources."

A consulting partner of another accounting firm who attended Mr. Page's mid-1987 meeting says that "dozens of partners at Big Eight firms are awaiting the outcome of the Arthur Young litigation. If Arthur Young loses, you may see a big exodus" of consultants from various firms.

CHAPTER 6

FINANCIAL FRAUD

The public's attention is often drawn to lead stories in print and electronic media on major frauds involving large companies such as Continental Illinois, E.S.M., E.F. Hutton and ZZZZ Best. These cases have affected thousands of stockholders, creditors, and individuals who use the services of these companies (particularly the financial services). Congress, in turn takes a serious look at the accounting profession and the quality of its work, particularly in reducing the incidence of fraud and so-called "audit failure."

The following articles provide insight into many of these fraud cases, which usually take several years to resolve. It is interesting to note that much of the fraud involves executive "override" of existing corporate control policies. The "Treadway" report cites executive override as one of its major concerns in its discussion of the "Tone at the Top."

FDIC Weighing Action against 5 Firms Involved in Audits of Banks That Failed

By Lee Berton

March 28, 1984

NEW YORK—The Federal Deposit Insurance Corp. said it is considering court action against five accounting firms involving the audits of banks that subsequently failed, were closed or were sold to other banks.

Furthermore, the FDIC said that, with insurance claims mounting, it will be considering filing more suits against outside auditors of such banks.

Cecil Underwood, an FDIC attorney with a special section on accountants' liability, confirmed the FDIC is considering court actions against CPA firms in the audits of six banks, but he wouldn't disclose the auditors or the banks. Sources said, however, that among the CPA firms being scrutinized are Peat, Marwick, Mitchell & Co. and Ernst & Whinney.

The FDIC is negotiating with some of the firms in an effort to reach out-of-court settlements, Mr. Underwood said. Both the FDIC and CPA firms prefer to settle disputes over bank auditing out of court. They believe that adverse publicity can prompt other suits by disgruntled depositors or by creditors of the closed or merged banks that had financial difficulties. Such out-of-court settlements often reach millions of dollars.

The investigation of Peat Marwick is said to involve Peat's March 1982 clean audit opinion on Penn Square Bank in Oklahoma City. Nearly four months later, federal regulators closed the bank and still are liquidating it. Peat Marwick, based in New York, audits about 600 banks.

Ernst & Whinney, a Cleveland-based accounting firm with about 400 bank clients, in January 1983 issued a clean opinion on the financial statement of United American Bank, the Butcher bank in Knoxville, Tenn. Twenty days later the bank was closed by federal regulators and has since been merged with another bank. Sources said the FDIC's investigation of Ernst & Whinney centers on the United American audit.

Sources said the FDIC hasn't yet begun negotiations with Ernst & Whinney but plans to begin talking with the CPA firm later this year.

Ernst & Whinney admitted the possibility that the FDIC was investigating possible court action, but said that "settlement discussions between our firm and the FDIC have never taken place." The CPA firm said "we've not been offered a settlement nor have we been approached" by the FDIC.

Peat Marwick officials said no negotiations had taken place between the CPA firm and the FDIC "nor can we confirm that any will take place." Added a spokesman: "These are delicate matters and we're not sure that publicizing rumors about them will be of any help."

The FDIC's Mr. Underwood said that, because of the huge losses being incurred in insurance claims, more suits will be considered against outside auditors, as well as directors and management, of banks that failed, were closed or forced to merge with other financial institutions.

Since 1981, the FDIC has reported insurance expense losses of over $2.6 billion. Before 1981, such losses were fairly small, ranging from $30 million to $100 million a year. Insurance expense losses are the amounts that the FDIC expects to pay out over future years to depositors and creditors of troubled banks.

Mr. Underwood said auditors in several cases will be charged with negligence in failing to follow generally accepted auditing standards in performing the audit for some of these banks.

In the Penn Square situation, the FDIC in July 1983 paid $89 million in dividends to uninsured depositors and other creditors, or about 20% of the outstanding proven claims against the bank.

Insurance sources said liability insurance rates for accounting firms have climbed sharply since the mid-1970s, with deductibles climbing to as high as $1 million for the so-called Big 8 firms from considerably less a decade ago.

SEC Expands Continental Illinois Probe to Examine Bank's Loan-Loss Provisions

By Lee Berton and Bruce Ingersoll

June 21, 1984

The Securities and Exchange Commission has expanded an investigation of Continental Illinois Corp. to examine the adequacy of the banking concern's loan-loss provisions over the past several years.

The investigation of the company, parent of Continental Illinois National Bank & Trust Co. of Chicago, is being conducted by the SEC's enforcement division, its chief accountant's office and its corporate finance division. While John Fedders, the SEC's director of enforcement, wouldn't confirm it, sources said the investigation was expanded one month ago. But they stressed that investigations don't necessarily result in enforcement action.

Continental disclosed in March 1983 that it was under SEC investigation for possible violation of financial condition disclosure requirements, and for possible insider trading violations. The initial inquiry was undertaken by the SEC's Chicago regional office. It's understood that SEC officials in Washington took over the investigation and broadened its scope shortly after the run on deposits at Continental began one month ago amid a flurry of rumors about the bank's deteriorating financial condition. The SEC also amended its original investigation order, giving its staff greater authority to pursue new lines of inquiry.

Federal regulators and other banks have been trying to help Continental with a massive infusion of capital.

Penn Square Loans
Charles M. Vincent, a vice president and bank analyst for Provident National Bank in Philadelphia, notes that Continental in-

Mr. Ingersoll is a staff reporter of THE WALL STREET JOURNAL.

creased its loan-loss provision from $35 million in 1982's first quarter to $262 million in the second quarter of 1982.

"Continental took a big hit in the second quarter because it was underproviding for reserves for some time prior to that," says Mr. Vincent. Continental's loan-loss reserve had declined as a percentage of total loans every year from 1975 through 1981. In 1982 it was disclosed that Continental had purchased about $1 billion of loans from Penn Square Bank, the Oklahoma City bank closed by federal regulators that year because of bad energy loans.

In 1982, according to a report by Continental's investment banker, Goldman, Sachs & Co., Continental was charging off or classifying as nonperforming a smaller percentage of its loans from Penn Square than other banks with large Penn Square loan exposure. At that time, Chase Manhattan Corp. charged off 21.2% and classified 35.4% as nonperforming, and Seafirst Corp. charged off 4.4% and classified 27.3% as nonperforming. Continental charged off 4.5% and classified 15.1% as nonperforming. A loan generally is listed as nonperforming if its interest is more than 90 days overdue.

Asked by Goldman Sachs about the differences, Continental management said at the time that it believed "our examinations support the determinations we have made." Since then Continental has written off about 35% of Penn Square loans and classified 47% as nonperforming

And all signs point to increased problem loans for Continental and therefore increased pressure on its loan-loss reserves. David G. Taylor, Continental's chairman and chief executive officer, has said nonperforming loans will rise in the second quarter of 1984 from the $2.3 billion level of the first quarter. In addition, as of March 31, the bank had more than $400 million in loans more than 90 days past due but not classified as nonperforming. Regulators are pressing banks to place loans of that status in the nonperforming category.

SEC officials said it is usual procedure for the agency's enforcement division during an investigation to look into the auditor's role in the financial reports. A spokesman for Ernst & Whinney, the Cleveland-based firm that is Continental's outside auditor, declined to comment on the investigation, saying only that it is the firm's policy to "cooperate with regulatory authorities."

Loan-Loss Evaluation

Thomas Macy, a partner with Price Waterhouse, an accounting firm, and chairman of the American Institute of Certified Public Accountants' banking committee, says the committee has been reviewing the adequacy of loan-loss evaluation for banks. "It's a logical area for the SEC to be looking into because so many banks are perceived to be in trouble," he adds.

The Continental Illinois inquiry underscores the SEC's increasing activism in the banking industry. The commission under chairman John Shad has taken enforcement action against eight bank holding companies and one thrift holding company, including five cases since October 1983. "Bank accounting and disclosure practices are one of the top priorities of our enforcement program," says commissioner James Treadway.

The SEC also has begun requiring greater disclosure on the part of bank holding companies. Under guidelines amended last summer, they must file disclosure reports with a new "risk elements" section, detailing past-due and nonaccrual loans, potential loan problems, and loan concentrations. In January the SEC directed bank holding companies to begin reporting material developments that affect their subsidiaries' foreign loans to countries that have liquidity problems.

Early Warnings:
Long Before the 'Run' at Continental
Illinois, Bank Hinted of Its Ills

But Mesmerized by Its Surge in Loans, Many Analysts Ignored Signs of Danger—'Building Skyscraper of Sand'

By Lee Berton

July 12, 1984

In Continental Illinois Corp.'s 1981 annual report, on page 32, line 10, is the number $289,169,000.

That number said a lot about Continental.

It was the bank holding company's reserve against possible loan losses at the end of 1981, and it showed that the reserve as a percentage of total loans was well below the ratio at most major U.S. banks. Moreover, raising Continental's reserve to the industry norm in 1981 would have nearly wiped out the increase in the company's profits from 1979 to 1981.

The figure showed an "inherent weakness" in the company, says Mark Alpert, a securities analyst with Bear, Stearns & Co. Continental, he contends, "was keeping its reserve low to inflate its profit."

Continental Illinois, the ninth-largest bank holding company in the United States, is the parent of Continental Illinois National Bank & Trust Co. of Chicago, which federal regulators and other banks now are trying to rescue through a huge infusion of capital and credit.

Penn Square Link

Financial analysts, bankers and regulators often say Continental's problems were well hidden until July 1982, when the bank was identified as the biggest buyer of energy loans from Penn Square Bank, which federal regulators had just shut down. And they say the extent of Continental's financial sickness is being determined only now, as regulators and potential purchasers comb through its books.

But a close examination of Continental's past financial reports indicates that long before Penn Square collapsed, Continental had been providing public warning signs—though not explaining its problems in a systematic way—and that over the past two years those signs have been growing more alarming. Its financial statements to shareholders and regulators, as well as public announcements by Continental officials, tell the story of a bank heading for trouble for perhaps longer than a decade.

Continental's numbers also hint at what is needed to revive the bank. Accountants and analysts believe that the bank's net worth is very low. Its asset base, which was about $41 billion on March 31, has already been reduced to about $37 billion and, they say, should be shrunk further to $25 billion to $30 billion by writing off or selling many of its bad loans and other assets.

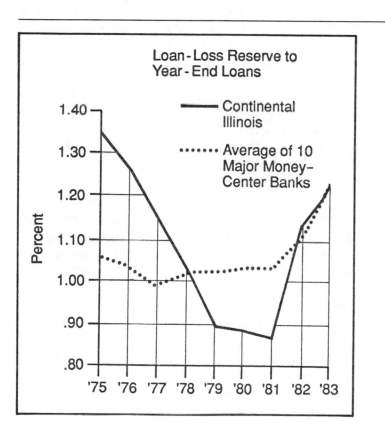

And in addition to $2 billion of capital already provided by the Federal Deposit Insurance Corp. and a group of banks, at least another $2 billion in capital may be needed to make Continental viable, they figure.

Finally, a financial examination of Continental tells much about how and why more banks are getting into hot water. So far this year, 43 FDIC-insured banks have failed; in all last year, 48 failed.

Hindsight, of course, makes a dissection of Continental easier. Many analysts, including Mr. Alpert of Bear Stearns, ignored the warning signs when they first appeared. And though analysts claim to have learned their lesson, they also agree that the lesson is easily forgotten when the fever of the moment overwhelms reason.

That fever apparently struck in the case of Continental. "The bank's loan growth was so spectacular in the late 1970s that everyone, including Continental's management, put on blinders when they saw danger signs," Mr. Alpert asserts.

Accountants point out that a bank normally has little equity and uses other people's money to generate income. Continental's 1983 annual report shows its equity at 4.33% of its total assets—about the same as for other money-center banks. This compared with 21% for Sears, Roebuck & Co., the big Chicago retailing and financial-services concern; 35% for Kaiser Aluminum Corp., and 50% for Goodyear Tire & Rubber Co.

Asset Problems

Because banks are so highly leveraged and their liabilities tend to be volatile, they must try to keep their assets fairly liquid. But Continental's assets were a lot less liquid than other banks', and thus it was more vulnerable to a run on its deposits. David Cates, a bank analyst, notes that in 1981, at the peak of Continental's loan growth, its relatively liquid assets, such as the short-term certificates of deposit that its overseas branches were buying from foreign banks, were only 14.5% of all assets earning interest. That compared with a median of 25.7% for 14 U.S. money-center banks.

Moreover, Continental's loans, which are the least liquid of a bank's assets, average 78.9% of its earning assets in 1981, compared with a median of 67% for its 14 peers.

The high leverage also demands that banks be careful that their asset growth doesn't outstrip their ability to fund loans or take in deposits. Instead, Continental chose a risky path to super growth in the 1970s. As disclosed in its financial reports, Continental's foreign and domestic loan growth from 1977 through 1981 averaged about 22% a year. In contrast, at Morgan Guaranty Trust Co., a major competitor in corporate lending, total loan growth averaged 17% a year and domestic loan growth only 13% a year. Domestic loan growth for the entire U.S. banking system during that period was just 12% annually.

Meanwhile, the liability side of Continental's balance sheet looked equally risky. According to Richard Hairsine, a former bank auditor who advised Continental on its accounting system in the early 1970s, the bank has been "walking a thin line for a long time." Tallying the bank's various accounts in 1971, Mr. Hairsine noticed even then that the bank had only 50,000 checking accounts. And even those few accounts were mostly from corporations, corporate executives and affluent depositors—all of whom shift deposits to other banks more quickly than small-business people and the less wealthy.

"Continental was borrowing money to finance an aggressive loan policy, and I was shocked it had practically a nonexistent consumer-deposit base," Mr. Hairsine says. For its aggressive loan growth, he estimates, Continental should have had at least 500,000 checking accounts. "It was building a skyscraper of sand that would eventually fall," he says.

From 1977 through 1981, the annual reports show, Continental's core deposits from individuals, partnerships and corporations remained static while, at the 20 largest U.S. banks, growth in such deposits averaged more than 8% a year. "Continental, which was limited to three branches by Illinois law, was trying to hit the ball over the fence by choking up on the bat," asserts Robert Walters, senior vice president of Sheshunoff & Co., an Austin, Texas, consulting firm in bank analysis.

Continental began to pursue consumer-deposit volume in a big way in 1982, its annual reports show, but by then it was too late to stem the big institutions' growing lack of confidence in the bank because of the Penn Square debacle.

Lacking a big consumer base, Continental was raising lendable funds by borrowing heavily in the overnight money market, by selling certificates of deposit both in the United States and abroad, and by selling commercial paper (short-term IOUs). Continental also was attracting deposits of other commercial banks, particularly overseas institutions, by in some cases paying them more interest than some other banks offered.

Foreign Banks' Deposits

From 1977 to 1981, for example, Continental's annual reports show that time deposits of foreign banks in Continental's foreign branches soared an ominous 91% to $12.8 billion. Morgan Guaranty's similar deposits rose 71% during the period, but the interest rate it paid was anywhere from one-quarter to two-thirds percentage point less than Continental's rate. That seemingly slight differential can substantially affect the bottom line.

"Continental didn't have the flexibility to protect against a run on its deposits because it was funding its loans with 'hot' money," maintains Charles M. Vincent, a vice president of Provident National Bank in Philadelphia and a bank analyst. Mr. Vincent notes that foreign banks quickly shift time deposits from U.S. banks' overseas branches if they suspect any problems. "A depositor that is a bank will run faster than any other depositor at the first smell of smoke," he adds.

As a result, Continental was getting squeezed from both sides. It was overcommitting its assets with heavy loan volume and financing them with more volatile, more expensive money. From 1979 to 1983, Continental's net interest margin—the total cost of all its funds contributing to earning assets subtracted from the yield of all its assets—was as much as three-quarters percentage point below the median for its 14 peers.

Paul R. Ogorzelec, a bank auditor with Arthur Andersen & Co. in Chicago, says he has been warning his bank clients for decades that too rapid loan growth using costly funds "can produce smoke that will lead to a fire sale."

Nonperforming Loans

In addition, Continental's loans—the main assets at the Chicago institution and any other bank—are of poorer quality than its competitors', the bank's most recent financial reports show. At the end of the 1984 first quarter, for instance, Continental's nonperforming loans—those 90 days or more past due on interest or principal—were 7.7% of its total loans compared with 2.7% for the 14 money-center banks. Continental's loan-loss reserves rose to 1.32% of its total loans at the end of the quarter from 1.21% at the end of 1983 and 1.11% at the end of 1982.

But people who watched Continental's financial statements and public announcements got hints that something was amiss with its loan portfolio long before this year's first quarter.

More than most banks, accountants say, Continental was notorious in the industry for "shooting craps" by lending to companies that other banks avoided. Among Continental's customers were once-ailing Chrysler Corp., International Harvester Corp. and Braniff International Corp. Yet, as Bear Stearns' Mr. Alpert notes, the bank seemed reluctant to increase its loan-loss reserve. While Continental was reducing its reserve as a percentage of total loans from 1.34% in 1975 to 0.87% in 1981, other money-center banks generally held that figure steady at an average 1.03%.

Continental comments, "During the period, we always provided more to the reserve than the actual credit losses." It adds that the reserve is always based on "the best information available" at the time.

Financial analysts also received indications that the bank's credit controls were inadequate. A Continental official admitted to a group of analysts in August 1982 that the bank's 454 loans from Penn Square came up for review by its senior management as "individual loans." In other words, he said, the top executives didn't know that the 454 loans were "all from Penn Square."

Lagging Writeoffs

Continental also lagged behind other banks in writing off and classifying as nonperforming the $1 billion of loans it bought from Penn Square. In mid-1982, soon after Penn Square was closed by federal regulators, Continental charged off only 4.5% and classified only 15.1% of its Penn Square loans as nonperforming, according to a report by Continental's investment banker, Goldman, Sachs & Co. In contrast, Chase Manhattan Corp. had by then charged off 21.2% and classified 35.4% as nonperforming, and Seafirst Corp. had charged 4.4% and classified

27.3% as nonperformers. "Continental just wouldn't face the music, which is now a drumbeat on its head," Mr. Vincent observes.

Aware of the slow write-offs, the Securities and Exchange Commission has expanded an investigation, begun last year, into Continental's possible violation of disclosure requirements to also examine the adequacy of its loan-loss provisions over the past several years.

At least until recently, Continental continued to be slow in classifying loans as nonperforming. Financial reports disclose that at the end of the 1984 first quarter, 1.3%, or $405 million, of Continental's total loan portfolio consisted of credits that had principal or interest 90 days overdue but weren't classified as nonperforming. While a few major banks had similar percentage figures last March 31, more conservative banks, such as Morgan Guaranty and Bankers Trust Co., keep this proportion far below 1%.

Accountants cite these disparities as evidence that Continental has been under pressure to increase sharply what it reports as nonperforming loans. Some accountants think that as much as $4 billion of Continental's loans may fall into that category.

Peat Loses Plea over Review of Penn Square

High Court Justice Declines to Delay Full Disclosure of Firm's Internal Study

By Lee Berton

January 3, 1985

Peat, Marwick, Mitchell & Co., a major U.S. accounting firm, must disclose completely an internal study of its 1981 audit of Penn Square Bank, which was closed by federal authorities in 1982.

Supreme Court Justice Byron R. White declined to postpone

an order issued last month by a U.S. district court judge in Oklahoma City, where Penn Square was based, that denied Peat the right to keep parts of the report confidential.

Attorneys for Peat and other major accounting firms said yesterday that Justice White's refusal may open all accounting firms to "self-incrimination" in cases where firms have been sued for failing to spot financial troubles at client companies.

The Peat internal study is being requested by at least 10 parties who are suing Peat for a total of more than $400 million. The plaintiffs claim that, among other things, they bought certificates of deposit from Penn Square after Peat gave the bank's 1981 financial statements a clean opinion. Penn Square was closed after many of its energy loans turned sour and the CDs became worthless.

Edwin Scott, associate general counsel for Peat, said such internal reports are done at the request of accounting firms' in-house counsel after litigation is begun. Often they are "quite candid and speculative," he added.

Mr. Scott said that to permit the plaintiffs to see the study "opens the door for more rulings" where accounting firms won't be able to claim "privilege" for material that "should be protected as the work product of the accounting firm's attorney."

Harris Amhowitz, senior partner and general counsel for Coopers & Lybrand, another major accounting firm, said failure to protect such studies "could lead to self-incrimination." It's a "scary development," he added.

Continuing Claims
Mr. Scott of Peat noted that the accounting firm will have to turn over the study to the plaintiffs immediately. But he said Peat still has a request before the Supreme Court on a procedural matter in the case. The firm is asking the court to consider whether a lower court should have ignored Peat's claim of privilege on certain documents because of procedural mistakes the lower-court judge says Peat made. It's unlikely the Supreme Court will be able to hear this issue before next month, attorneys at accounting firms said.

In the Penn Square litigation, U.S. District Court Judge Lee West late last year ruled that Peat couldn't protect the study because the accounting firm didn't specifically list it as "privileged" at certain times when the cases came before him. Last Monday, Peat, in an emergency request, asked the Supreme Court to set aside Judge West's ruling until the full court could decide the procedural issue.

Each Supreme Court justice is assigned a specific circuit court for such "temporary stay" issues, and Justice White handles the federal appeals court in Denver, which includes Oklahoma City in its jurisdiction.

Two Review Types
Accounting firms usually perform two types of reviews after an audit is over. Attorneys at accounting firms believe that the first, done randomly by partners for quality control, isn't protected from disclosure by the courts. But they are adamant that studies of audits requested by in-house counsel after litigation is begun should be "privileged."

"Otherwise, you may find that accounting firms will have to ask their trial counsels to have other outside accounting firms review their audit engagements to retain the protection of privilege," said Coopers & Lybrand's Mr. Amhowitz.

Peat's attorneys in their filings have called the Penn Square internal study "a compendium of professional opinion, favorable and unfavorable, concerning the audit." They said the study contains "candid conclusions."

SEC Is Probing Alexander Grant Audits of Collapsed ESM's Books, Sources Say

By Lee Berton

March 15, 1985

NEW YORK—The Securities and Exchange Commission is investigating the performance of Alexander Grant & Co., a Chicago-based accounting firm, in auditing the collapsed E.S.M. Government Securities Inc., accounting industry sources said.

Both Grant and the SEC declined to comment on the report.

Meanwhile, an accountant working for the court-appointed receiver of E.S.M. Government Securities asserted it should have been obvious to Grant that E.S.M. Government Securities and its parent, E.S.M. Group Inc., were keeping two sets of books that "don't agree."

Jack Goldstrich, a partner with Holtz & Co., a Miami accounting firm, said E.S.M. Government Securities kept its books clean by making only brief journal entries for itself and "booking the real activities for the parent company."

Avoiding Losses

Thomas Tew, the court-appointed receiver for E.S.M. Government Securities, explained that the subsidiary thus was able to avoid showing losses in dealing in repurchase agreements backed by government securities. In effect, this means that the parent rather than the subsidiary took all the risk and that the subsidiary's assets allotted to its repurchase-agreement business remained frozen since 1983, Mr. Tew said.

In dealing with customers, E.S.M. Government Securities typically put up government securities as collateral for cash loans from customers, with the agreement to buy the securities back from the customers later at a higher price. In a "reverse repurchase agreement," the customer, often a brokerage firm, borrowed money from E.S.M., using government securities as collateral; the customer agreed to buy the securities back later at a higher price.

Borrowers of cash under such arrangements bet that the price of the government securities will rise while lenders hope that the securities' price will fall.

'Mirror-Image' Transactions

Mr. Tew asserted that E.S.M. Government Securities was able to avoid showing losses in these dealings by "booking mirror-image" transactions with the parent. For example, if the subsidiary did a repurchase agreement with a customer for $1 million, it would book a $1 million reverse agreement with its parent. Thus, the unit would appear to have no chance for a loss or gain, and any risk would fall on the parent.

But, according to Mr. Tew and Mr. Goldstrich, the parent passed off any losses to an affiliated company, E.S.M. Financial Group Inc., and created the illusion that the parent had made profitable trades.

Mr. Tew said he didn't understand how Grant, E.S.M. Government Securities' outside auditor, could miss the significance of the mirror transactions. Grant has been the subsidiary's auditor for several years, but only prepared the annual tax returns of E.S.M. Group and E.S.M. Financial Group, Mr. Goldstrich noted.

The parent and E.S.M. Financial Group didn't have outside auditors, Mr. Goldstrich added.

Robert A. Kleckner, Grant's executive partner, declined to comment on the likelihood of any SEC action. "It would be inappropriate for me to comment on matters involving a client at this time," he said.

Accounting Parallels

Accountants said they see parallels in the E.S.M. collapse with auditing failures at Continental Vending Corp. in the late 1960s, Equity Funding Corp. of America in 1973 and Drysdale Securities Corp. in 1982. At Continental Vending and Equity Funding, parents and subsidiaries had separate auditors, while Drysdale allegedly passed off losses in government securities to a unit set up for that purpose.

"The government securities business is volatile, and an auditor looking at it should make sure that he understands all transactions" among parents, units and affiliates, said Allan Ackerman, a partner of KMG Main Hurdman, a New York-based accounting firm.

Douglas Carmichael, an accounting professor at Baruch College here and former director of auditing standards for the American Institute of Certified Public Accountants, said that an accounting firm auditing a subsidiary whose parent it doesn't audit is "put in a difficult position." Auditing rules require the subsidiary's auditor to understand the purpose of transactions with the parent. The auditor must examine business documents behind such transactions, the rules also say.

"If there's any suspicion of covering up problems," the auditor should examine all dealings between parent and subsidiary, Mr. Carmichael said. Mr. Goldstrich of Holtz & Co. said that in looking through E.S.M.'s books, he didn't see any indication that Grant did this. Grant declined to comment on this aspect as well.

Rare Public Dispute between CPA Firms Involves Liability in Brokerage's Failure

By Bruce Ingersoll and Lee Berton

March 28, 1985

A dispute between two accounting firms over which should be held more liable for failing to detect fraud in the costliest U.S. brokerage-firm collapse comes to a head at a federal bankruptcy court hearing today in Toledo, Ohio.

The dispute is remarkable both because of the sums involved and because accounting firms rarely point fingers at each other in public after client business failures. Liability insurance rates are soaring for all of them, and auditors fear that such

Mr. Ingersoll is a staff reporter of THE WALL STREET JOURNAL.

public acrimony invites still more of the lawsuits that increasing numbers of disgruntled creditors are filing.

The brokerage firm, Bell & Beckwith, based in Toledo, was put into bankruptcy early in 1983 after it showed a capital deficiency of more than $40 million.

Patrick A. McGraw, a court-appointed trustee overseeing its liquidation, has sued Frederick A. Todman & Co., a relatively small New York-based accounting firm that was Bell & Beckwith's auditor from 1977 until its collapse, for $65 million in damages.

At the same time, Mr. McGraw has offered to settle for $388,512 a claim against Arthur Young & Co., Bell & Beckwith's auditor from the early 1960s until it was fired by the brokerage firm in 1976. That settlement is the subject of today's hearing.

Mr. McGraw says both Todman and Arthur Young failed to uncover the misdeeds of Bell & Beckwith's high-living managing partner, Edward P. Wolfram, Jr., because they didn't follow generally accepted auditing standards. Mr. Wolfram is serving a 25-year term in federal prison for securities fraud.

Trustee's Goal

The trustee hopes to collect from the two accounting firms enough money to pay off Bell & Beckwith's creditors and reimburse Securities Investor Protection Corp., which has paid out about $40 million to the brokerage firm's customers.

Both Todman and Arthur Young deny any wrongdoing or liability in the Bell & Beckwith failure. The Todman firm, in turn is challenging the proposed settlement with Arthur Young in the federal bankruptcy court. Also challenging it are a group of former Bell & Beckwith partners, a one-time limited partner and a Toledo firm whose losses were only partly covered by SIPC.

Bernard Weiner, Todman's senior managing partner, says the trustee of Bell & Beckwith should be suing Arthur Young for a greater amount instead of settling out of court. "If Arthur Young had done their job, Bell & Beckwith would have been closed in 1976 for insufficient net capital," he asserts.

Eugene Erbstoesser, associate general counsel for Arthur Young, disagrees. He notes that Arthur Young "was fired in 1976 as the brokerage firm's auditor after informing the Securities and Exchange Commission that Bell & Beckwith had material inadequacies in its internal accounting controls."

Firms' Insurance Coverage

Mr. Weiner says that $10 million in liability insurance for Todman was canceled by American Home Assurance Co. in November 1983 after Bell & Beckwith's problems surfaced. "We now carry $2 million in liability insurance with Connecticut Underwriters through a White Plains, New York, broker, and were fortunate to get it," he says. On the $2 million policy, the first $85,000 is deductible.

Arthur Young, on the other hand, is insured with the other Big Eight accounting firms by Lloyd's of London, most of them through a Montreal broker, and its liability limits are much higher. "Those suing us in this case obviously look at us as a 'deep pocket' from which they can draw money if the companies we've audited no longer exist," says Carl Liggio, general counsel of Arthur Young, the sixth-biggest U.S. accounting firm based on 1984 revenue.

For Todman, which has only eight partners and 60 staff members, compared with more than 700 partners and a staff of more than 7,000 for Arthur Young, the disposition of claims involving Bell & Beckwith could spell its survival or demise. Todman's Mr. Weiner notes that its annual fee revenue has declined to $3 million from $6 million as recently as 1979. "We audit more than 60 brokerage firms among our 300-plus clients, and recent mergers on Wall Street have depressed our business," says Mr. Weiner.

Last August the SEC censured Todman in connection with the Bell & Beckwith collapse, and said that Todman couldn't take any more brokerage-firm clients until it underwent a "peer review" by another accounting firm and took other steps to upgrade the quality of its practice.

The peer review of Todman was begun by Chicago-based Alexander Grant & Co., the 11th-biggest U.S. accounting firm, which has been having its own problems in the collapse of E.S.M. Government Securities Inc. in Ft. Lauderdale, Florida. The SEC has charged that a Grant auditor, no longer with

Grant, took $125,000 in illegal payments from three E.S.M. officers.

Arthur Young's attorney, Mr. Erbstoesser, said that when Todman took over the Bell & Beckwith audit in 1977 it didn't consult with Arthur Young as to its problems with the brokerage firm. Auditing standards require such consultation on "facts that might bear on the integrity of management (and) on disagreements with management" on accounting or auditing.

Mr. Weiner says he doesn't recall if "such contacts were made with Arthur Young" in 1977.

In its censure of Todman, the SEC alleges that the accounting firm failed to disclose that receivables from customers and from Mr. Wolfram and his wife were collateralized by stock of a Japanese plumbing fixture company that Bell & Beckwith financial statements valued at as much as $96,000 a share. The shares should have been valued at only $1.80 each, the SEC says.

Alexander Grant, ESM's Auditor, Faces at Least 12 Suits; Fox Merger Is Stalled

By Lee Berton

April 5, 1985

NEW YORK—At least a dozen lawsuits have been filed against Alexander Grant & Co., auditor of E.S.M. Government Securities Inc., for alleged failure to uncover fraud at E.S.M. over the past four years, the Chicago-based accounting firm disclosed.

And in the wake of the E.S.M. collapse, Grant said yesterday it has sponsored two investigations of auditing orperations at its Miami and Fort Lauderdale, Fla., offices. One investigation is being handled by Grant partners from other cities. The other is by the special investigations committee of a unit of the American Institute of Certified Public Accountants.

As previously reported, the Securities and Exchange Commission has sued Jose Gomez, former managing partner of Grant's Miami and Fort Lauderdale offices, for allegedly receiving $125,000 from three E.S.M. officials for certifying false financial statements of the Fort Lauderdale securities dealer.

In another development, Grant's anticipated merger with Denver-based Fox & Co. has been put on hold because of the E.S.M. situation. Norman E. Klein, managing partner of Fox, said in an interview yesterday that questions being raised by Fox partners were temporarily delaying the merger talks. "Our partners are entitled to know what happened so we're not pushing for the merger right now," said Mr. Klein.

Peter Skomorowsky, managing partner of Grant's New York office, noted that plaintiffs against Grant include three municipalities and two thrifts. The plaintiffs assert that they invested through E.S.M., which collapsed last month, because Grant had given E.S.M.'s financial statements clean opinions since 1980.

Plaintiffs include shareholders of American Savings & Loan Association of Florida; the conservator of Home State Savings Bank, Cincinnati; Pompano Beach, Fla.; Toledo, Ohio; and Beaumont, Texas. Thomas Tew, court-appointed trustee of E.S.M., also has sued Grant.

Home State is owned by Cincinnati financier Marvin L. Warner, a business associate of a former director of E.S.M., which was headed by a former American savings director.

Amounts Sought in Suits

Mr. Tew is asking for $300 million, while the other plaintiffs are asking for lesser amounts. The total could exceed $1 billion, according to Alvin Stein, an attorney for Grant. But he added that many of the suits are "repetitive," so that the actual amount of claimed losses would be closer to $300 million.

In a detailed report filed earlier this week with federal bankruptcy court in Miami, Mr. Tew accused Grant of helping E.S.M. cover up huge losses and create phantom assets through intricate journal entries among related companies of E.S.M. Group Inc., parent of E.S.M. Government Securities. Grant audited the books of E.S.M. Government Securities, but not those of the parent.

In his report, Mr. Tew accused Grant of failing to ensure that E.S.M.'s financial statements were examined by personnel with "adequate technical training and proficiency as auditors." He also said that Grant failed to properly supervise and oversee the E.S.M. audit. He said he anticipates that "ultimately every creditor of (E.S.M.) will file a direct action against Grant."

In addition to the three cities that have sued Grant, other creditors include Harrisburg, Allentown and Dauphin County, Pa.; and Chellan, Clallam and Jefferson counties in Washington.

Mr. Tew has said the cities and counties lost money through transactions with E.S.M. that involved complex "repurchase agreements," in which they in effect loaned money to E.S.M., which was to post government securities as collateral. According to Mr. Tew, the lenders in many instances didn't take possession of the securities, which wrongfully were pledged as collateral for other transactions.

"We're sure this is going to be a litigating circus," said Mr. Skomorowsky of Grant.

In a statement, Robert Kleckner, executive partner of Grant, said that Mr. Gomez, the former Grant partner in Miami sued by the SEC, seemed to be "a highly qualified and faithful professional, family man and trusted member of the community. . . ."

Mr. Kleckner added: "Until mid-March, we had no reason to believe that this perception of Jose Gomez was not well founded." If allegations against Mr. Gomez are proven, then he "abandoned his professional responsibilities and violated our firm's rules. . . ," Mr. Kleckner said.

Mr. Kleckner said Grant's Miami and Fort Lauderdale offices have a total of 70 employees, including nine partners.

Invitation from Grant
Robert A. Mellin, chairman of the special investigations committee of an AICPA membership unit for accounting firms, said that the panel, at Grant's invitation, will "do a special review" of the work of Grant's Miami and Fort Lauderdale offices during the next few weeks. "Our goal is for corrective action and improved systems of quality control, not for punitive action," said

Mr. Mellin, senior partner of Hood & Strong, a San Francisco accounting firm.

"I've been in this accounting profession for 35 years and this is the first time I recall that a CPA firm partner is accused of taking money" to falsify the books, said Mr. Mellin. "It's a black mark for the profession."

Billionaire Investor Loses Recent Battle with an Auditor

Peat Marwick Tells Buffett to Restate Firm's Net or Get Qualified Opinion

By Lee Berton

April 26, 1985

NEW YORK—Billionaire investor Warren Buffett is a consummate winner. His investment company, Berkshire Hathaway Inc., founded in 1956, never has had a down year on Wall Street, not even in the worst of bear markets.

But Berkshire Hathaway's 1984 annual report reveals that Mr. Buffett lost a recent battle with the company's outside auditor, making the Omaha, Nebraska–based company a little less of a winner the past two years.

An analysis of the annual report shows that the auditor, Peat, Marwick, Mitchell & Co., required Berkshire Hathaway to report almost 8% lower per-share earnings for 1984 than it would have liked to. Peat also made the company restate 1983 per-share profit, reducing it by slightly more than 1% from the previously reported amount.

Mr. Buffett isn't happy about it.

Taking close to a full page in the 1984 report, he expounds on why he thinks Peat is wrong. "We disagree with . . . (Peat's) position from both the view of economic substance and proper accounting. But, to avoid a qualified auditor's opinion, we have adopted herein Peat Marwick's 1984 views, and restated 1983 accordingly," he writes.

The dispute arose this way: In 1983, Berkshire Hathaway tendered 350,000 Geico Corp. shares to Geico for $21 million and treated it as a dividend. In 1984, Berkshire Hathaway sold to General Foods Inc. on several occasions "a quantity of shares" of General Foods for a total of $21.8 million. In both years, the percentage of Berkshire Hathaway's ownership of Geico and General Foods remained the same after the sales.

The argument between Mr. Buffett and Peat centers on a question that is unresolved in the accounting profession: If company A sells shares it holds in company B back to B, but retains the same percentage of ownership, is A's transaction a sale of shares or a dividend from B?

If the transactions are treated as dividends, the entire receipts from the sales would be considered profit. But under accounting rules, if the transactions are stock sales, the purchase prices of the stocks must be deducted from the sale prices before determining profits.

The company said that both of the transactions are treated as dividends for tax purposes.

As explained by Mr. Buffett, Peat's Omaha office and a reviewing partner from Chicago permitted Berkshire Hathaway to treat the Geico item as a dividend in 1983. But for 1984, Peat's New York headquarters disagreed on the Geico treatment. It also called the General Foods transactions stock sales, and forced Berkshire Hathaway to restate 1983 net and scale down net for 1984.

Thus, under Peat's latest decision, Berkshire Hathaway's reported profits were less: per-share net in 1984 was $129.82 instead of $140.60; net for 1983 was restated to $105.15 a share from $106.40 a share.

Peat Marwick wouldn't say much on the dispute. Clifford E. Graese, a vice chairman, said "It's the client's prerogative to disagree. Our report speaks for itself."

Arthur Young's Work for Hutton Probed by SEC and Two Congressional Panels

By Andy Pasztor and Lee Berton

July 18, 1985

The Securities and Exchange Commission and two congressional subcommittees are conducting separate investigations of Arthur Young & Co.'s role in advising E.F. Hutton & Co. on its cash management practices.

A common focus of the three inquiries is Arthur Young's role in helping to defend Hutton against criminal prosecution for bank overdrafts and also serving as a consultant to recommend changes in Hutton's cash management procedures, investigators said. Some accountants worked on both projects at different times, Arthur Young said.

Arthur Young, a big accounting firm based in New York, has given investigators certain internal documents relating to consulting work it performed for Hutton starting in the summer of 1982, and a number of its senior officials have been interviewed in the past few weeks about that work. But Arthur Young officials said that Hutton ordered them not to give investigators copies of confidential papers relating to the accounting firm's work to assist Hutton's attorneys defending the brokerage house from criminal prosecution.

Some of the investigators and several accounting professors contend that the dual role has at the very least created the appearance of a conflict of interest that may pull the accounting firm into the escalating controversy around Hutton's illegal check-writing practices. In May, Hutton pleaded guilty to 2,000 counts of mail and wire fraud in connection with the check overdraft scheme involving many of its 400 banks nationwide.

The investigation of Arthur Young's relationships with Hutton also raises a number of legal and ethical questions about

---

Mr. Pasztor is a staff reporter of THE WALL STREET JOURNAL.

whether auditing firms should provide such a broad array of consulting services to clients, especially those under criminal investigation.

'Absolutely Pristinely'

Paul J. Ostling, Arthur Young's associate general counsel, said in an interview that the firm is convinced it behaved "absolutely pristinely" in fulfilling both roles and did everything possible to avoid any conflict of interest. Mr. Ostling confirmed that Arthur Young continues to assist Hutton's attorneys representing the brokerage during the federal investigations.

Hutton contends that Arthur Young documents or computations relating to such work contain privileged attorney-client material. Congressional investigators said Arthur Young officials also have refused to answer certain questions for the same reasons.

To preserve the independence and impartiality of the consulting effort, Arthur Young maintained it used separate teams to perform the two different types of work for Hutton. Since both teams "were performing services for the same side," there wasn't any conflict of interest, according to Mr. Ostling.

But investigators from the House Judiciary Subcommittee on Crime and the House Energy oversight and investigations subcommittee have questioned Arthur Young's assertions. In addition, the SEC has subpoenaed certain documents from Arthur Young relating to its work over the years for Hutton. And Griffin Bell, hired by Hutton for an independent inquiry into the overdrafting violations, has asked for Arthur Young work papers previously withheld from government investigators.

Case Is Called Borderline

Robert Chatov, an associate professor of management at the State University of New York at Buffalo, said Arthur Young's dual role is "a borderline case" that raises possible ethical conflicts. Accounting firms tend to "get into trouble when they wear too many hats," Mr. Chatov said, adding that the rules for determining the propriety of such activities are open to large differences in interpretation.

Abraham Briloff, professor of accounting at the City University of New York and an industry critic, maintained that Arthur Young's work defending Hutton raises "a major contradiction" about its impartiality as a cash management consultant. "I don't conceive of Arthur Young as being independent in any respect. They are advocates for Hutton down the line, regardless of what the company claims," Mr. Briloff asserted.

Hutton has indicated it originally hired Arthur Young in July 1982 as a "nationally recognized cash management specialist" to provide an independent review of bank withdrawal practices. Hutton has said it relied on Arthur Young's advice in revising its companywide banking procedures. "They're considered the most successful firm in advising cash management," according to Hutton's chairman, Robert Fomon.

Mr. Ostling, however, disclosed that before Young was hired as a consultant, Hutton's attorneys sought and obtained Arthur Young's informal approval of the revised procedures the brokerage house wanted to put in place. Hutton was under criminal investigation at the time, and sought to continue some bank overdrafting practices that it considered legal.

Expert Witness

Two years later, when the Justice Department was ready to seek an indictment against Hutton, charging it defrauded many of its banks through arbitrary and excessive withdrawals, Hutton again turned to Arthur Young for assistance. This time, William Renshaw, one of the senior Arthur Young officials who worked on the original consulting contract, was an expert witness for Hutton.

Mr. Renshaw said that from 1982 until earlier this year, Arthur Young advised Hutton it was entitled to draw down uncollected balances in branch bank accounts without first informing the affected banks. Mr. Renshaw said he now advises clients to notify all banks that may be unaware of such drawdowns.

Florida Accounting Board Considers Imposing Sanction on Alexander Grant

By Lee Berton

July 24, 1985

The Florida State Board of Accountancy is weighing an order that would suspend Alexander Grant & Co., a major accounting firm, from obtaining new audit clients in the state for 60 days.

The proposed sanction, which has been recommended by a panel of the Florida board, arises from Grant's audits of E.S.M. Government Securities Inc., a Fort Lauderdale government securities dealer that failed earlier this year.

The three-member panel also has recommended that the accountancy board impose a 60-day sanction against Fox & Co., a large Denver-based accounting concern that was merged into Chicago-based Grant last May. The proposed action against Fox stems from the concern's 1979 audit of Saxon Industries Inc., a New York–based paper and business machines maker.

The Securities and Exchange Commission earlier this year charged that a former Grant partner took a $125,000 bribe from E.S.M. officials to permit E.S.M. to issue fraudulent financial reports. Two years ago, the SEC charged Fox with violating federal securities law in connection with its audit of Saxon's books, which included nonexistent inventories of photocopiers.

Action Is Rare

The proposed sanctions, which the Florida board will vote on tomorrow, are highly unusual for the nation's state boards of accountancy. These boards, which license and regulate accountants, generally impose mild penalties on CPA firms or accountants who are found to have violated federal or state laws or ethics of the accounting profession. In Florida, for example, errant accountants are frequently only required to take continuing professional education courses, according to Martha Willis, executive director of the Florida board.

The proposed action against Grant and Fox by the Florida board is a major development in "a trend by state accountancy boards to be more aggressive in disciplining major CPA firms," says Sandra Suran, president of the National Association of State Boards of Accountancy and a partner in the Portland, Oregon, office of Peat, Marwick, Mitchell & Co.

Robert Kleckner, executive partner of Alexander Grant, said the firm wouldn't comment until the Florida board has voted tomorrow. According to accountancy board officials, both Grant and Fox have signed preliminary "stipulations" agreeing to the 60-day sanctions.

Function of Boards

State accountancy boards function much like other state boards for physicians, dentists and architects. Such groups aren't regulatory agencies in the usual sense because they generally are composed of industry professionals. They aren't, however, simply self-regulatory groups because their authority is based on state legislation. Over the years, more active state legislatures have pushed state boards of accountancy to select public members instead of only accountants. The nine-member Florida board, for example, has two public members.

Sunset laws requiring legislative approval to reinstitute state boards have begun lumping boards for various professions under state umbrella agencies such as Florida's Department of Professional Regulation. These departments also have put pressure on the boards to be tougher on the professions they regulate.

The Florida State Board of Accountancy is considered one of the more aggressive state boards in the enforcement area, but this is the first time it has considered temporarily barring a major accounting concern from accepting new audit clients. Grant, after its Fox merger, is the 10th-biggest U.S. accounting firm, with 82 U.S. offices and 4,000 employees.

Britain to Claim that Arthur Andersen Doubted Some of De Lorean's Transfers

By Lee Berton

August 2, 1985

NEW YORK—In a court brief to be filed here today, the British government will say it has evidence that Arthur Andersen & Co. had grave doubts about the legality of certain fund transfers of John Z. De Lorean's sports car company.

Arthur Andersen, the biggest world-wide accounting firm that was the company's outside auditor, continued to express such doubts while giving clean audit opinions about financial reports of Mr. De Lorean's company over a four-year period that ended in 1981, the court papers will show.

Attorneys for the British government said the brief to be filed today in U.S. district court here is in response to a motion by Arthur Andersen to dismiss a British government complaint on jurisdictional grounds.

De Lorean Motor Co. was placed into receivership by the British government in February 1982. Britain's Department of Economic Development, which invested in the company, last February sued Arthur Andersen in U.S. district court here.

Britain is claiming $260 million in damages from Andersen, which includes triple damages under U.S. law.

Court papers allege that De Lorean Motor transferred more than $5 million of British government money in 1978 from Belfast to a Geneva, Switzerland, company called GPD Services Inc., which was registered in Panama. The British government charges the transfers were made to GPD's Swiss bank accounts in violation of British exchange-control regulations.

Britain also has charged that more than $12 million invested by private U.S. investors was diverted from Mr. De Lorean's auto company.

Britain has charged that Arthur Andersen knew of "or would have discovered" a fraud being committed by De Lorean Motor against its investors if it hadn't "recklessly disregarded other facts known to it and the standard of care which it was required to exercise." Arthur Andersen has denied these allegations.

A 1978 memo written by Ian Hay Davidson, then senior partner of Arthur Andersen in London, and Frank Barrett, a senior partner in the firm's Dublin, Ireland, office, said that Arthur Andersen "may have to qualify our audit report on the grounds that we would have some doubt as to the ability of the company to survive. If this happens, of course, the game is up and the scandal is out in the open."

The memo—published in a British newspaper—also suggested that Arthur Andersen might have to resign, but noted this would be difficult because the accounting firm then would have to disclose the reason for the resignation, possibly triggering "a public scandal."

In Chicago, Duane Kullberg, managing partner of Arthur Andersen, confirmed the memo and said it "reflects normal internal questioning that goes on in any audit process where all our partners try to play the devil's advocate." Mr. Kullberg said the firm expressed these doubts to De Lorean Motor's board and the British government in 1978. "Based on their reassurances, we were able to give the company's financial statements clean opinions," he said.

Don Hanson, Arthur Andersen's current senior partner in London, has said that by the time the firm began the 1978 audit, the payment had been made from De Lorean Motor to GPD.

In an earlier court filing, Arthur Andersen claimed that U.S. courts don't have jurisdiction in the case because De Lorean was a foreign company and didn't issue U.S. securities. In its latest filing, the British government said that Arthur Andersen is a world-wide partnership and that its British and Irish affiliates should therefore be liable to U.S. law.

Grant Thornton Finds Itself in Disarray

Suit over E.S.M. Shows Partners' Vulnerability

By Lee Berton

April 4, 1986

When Steve L. Hipp was invited early last year to join Alexander Grant & Co., he jumped at the chance. Mr. Hipp had been a partner at the troubled accounting firm of Fox & Co., which was being absorbed by Grant. Chicago-based Grant, now known as Grant Thornton, was a bigger firm and long regarded as the Mr. Clean of the accounting profession.

But a few months later, Mr. Hipp received a rude shock. Jose Gomez, Grant's managing partner for southern Florida, was accused of taking a $125,000 bribe from E.S.M. Government Securities Inc. in return for certifying false financial statements for at least four years. Mr. Gomez later pleaded guilty. Grant was sued for $300 million in actual damages and as much as $1 billion in punitive damages by parties that said they lost money in transactions with the now-collapsed Fort Lauderdale securities firm.

The total damages sought are more than five times Grant's malpractice insurance coverage and almost 50 times partners' capital.

Aware that a partner in a professional firm can be held liable for frauds proven against other partners, Mr. Hipp chose to become a manager in Grant rather than a partner. While he won't disclose the loss in potential income, he acknowledges the step-down is a "big sacrifice." But he adds, "It will save me a lot of liability worries."

Turmoil at Firm

Grant itself is in turmoil. The nation's 11th-largest accounting firm is having problems obtaining new clients and partners, retaining current clients and keeping its executive suite intact.

Recently, Grant's top partner said he will step down, and the No. 2 partner already left. "It's been rough times," says Peter Skomorowsky, regional managing partner in New York and the firm's official spokesman.

The firm's travail illustrates the pressures on a professional firm—whether it be in accounting, law, architecture or another field—when its reputation is threatened by a major liability suit. The problem is particularly significant for an accounting firm because, as an auditor, it is expected to be its clients' financial conscience.

"The E.S.M. case is the most dramatic example of how vulnerable professional partners are to mistakes made by colleagues in their firm," says Newton Minow, a partner in the Chicago law firm of Sidley & Austin and a former adviser to Arthur Andersen & Co., the biggest U.S. accounting firm. "This suit could be severely damaging to the firm."

To add to Grant's woes, the plaintiffs are suing more than 400 Grant partners who were served with court papers saying that their personal assets could be attached by the court in any settlement of the E.S.M. case. Some Grant partners considered shifting personal assets to wives or relatives, but Grant told them this isn't necessary.

"As far as I'm concerned, there's a better chance their wives will file for divorce than that they will lose their shirts because of E.S.M.," says Alvin Stein, a New York lawyer representing Grant.

Grant Thornton
(Formerly Alexander Grant & Co.)

Headquarters	Chicago
U.S. offices	77
U.S. partners	450
U.S. revenues	$175 million*
Major clients include:	Sunstrand Corp., Southmark Corp., Republic Airlines Inc., Orange & Rockland Utilities Inc.

*Year ended July 31, 1985.

Since E.S.M., Grant has found it difficult to attract new tax partners in south Florida and Washington, D.C., two important areas for its practice, says Grant's Mr. Skomorowsky. In recent months, Grant has lost a dozen public clients, compared with only two or three for firms of comparable size, says Arthur Bowman, editor of Public Accounting Report, a newsletter.

Mr. Skomorowsky insists that any loss of clients hasn't been because of the E.S.M. case. A half dozen former clients confirm this, including one of the biggest, Baxter Travenol Laboratories Inc., a Grant client for 32 years that moved to Price Waterhouse in September.

But Mr. Skomorowsky concedes that the firm is "getting somewhat fewer opportunities for new business." He says, "There's no question that E.S.M. was a disaster for our image. But as Mark Twain said, 'The reports of our death are premature.'"

However, the E.S.M. case caused Grant to lose some Fox business and partners that it otherwise would have picked up in the combination. Walter Knepper, who ran Fox's office in St. Louis, says that "as a result of the E.S.M. case, we lost a big client" just before the Grant-Fox combination May 1. He says the loss cut the office's annual revenues 20% and spurred Fox's St. Louis office to join Houston-based Pannell Kerr Forster, the 14th biggest accounting firm. "We're working hard to regain the reputation we lost when Fox had so many audit failures," says Mr. Knepper. "Why should I move from one firm with problems into another firm with problems?"

The Securities and Exchange Commission in mid-1983 prohibited Fox from accepting new publicly held clients until early 1984 because of problems with certain audits.

Early Departure

In Grant's executive suite, Robert Kleckner decided to step down as executive partner this year instead of in 1988, as he had told other partners when the Fox combination was announced in late 1984. And Herbert Dooskin, named Grant's chairman several months ago, recently resigned to take a post in industry.

Both men maintain that the E.S.M. case didn't influence their actions, and they insist that Grant's future is bright. "Our standards of quality and performance are still outstanding, and from the 25 phone calls I've personally received from clients, they're all standing behind us," says Mr. Kleckner.

Mr. Dooskin says he's leaving the firm because a Grant client, Ply-Gem Industries Inc., a New York–based maker of specialty wood products, "made me an offer I couldn't refuse;" he says Ply-Gem will pay him a higher salary. "It was a difficult decision," Mr. Dooskin says. "I've been with Grant for 22 years and it's been like family."

Grant was founded in 1924 by Alexander Grant, an accountant from Cameron, Missouri. Last January, Grant and its British affiliate, Thornton Baker, adopted the uniform Grant Thornton name.

"Grant was once considered one of the best-run firms in the profession," says James Emerson, publisher of the Big Eight Review, a Bellevue, Washington, newsletter. "Since E.S.M., it has come down several pegs."

A former Grant partner, who requests anonymity because he hasn't recovered all his capital from the firm, says he joined another firm in mid-1985 because he felt "it would be difficult to continue to try to sell my services after E.S.M." He adds, "Clients were already beginning to ask me embarrassing questions."

Counterattacking

Grant is counterattacking. Mr. Stein, the firm's New York attorney, says he is confident that Grant can reduce the impact of the E.S.M. claims because some of the parties suing Grant were themselves involved in the E.S.M. fraud. Mr. Stein recently filed a 200-page third-party complaint in a federal court in Fort Lauderdale claiming unspecified damages from eight entities and 22 people.

And in an unusual step for an accounting firm, Grant named another accounting firm, Arthur Andersen, in its third-party suit. Arthur Andersen was auditor of Home State Savings Bank, a Cincinnati thrift put up for sale after a run on its deposits spurred by its investment in E.S.M. Home State had sued Grant for more than $117 million for money allegedly lost in government securities trading with E.S.M. Grant claims Arthur

Andersen conspired with Home State to withhold information from Grant that would have been damaging to E.S.M. Arthur Andersen denies this.

Harold Cunningham, Andersen's partner for legal affairs, says the Grant suit is "a desperation move," and that "Grant is groping for anything to get another accounting firm or other people involved to ease the claim against themselves."

Mr. Stein says he is telling executives at Grant that he can keep awards against Grant below the firm's liability insurance coverage because a lot of the parties didn't exercise sufficient diligence in transactions with E.S.M. And he is trying to reach a settlement before the trial starts Oct. 1.

'Strong Medicine'

Dan L. Goldwasser, a special counsel for the New York State Society of Certified Public Accountants, says the E.S.M. liability suit could cripple Grant. "A partner admitting to a payoff is awfully strong medicine for any judge or jury," he says.

Some Grant partners continue to worry that the E.S.M. case can do long-term damage to the firm's image and financial outlook. "Two clients have asked me if the firm will continue to be in existence," says Ronald Berman, a Grant tax partner in Madison, Wisconsin, who has been with the firm a dozen years. "It's not a happy question to have to answer."

And Norman Essman, a Grant partner in St. Louis since 1969, says that while the E.S.M. case probably won't sink Grant, "It'll cost us a hell of a lot of money to defend. I'd like clients to call and hire us because Grant Thornton is as well known as a Big Eight firm but that just isn't happening. As partners, we have to establish our own reputations."

Arthur Andersen Loses Appeal of Award to Bank in Suit over Drysdale Collapse

By Phillip L. Zweig

September 9, 1986

NEW YORK—A federal appeals court upheld a $17 million judgment against accounting firm Arthur Andersen & Co. in connection with the 1982 collapse of Drysdale Securities Corp., a government securities firm.

A federal jury had awarded the judgment in March 1985 in a civil suit brought by Manufacturers Hanover Trust Co. The New York bank had contended that Andersen violated federal securities law and committed fraud and negligence in certifying financial statements for Drysdale and its Drysdale Government Securities Inc. unit.

Although the decision didn't appear to set major new legal precedents, an attorney familiar with the ruling said it was important because it explored the possible connections between an accountant's statements for a client and the ultimate use to which that information is put by a third party. Specifically, the decision addressed accountants' liability for violations of federal securities laws, particularly section 10(b) and rule 10b-5 concerning fraud in connection with the purchase or sale of securities. Only a few appellate court decisions have covered that area of the law, he said.

Accountants have been the subject of increasing numbers of lawsuits in recent years in the wake of several large financial collapses of banks, government securities dealers and other financial institutions.

In Chicago, a spokesman for Andersen said, "We believe the merits of our appeal are well-founded and (we) are extremely disappointed with the decision. We are reviewing the opinion to determine what options are available to us." The spokesman de-

---

Mr. Zweig is a staff reporter of THE WALL STREET JOURNAL.

clined to indicate whether the Big Eight firm would appeal to the Supreme Court.

Although the Second Circuit appeals court upheld the $17 million judgment, it vacated an award of pre-judgment interest and sent back to the trial court the question of whether payment of such interest was appropriate. However, post-judgment interest at 9% a year from the date of the judgment still stands.

The court denied Manufacturers Hanover's request for proceedings to seek punitive damages against the accounting firm.

Drysdale collapsed and created near panic in the financial markets when it failed to meet $180 million of interest payments due Chase Manhattan Bank, Manufacturers Hanover and other dealers. Both banks sued Arthur Andersen; the accounting firm settled with Chase in October 1984, reportedly for nearly $50 million.

The appeals court examined in some detail the question in the trial of whether Andersen's actions in issuing statements on a new Drysdale unit caused the bank's losses. The court noted that the financial community had "come to mistrust (Drysdale Securities') solvency before the Andersen report was issued. In this context, the Andersen report portrayed a new, highly capitalized company on whose promises" the bank could rely, the opinion said. By misrepresenting the new unit's financial status, the court said, the accounting firm "may reasonably have been found to have induced" the bank to enter into repurchase agreements with Drysdale, despite earlier misgivings by the bank.

The court rejected Andersen's assertions, on appeal, that, among other things, the district court lacked jurisdiction in the case, that the bank had caused its loss by its own recklessness, and that the trial judge had submitted improper instructions to the jury.

In a related case, the Supreme Court in June let stand a federal appeals court ruling that reinstated a civil action by the Securities and Exchange Commission against Warren Essner, a former Andersen partner. Mr. Essner had been retained to help Drysdale spin off its government securities business. After Drysdale collapsed, the SEC charged him with fraud for giving the government securities unit an unqualified opinion. A federal appeals court ordered a trial of the SEC's complaint after a federal court had dismissed the case. The high court's refusal to hear Mr. Essner's appeal cleared the way for a trial.

Former Auditor at KMG Main Is Investigated

New York City Prosecutor Probes a Possible Role in Wedtech Corp. Case

By Lee Berton

February 9, 1987

NEW YORK—The Manhattan district attorney's office has begun investigating whether a former KMG Main Hurdman auditor concealed fraud by Wedtech Corp., a former KMG client currently involved in a corruption scandal.

Parallel investigations are being conducted by KMG and a self-enforcement arm of the American Institute of Certified Public Accountants into the possible role of the former auditor, Richard Bluestine, in the fraud case.

An institute official said that at least four lawsuits have been filed by Wedtech shareholders accusing KMG, the ninth-biggest U.S. accounting firm, with failing to discover fraud in its audits of Wedtech. The company filed Dec. 14 for Chapter 11 bankruptcy-law protection from creditors.

Unusual Case

Though accounting firms often are sued when their client companies encounter business problems soon after a clean audit, it's rare that outside auditors are questioned about receiving improper payments from client companies.

In the Wedtech case, KMG and an investigations arm of the institute are seeking to determine whether KMG's internal control systems were sufficient to detect any lack of auditor independence.

And Manhattan district attorney Robert M. Morgenthau's office is investigating to determine whether Mr. Bluestine's independence was compromised when he accepted in 1983 stock and loans from the Bronx-based defense contractor and maker of pontoons, spare parts and small engines.

Mr. Bluestine left Wedtech last year and joined the accounting firm of Grant Thornton here six months ago. He hasn't been charged with any crime.

KMG said Mr. Bluestine was the engagement partner on the Wedtech audit when he resigned from KMG on Sept. 6, 1983, to join Wedtech. Prior to his resignation, KMG certified Wedtech's prospectus for a public stock offering in August 1983, according to both KMG and Mr. Morgenthau.

Wedtech officials have admitted that they falsified invoices in seeking reimbursements from the government and to obtain added contracting business. They also admitted bribing city officials.

Mr. Morgenthau has said that during 1983 Mr. Bluestine got $1.5 million in Wedtech stock and $900,000 in low-interest loans from Wedtech.

Yesterday, Mr. Morgenthau said that Mr. Bluestine agreed to obtain the stock and loan prior to leaving Main Hurdman. He also said that in January 1983, months before Mr. Bluestine joined Wedtech, Mr. Bluestine went to Japan with two Wedtech officials to help the company sell a license for a coating process.

According to Mr. Morgenthau, Mr. Bluestine paid for the air transportation of the two Wedtech officials and himself and later was reimbursed for the entire amount, including his own fare. Under professional ethics rules, an independent auditor is forbidden from accepting gifts or money beyond his firm's fee for the audit.

Irregularities Found in 1983
Several telephone messages left for Mr. Bluestine at his Long Island, New York, home weren't returned by him, nor could his attorney be reached. But his wife said: "There are two sides to

every story and the other side will surface with a lot of stuff coming out."

John Thompson, chairman of KMG, said the firm discovered some irregularities in Wedtech's books in 1983 while Mr. Bluestine was Wedtech's auditor. "We reported these to the company and its outside legal counsel," he added.

Another KMG official said Wedtech's legal counsel, Biaggi & Ehrlich, told KMG at that time that Wedtech had discussed the irregularities with the proper government officials and assured KMG the irregularities would be stopped.

Earlier this month, Bernard C. Ehrlich, a partner at Biaggi & Ehrlich, was indicted in a state court in Manhattan on charges of bribing a state official on behalf of Wedtech. He pleaded innocent.

Wedtech discharged KMG as its auditor in mid-1985 and switched to Touche Ross & Co. KMG officials said another former KMG employee, Anthony Guariglia, left the firm in June 1983 to join Wedtech. Mr. Guariglia, who became Wedtech's president and chief financial officer, along with other former top Wedtech officials, pleaded guilty last week to bribing a city official and misappropriating money from Wedtech.

Peter Skomorowsky, managing partner of the New York office of Grant Thornton, where Mr. Bluestine now works, said Mr. Bluestine has told Grant Thornton "he firmly believes he is innocent" of any wrongdoing.

Bear Stearns, Moseley Securities Sued by Wedtech Holders over Underwritings

By Lee Berton

February 11, 1987

NEW YORK—Two major Wall Street brokerage firms have been drawn into the widening corruption scandal involving Wedtech Corp., the Bronx-based defense contractor.

The firms are Bear, Stearns & Co. and Moseley Securities Corp., formerly called Moseley, Hallgarden, Estabrook & Weeden. Three lawsuits filed by Wedtech shareholders allege that the securities firms misled investors in selling Wedtech securities. Bear Stearns denied the allegations and Moseley wouldn't comment.

Wedtech collapsed and filed for Chapter 11 bankruptcy-law protection in December. Wedtech officials have admitted that they falsified invoices in seeking reimbursements from the government and to obtain additional contracting business. They also admitted bribing city officials.

Suits against Auditor

Of eight lawsuits filed against KMG Main Hurdman, Wedtech's outside auditor until mid-1985, by Wedtech stock or bond holders, one suit names Moseley and two name both Moseley and Bear Stearns.

Marion P. Rosner, a New York attorney heading the committee of nine law firms representing the plaintiffs, said that Moseley and Bear Stearns separately and together have underwritten issues of $115 million in debt and $38.9 million in equity of Wedtech since August 1983.

The suits seek unspecified damages, including punitive amounts, and the total may reach into the millions, Ms. Rosner said.

Ms. Rosner said that Moseley and Bear Stearns failed to exercise "due diligence" in issuing the securities, which she said contained false and misleading data about Wedtech's sales, earnings and receivables. Several Wedtech officials have admitted to using false invoices to alter Wedtech's books in recent court cases against the company.

Paul Hallingby, a Bear Stearns managing director who was elected to Wedtech's board in mid-1985, said he resigned around the end of 1986 but didn't elaborate on the reasons. Asked if Bear Stearns exercised "due diligence" in underwriting three of Wedtech's debt and equity issues, Mr. Hallingby said "of course" and went into a meeting.

When asked, Moseley said that a former Moseley official, Frederick Moss, was on Wedtech's board. But a woman who identified herself as secretary to Howard Berg, Moseley's president, declined to comment further. "Mr. Berg says we'd prefer not to say anything," she said.

Touche Ross Papers Subpoenaed

Meanwhile, Touche Ross & Co., a major U.S. accounting firm that succeeded KMG as Wedtech's auditor in mid-1985, said that its work papers involving audits of Wedtech's books have been subpoenaed by a Manhattan grand jury. The grand jury is apparently trying to find out how Wedtech obtained clean opinions on its financial statements at least nine months before it filed for Chapter 11 last December 14.

Richard H. Murray, Touche Ross's general counsel, said that the accounting firm became aware of "possible inaccurate prior reporting" of financial data by Wedtech and the company's "declining fortunes" last fall.

Mr. Murray said that the problems were reported to the audit committee of Wedtech's board and that Touche was then asked to do "special reviews" of Wedtech's books. After Touche resigned as Wedtech's auditor, it informed the Securities and Exchange Commission that Wedtech losses as of September 30 appeared to total at least $90 million, which would create a negative net worth, or assets minus liabilities, of at least $30 million.

Bear Stearns's Mr. Hallingby was chairman of Wedtech's audit committee until he resigned from Wedtech's board at the end of last year.

KMG, Wedtech's auditor before Touche, has been hit by five lawsuits alleging the auditor wasn't independent and asking damages. KMG has said it discovered discrepancies in Wedtech's books in 1983, informed Wedtech and was told by Wedtech's attorneys that the matter was referred to two government agencies and would be corrected. KMG has said it was satisfied with its audits and followed "extended procedures" after discovering the discrepancies.

Arthur Siskind, a partner of Squadron, Ellenoff, Plesent & Lehrer, said the firm resigned as Wedtech's outside attorneys early last December. "At that time, we felt we didn't have enough information about what was happening at Wedtech," Mr. Siskind said.

Mr. Siskind said that when questions were raised about Wedtech's financial statements in 1983, when the company had a $21.5 million equity offering, KMG told the law firm that any irregularities had been referred to two government agencies and weren't consequential.

The Manhattan district attorney's office has said it is probing whether a former KMG partner, Richard Bluestine, who was Wedtech's outside auditor in 1983 before joining Wedtech in September 1983, concealed fraud by Wedtech. No charges have been filed against Mr. Bluestine.

Continental Illinois Officials Are Slated to Give Accounts of Collapse under Oath

By Jeff Bailey

February 17, 1987

CHICAGO—Executives who presided over the collapse of Continental Illinois Corp. are expected for the first time to answer questions publicly about the banking concern's collapse beginning this week in federal court.

Mr. Bailey is a staff reporter of THE WALL STREET JOURNAL.

They will appear neither as the accused nor accuser in connection with history's biggest banking collapse, but as witnesses who have been subpoenaed to help a jury decide whether the banking concern's former auditors, Ernst & Whinney, did shoddy audit work on Continental's 1981 financial statement.

The lawsuit is part of a massive 4½-year-old shareholder action arising out of the losses that led to Continental's collapse in 1984.

The former chairman and chief executive officer, Roger E. Anderson, is expected to be called to testify, along with several of his subordinates and perhaps some fellow board members— nearly all of whom have refused to speak publicly about their roles in Continental's downfall.

"You'll get a revisit with the 1981-82 Continental management team in this case," promised Nicholas E. Chimicles, one of the lawyers who represents former shareholders. "This is the ultimate audit."

The shareholders and the Federal Deposit Insurance Corp., which bailed out Continental and took on most of its worst loans, are expected to seek several hundred million dollars from Ernst & Whinney, lawyers close to the case said.

Mr. Chimicles and Lowell E. Sachnoff, a lawyer working for the FDIC, wouldn't comment on damages. The FDIC's cost of rescuing Continental is expected to exceed $1 billion. The FDIC inherited the claim against the auditors as part of the bailout.

The agency and former holders charge Ernst & Whinney with massive failure in its audit of Continental's 1981 books. The following July, Penn Square Bank of Oklahoma City was closed by federal regulators and Continental began disclosing that the $1 billion in oil and gas loans it bought from the smaller bank were mostly bad.

"We stand behind our audit," an Ernst & Whinney spokesman said. "We didn't do anything wrong." Continental's government-appointed management team replaced the Cleveland-based firm in 1985 with Price Waterhouse.

Ernst & Whinney's lawyer, Daniel F. Kolb, wouldn't comment. But in papers filed Friday in U.S. District Court here, he said the FDIC should be barred from any recovery because Continental officials withheld important information from the auditors, including a bank investigation that was underway at the time of personal loans made by Penn Square to Continental vice president John Lytle.

Mr. Lytle has since been indicted on wire and bank fraud charges and federal prosecutors have said the Penn Square loans were instead part of a kickback scheme. Mr. Lytle denied the charges.

Ernst & Whinney contends that by keeping its original probe of the loans from its auditors, Continental interfered with the audit. The audit firm also will seek to hold Mr. Anderson and his crew responsible. "Ernst & Whinney did not run the bank, make loans, supply information for lending purposes, advise on business risk or render long-term economic forecasts," the firm's lawyers said. "Ernst & Whinney was no more and no less than Continental's auditor."

Mr. Anderson and the other individuals who were defendants in the shareholder and FDIC suits have settled, though insurance companies that wrote Continental's directors-and-officers liability policy are refusing to pay under the settlement. They say they, too, were misled by Continental management.

FDIC and shareholders' lawyers said in a filing Friday that they'll show that Ernst & Whinney knew that Penn Square had been criticized by its own auditors and by regulators and—because the Oklahoma Bank was responsible for much of Continental's rapid loan growth—the auditors should have looked more carefully at the loans.

Also, they charge that Ernst & Whinney's sampling of loans to test Continental's internal auditing didn't include any Penn Square loans or any loans made after August 31, 1981—though much of the loan growth for the year occurred after that time.

Wedtech Used Gimmickry, False Invoices to Thrive

Accounting Method Said to Have Been Misused to Fuel Firm's Rise

By Lee Berton

February 23, 1987

NEW YORK—Wedtech Corp., a Bronx-based defense contractor, was once hailed as the first major hirer of long-unemployed minorities in the South Bronx slums. Its rapid growth, fueled by no-bid defense contracts available to a minority-controlled business, turned it into a highflier on the New York Stock Exchange.

But late last year, the company collapsed. And now the company is entangled in a scandal involving political payoffs that Wedtech officials admit they made to get those contracts.

Wedtech lost its status as a minority business early last year. As government contracts began petering out during the year, federal and state investigators began looking into the political payoffs. The company's profits and stock price plummeted and, in December, it filed for Chapter 11 bankruptcy-law protection from creditors.

Earlier this month, four Wedtech officials pleaded guilty to a scheme that inflated the company's earnings through false invoices and flagrant accounting gimmicks, as well as to bribing officials. Law enforcement officials say more indictments will follow.

Wall Street analysts and thousands of investors in more than $160 million of Wedtech's stock and bonds are puzzled and upset about Wedtech. A major question being asked is how did Wedtech fool so many people for four years about its earnings?

They wonder how Wedtech's books could have received clean bills of health from the time the company went public in late 1983, since subsequent investigations have shown that earnings were being inflated.

Profit-Booking Technique

Financial analysts and accountants say Wedtech was able to accomplish this by adopting an extremely complex profit-booking technique known as "percentage-of-completion" accounting, which can lend itself to questionable financial reporting when abused by company management.

The scheme to which the four officials pleaded guilty involved issuing false financial statements, law enforcement officials say. According to Thornton O'glove, publisher of the *Quality of Earnings Report* for institutional investors, the company pumped up its earnings by overstating work expected from the government that apparently never materialized.

"Wedtech became skilled at using 'ghost' accounting to create earnings that didn't exist," Mr. O'glove says. "When revenues dropped sharply last year, the company just couldn't scramble fast enough to cover up the empty holes that surfaced from previous years."

Help from Auditor

Wedtech got a lot of help in disguising earnings from a former member of its previous outside auditing firm, KMG Main Hurdman. Anthony Guariglia, who left KMG in mid-1983 after working on the Wedtech audit, later became Wedtech's president. Earlier this month, Mr. Guariglia pleaded guilty to bribing government officials and to defrauding Wedtech shareholders through falsifying financial statements, thereby inflating profits.

Another KMG partner with close ties to Wedtech was Richard Bluestine, who was in charge of Wedtech's audit in 1983. Mr. Bluestine left KMG to join Wedtech in September of that year. The Manhattan district attorney's office says Mr. Bluestine, before leaving KMG, allegedly agreed to receive $1.5 million in Wedtech stock and a $900,000 loan from Wedtech. The district attorney's office has said it is probing whether Mr. Bluestine was truly independent of Wedtech when he audited its books. Mr. Bluestine, who declines to comment, hasn't been charged with any crime.

Ten civil suits have been filed against former Wedtech officials. Seven of them are also directed against KMG and allege

Wedtech Corp.
Consolidated statements of income (in millions of dollars)

	Net Revenues	Net Profit	Per Share[1]
1986[2]	$ 72.2	$4.6	42
1985	117.5	9.7	99
1984	72.4	4.7	53[3]
1983	27.4	4.9	67[3]
1982	20.5	3.1	48[3]

[1]Cents per share.
[2]Ended June 30; Wedtech's last audited financial results. A filing with the Securities and Exchange Commission says that by September 30, 1986, Wedtech had a loss of at least $90 million.
[3]Adjusted for a 3-for-2 stock split on September 18, 1985.

fraud in the accountant's failure to discover the false invoices and the bribes, which KMG denies. Five suits are against Wedtech's underwriters, Bear, Stearns & Co. and Moseley Securities Corp., which allege that the securities firms, in selling Wedtech securities, misled investors about Wedtech's financial results. Bear Stearns denies the allegations and Moseley won't comment.

But how did Wedtech manage to avert the scrutiny of Wall Street financial analysts for so long? Its stock jumped to $24 (equivalent to $16 after a 3-for-2 split in September 1985) in the over-the-counter market early in 1984, from only $16 when it went public 15 months earlier. And although at least $25 million of its profits were created through fancy accounting gimmickry since 1981, the company wasn't forced to file for Chapter 11 bankruptcy-law protection until last December.

Favored Treatment
First, to get sales dollars flowing into its coffers, Wedtech had to get favored treatment as a government contractor. The modus operandi was simple and dishonest, law enforcement officials say. Claiming that its founder, John Mariotta, a Hispanic, controlled the company, Wedtech qualified for special "small busi-

ness status." This enabled it to get favored government business without bidding.

Actually, after Wedtech went public in August 1983, Mr. Mariotta no longer controlled the company. "He simply had an option to buy stock that would bring him up to 51% control if he exercised it," says an accountant who has scrutinized Wedtech's books and management files. "But other company officials had the contractual right to fire him if he tried to exercise it."

Then, accounting gimmickry became the keystone of the company's scheme to falsify earnings, according to law enforcement authorities. Wedtech, as a defense contractor—it sold bridge supports, small motors and spare parts to the military— was able to use "percentage-of-completion" accounting. Such accounting, used legitimately by many firms, permitted it to record earnings based on its current costs, the estimated costs to complete a project and whether it believed the entire contract price would be received by the company.

Example of Accounting Trick

For example, say Wedtech was making 10,000 bridge pontoons for the Army over three years at a cost of $100 million in material and labor and was charging the Army $110 million for all the supports, making a $10 million, or 10% profit. If its costs in the first year were $25 million, under percentage of completion it would record a profit of $2.5 million, or 10% of its costs.

In the contract's second year, if Wedtech spent $50 million, it would record $5 million in profit. This would leave $25 million in costs and a profit of $2.5 million for the third year of the contract.

Law enforcement officials and accountants say Wedtech was improperly accelerating its contract receipts and recognizing profits it never received.

If the Army, for example, later decided that it only wanted a total of $50 million of the bridge supports, Wedtech would only be able to record profits of $2.5 million the first year, $2.5 million the second year and none the third year. That's a total of only $5 million, or half the previous total. But, in this hypothetical example, Wedtech would have booked the entire $10 million.

The company actually should have been using "completed-contract" accounting because it wasn't certain that it would get the entire amount in a contract, Mr. O'glove says. Under this accounting method, Wedtech wouldn't have been able to record any profit until the end of the three years in the contract.

Falsifying Invoices

Law enforcement officials say that the falsified invoices that Wedtech officials admitted using in seeking reimbursements from the government totaled $4.7 million during 1981 and 1982. This, in part, explains why a prospectus for Wedtech's $30.4 million equity issue in late 1983 shows a jump in receivables to $12.8 million at the end of 1982 and to $15.6 million as of April 30, 1983, from only $2.8 million in 1981.

In its financial report for 1984, Wedtech listed net income of $4.7 million. In fact, say law enforcement officials, this profit included portions of a $20 million contract to supply cooling and suspension kits for Army vehicles in West Germany. Law enforcement officials say that Wedtech never got this contract.

How did Wedtech's auditors, KMG, miss this overstatement?

KMG notes that when it turned up falsified invoices on Wedtech's books in 1983, it informed the company and its outside attorneys, Biaggi & Ehrlich, who said the matter had been referred to government regulators and assured KMG the irregularities wouldn't recur. (Earlier this month, Bernard C. Ehrlich, a partner in the law firm, was indicted in a state court in Manhattan on charges of bribing a state official on behalf of Wedtech. He pleaded innocent. The other partner in the law firm, Richard Biaggi, who hasn't been charged with any crime, is the son of U.S. Rep. Mario Biaggi.)

KMG says that in 1983 it followed "extended" audit procedures and was satisfied that any irregularities had been stopped.

As to the 1984 report, a KMG spokesman says that recent guilty pleas by the Wedtech officials to bribery and business fraud indicate that "pervasive fraud" permeated former Wedtech management.

"We took tough positions with Wedtech in auditing and accounting issues, which ultimately led to our dismissal" in mid-1985, says John A. Thompson, KMG's chairman and chief executive. KMG declined further comment because of the civil litigation against it filed by Wedtech shareholders.

After KMG was replaced as auditor in mid-1985, the new auditor, Touche Ross & Co., gave Wedtech's 1985 financial statement—reporting net of $9.7 million, or more than double a year earlier—a clean opinion.

Touche Ross officials say they relied somewhat for their clean opinion on Wedtech's 1985 financial report on auditing work that KMG had done in the early part of that year. "KMG assured us there was no reason to doubt the integrity of Wedtech's management," says Richard Murray, Touche's general counsel.

By the time Wedtech's stock moved to the New York Stock Exchange in January 1986, its price had spurted upward 50% to $24.

Early in 1986, about the time that Wedtech lost its minority-business status—spelling an end to its no-bid contract privilege, Wedtech's founder, Mr. Mariotta, was forced out of the company. Law enforcement officials say he and another Wedtech executive, Fred Neuberger, who recently pleaded guilty to payoffs of government officials and business fraud, would throw cups of coffee and chairs at each other during hectic Wedtech board meetings late in 1984 and early 1985.

Phone messages left at the homes of Messrs. Mariotta and Neuberger weren't returned.

Last August Wedtech floated a $75 million issue of 14% junk bonds just as reports about its influence peddling began to surface.

Contracts Withdrawn

After the federal government last year withdrew a sizable number of military contracts from Wedtech, the company had to fire most of its 1,400 workers, reducing its work force to under 200. In mid-December, the company filed for Chapter 11 bankruptcy-law protection from creditors.

After Wedtech's business began to fall apart, Touche Ross withdrew as its auditor but, in a Securities and Exchange Commission filing, it noted that the company's losses as of last September 30 were at least $90 million and that Wedtech had a negative net worth (assets minus liabilities) then of $30 million.

Manhattan and Bronx district attorneys and the U.S. attorney here are investigating fees paid by Wedtech to politicians. They say more indictments will follow.

Wedtech's current president, Joseph Felter, a retired U.S. Army colonel who was brought in by the company's creditors, says Wedtech plans to rehire about 30 employees because a few new Army contracts are beginning to filter in. Following the receipt of these new government contracts, Wedtech's stock price, which had gone as low as 25 cents, in recent weeks underwent a run-up. It reached a high of $1.75 a share Friday before closing at $1.50.

Laventhol & Horwath, Wedtech's new auditor, is trying to put the company's financial records back together again, and another auditor, Arthur Young & Co., is going over its books as a representative of the creditors.

"We're scrubbing the company from top to bottom and are restoring proper accounting systems," says Mr. Felter. "What happened in the past here was incredible, but we want to restore credibility. We have to in order to survive."

Harry Tavitian, Wedtech's current controller, adds: "We trusted former management and they let this company go down the drain. It really hurts because we have a lot of potential."

KMG Main Hurdman Censured by SEC for 'Improper' Conduct in Two Audits

By Cynthia S. Grisdela and Lee Berton

March 26, 1987

The Securities and Exchange Commission censured KMG Main Hurdman, a New York–based accounting firm, for "improper professional conduct" in connection with its audits of First National Bank of Midland, Midland, Texas, and of Time Energy Inc.

The SEC also imposed sanctions on the accounting firm requiring it to tighten its internal control procedures, among other things.

Main Hurdman settled the agency's charges without admitting or denying any wrongdoing. As part of the settlement, the accounting firm agreed to the censure and said it would take steps to put it in place and maintain adequate internal controls.

Main Hurdman has an agreement to merge with Peat Marwick Mitchell & Co. next Wednesday, and the SEC order addresses that. It specifies that if Main Hurdman merges with a larger accounting firm this year, the combined firm must have internal controls that comply with the procedures the agency is requiring Main Hurdman to adopt, as well as adequate quality control reviews and training programs.

In its administrative proceedings, the SEC alleged that Main Hurdman's audits of First National Bank of Midland in 1982 and its audits and reviews of the financial statements of Time Energy from 1983 through the second quarter of 1985 "were not conducted in accordance with generally accepted auditing standards."

Some critics of faulty auditing say such SEC administrative actions are "mere wrist slaps" and they call for harsher discipline against major firms.

But SEC officials say that the purpose of these censures is

Ms. Grisdela was a staff reporter of THE WALL STREET JOURNAL.

"remedial rather than punitive." Also, the SEC notes that it has initiated more censures of major accounting firms in recent years. In the fiscal year ended last September 30, the SEC censured 14 major accounting firms for faulty audits and other alleged misconduct. In some SEC actions over the past few years, accounting firms have been suspended from practicing before the SEC until remedial actions, such as peer review or education for professionals, have been completed.

The SEC also charged that Main Hurdman failed to exercise "due care" and "adequate professional skepticism" in its audits of the two companies, both of which were experiencing financial difficulties.

In New York, John Thompson, chairman of KMG Main Hurdman, said the firm has reviewed the work performed in the audits of the bank and Time Energy and "stands behind it."

"We felt that it was desirable to settle these disputes and put them behind us" with the merger with Peat Marwick pending, he said. "Under any other circumstances, we would have contested vigorously."

First National Bank of Midland, which had a large portfolio of loans to the oil and gas industry, was declared insolvent on October 15, 1983, and placed under the receivership of the Federal Deposit Insurance Corp., the SEC said.

Houston-based Time Energy, an energy management company, last year agreed to restate its earnings from 1983 through 1985 to settle SEC charges that it issued "materially false and misleading" financial statements during that period.

Officials at Time Energy couldn't be reached for comment yesterday.

Although the audits were performed by Main Hurdman's field offices in Midland and in Houston, the SEC also faulted the firm's New York office. The New York office, it said, failed to require a more critical analysis of the circumstances in both cases and failed to adequately document the consulting process between the offices.

Accounting Suit Is Thrown Out in Key Decision

Ruling Favors Mann Judd, Makes Clear Distinction between Audit, Review

By Lee Berton

March 27, 1987

NEW YORK—In a landmark decision that could affect the entire accounting profession, a New York appeals court dismissed allegation of negligence involving a review by Mann Judd Landau, a major New York–based accounting firm.

The court made a clear distinction between audits and reviews, suggesting that accountants have less liability for the results of the reviews, which unlike audits don't check inventories and receivables at first hand. Reviews generally cost 20% to 40% less than audits.

The lawsuit, which sought $2.5 million in damages, was filed in New York Supreme Court in early 1985 by William Iselin & Co., a New York factor—a concern that buys accounts receivable and takes over the job of collecting them—that extended $2.5 million in loans and credit to Suits Galore Inc., a Miami-based garment maker.

Iselin is currently a unit of Manufacturers Hanover Corp.

The suit noted that Mann Judd "reviewed" financial reports of Suits Galore in 1982-84, just before the company sought protection from creditors under federal bankruptcy laws. Mann Judd, the suit claimed, failed to follow proper professional procedures in performing the reviews. Suits Galore has since reorganized.

Appeals-Court Position

In dismissing the complaint, the appeals court said third parties can't rely on reviews as they can with audits to assure themselves that a company is financially healthy.

"This decision will give great comfort to many accounting firms which in the past felt compelled to settle out of court in fear of an unfavorable jury decision," said Dan Goldwasser, special counsel for liability matters for the New York Society of Certified Public Accountants.

The New York Supreme Court had ruled the case had merit, but its appellate division, by a 4-1 vote, dismissed the negligence case against Mann Judd. The appeals court said the review reports didn't represent certifications and that "no opinion was expressed."

'Very Vague' Standards

Louis Strassberg, a New York attorney representing Iselin, said the company is considering an appeal. He said that if the appeals-court ruling isn't overturned, "accountants and their clients will find that reviews are useless, since no one can rely on them."

Attorney Goldwasser noted that several accounting firms in the past had preferred to settle out of court rather than risk an adverse jury trial in cases involving charges of negligence in performing reviews. "The technical standards for reviews, unlike those for audits, are very vague," Mr. Goldwasser said.

Other attorneys said that courts in California, New Jersey, Wisconsin and New Hampshire in the past have been more favorable to plaintiffs who file negligence claims against accounting firms, alleging faulty audits or reviews. Early in 1986, a three-judge appeals panel in California upheld the right of third parties, such as lenders, investors and business partners, to sue accountants when companies audited by the accountants later run into financial problems.

In 1985, however, a New York court reached a decision contrary to the California finding, sharply limiting the ability of third parties to sue accountants in such instances. The latest appeals decision relied on the 1985 decision, which limited negligence to third parties only if the auditors issued their reports specifically for the parties' use.

California Wants KMG Main Hurdman Disciplined for Technical Equities Audit

By Lee Berton

April 8, 1987

California called for the revocation or suspension of KMG Main Hurdman's right to practice accounting in the state, charging negligence in the audit of a company that collapsed and cost investors about $100 million.

The California action also could affect KMG Main Hurdman's new parent, Peat Marwick, state officials said. New York–based KMG Main Hurdman last week merged with Peat, Marwick, Mitchell & Co. to form Peat Marwick, the world's largest accounting firm.

In San Francisco, John E. Barsell, Jr., a deputy state attorney general, said he filed the complaint with the state accountancy board in Sacramento, pending the issuance of an opinion by an administrative law judge. The complaint charges KMG Main Hurdman with "gross negligence" when it issued a clean audit opinion on the 1985 annual report of Technical Equities Corp., a San Jose–based investment firm.

Technical Equities sold about $100 million of partnerships in real estate and other businesses to hundreds of investors, including many sports figures and wealthy individuals.

The company collapsed last year after a cash-flow crisis and sought protection under federal bankruptcy laws. Many investors sued the company and its former president, Harry C. Stern, and some filed negligence suits against KMG Main Hurdman.

As the successor to KMG Main Hurdman, Peat Marwick has 15 days in which to respond to the state's charges, which will be heard before an administrative law judge, Mr. Barsell added. He said the administrative law judge will forward a recommendation to the accountancy board, which can accept or reject the recommendation. Mr. Barsell added it is "unusual" for an action to suspend or revoke a license to be filed against a major accounting firm.

Richard I. Miller, KMG Main Hurdman's former general counsel and now an associate counsel of Peat Marwick, said he didn't believe the action would affect operations of Peat Marwick in California. He said he was "disappointed" with the state's charges, claiming that they are "filled with technical inaccuracies."

Mr. Barsell also said the action could hinder the newly combined Peat Marwick from practicing in the state.

"The new partnership will have to file an application with the California State Board of Accountancy to practice in the state within the next 30 days," Mr. Barsell said. "When it does, that license application will have to be reviewed in light of the current action."

Revenue of Peat Marwick in California is sizable, amounting to $71 million in the San Francisco area alone, a spokesman for the accounting firm said. The firm's U.S. revenues total $1.35 billion.

The California action also names two former KMG Main Hurdman partners, Marylee Lau and Robert Nilssen; a former KMG Main Hurdman audit manager, Kirstin Toleme; and another accountant working for the firm, Donald F. Oliver.

The four people couldn't be reached for comment. A Peat Marwick spokesman said Ms. Lau and Mr. Nilssen currently are employed by Peat Marwick.

FDIC Sues Ernst & Whinney over Audit of Four Butcher Banks, Seeks $250 Million

By Lee Berton

May 21, 1987

The Federal Deposit Insurance Corp. sued Ernst & Whinney, seeking $250 million from the accounting firm for its allegedly faulty audit of four collapsed Tennessee banks owned by the Butcher brothers.

The lawsuit, filed in U.S. district court in Knoxville, is by far the biggest the FDIC has filed against accounting firms since it began such suits in 1980. Ernst & Whinney is the third biggest U.S. accounting firm, with U.S. revenue of $900 million in its latest fiscal year.

Cecil Underwood, an FDIC attorney in Washington, said the agency believes that Ernst & Whinney was "extremely negligent in the audits and that the suit represents substantial liability exposure on the part of the accounting firm." Mr. Underwood said the funds would replace money in its insurance reserves that the FDIC has already given to thousands of depositors of the four banks.

Ray Groves, chairman of Cleveland-based Ernst & Whinney, said the firm will "vigorously defend itself against these allegations." The suit, he added, is "another example of the FDIC attempting to push off to an auditor its own regulatory obligation."

Mr. Groves said that when the FDIC did its concurrent audit of the Butcher banks in 1982, it wouldn't tell outside auditors the results of its examination, which revealed "intricate collusion and fraud among the many Butcher banks."

Collapse in 1983
The banks, run by Jake Butcher, and his younger brother, C.H. Butcher, Jr., collapsed in 1983. In the case of one of the banks, United American Bank in Knoxville, Ernst & Whinney issued a clean audit opinion on its financial statement in January of that year. Twenty days later the bank was closed by federal regulators and has since been merged with another bank. Both Butcher brothers are serving jail terms on fraud charges.

The suit alleges that Ernst & Whinney's partner in charge of Butcher bank audits, Walter Boruff, borrowed $53,000 from Butcher banks during the years the accounting firm performed the audits, and at other times. The borrowings, the suit declares, impair "Ernst & Whinney's independence."

Reached at his Knoxville office, Mr. Boruff declined to comment, referring any queries to Mr. Groves.

Asked about the loan, Mr. Groves declined comment, saying he hadn't yet had time to study the details of the suit.

Allegations of Suit

The suit charges that Ernst & Whinney violated auditing standards by relying on internal audit staffs of the banks for confirmations of commercial loans. It also alleges that the accounting firm discovered that the banks forgot to mail confirmations covering $16 million of such loans.

Legal experts in the accounting profession see the latest FDIC suit against Ernst & Whinney as an escalation of the government effort to regain funds for failed financial institutions. "This new FDIC suit is definitely upping the ante and could present a major liability and insurance problem for accounting firms," said Dan Goldwasser, special counsel for liability matters for the New York Society of Certified Public Accountants.

Ernst & Whinney already is facing a lawsuit by the FDIC seeking $180 million involving the accounting firm's audits of the troubled Continental Illinois Corp., the Chicago-based bank holding company. A trial in that suit has entered its 13th week.

Since 1980, the FDIC has filed lawsuits against eight accounting firms involved in failed banks. Last year Peat Marwick, currently the biggest U.S. accounting firm, settled out of court with the FDIC on a suit asking for $88 million in the failure of Penn Square Bank in Oklahoma City in 1982. Peat, which was Penn Square's auditor, paid $18.5 million to settle the FDIC suit.

In this suit against Ernst & Whinney, the FDIC has chosen Melvyn I. Weiss, a New York attorney who has been extremely successful in negligence suits against accountants, as its attorney. Mr. Goldwasser said the FDIC's choice of attorney indicates the intensity of its effort to avoid the fate of the Federal Savings & Loan Industry Corp., which has seen its funds severely depleted by thrift failures.

The FDIC wants to maintain its strength as an insurer and "is dead serious in seeking major return of funds from accounting firms," Mr. Goldwasser said.

Jury Rejects FDIC Claim of Negligence in Ernst's '81 Continental Illinois Audit

By Alex Kotlowitz and Lee Berton

July 3, 1987

A federal jury in Chicago dealt U.S. banking regulators a big setback in finding that Ernst & Whinney wasn't negligent in a 1981 audit of Continental Illinois Corp.

The losses that year eventually led to Continental's 1984 collapse and subsequent government bailout.

After a day and a half of deliberations, the eight-person jury concluded that the Cleveland-based accounting firm wasn't negligent in its audit of Continental's 1981 financial statement. The civil suit had been brought by the Federal Deposit Insurance Corp. and some former Continental shareholders.

Ernst & Whinney's victory could make the FDIC less aggressive in seeking big damages against auditors of failed banks. The federal agency, which sought nearly $200 million in this case, is seeking about $250 million from Ernst & Whinney in a case in Knoxville, Tennessee, involving the collapse of banks owned by the Butcher brothers.

An FDIC spokesman said the agency was "disappointed" with the case's outcome and added that it was "evaluating" the possibility of appealing the verdict. The agency won't make a decision on whether to appeal for a few weeks, he said.

The shareholders' attorney, Nicholas E. Chimicles, couldn't be reached for comment.

'We Are Pleased'

Ernst & Whinney Chairman Ray Groves said, "We are pleased with the verdict and the jury's recognition of the quality of our audit."

Legal experts familiar with accountants' negligence prob-

Mr. Kotlowitz is a staff reporter of THE WALL STREET JOURNAL.

lems said the jury's exoneration of Ernst & Whinney is positive for the entire accounting profession. "It's a plus for accountants in that it renews their faith that future juries won't hold them to impossible standards," said Dan Goldwasser, a New York attorney who consults on legal matters for the New York State Society of Certified Public Accountants.

Mr. Goldwasser also said that the decision will take some of the pressure off the major accounting firms in the future to settle out of court, "when they believe they have a good case."

Since 1981, major accounting firms have made out-of-court settlements totaling more than $250 million in negligence cases filed by investors, vendors and suppliers of companies they have audited. In most instances, the suits were filed after the CPA firms issued a clean opinion on financial statements of companies which soon afterward encountered severe business problems or filed under federal bankruptcy statutes.

As previously reported, sources have said the FDIC once offered to settle with Ernst & Whinney for $20 million, and that the accounting firm offered the FDIC about $2.5 million.

Cecil Underwood, assistant general counsel for the FDIC, believes yesterday's decision "is going to further hamper our efforts to settle these kinds of cases out of court."

The FDIC, however, had a tough case to prove. The agency and former shareholders charged Ernst & Whinney with massive failure in its audit of Continental's 1981 books. The following July, Penn Square Bank of Oklahoma City was closed by federal regulators, and Continental began disclosing that the $1 billion in oil and gas loans it bought from the smaller bank were mostly bad.

Trial of 19 Weeks
In the 19-week trial, Ernst & Whinney argued that the FDIC should be barred from any recovery of damages, because Ernst said Continental officials withheld important information from the auditors. That included a bank investigation, under way at the time, of personal loans made by Penn Square to Continental Vice President John Lytle.

As previously reported, Mr. Lytle has since been indicted on wire and bank fraud charges, and federal prosecutors have said the Penn Square loans were part of a kickback scheme. Mr. Lytle has denied the charges.

FDIC attorneys argued that those charges were irrelevant to whether Ernst & Whinney did an adequate job of auditing Continental, Mr. Underwood said.

Grant Thornton Nears $80 Million Pact with Ohio Officials in E.S.M.-Thrift Case

By Lee Berton and Richard Koenig

September 15, 1987

Grant Thornton, a major accounting firm, is close to an $80 million out-of-court settlement with Ohio regulators in the E.S.M. Government Securities Inc. case, according to court officials and Grant attorneys.

When reached, the settlement would bring the total payments by Chicago-based Grant Thornton to $160 million in the slew of lawsuits that have been filed against the firm by parties that lost money as a result of E.S.M.'s collapse in early 1985. Grant Thornton, the 10th-largest U.S. accounting firm, was formerly known as Alexander Grant & Co. and was E.S.M.'s auditor.

The collapse of Fort Lauderdale, Florida–based E.S.M. triggered a run on thrift institutions in Ohio and caused investment losses for 17 municipalities around the country that had done business with E.S.M.

Judge Richard Niehaus of the Hamilton County Common Pleas Court in Cincinnati said in an interview that $65 million of the $80 million in the proposed settlement would go to the Depositors Assistance Corp. Depositors Assistance is an Ohio state agency that was set up to pay depositors of Cincinnati-

---

Mr. Koenig is a staff reporter of THE WALL STREET JOURNAL. *Thomas Petzinger, Jr., contributed to this article.*

based Home State Savings Bank, which had $147 million in losses from investments it made with E.S.M. The rest would go to 69 Ohio thrifts that supported a private guarantee fund for thrift depositors.

Alvin M. Stein, a New York attorney representing Grant, said several points still must be ironed out with plaintiffs in Ohio before the final settlement is made. "We're actively working toward a settlement and are hopeful it will be consummated soon," Mr. Stein said. "This is the final leg in putting all the problems of E.S.M. behind us."

Jose L. Gomez, formerly Grant's managing partner for southern Florida, has admitted taking $200,000 in bribes from E.S.M. officials for certifying false financial statements. Mr. Gomez pleaded guilty to fraud charges early last year and was sentenced to prison last January.

The $160 million in completed and potential settlements "is an unprecedented amount to be paid in a malpractice suit against any accounting firm and is the biggest black eye suffered by any CPA firm in history," says Arthur Bowman, editor of a monthly accounting newsletter published in Atlanta.

Insurance 'More Than Adequate'

In Chicago, Burt K. Fischer, Grant's executive partner, said, "We are delighted to be on the verge of clearing up the claims against us in the E.S.M. case." Mr. Fischer said Grant's $195 million in malpractice insurance coverage was "more than adequate to cover the claims." Grant partners had to pay for a $500,000 deductible under a policy underwritten by a Lloyds of London syndicate and other insurers.

Mr. Fischer said Grant has been able to obtain continued liability insurance with a new deductible of more than $3 million. The lead insurer continues to be Lloyds, with several other European insurance companies providing added coverage, he said.

The initial claims against Grant involving E.S.M. totaled more than $250 million, and some attorneys close to accounting firms initially feared that the E.S.M. suits might sink Grant. But Mr. Fischer said Grant "is doing extremely well and is in no danger of going out of business."

He noted that Grant has obtained a number of new clients

over the past year, including Herman's Sporting Goods Inc., Snelling & Snelling Inc., and Integon Life Insurance Co. "It's true that we lost about a half-dozen clients because of the E.S.M. scandal, but we've been able to keep the vast majority of all our other clients while gaining new business," Mr. Fischer said.

In the wake of the E.S.M. case, Grant has shrunk, selling 12 of its 67 offices over the past year. As a result of these sales and of retirements, the number of Grant partners has fallen to 374 from 414 a year ago, Mr. Fischer said. However, he added that Grant's revenue for the fiscal year ended July 31 rose 8% to $210 million for its remaining 55 offices. "Those partners who are left are thriving," he declared. Average income per partner, he said, is up more than 18% from a year ago.

Limits Are Sought

As malpractice suits have mounted against accounting firms since 1980, some attorneys have called for limits or restraints on settlements, which they feel threaten the existence of professional firms. "This settlement (by Grant) shows why it's so important that liability exposure be reduced in the courts or by state legislators," said Kenneth Bialkin, a senior partner of Willkie, Farr & Gallagher, a law firm that represents the American Institute of Certified Public Accountants, the leading professional group for CPAs.

Since 1980, major accounting firms have paid out more than $300 million in out-of-court settlements to settle malpractice suits following the collapse of client firms to which the CPA firms had given clean audits. Two years ago, the eight largest U.S. accounting firms organized their own offshore captive insurance company after malpractice insurance rates for accountants more than doubled and coverage levels were sharply reduced by Lloyds and other major insurers.

Separately, in Houston, a federal court jury hit Coopers & Lybrand with a verdict of $5 million after finding that the accounting firm had knowingly approved false financial statements of Rapada Corp., a former oil and gas company in Houston.

In the litigation, four purchasers of Rapada preferred stock, including a unit of Security Pacific Bank, had blamed Coopers

& Lybrand for certifying that the oil company had had a 1980 profit of $55,000, when it actually had a deficit of $2.4 million and for certifying that the company had a positive net worth of $1.6 million when it actually had a negative net worth of about $1 million.

After a five-week trial, the jury found that the accounting firm "acted knowingly with intent to defraud, or with severe, reckless disregard to the truth," in certifying the company's financial statements.

Lawyers for Coopers & Lybrand didn't immediately return telephone calls seeking comment.

Touche Ross Could Face Liability Risk on Solvency Letter in Southland Deal

By Lee Berton

November 11, 1987

NEW YORK—Touche Ross & Co., outside auditor of Southland Corp., may face a liability risk if Southland's planned leveraged buy-out falls through, say attorneys familiar with liability problems for accountants.

Southland already has purchased two-thirds of its stock, using borrowed money.

Because of volatile securities markets, Southland's plan to go private appears to be in jeopardy. Touche, the eighth largest U.S. accounting firm, played an important role in the proposed buy-out financing by providing Southland's lenders with a little-known service known as a solvency letter.

In leveraged buy-outs, companies go private using borrowed funds to buy out public shareholders. The debt is designed to be paid by future cash flow or sale of assets. Solvency letters have been quietly requested in increasing numbers in the past two years by lenders who want to be assured that the buy-out can be completed and that the debt incurred by companies going private through buy-outs won't push the companies into insolvency.

Richard Murray, executive director of Touche Ross International and Touche's former general counsel, declined comment on the Southland transaction. But he acknowledged that the writing of solvency letters by accounting firms generally "is risky because it deals with future events that can change very quickly in the current stock market environment." He added, "That's why we do any solvency letter with extreme care."

Five banks, led by Citibank, asked Southland's investment bankers, Goldman, Sachs & Co. and Salomon Brothers Inc., earlier this year to obtain a solvency letter from Touche. The accounting firm was asked to attest that Southland could pay back the banks and other creditors.

On the basis of a solvency letter from Touche and Valuation Research Corp., a Milwaukee consulting firm that does asset valuation, the banks lent $2.1 billion to Southland, investment bankers said. Citicorp Industrial Credit Inc., a Citicorp unit, is the lead banker. The other banks are Manufacturers Hanover Trust Co., Bankers Trust Co., Security Pacific National Bank and Canadian Imperial Bank of Commerce. A spokesman for Citicorp declined comment on the Southland transaction.

Without such a letter, the banks told Southland they wouldn't extend the loans, the investment bankers added.

If Southland were unable to pay some debts to the banks or other creditors because the buy-out is in limbo or for other reasons, the banks or these creditors could accuse Touche of negligent practice in giving them assurance that the transaction could be completed, say attorneys familiar with such transactions.

According to these attorneys, the banks also wanted these letters to protect themselves from possible litigation down the road from other unsecured debtors of Southland. The attorneys say that even if the buy-out is completed but the company later collapsed under the burden of new debt, the unsecured creditors of Southland, such as suppliers and vendors, could accuse the banks of "fraudulently conveying" Southland's assets to themselves.

Solvency letters were almost unheard of several years ago, but a recent spate of leveraged buy-outs, mergers and corporate restructurings has spurred lenders to ask accounting firms and other appraisers of corporate assets for them.

Dan Goldwasser, an attorney and consultant to the New York State Society of Certified Public Accountants, said the solvency letters is a "dangerous extension of the liability exposure of all accounting firms." He added, "With all the liability problems that accounting firms have had over the past seven years, the solvency letter could put one more nail in the malpractice coffin that the profession may be fashioning for itself."

Since 1980, major accounting firms have paid close to $300 million in out-of-court settlements to disgruntled shareholders, suppliers and lenders of companies that encountered severe business problems soon after their financial statements were given audits certifying their financial health.

Partners of major accounting firms privately acknowledge that providing solvency letters to companies in leveraged buy-outs, mergers and other corporate restructurings is extremely risky. But they note that if they don't provide such letters, clients would find new auditors who would.

Recognizing the increased risk of providing such letters, accounting firms are asking consultants who do asset valuations to also sign the letters.

Robert Simpson, managing director of Valuation Research's New York office, which shared the Southland evaluation, acknowledges that providing solvency letters for buy-outs and other corporate restructurings is "a tricky business." Asked whether Valuation Research has any liability exposure because of the letter to Southland's lender, Mr. Simpson said, "We did the letter for a fee and did the best we could. I'd rather not try to guess where this Southland deal will turn out."

Low-Tech Steps Can Help Guard Computer Data

By Lee Berton

December 28, 1987

Attention, computer users using a password to protect valuable and confidential data. "Black night" can protect *you*.

"Black night" isn't some electronic box attached to a computer or elaborate software costing a small fortune. It's an example of a simple but safer system for remembering a computer password, according to computer security specialists.

As computer storage of information such as proprietary business plans and executive payroll lists proliferates, protecting such data from theft is becoming more complex, and more costly. Companies increasingly are using expensive systems that recognize an individual's voice or fingerprints, for example, to screen access to the computer's data.

High Tech Unnecessary?

But these high-priced systems defeat the purpose of the simple and inexpensive passwords, specialists say. Moreover, they add, there are a number of simple and inexpensive ways to safeguard passwords.

"It isn't necessary to go to high tech to protect your passwords," says Donn Parker, a computer security consultant with SRI International, Menlo Park, California.

Security specialists warn that many passwords can be discovered easily and quickly by running through the computer a "dictionary" program that uses an alphabetical list of words to search for password possibilities. The specialists also caution that numbers used as passwords are very vulnerable to security violators: They're often posted openly, since they're harder to recall.

"Too many computer users openly list their passwords or identification numbers in their Rolodex files, on pullout shelves in their desks or under desk blotters," says David R. Wilson, national director of computer security for the Cleveland-based accounting firm Ernst & Whinney.

A survey of some 500 companies last year by Ernst & Whinney shows that 12% of them lost valuable data as a result of faulty computer security, mostly through loose password protection.

How It Works
The "black-night" system combines the advantage of words in being easier to remember and the greater security of numbers in being absolutely random and therefore more difficult to break with a "dictionary," says Ira Gottfried, a partner of the accounting firm Coopers & Lybrand.

Here's how it works, according to Mr. Gottfried. First, find an easy-to-remember word or phrase with 10 different letters, like "black night." Each letter represents, for example, a number running from 0 to 9. Using "black night," "b" is 0, "l" is 1, "a" is 2 and so on, ending with "t," which is 9. Thus, a numerical password like 385 is represented in "black night" by the letters "chn."

"Since no one but you knows the memorized number generator—in this case 'black night'—you can openly post password and letters and only you can decipher it," says Mr. Gottfried, who advises many companies and organizations on how to boost computer security.

Graphic passwords are another good way to tighten security, says Mr. Parker of SRI International. One graphic password, for example, would depict an automobile shown on the computer screen. "To get into the system, the user must pick the proper sequence of car parts with an electronic pointer," he explains.

Say the password is "left front wheel, rear license plate, front headlight." "This sequence is a lot easier to remember than a number and most people can recall it because it relates to their own car," Mr. Parker says. Also, the possible combinations of such parts are almost infinite and therefore very difficult and time consuming to decipher, he says.

Changing Frequently
Ernst & Whinney's Mr. Wilson says that the hardest-to-break passwords combine numbers and letters in upper and lower case—which some computers can differentiate—like R2t6z. "But

these are the toughest to remember and therefore the most frequently posted openly," he concedes. Also, passwords can be
changed frequently, which makes them harder to break but also
harder to remember.

Some computers can be programmed to formulate passwords that work only if responded to by associated passwords.
At one company, for example, the computer displayed the word
"swordfish" when one individual inserted a security card to request access.

This user then had to recall that in an old Marx Brothers
movie about the prohibition era of the 1920s, "mute" Harpo
Marx carried a live swordfish as a password to enter a speak-
easy.

The user gained access to the confidential data by plugging
in the proper response: "Harpo."

Accountants Who Specialize in Detecting Fraud Find Themselves in Great Demand

By Daniel Akst and Lee Berton

February 26, 1988

Douglas Carmichael normally deals with numbers. But when he
discusses one particular facet of his work, he sounds more like
a man who deals with murder.

"When the death of a company (occurs) under mysterious
circumstances, forensic accountants are essential," he says.
"Other accountants may look at the charts. But forensic accountants actually dig into the body."

So-called forensic accountants—investigators who specialize in uncovering fraud in the ledgers of businesses—are finding
their talents much in demand these days. Huge fraud cases—
like the one involving ZZZZ Best Co. in California—and an increase in the number of malpractice suits against mainstream

accounting firms have brought Mr. Carmichael, an accounting professor at City University of New York-Baruch College, and his fellow investigators into the limelight.

"Forensic accounting is big business," says James Loebbecke, an accounting professor at the University of Utah.

Looking for Fraud

Ideally, a company's regular accountants are supposed to guard against financial finagling. Indeed, the Auditing Standards Board of the American Institute of Certified Public Accountants recently adopted rules that specifically require auditors to look for fraud.

But critics say accountants often muzzle themselves; they are too dependent on the big audit fees that come from the clients they are supposed to police. And when fraud is suspected or a big accounting firm is sued for malpractice, other accounting firms are usually reluctant to assist prosecutors. The reason: Opposing a big firm can jeopardize business opportunities.

That's when forensic accountants are called in. Such individuals are often retirees or professors or are found in small accounting firms. But their work goes far beyond a routine auditing.

In a standard audit, accountants test samples of inventory, receivables and payables. They ask banks to confirm the amount of cash in a company's account and send form letters to outside firms that have contracts with the company being audited. The idea is to make sure the other company exists and the contract is real.

But a firm like John Murphy & Associates Inc. in Santa Ana, California, goes much further. Digging into the affairs of a hypothetical Jones Corp., for example, Murphy accountants and investigators in many cases will examine each and every document. If there is a contract between Jones Corp. and an equally hypothetical Smith Corp., Murphy will find out who owns Smith. And then the questions begin. Is that person related to someone inside Jones? Is there collusion? Kickbacks?

Last May, the Murphy firm was hired to unravel the tangled affairs of ZZZZ Best, the Reseda, California, carpet-cleaning company. Murphy's efforts in that case illustrate the difference between a routine audit and the sleuthing done by forensic accountants to uncover fraud.

Now bankrupt, ZZZZ Best left lenders and shareholders with as much as $70 million in losses, prosecutors say. Its founder, Barry J. Minkow, is in prison, awaiting trial on charges of fraud, money laundering and racketeering.

The Murphy firm was hired after ZZZZ Best board members unaligned with Mr. Minkow became aware of credit-card abuses within the company. The president of the Murphy firm, John Murphy, assigned accountants and conventional investigators to the case.

> *The difference between a routine audit and the work of so-called forensic accountants is illustrated in the investigation of ZZZZ Best.*

The investigators first prepared a written profile of every key person involved with the company, including corporate officers, employees and vendors. The investigators relied heavily on vast computer data bases, which are available commercially and can be tapped using a personal computer. Those data bases allowed Mr. Murphy's team to track, among other things, licenses, property records, civil and criminal court cases and liens.

Mr. Murphy says the background work enabled his investigators to learn that several individuals involved with ZZZZ Best had a shady past. He further determined that two key figures in the case owned a separate business, and that one of them lied about it on his 1985 federal income-tax return. The individual who falsified his taxes, Mr. Murphy alleges, teamed up with a third ZZZZ Best figure to try and defraud a major insurance company.

The accountants then began their work in earnest, scrutinizing ZZZZ Best ledgers, contracts, and bank statements. Company checks—there were thousands—were particularly suspect, says William A. Davey, a Murphy accountant, because they tended to be written by hand, in large round numbers, and were often payable to cash.

To facilitate the investigation, the information from every check was entered into a computer equipped with special software. That made it easy to see who received what: Checks made out to different people or firms but paid into the same account could be discovered, and the amounts matched to other documentation, says Drew Maconachy, an accountant on Mr. Murphy's team.

Mr. Maconachy and his associates also analyzed the flow of funds in and out of ZZZZ Best and to two other companies: Interstate Appraisal Services, which gave ZZZZ Best the lucrative building refurbishing jobs that accounted for nearly 90% of its business, and Marbil Management Co., a contractor that was supposedly working on jobs for ZZZZ Best.

The investigative accountants paid close attention to the timing of deposits and withdrawals and soon became convinced there wasn't much in the way of genuine sales at ZZZZ Best. Says Mr. Murphy: "I felt what we had was a monstrous check kite. It was a cash race track."

A Circular Cash Flow?

Murphy accountants say the amounts, dates, and destinations of various checks and deposits indicated that the same money—obtained from ZZZZ Best investors and lenders—was going around and around: from ZZZZ Best to Marbil, back to Interstate, and apparently back yet again to ZZZZ Best.

The purpose of all this movement was to make ZZZZ Best look like a legitimate business, investigators say. Based on that appearance, the company persuaded Drexel Burnham Lambert last year to raise a reported $40 million for it. But the financing fell through last May.

Perhaps the most unsettling discovery made by Mr. Murphy's team was that ZZZZ Best's major source of revenue—its building-refurbishing contracts—appeared to be bogus.

Purportedly, ZZZZ Best had major contracts to refurbish buildings that had been damaged by fire. So Murphy investigators visited supposed refurbishing jobs in Sacramento, San

Diego, Santa Barbara, and Dallas. They also contacted local fire and police departments. Their conclusions: There were no fires and no jobs.

Ernst & Whinney, ZZZZ Best's regular auditor, resigned last June after it suspected that one of the company's major contracts was nonexistent. The firm is now one of about 50 defendants being sued by disgruntled shareholders for alleged violations of federal securities and state law. Ernst & Whinney denies wrongdoing and says there isn't any basis for the suit.

Battle of the Books:
Audit Firms Are Hit by More Investor
Suits for Not Finding Fraud

Is Their Opinion a Guarantee? Work on
Regina's Report Is Haunting Peat Marwick
SEC May Tighten Its Rules

By Lee Berton
Staff Reporter of THE WALL STREET JOURNAL

January 24, 1989

When the stock of Regina Co. suddenly collapsed, Howard Schwarzman was shocked. Profits of the Rahway, New Jersey, maker of vacuum cleaners had skyrocketed since it had gone public in 1985, and the 61-year-old white-bearded magician from Baltimore had seen the value of his Regina stock, bought for $18,000 over the years, climb to $54,000.

But last September, only a month after Regina issued its annual report, Peat Marwick, a major accounting firm, withdrew its stated opinion that the report fairly represented Regina's financial condition. Regina's chief executive quit, and its new management alleged that the prior report was incorrect and probably fraudulent. With the stock plunging, Mr. Schwarzman, far from pulling a fat profit out of the hat, sold his shares at an $8,000 loss.

"Unsophisticated investors like me just can't put a lot of faith in an auditor's opinion. It's not magic," says Mr. Schwarzman, one of many investors suing Peat Marwick over its allegedly faulty audit.

Investors' Question

Like Mr. Schwarzman, many investors wonder how an outside auditor can give a clean opinion to financial results that so quickly turn sour. They have long believed that a clean opinion—one not citing any severe corporate problems—is like the Good Housekeeping Seal of Approval.

But it isn't, accountants say. Though recently acknowledging a responsibility for catching "material fraud," accountants have long argued that the financial statement is management's responsibility. Primarily, the auditor checks to see whether the company's reports follow generally accepted accounting principles, the admittedly permissive rules for financial reporting. Beyond that, all the auditor can do is "to provide reasonable assurance, not a guarantee, that the financial statements are free of material misstatement," the American Institute of Certified Public Accountants said in a recent pamphlet.

Some Peat Marwick partners say a company management bent on fraud can easily bamboozle the auditor. "We're only human and prefer to trust the people we're auditing," one partner comments.

High Cost Cited

Accountants also cite the problem of cost. "It is not economical to examine 100% of the financial-statement support," the CPA institute says. Carl Liggio, general counsel for Arthur Young & Co., another major accounting firm, says an audit that would catch all fraud would be too expensive—perhaps four to six times the cost of current audits, which run from several thousand dollars for small companies to more than $1 million for major corporations. "Who would pay for such perfection?" Mr. Liggio asks. "Likely, the public," he volunteers.

Nevertheless, the Securities and Exchange Commission is pushing auditors to become more active "in detecting management fraud and in improving disclosure," says Joseph Aleknavage, the associate chief accountant for the SEC's division of corporate finance. Within two weeks, he adds, the SEC probably will issue a new rule forcing outside auditors to report accounting disagreements with managements within 15 days rather than the current 45 days. And he says it is likely to propose that auditors be required to check quarterly financial statements soon after they are issued, not months later during the annual audit.

Meanwhile, more and more investors, like Mr. Schwarzman, are suing auditors. All the Big Eight accounting firms have been sued repeatedly for faulty audits over the past two decades. But Peat Marwick, with some $900 million in annual audit revenues, has the largest U.S. audit practice and appears to be the biggest target for disgruntled investors.

Extensive Litigation

The accounting firm is being sued over its audit of Allegheny International Inc., a producer of appliances and industrial products whose former management allegedly hid improper use of corporate aircraft, a London townhouse and $113,000 of wine bought by the company.

Peat Marwick also is being sued over three audits done by KMG Main Hurdman, a smaller accounting firm that it acquired in 1987. These audits involved Crazy Eddie Inc., an electronics-store chain whose former management is accused of creating "phantom" inventory and profits and of destroying records; Coated Sales Inc., a textile converter whose former management allegedly used bogus receivables to create fake profits; and American Biomaterials Corp., a maker of medical and dental products whose former management allegedly failed to disclose improper payments and gifts to its executives.

The Regina case, however, may prove the most nettlesome. The U.S. attorney's office in Newark, New Jersey, is investigating possible criminal charges against former Regina executives. And the SEC has begun studying Regina's financial statements. "Where there's been a big change in numbers, the SEC normally looks at the accountants," one SEC attorney says.

Under pressure from a surge in class-action negligence suits last year, accountants acted to strengthen audits. But ironically, some critics say these very efforts eroded the sharpest warning to investors—the "subject to" opinion. Using that format, an auditor finding that a client company had a major problem, such as pending litigation, would certify the financial statement "subject to" resolution of the problem. Since mid-1988, auditors' opinions require more careful reading because they no longer use that format; they simply include an extra paragraph explaining the problem without the words "subject to."

"The explanatory paragraph carries less wallop than the 'subject to' opinion, which was a bright red flag," contends Lee J. Seidler, a senior managing director of Bear, Stearns & Co. and a former accounting professor. In changing the format, moreover, the CPA institute reiterated that "an auditor is not trained to detect forgeries, nor will customary audit procedures detect all conspiracies."

Although Regina's report wasn't affected by the change, the inability of an average stockholder to anticipate the company's collapse shows the public's vulnerability in relying on auditors' opinions. "Only the court can protect my interests now," Mr. Schwarzman says.

John Shank, an accounting professor at Dartmouth College's Amos Tuck School of Business Administration, says, "At the very time an auditor should be the most cynical and skeptical about a company is when his client is applying the most pressure."

Ignoring 'Danger Signs'

Edward Grossman, an attorney representing Mr. Schwarzman and other shareholders in class-action suits against Regina's former management and Peat Marwick, says, "Auditors can close their eyes to danger signs." Mr. Grossman adds that in some of his lawsuits, he has found that lower-level accountants had discovered signs of fraud or impropriety but were ignored by their superiors. "The higher-ups at accounting firms usually seem to be willing to give management a chance to get its house in order," he says.

In response, Arthur Young's Mr. Liggio says accounting firms check out suspicions of lower-level staffers even if the partner in charge of the audit doesn't agree. "But more often than not, these suspicions don't prove to be true," Mr. Liggio says. "In one instance, we even spent $40,000 of our own money for a second review, and no problem was found."

Peat Marwick is still working on a new audit of Regina, which recently turned its $10.9 million profit for the year ended last June 30 into a $16.8 million loss for the 15 months ended September 30. Regina's new management says· its review has turned up fraud and negligence: Returns of faulty products weren't deducted from sales, some sales invoices were fakes, and revenue was inflated. William Murray, the Peat Marwick partner in charge of the Regina audit, declines to comment.

Distrustful Expert

Unlike Mr. Schwarzman, David Rocker, a Wall Street money manager who runs his own hedge fund, has long distrusted auditors. When Regina issued its fiscal 1988 results, Mr. Rocker subtracted its nine-month figures and discovered that although indicated fourth-quarter sales rose 28% from a year earlier, receivables had soared 84%, total inventories 100% and inventories of finished goods alone 74%. At the same time, fourth-quarter outlays for research and development fell 37% and depreciation 88%.

"Goods were backing up in the pipeline, and the lower depreciation charges showed earnings weren't for real," Mr. Rocker says. "Obviously, the auditors weren't asking the right questions. Regina's report raised more red flags than I'd seen in a long time"—so many that he sold more than 100,000 Regina shares short; that is, he sold borrowed shares that he later repurchased at a much lower price and returned to the lender. "I made a bundle of money," he says. Peat Marwick won't comment on his remarks.

As for auditors in general, Mr. Rocker comments, "They aren't paid to blow the whistle against companies. They are paid by the very companies they oversee."

How did that come about? Because in the early 1930s, when Congress wanted public companies audited by independent parties, accountants volunteered to do the job. But the securities laws that gave it to them didn't provide funds to pay them. So, the companies pay the watchdogs.

Mr. Liggio of Arthur Young, admitting that auditors are

often "taken in by dishonest managers," recalls one auditor-negligence case in which the company's owner sent his pilot by plane to intercept confirmation requests on cash and assets that the auditor had express-mailed to lenders and suppliers. "The pilot signed off on the confirmations and sent them back to the auditor," Mr. Liggio says. "How could an auditor catch something like that?"

Extra Caution Needed

However, Mr. Liggio concedes that auditors sometimes can be gulled if they don't take "that extra step needed when they suspect fraud." He cites the chief executive of one company who insisted that he paid for spare parts in cash—a practice apparently common in the industry. In reality, the cash was used to bribe the buying agents of several large customers. "But the auditor didn't check to see that the spare-part inventory was increasing during that period," Mr. Liggio says.

In Regina's case, company executives were issuing glowing reports just as its house of cards was crashing down over their heads. As recently as last July, Regina was telling investors to "look forward to some significant new announcements in the next few months which we believe will further enhance our growth." For the prior three years, Regina had reported profit gains of 300%, 75% and 54%.

But in late July, the lawsuits say, Regina was getting back huge returns of vacuum cleaners from its distributors, some plastic cleaner parts were melting, and many of its sales were fictitious. A TV commercial in which a Regina cleaner picked up corn flakes from the floor better than rival cleaners had to be withdrawn after Hoover Co., a competitor, sued.

"These are the kind of warning signs that an auditor just can't afford to miss," Prof. Shank says.

As to the lawsuits recently hitting Peat Marwick, Leonard P. Novello, its general counsel, calls them "separate, unconnected matters involving companies in different industries." He adds: "As a public accounting firm with the largest audit practice in the country, we are not surprised by the number of lawsuits filed against accounting firms, including ours—most of which have little basis in fact."

But some Peat Marwick officials privately worry that the SEC may again make the firm an "object lesson" to the entire auditing profession. In 1975, the SEC strongly censured Peat Marwick for failing to perform proper audits for five companies that collapsed soon after getting clean opinions.

The SEC ticked off a litany of some of the worst audit problems of the 1970s: National Student Marketing Corp., which improperly inflated sales and profits; Talley Industries Inc., which improperly recorded defense-contract costs; Republic National Life Insurance Co., which manipulated investments; Penn Central Co., which created fraudulent profits through fake shipments of modular homes.

Peat Marwick was suspended from taking new public audit clients from May through October 1975, and was forced to undergo a peer review of its audit procedures by outside accountants that year. Additional but limited reviews were conducted in 1976 and 1977.

Is Peat Marwick worried about the current spate of suits? "We believe our litigation posture is no better or worse, on a relative basis, than other firms, and it is unfair to single us out," Mr. Novello says.

CHAPTER 7

CRITICISM OF THE
FINANCIAL ACCOUNTING
STANDARDS BOARD

About 15 years ago, the Financial Accounting Standards Board (FASB) was organized to replace the Accounting Principles Board that determined accounting practices and policies for almost two decades. The Accounting Principles Board was composed exclusively of members of the public accounting profession involved in independent auditing. As a result of the recommendations of the Wheat Commission and the Cohen Commission, the rule-making process was opened up to include representatives from industry and from government.[1]

The FASB rule-making activities involve extensive "due process." All meetings are public, and the statement development process is designed to encourage involvement by interested parties. In contrast to the previous rule-making group, the FASB members are salaried and must sever relationships with their previous employers. This was done to enhance the independence and credibility of the Board.

As should be expected, the FASB is under fire from industry, from the accounting firms, from the SEC, and even from government because of its sensitive "balancing act" role—the key element in this self-regulated industry. Reflecting on this thankless role, Charles Horngren, noted professor and author described the Board's position in the world as that of a lone tree on a deserted island inhabited by a pack of wild dogs.

---

[1]See Chapter 1.

Numbers Game: FASB, Which Decides Accounting Questions, Sparks Much Criticism

Rule-Making Panel Is Said to Act Too Slowly, Issue Costly, Useless Standards—But 'Due Process' Is Upheld

By Lee Berton

April 30, 1984

STAMFORD, CONN.—The Financial Accounting Standards Board meets here each week, in a three-story white building amid acres of trees, to set accounting rules for American industry. The bucolic setting appears peaceful and harmonious, but looks can be deceiving.

Actually, critics all over the country are bombarding the seven-member board with a cacophony of complaints.

Accountants increasingly accuse the FASB of moving too slowly—and of producing little of substance when it finally does act. Some securities analysts gripe that the FASB has ducked accounting changes that would have improved financial disclosures by public companies. Businessmen say accounting rules are unnecessary, complex and costly. And the counsel of one congressional subcommittee is talking about scrapping the FASB and replacing it with a government body.

"I seriously question whether the FASB is going to make it," says the chairman of one large accounting firm.

Major Threat

The current turmoil could radically change or destroy a unique organization—a private standards-setting professional body that, in effect, makes "the law of the land" for thousands of American corporations. Although the Securities and Exchange Commission retains the right to overrule FASB decrees and can issue its own rules, it generally leaves the rule-making job to the FASB.

How the FASB works—or doesn't work—is especially important now because it faces an unusual number of difficult but crucial issues. Its decisions will affect nearly every company in the United States by determining how much profit or loss the companies report and how much debt they must list on their balance sheets.

"The morsels on its plate are so big right now," says the accounting firm chairman, "I wonder whether it will choke on them."

The biggest morsel for the FASB to digest concerns pension accounting. Currently, companies don't put unfunded pension liabilities on their balance sheets as debt, but the FASB has proposed that they all do so. Inclusion of hundreds of billions of dollars of such projected pension costs would severely damage corporate debt-to-equity ratios. Seven of the "Big Eight" accounting firms and practically every major U.S. corporation disagree with the FASB, which is expected to issue a draft rule this year and a final rule in 1985.

Deferred Taxes

Another big issue involves deferred taxes. By next year, the FASB must decide whether to continue to permit companies to speed up reporting of their income-tax expenses to shareholders, even though a return for those taxes may not yet have been filed with the government. Utilities, for example, want the current rule retained because it lowers their reported earnings and thus enables them to seek higher rates. But some accountants argue that taxes reported should equal taxes paid.

The stakes are huge. By one estimate, the reported earnings of 338 major U.S. companies for fiscal years ended between July 31, 1982, and June 30, 1983, would have soared $8.2 billion if the deferred-tax accounting treatment had been eliminated.

The third big issue concerns the current rule that companies don't have to report debt in joint ventures in which they hold less than a 50% interest or to consolidate finance subsidiaries. The proponents of a change say, among other things, that the current rule enables some companies to hide their true debt load. But others contend that acknowledgment of the additional debt could bury some capital-intensive companies or turn investors away from successful retailers and manufacturers that offer enormous amounts of credit to their customers.

'Junior Securities'

The FASB also is dealing with some less important but still noteworthy issues. For example, it is proposing to put a damper on "junior securities," cut-price stock that companies offer to key executives as an incentive. If the rule is approved, as expected, companies will have to deduct that compensation from their profits. R. Terry Duryea, a partner at Deloitte Haskins & Sells, a big accounting firm, says the proposed rule could reduce reported earnings of 10 of his high-technology client companies by an average of 24% a year over the next four years.

Whatever the FASB decides about such issues will become, in effect, "laws" because the SEC has said they are. The SEC has told publicly held companies that unless they follow FASB rules, they will fail to gain SEC approval of their financial reports. Without SEC approval, trading in the companies' securities would be impaired.

The roots of this vast, unusual power go back to 1938, when the SEC decided to let the accounting profession set its own rules. From that year until 1973, those rules—or "principles," as accountants call them—were set by one body and then another. Both bodies were part of the American Institute of Certified Public Accountants, a national group of CPAs.

But in the 1960s, CPA firms were criticized for too often allowing companies to "shop" for accounting principles that would increase their profits and stock prices. So, the institute appointed a blue-ribbon committee to examine the issues. The committee recommended that a separate standards-setting body be set up with representation from industry, government and Wall Street as well as from accounting.

Out of that, the FASB was born in January 1973. Its annual budget has since tripled to almost $10 million, and its staff has grown to 125. Its chairman earns $225,000 a year, with the other six board members getting $185,000 each. Over the years, the FASB has issued 79 standards. By one estimate, it mailed out more than three million documents last year and more than

100,000 letters. It receives up to 600 phone calls daily, many seeking advice on how to interpret its complex rules.

"It's become a full-blown bureaucracy that would do credit to any federal agency," says Thornton O'glove, a securities analyst who writes a report on the quality of corporate earnings. And critics add that the FASB's resemblance to a government body goes beyond mere staff size and paper pushing; they say it is a model of bureaucratic inefficiency and indecisiveness.

The trouble arises partly because the seven-member board, which includes five CPAs, is a democracy that, like the accounting profession, is sharply divided on many issues. Ralph Walters, a partner in the big accounting firm of Touche, Ross & Co. and a board member from April 1977 through last year, admits that the FASB "drags its feet." He explains that all its decisions must be subjected to tortuous "due process," involving discussion memos, exposure drafts and hearings.

"It was one of the most frustrating experiences of my life," he says. "Discussion of specific rules goes on for years."

An Agonizing Debate
Mr. Walters recalls how the board debated for months in mid-1982 about whether corn stored by a hog farmer should be priced at cost or adjusted for inflation; the latter method would cut the farmer's profits.

"Three members of the board, including myself, voted for current value," Mr. Walters says. "Three others wanted historical cost. One board member said that once a farmer made up his mind to feed the corn to the hogs, its cost should be fixed to the market price at that time from then on. It was mind-boggling."

The issue still hasn't been decided.

Due process doesn't only force the FASB to waste time on minutiae, critics charge; it also forces the board too often to produce unworkable rules that, by trying to satisfy everybody, end up being costly for companies to implement and ineffective as well.

An eight-year-old FASB rule, for instance, requires companies to capitalize certain leases. The rule's intent was to force more companies to label such leases as debt. But the rule, which runs 226 pages and includes seven amendments, six interpretations and nine staff bulletins, has so many loopholes that most major companies have figured out ways around it.

Price of Due Process
Many accountants acknowledge such problems but believe that that is the price of due process. "A dictatorship in accounting standards might move a lot more quickly, but it would ride over everyone's doubts and opinions," says Michael Alexander, a Touche Ross partner who was the FASB research director from 1978 to 1982. "In a democratic organization like the FASB, delays and disagreements are the price we pay. It can be exasperating, but I think it works."

But critics say due process isn't the only problem. Lee Seidler, a professor of accounting at New York University's Graduate School of Business Administration, contends that the FASB suffers principally from a lack of leadership. "There doesn't seem to be a good horse trader on the board who can push standards through faster," he says. "It's a group of equals, and you really need a strong leader."

In response, Donald J. Kirk, the FASB chairman since 1978, says: "All the evidence I've seen indicates that the public wouldn't accept [accounting] standards that appeared to be arrived at hastily, or arbitrarily, or as the obvious result of internal 'horse trading.' There has to be a more judicial approach, as distinct from a legislative-deadline type of approach."

'Conceptual Framework'
Critics of the FASB also accuse it of wasting time trying to construct a "conceptual framework" for all future accounting rules. The FASB believes that such a framework—which some accountants envision as a sort of "constitution" for the profession—is important for "providing guidance in resolving new or emerging problems" in accounting. "But we don't believe it will be the panacea for all future accounting problems," an FASB staff member says. "Some people want a computer where you can punch keys and come up with the right answer every time, and the framework just won't do that."

But others say the framework isn't worth the effort, largely because it can never be constructed. "It's a quest for a Rosetta stone that doesn't exist," says Abraham Briloff, an accounting professor at Baruch College in New York City. Adds Prof. Seidler: "The notion that a few board members and staff . . . could develop a conceptual framework for accounting has demonstrated the vanity of ignorance."

As evidence, he cites the problems that the board has been having with such basic questions as whether to measure financial events by historical cost or current value. Unless the FASB can answer that, most accountants say, the framework is useless.

Problem of Inflation
After many years of debate, during which inflation has become a significantly less relevant issue, the FASB issued a draft last December on "recognition and measurement" of price-adjusted data. The draft says current price data should be recognized "if it is sufficiently relevant and reliable to justify the costs involved." But if such data is unclear or disputed, the draft says, its application can be decided "in the light of the circumstances of each case."

Mr. Walters concedes that the draft "says almost nothing." But he explains that the board was "hopelessly deadlocked" and that it was the best the members could do. And FASB Chairman Kirk says outsiders mistakenly hoped that the draft would "produce indisputable answers to questions" about how certain events should be measured for financial statements. "Concepts are not intended to solve specific problems directly," Mr. Kirk says. "They are meant to provide tools for helping to solve problems."

Such responses, however, haven't satisfied Rep. John D. Dingell, a Michigan Democrat who last year asked the General Accounting Office to see whether the FASB or the SEC is issuing effective and timely standards. Rep. Dingell is the chairman of the Oversight and Investigations subcommittee of the House Commerce Committee, which this summer plans to hold hearings on the setting of accounting standards.

"If standard setters were really doing their jobs, we wouldn't have Penn Squares or Drysdales popping up without fair warning," says Michael F. Barrett, the subcommittee's chief counsel. "Maybe if the government set all accounting standards and was tougher, we wouldn't need an FASB." In mid-1982, both Penn Square Bank and Drysdale Government Securities Inc. went bankrupt after getting clean bills of health from their outside accountants.

SEC Pressure

Most critics of the FASB expect it to continue to waffle on major issues unless the SEC puts more pressure on it to take stronger stands. In January, for instance, the FASB decided against requiring companies to issue quarterly financial data on their separate lines of business. As a result, the SEC proposed that requirement a month later and has asked for comment on the proposal.

"What is needed is a smaller group with more political power," says John C. Burton, a former chief accountant of the SEC and now the dean of Columbia University's Graduate School of Business. He notes that there are two openings on the five-member SEC, and those two new members could force changes in rule-making for accounting. Although Mr. Burton doesn't expect that to happen, he concedes, "If the FASB continues to be ineffective, it could mean we'll get a government body setting standards."

But whatever the criticism of the FASB, the prospect of the government setting standards scares many businessmen and accountants. They say that in countries such as West Germany and Japan, where lawmakers and government agencies more actively set accounting rules, disclosure of financial data by publicly held companies is poor.

"The FASB at best does a mediocre job," says Theodore Eggert, the vice president for research at A.G. Becker Paribas, a Wall Street brokerage firm. "But a government agency setting accounting rules . . . might be even worse. At least businessmen know whom to complain to at the FASB or who can get their message to the FASB through their accounting firm. With a government agency, there would be little if any redress. Government agencies are usually faceless."

Role of Business on the FASB Irks Some Accountants

Clout of Industry Appears to Grow as IBM Ex-Aide Named Representative

By Lee Berton

October 31, 1985

NEW YORK—Businessmen appear to be getting a bigger role on the Financial Accounting Standards Board, the chief rule-making body for accountants. And some accountants don't like it.

Under pressure for more than a year to give businessmen more representation in its standards-setting process, the Financial Accounting Foundation, a supervisory and funding body for the FASB, has appointed a second representative of business and industry to the FASB.

He is C. Arthur Northrop, former treasurer of International Business Machines Corp. Since 1973, when the FASB was founded, it has had only one representative from business and industry. But a year ago, the Business Roundtable and the Financial Executives Institute began lobbying for more representation.

Businessmen say they are particularly upset by an FASB pension accounting proposal that would increase their reported debt and an FASB inflation accounting rule that raises the costs of preparing financial statements.

Some accountants believe that business would like to pack the FASB with more businessmen to water down some strict accounting rules. "But it's not a good idea to have rules made by those who should be governed by them," says George H. Sorter, a professor of accounting at New York University's graduate school of business.

But John J. Quindlen, a senior vice president and chief financial officer of Du Pont Co. who heads a committee of the institute on accounting standards, doesn't agree. "We only feel that the FASB has made some mistakes that the benefit of real business experience could avoid," says Mr. Quindlen.

Mr. Northrop, 62 years old, says he won't represent the views of business alone on the FASB but will work with other FASB members to develop the best accounting rules possible.

The Financial Accounting Foundation also appointed Robert J. Swieringa, a professor of accounting at Cornell University's graduate school of management, to the FASB. Both appointments, effective January 1, are for five years. Messrs. Northrop and Swieringa will succeed Robert T. Sprouse, a former academic, and Frank E. Block, a former president of the Financial Analysts Federation, on the FASB.

The other FASB member currently representing business and industry is Victor Brown, a former executive of Firestone Tire & Rubber Co. and Standard Oil Co. (Indiana).

SEC, Reportedly Pressed by Business, Studies Need for an Overhaul of FASB

By Lee Berton and Thomas E. Ricks

August 3, 1988

The Securities and Exchange Commission, under pressure from business, is quietly investigating whether the Financial Accounting Standards Board needs an overhaul, accountants and businessmen said.

Since last May individual members of the Business Roundtable, a powerful lobbying group, have been criticizing the FASB in meetings with managing partners of major accounting firms and SEC members. Roundtable members have told the SEC that some rules of the chief rule-making body for accountants aren't effective and are too costly for companies to implement.

In Washington, the SEC's chief accountant's office con-

Mr. Ricks is a staff reporter of THE WALL STREET JOURNAL.

firmed that it is reviewing the FASB as part of its oversight responsibilities. The seven-member FASB, based in Norwalk, Connecticut, derives its power to set standards from the SEC, which under congressional direction must maintain oversight of the body. But business contributes about $3 million a year to a foundation that funds the FASB, whose annual budget is about $11 million, and so has considerable clout in accounting rule-setting.

SEC watchers say that while commission members may be more amenable to the pressures of business, the SEC staff wants to resist more involvement in accounting rule-setting. All four current SEC members are Reagan administration appointees, and the majority is likely to be sympathetic to business complaints about burdensome rule-making.

The SEC review is bound to be looked at closely by Congress. Rep. Ron Wyden, a member of the House Energy and Commerce Committee's oversight and investigations panel, which has held a score of hearings on accounting issues in recent years, said he wasn't familiar with the SEC review of FASB, but added that his prime concern is that the FASB take an aggressive approach to fraud issues. "Nobody wants things that add to business cost, but we certainly want them to be activist on financial fraud," the Oregon Democrat said.

Glen Davison, the SEC's deputy chief accountant, said the SEC is "always overseeing the FASB processes and keeping an eye out for criticisms of standard-setting bodies and ways they can be improved." Mr. Davison said the chief accountants office is "currently monitoring suggestions raised that the FASB consider changes in the rule-making process."

He said that the SEC will look at suggestions by business that the FASB field-test more of its proposals with companies before adopting rules, and that the FASB use more advisory task forces from business, accountants and other users of financial statements.

'Cookbook' Approach
John Reed, chairman of Citicorp and chairman of the Roundtable's accounting-principles task force, has been criticizing the FASB in meetings with SEC commissioners and managing partners of major accounting firms, according to accountants and

businessmen. A Citicorp official working with the task force confirmed that such meetings had taken place, and added that
three members of the task force had attended them. He declined
to identify the three members.

Other members of the task force include top officials of Du
Pont Co., Eastman Kodak Co. and CSX Corp. None could be
reached for comment.

According to accountants and businessmen, Roundtable
members are telling the SEC that some FASB rules use a "cook-
book" approach and are so narrow and detailed as to make implementation prohibitively costly. They have cited rules on pension costs and deferred taxes.

'Natural Creative Tension'

The pension-costs rule forces some companies to set up profit-
reducing reserves for future retirements. The tax rule requires
complex adjustments in financial reports every time corporate
tax rates are changed.

Dennis Beresford, FASB chairman, said the SEC review is
an "internal type of thing that won't result in a report" to the
public. As to criticism from the Roundtable, Mr. Beresford said
that the FASB "feels pressure from lots of people all the time
that suggest changes in the standard-setting procedure. It's a
natural creative tension."

But Arthur Wyatt, who quit the rule-making body's board
last year because he said he was frustrated over the growing role
of business in accounting standard-setting, said that business
pressure continues to be a major problem for the FASB.

Accounting-Board Rulings Make Business See Red

By Lee Berton

March 21, 1989

"If the FASB doesn't listen to reason, a lot of businessmen like myself are prepared to scramble the pilots and let loose the bombers," asserts a financial executive of one major Midwest industrial corporation. Asked what this warning implies, the executive says: "If the FASB doesn't recognize the damage it can cause to U.S. industry, Congress would. Congress can't afford to let some ivory-tower accountants take the steam out of the economy."

Running to Congress is a step most businessmen would prefer to avoid because they don't trust the instincts of lawmakers in accounting matters. However, the economic stakes in new accounting rules and proposals by the Financial Accounting Standards Board, the chief rule-making body for accountants, have become so big that some businessmen now privately say they may have no choice.

For example, a new accounting proposal, which will be the subject of extensive hearings this year, could wipe out major portions of the reported profits of most big major U.S. corporations starting in 1992 by forcing them to begin accruing—or deducting in advance from reported profits—for retirees' medical and insurance benefits. Currently, companies deduct such costs each year as the benefits are paid. The vast majority of U.S. companies don't prefund such massive benefits right now because such prefundings aren't tax-deductible like pension-fund costs.

A recent accounting rule taking effect this year forces U.S. companies to consolidate unrelated financing subsidiaries, skewing key financial ratios. One particularly vexing accounting rule, say financial executives, goes into effect in 1990. It bars companies from offsetting certain massive liabilities with credits for future taxes as had been done for decades; the rule eliminates deferred-tax credits and debits on the balance sheet.

The FASB says such accounting changes are needed to improve disclosure to investors, to provide better comparisons of financial data among companies and industries, and to require companies to accrue for expenses they promise to pay. "We are most concerned about proper accounting and disclosure," says Dennis Beresford, chairman of the FASB. "And while we are aware of public-policy and economic consequences, they cannot be our main thrust. Otherwise, the standard-setting process would become too politicized."

Corporate executives are getting increasingly upset that these rules are set in an economic vacuum. "The FASB doesn't seem to care what it does to the U.S. economy, and its credibility gap with business is growing," maintains Eugene Flegm, assistant controller of General Motors Corp. GM's reported annual profits after 1992 could come close to being wiped out by the FASB's latest proposal on accruing for retirees' medical and insurance benefits, say some accountants.

And Thomas Jones, Citicorp's senior vice president, finance, says "the real problem with the FASB is that it is its own prosecuting attorney, defense lawyer, jury and judge." Mr. Jones is particularly unhappy with the FASB's deferred-tax rule, which he estimates is costing the bank about $3 million to implement in terms of manpower and paper work.

"The FASB's tax standard is requiring us to figure out complex tax schedules for operations in 90 countries and at least 30 states and has taken up to 15 people at the bank almost 12 months to calculate," says Mr. Jones.

Such discontent with the FASB has spurred such powerful lobbying groups as the Business Roundtable to ask for more of a voice in FASB deliberations. Indeed, the Roundtable late last year urged the Securities and Exchange Commission to consider forming an oversight body with greater input from business that would help set the FASB's rules agenda.

In a letter to SEC Chairman David Ruder, John Reed, chairman of the Roundtable's accounting principles task force, asserts that the FASB has "made significant changes to a set of accounting rules that already work well." Mr. Reed, Citicorp's chairman, was speaking for such task force members as Du Pont Co., Eastman Kodak Co. and Martin Marietta Corp.

The SEC has rejected the idea of another oversight body for

the FASB; the FASB already has several advisory bodies with business representatives that give it advice but don't set its agenda. But SEC accounting specialists have in recent months been huddling closer with corporate executives and more carefully monitoring the FASB's proposals. "We can't turn a deaf ear to what business is saying," says Edmund Coulson, the SEC's chief accountant.

In response to pressure from business, the FASB is already making some changes in its procedures that business should welcome. For example, FASB task forces are now being chaired by board members rather than FASB staffers, who tend to be more doctrinaire about accounting concepts. And it's likely that major FASB proposals from now on will be field-tested by major companies before being proposed. In addition, the FASB, founded in 1973, may soon be asked to pass rules that receive a lot of negative comment from industry by a 5-2 vote, as it once did, rather than the current 4-3 vote.

If all this doesn't satisfy the critics, there seems to be little question that some disgruntled businessmen will take their case to Congress, asking for some form of relief. And that doesn't sit well with the FASB. "If people keep running to Congress because they get an accounting answer they don't like, they're going to wreck the standard-setting process," says Timothy Lucas, the FASB's research director.

There are ample precedents for seeking congressional aid from onerous accounting rules. Business in the past has persuaded lawmakers to give companies the right to get the benefits of the investment tax credit immediately rather than defer them as accounting standard-setters had ruled. Critics of congressional interference say this meddling helped undermine the power of the FASB's predecessor, the Accounting Principles Board, and led to the board's demise. And under pressure from business, lawmakers asked regulators to give oil and gas producers more time in writing off dry holes rather than expensing them immediately under a new accounting rule. Many accountants say this gave oil and gas producers free rein to report expenses any way they wished and obscured comparability in the industry.

But despite all the recent emotion generated by business

about accounting standards, the best minds in the profession still agree that standard-setting should remain in the private sector. "As faulty as accounting rule-making may be, it's still better to keep Congress out of the act," says John Burton, an accounting professor at Columbia University's Graduate School of Business and former chief accountant of the Securities and Exchange Commission. "Otherwise politics would take over and there'd be no chance for standard-setters to come to their senses now and then."

PART 2

THE IMPACT OF THE FINANCIAL ACCOUNTING STANDARDS BOARD

CHAPTER 8

ACCOUNTING FOR INCOME TAXES

The FASB's Statement No. 96, Accounting for Income Taxes has been referred to the most wide-reaching and complex accounting standard in recent history. There is a high degree of interest in the statement not only by accountants, but by top executives and managers whose decisions are affected by tax rules. Statement No. 96 is a radical departure from the existing generally accepted accounting principles on income tax accounting. It is the product of a five-year project by the Financial Accounting Standards Board, during which the fundamental concepts underlying income tax accounting were completely reexamined and evaluated. The result is sweeping changes in our present approaches that affect:

- Computing tax liability.
- Classifying taxes on the balance sheet.
- Accounting for the tax effects of business combinations.
- Accounting for changes in the tax laws.
- Evaluating the appropriateness of tax assets and liabilities.

Statement No. 96 affects not only publicly held companies, but also privately held, taxable entities in all industries. It even extends into the future, as in the case of publicly traded, master limited partnerships that will be taxed as corporations beginning in 1997. The fundamental concept underlying this new requirement is an accounting for tax effects of *all* transactions, be they transactions affecting current transactions affecting future years' returns and profits. The following articles illustrate the interplay between the corporate accounting community, the independent audit firms, and the FASB in its rule-making capacity in developing this challenging pronouncement.

FASB to Consider Deferred-Tax Changes as Companies Begin to Mount Opposition

By Lee Berton

March 16, 1984

NEW YORK—The Financial Accounting Standards Board next month will begin considering changes in deferred-tax accounting that could sharply boost reported profits and lower liabilities for most U.S. companies.

While the rule-making body for accountants won't make up its mind on the issues until late next year, many U.S. companies are beginning to mount extensive campaigns to convince the FASB that it shouldn't change the rule.

One of the first big efforts comes today as the National Association of Accountants, an organization of 97,000 management accountants, holds a much ballyhooed conference here on the deferred-tax issue. Both the National Association of Accountants and the Financial Executives Institute, an organization of 12,500 U.S. financial executives, have recently informed the FASB that they oppose any major changes in the treatment of deferred-tax accounting.

"Deferred taxes is one of the biggest accounting issues on the horizon because of its tremendous impact on earnings, and most companies are extremely worried that the FASB can, in any new accounting treatment, create a lot of problems for them," says Leopold Bernstein, an accounting professor at Baruch College, New York.

Favored by Utilities

Companies currently can speed up their reporting of income tax expenses to shareholders, even though a return for these taxes generally hasn't yet been filed with the government. Utilities strongly favor such accruals of unpaid taxes, which are listed as liabilities on the balance sheet, because they lower reported earnings and help utilities persuade regulators to boost rates.

But some accountants and small companies say that it is too costly and complex to set up a deferred-tax account. And other accounting theorists say the taxes that are accrued are generally never paid by capital-intensive companies, because the continuous depreciation generated by building new plant and equipment continues to accumulate new tax deferrals.

If the FASB eliminated the deferred tax treatment, these huge amounts of deferred taxes would be wiped out, sharply boosting earnings and lowering liabilities. The FASB is considering a range of changes in the deferred tax area, most of which would result in higher reported earnings and lower liabilities.

The stakes in the deferred-tax issue are high for almost all major corporations, because of the huge accruals they have built up over the years on their balance sheets. A research study done by Mr. Bernstein, for example, shows that the reported earnings of 338 major U.S. companies for years ended between July 31, 1982, and to June 30, 1983, would have jumped $8.2 billion if the deferred-tax accounting treatment is eliminated.

Du Pont and GM

According to Mr. Bernstein, the reported earnings of Du Pont Co. for the year ended December 31, 1982, would have soared almost 50%, while the per-share profit of General Motors Corp. for the same year would have increased about 15% if deferred-tax accounting for accelerated depreciation had been eliminated.

While most accountants would prefer to discuss deferred-tax theory, a few concede that some companies that had favored change now oppose it because the economy has turned around.

"Two years or so ago when the FASB began considering deferred taxes, the recession was holding down earnings, but now that we're in a recovery, most companies of major size don't want an infusion of instant earnings," says a CPA with a major accounting firm. Frankly, he says, companies are worried that if reported earnings balloon, Congress may boost taxes, unions may demand higher pay raises and shareholders may want higher dividends.

The FASB says that of 400 comments it has received, most of them from corporations and accounting firms, on deferred-tax accounting treatment, most generally favor the status quo. After the hearings next month, the FASB will issue an exposure draft on the issue late this year and is expected to issue the new rule late in 1985.

FASB Proposal Will Result in Big Gain in Profit and Net Worth for Many Firms

By Lee Berton

July 31, 1986

NEW YORK—Many U.S. companies will enjoy big one-time gains in reported profit and net worth from a new accounting rule on deferred taxes that will soon be proposed by standard setters.

The proposal by the Financial Accounting Standards Board would convert any decline in the tax rate into a big profit spurt. Specifically, the new rule would allow a reduction, or "debit" of the liability on the balance sheet that has been accruing for future tax payments. Meanwhile, accepted accounting principles would allow this amount to be assigned, or "credited" to earnings.

For companies eager to apply the rule, the only problem is that while the FASB expects to issue a proposal by September, it won't be enacted as a rule, and therefore be beneficial, until late next year.

Boost of $160 Million

Frank Westover, senior vice president and controller at Chicago-based IC Industries Inc., a railroad and consumer products producer, said the proposed one-time gain could boost IC's annual reported earnings by about $160 million. That's nearly as much as the $163 million, or $1.50 a share, the company earned in all 1985.

Following a recapitalization, Chicago-based FMC Corp. has a negative net worth of $600 million. Arthur Lyons, vice presi-

dent and controller of the maker of defense products and industrial and agricultural chemicals, says the proposal could reduce
that by $20 million to $25 million in the year it is applied.

A number of companies that would be favorably affected argue that the FASB should move more quickly. "The FASB has
been considering changing the accounting treatment of deferred
taxes for several years and now that Congress is on the verge of
sharply lowering tax rates, it should move quickly," asserts IC
Industries' Mr. Westover. Otherwise, he says, the tax liability
recorded on the balance sheets of U.S. companies will be billions
of dollars higher at the end of 1986 than it should be.

Ray Simpson, a project manager for the Stamford, Connecticut–based FASB, the chief rule-making body for accountants,
said the FASB plans to hold hearings on the deferred-tax proposal in early January, with the rule expected to take effect by
mid to late 1987. "This is a very controversial proposal with
many facets, and we prefer not to rush it," he says.

Deferred-tax liabilities accumulate on companies' balance
sheets because companies speed up reporting of income tax expenses to shareholders, even though these taxes haven't yet
been paid to the government. Some opponents of deferred taxes
say the accrued taxes are generally never paid by capital-intensive companies. That occurs because the continuous depreciation generated by building new plant and equipment continues
to pile up new tax deferrals.

Some Favor Elimination
Because this accrued tax liability is never paid by many companies, some accounting theorists have long urged the FASB to
eliminate it entirely. But the FASB said it has tentatively decided to keep the liability on the balance sheet and, instead, reduce or increase it each time tax rates are changed.

Mr. Simpson points out that under the FASB proposal, companies would have the option after tax rates are lowered of taking a big one-time boost toward 1987 or 1988 earnings, or of
restating prior years' earnings. The profit increase would be
placed on a single line in the financial statement below the line
for extraordinary income.

Some companies oppose changing the current rule on deferred taxes because they believe the new proposal is too complex. "The new proposal would be onerous to administer, difficult to understand and artificial in nature," says Con Noland, director of accounting policy for Du Pont Corp., the Wilmington, Delaware-based chemical concern.

Du Pont and other companies also oppose the proposal because, while it could provide a one-time boost to profits, it would lower profits in succeeding years. That is because it would require companies to accrue a liability for taxes payable on profits of foreign subsidiaries in the year they are earned.

When U.S. taxes exceed the foreign rate, profits brought back to the United States generally are taxed at the difference. Many companies believe they shouldn't have to reserve a tax liability for foreign earnings that may never be returned to the United States.

But most big industrial companies favor the proposed rule because of the big boost it will give to profits when tax rates are lowered. And they plan to put more pressure on the FASB to approve the proposal as a rule this year.

"With the tax rates due to be sharply lowered this year, the FASB should seriously consider getting the deferred-tax rule issued this year," says Edmund L. Jenkins, a partner of Arthur Andersen & Co., the biggest U.S. accounting firm. "Otherwise, the board will have serious trouble maintaining its credibility with the corporate community," he adds.

FASB Rule to Cut Companies' Profits in Fourth Quarter

By a Wall Street Journal Staff Reporter

October 23, 1986

NEW YORK—The Financial Accounting Standards Board, as expected, issued a rule that—as a result of the tax-overhaul bill signed into law yesterday—will depress fourth-quarter profits of many companies.

The rule requires companies to reflect in the current quarter the entire impact of canceling the investment tax credit for all of 1986. This reduces earnings far more in the quarter than if companies, as many requested, had been allowed to restate previous quarters to reflect elimination of the tax credit. The new tax law cancels the investment tax credit retroactive to last January 1.

Congressional tax experts have estimated that the reduction in earnings this quarter for all companies that have used the investment tax credit this year may total $10 billion.

Financial analysts caution that investors will have to look carefully at the footnotes of 1986 annual reports to see which companies are affected.

"It's hard to predict just which companies will be hurt," says Pat McConnell, an accountant and an associate director of the securities firm Bear Stearns & Co. She noted that the tax bill will permit certain companies to retain a phased-down investment tax credit, as well as a tax credit for projects firmly committed to by last December 31.

The FASB, the chief rule-making body for accountants, again rejected a proposal many companies had sought to help offset loss of the investment tax credit. The proposal would have given companies a big one-time profit increase in the fourth quarter, reflecting the decrease in the corporate tax rate and the resulting change in the amount of tax credits to be accrued.

A final rule on deferred taxes isn't expected until late in the second half of 1987, after public hearings in January. "Until then, companies should continue to compute deferred taxes under existing accounting standards," said Neil McGrath, an FASB project manager.

The rule on the investment tax credit is effective for quarterly and annual periods ending on or after last January 1, the FASB said.

SEC to Issue Rules for Firms' Tax Disclosures

Companies Given Flexibility on Including Some Data on Deferred Liabilities

By Cynthia S. Grisdela

October 24, 1986

WASHINGTON—The Securities and Exchange Commission voted to issue guidelines on disclosures companies must make on their financial statements concerning effects of the revised tax law.

In an unusual move, the agency also agreed with a staff recommendation to let companies include supplemental information on recorded deferred income-tax liabilities as though the change in corporate tax rates took effect at the end of this year. Under the new law signed Wednesday by President Reagan, the top corporate tax rate will drop to 34% from the current 46% in the middle of next year, resulting in a "blended" rate for 1987 of 40%.

Some companies that have deferred income taxes at the current 46% top rate could pay at a lower rate when the taxes become due, resulting in higher reported income. Overall, however, the extra tax bite on business will be substantial next year because many corporate tax breaks will be eliminated on or before January 1, 1987.

The Financial Accounting Standards Board, which establishes standards for the accounting industry, is seeking comments on a proposal to adjust deferred income taxes for corporate tax rate changes, among other things. But the issue is controversial among accountants and a final standard isn't expected until mid-1987, the SEC staff said.

Current accounting rules provide for deferred income taxes to be stated at the tax rate in effect for the current year, without adjustment for subsequent tax rate changes. Consequently, the

---

Ms. Grisdela was a staff reporter of THE WALL STREET JOURNAL.

amount of deferred tax that will actually have to be paid in future years is overstated when corporate tax rates are reduced.

The agency normally wouldn't permit companies to change accounting methods until a final standard is adopted by the FASB, but the commission expressed impatience with the FASB's timetable. The SEC directed its chief accountant to convey "a sense of urgency" to the FASB and encourage implementation of the proposal sooner.

The commissioners, approving the guidelines on a 4-0 vote with Commissioner Charles Cox absent, emphasized that the supplemental information on deferred taxes is encouraged, but not required, for 1986 financial statements. But under current law, publicly traded companies are required to address other potential effects of the new tax law in their 1986 financial reports.

Earlier this month, J. Roger Mentz, an assistant secretary at the Treasury Department, wrote to SEC Chairman John Shad asking for the commission's assistance in "persuading" the FASB to accelerate action on the proposed standard. Alternatively, Mr. Mentz wrote, the commission should require public companies to include pro forma disclosures on deferred income taxes in their 1986 financial statements.

FASB Is Expected to Issue Rule Allowing Many Firms to Post Big, One-Time Gains

By Lee Berton

November 1, 1987

NEW YORK—The Financial Accounting Standards Board is expected to issue a rule early next month that would allow many companies to report big, one-time profit gains.

The boosts would result from the recently changed tax law, which lowered the corporate tax rate to 40% this year and 34% thereafter, from 46%. At many corporations, that freed a large chunk of money that had been accumulated to pay deferred taxes at the former, higher rate.

The FASB likely will require that corporations adjust their deferred tax account this year, or in 1988 or 1989. Many companies that would benefit from the new tax rate say they will take the windfall this year.

In Stamford, Connecticut, James Leisenring, research director and a member of the seven-member FASB, said the chief rule-making body for accountants will likely issue a rule on deferred taxes the first half of next month. "I'd say the odds are 90% that the board will issue the rule because a lot of companies are anxious to see us move on this issue," Mr. Leisenring added.

"This FASB action could result in billions of dollars in reported profits for most major companies if the FASB issues its deferred-tax statement next month, and if the companies elect to make the rule effective this year," said Pat McConnell, an accountant and an associate director of Bear, Stearns & Co., a New York securities firm.

But some companies may hold off until next year or the year after "in fear that Congress will raise tax rates and force them to take a hit to profits next year for the earnings benefit they received this year," Ms. McConnell noted.

Bernard R. Doyle, manager of corporate accounting services for Fairfield, Connecticut–based General Electric Co., said that if the FASB issues the rule on deferred taxes, it would result in a "significant boost" in GE's reported profit. "But we still haven't decided whether to take the benefits this year or next," he added. "We first want to see what the FASB is going to do."

While many companies would benefit from the new rule, several banks and property and casualty insurance companies might have to report lower earnings. Banks and insurance companies are restricted from building up reserves for future taxes or for loan losses by regulators and by the tax law. The rationale is to prevent them from lowering their profits and thereby reducing their taxes.

Because many companies have built up huge deferred tax credits on their balance sheets over the past few years, the FASB rule, if enacted, would mean that many would get massive infusions to reported earnings. The proposal would require such companies to readjust reserves for future taxes using the lower tax rates.

At Ryder Systems Inc., a Miami-based vehicle leasing company, the rule would permit the company to add as much as $100 million, or $1.25 a share, to profit from the $518 million deferred tax credit on its balance sheet, says Terry Ashwill, senior vice president and controller.

For the first nine months of 1987, Ryder reported that net income after preferred dividends rose 21% to $138 million, or $1.73 a share, from a year earlier. In 1986, net was $156 million, or $2.09 a share, after preferred dividends.

"We'll likely take the benefit of the FASB ruling this year, even though we have a strong balance sheet and don't really need it," Mr. Ashwill said. "A lot of companies in heavy capital-intensive industries with weaker balance sheets will be jumping for joy." He said that many companies would have a chance to offset charges from restructuring and from "losses suffered in the stock market from investments in other companies."

Robert A. Orben, vice president and controller of Cummins Engine Co., which reported a loss of $107 million in 1986 after taking some write-offs in a corporate restructuring, said the rule could not boost the Columbus, Indiana–based company's profit 20% in 1989. "We've used up a lot of our deferred tax credits in special charges the past two years, so we don't have a reserve to draw from now," Mr. Orben points out. But he added, "If Congress doesn't increase taxes, the rule will be a big help to us the year after next, when we again build up the deferred tax credit on our balance sheet."

Large Insurance Firms, Banks Seeking Relief from Costly Accounting Proposal

By Lee Berton and Karen Slater

November 20, 1987

NEW YORK—Some large insurers and banks are seeking help from Congress and the Securities and Exchange Commission to sidestep an accounting proposal that would hurt their earnings.

The companies are seeking to generate additional pressure on the Financial Accounting Standards Board, the chief rule-making body for accountants.

So far, Sen. Robert Dole (R., Kansas) has agreed with the insurers, and has asked the SEC to examine the proposal's impact on the industry. Officials at the SEC, which also was contacted directly by the banks and insurers, declined to comment; the agency has the authority to establish accounting rules but prefers to defer to the private-sector FASB.

Some accountants warn an appeal to the government could set a dangerous precedent that might erode the private sector's ability to set its own accounting rules.

"Business can't have it both ways," said Arthur Wyatt, a partner of Chicago-based Arthur Andersen & Co., a major accounting firm. As previously reported, Mr. Wyatt recently quit the FASB in protest against what he perceives as the increasing power of business to influence that body's decisions.

The proposal expected to be adopted by the FASB next month would require all companies to adjust their balance sheets to reflect new, lower tax rates—40% this year and 34% thereafter compared with 46%. Many companies would get a profit boost because the change frees up a large chunk of money accumulated to pay deferred taxes at the higher rate.

But it would severely hurt property and casualty insurance companies and banks, whose earnings would be penalized because they generally haven't been able to build up such reserves.

Ms. Slater is a staff reporter of THE WALL STREET JOURNAL.

Currently asking for some relief from that measure are more than a dozen big insurance companies—led by American International Group Inc., Travelers Corp. and ITT Corp.'s Hartford Insurance Group—and the New York Clearing House Association, which represents 12 of the country's largest banks.

The FASB proposal is "grossly unfair" and would distort the reported earnings of insurers, said Howard I. Smith, senior vice president and comptroller at American International Group. Requesting assistance from Mr. Dole and other senators "was our last avenue, our last resort," said John R. Berthoud, vice president for corporate finance at Travelers, which heads the insurers' lobbying group on the issue.

But James Leisenring, an FASB member and research director, said the insurers and banks have had "plenty of opportunity to comment on this proposal," and are simply trying to "bypass the private sector standard-setting process."

When business leaders asked Congress in the past to influence accounting standards-setting, the resulting rules permitted companies to continue disparate accounting treatments, Mr. Leisenring said. And Congress in the mid-1950s passed legislation that overrode accounting standards and gave businesses great latitude in selecting when to reflect the investment tax credit on their financial statements, he noted.

FASB officials said they are moving quickly to issue the tax-rate rule because of increasing pressure from big manufacturers who want the option of showing the tax benefit as soon as possible. But "just because the FASB is moving quickly doesn't mean it is right," said Richard Belas, chief counsel for Mr. Dole, the Republican Senate minority leader and a presidential aspirant.

Ray Simpson, an FASB project manager, said the agency's response to an SEC inquiry—which in turn was prompted by Mr. Dole's letter—is slowing the tax-rule proposal. Originally, the FASB thought it would issue the final rule in the first week of December; it now believes the rule—first proposed last year—will be issued by the middle or end of the month, Mr. Simpson said.

Even among companies that will be hit by the accounting change, some oppose the decision to appeal to the SEC and Congress. For instance, Aetna Life & Casualty Co., an original member of the insurers' lobbying group, said it isn't participating in subsequent efforts. "I don't think it should be thrown into the public arena," said J. Heath Fitzsimmons, vice president and corporate comptroller for the largest stockholder-owned insurer.

If enacted, the proposal would permit adoption by companies either this year or in 1988; it would be mandatory by 1989. The change would officially be effective for fiscal years beginning after December 15, 1988, Mr. Simpson said.

FASB Proposes to Delay Rule on Tax Deferral

Accounting Board Responds to Protests about Cost in Fixing Balance Sheets

By Lee Berton

November 24, 1987

NEW YORK—The Financial Accounting Standards Board proposed delaying for a year a complex accounting rule on deferred taxes. The chief rule-making body for accountants acted after a storm of corporate criticism arose over the high costs of implementing the rule.

The rule would require companies each year to adjust liabilities on their balance sheets to reflect any new federal, state or local income tax rate, rather than use a uniform tax rate over a long period of time, as has been permitted.

And it would force companies to figure such liabilities for separate subsidiaries, separate tax jurisdictions and for each overseas operation. Previously, the company could estimate this liability on a consolidated basis.

Lee Seidler, senior managing director of Bear Stearns & Co., a major securities firm, said the FASB rule on deferred taxes "is violently controversial because it caused companies to expend such an enormous amount of effort for such little improvement in the quality of data."

Mr. Seidler, an accountant, continued: "By delaying this rule, the FASB is responding to a lot of angry and furious corporate chief financial officers and controllers."

Timothy Lucas, research director of the Norwalk, Connecticut-based FASB, said "there has been a lot of comment and some controversy" over the FASB's rule. He said that within the past week, at least 15 major corporations had suggested delaying it.

Issued in late 1987, the rule would have required companies to implement it for fiscal years beginning after December 15, 1988. But the FASB now has proposed delaying such implementation for fiscal years beginning after December 15, 1989. Interested parties have 30 days to comment on the proposal.

Mr. Lucas said the new rule was issued, because under the previous accounting treatment, huge unexplained liabilities were building up on corporate balance sheets. "The new rule, although complex, is a better reflection of current tax rates," he stated.

Gaylen Larson, group vice president and controller of Chicago-based Household International Inc., said the rule will cost the financial services company up to $300,000 in added labor costs to implement, mostly in additional computation time. "That's a one-time cost, but we also figure that it will cost an estimated $30,000 a year to put into effect," he said.

Mr. Larson said he was "shocked at the time requirements and complexity of the rule." He added: "Corporations just didn't have enough time to make sense of it and need more time." Mr. Larson is chairman of the committee on corporate reporting of the Financial Executives Institute.

Robert D. Buchanan, senior assistant controller of Aluminum Co. of America, said the deferred tax rule would require Pittsburgh-based Alcoa to add two people to its controller's staff because of the welter of complex and diverse data the company will have to collect in the future.

Mr. Buchanan, who is a member of a tax implementation task force of the FASB, said that his group had presented 150 complicated implementation questions to the standard-setting body. "For companies that have subsidiaries in various states and countries with differing tax rates, the rule creates a lot of implementation problems," Mr. Buchanan said.

The delay in implementing the rule is also something of a reprieve for banks and insurance companies, which had complained that the rule would generally force them to report lower profits in the future. Under previous accounting rules, banks and insurance companies could create balance-sheet assets that anticipated future tax deductions to be permitted by governments. The new rule would eliminate such assets, which in the past boosted reported earnings.

"Our thinking in this matter is that if a company can't be sure it will have future income, the deductions may not be worth anything down the road," said the FASB's Mr. Lucas.

CHAPTER 9

ACCOUNTING FOR POST-EMPLOYMENT BENEFITS OTHER THAN PENSIONS

On February 14, 1989, the FASB issued a 476-paragraph exposure draft on a new disclosure requirement that will, for the first time, require recognition for liability associated with retiree health benefits. The financial media has reported that liabilities amounting to $1 trillion could be added to corporate balance sheets as a result of this new requirement.

The requirement was originally an element of the FASB pension accounting project that began many years ago. It was broken off in order to deal with pension accounting requirements in a more efficient way due to the complexity of the pension accounting treatments. Some critics have raised the possibility that stock prices will erode as a result of booking this new, large liability—particularly for those corporations with older, labor-intensive work forces. Others counter that knowledgeable financial analysts have for years discounted the net worth of companies for their prospective liabilities and related cash outflows involving this type of health plan. Other voices maintain that the whole nature and structure of employee benefits program will change as a result of this new rigorous but theoretically consistent accounting requirement.

Accounting Board Seeks Footnote Rule on Firms' Post-Employment Insurance

By Lee Berton

July 5, 1984

NEW YORK—The Financial Accounting Standards Board proposed a rule that would require companies to disclose in footnotes to financial statements the costs of post-employment health and life insurance benefits.

Unlike pension costs, which are continually funded in advance by companies, post-employment insurance benefits generally are recorded only when they are paid. Many accountants consider post-employment insurance costs to be significant enough to be separately noted for investors.

The FASB, which is the accounting profession's rule-making body, hasn't proposed how to measure post-employment insurance benefits in advance. Moreover, the board said it may still decide to require companies to put the cost on the balance sheet. These decisions will be made later this year or in 1985, according to Betsy H. Cropsey, the board's project manager.

The board received a storm of protests last year when it proposed that the cost of future pension benefits be listed as a liability on corporate balance sheets. Many corporations and seven of the Big Eight accounting firms disagreed with the board's views. They said the proposed change, which is still being discussed, would increase reported liabilities substantially.

But some accountants believe the post-employment insurance-benefit issue could be much more explosive than the pension-benefit issue. "If the FASB decides to put a liability on the balance sheet for these post-employment benefits, it might be far bigger than the liability for pension costs," said Harold Dankner, a partner in Coopers & Lybrand, a Big Eight accounting firm.

Mr. Dankner said that post-employment insurance benefits, unlike pension benefits, aren't funded in advance. That means the potential liabilities are much greater than with pension benefits—perhaps as much as 100 times greater for some companies, Mr. Dankner said.

Last February, the board separated the post-employment benefit issue from the pension issue. Some accountants felt the FASB was spinning off the project so it could set less punitive rules for post-employment benefits.

But Tuesday's announcement by the board suggests this may not be so. The board said that this is an interim step, and that it will continue to study the appropriate measure of the employer's cost and obligation with respect to post-employment benefits. Comments on the proposal are due by September 21.

Under the FASB proposal, a company would be required to disclose in footnotes to financial statements issued for periods ending after December 15, 1984, data on health care and life insurance benefits in the United States and overseas. If unavailable for foreign operations, the information may be disclosed by June 15, 1985.

The footnotes would include a description of the post-employment benefits, the cost of benefits included on the income statement for the period and a description of the current accounting and funding policies for those benefits.

The board and its staff have been discussing requiring companies to accrue or accumulate in advance the costs of such post-employment benefits, as has long been done for pension costs.

Meanwhile, in the pension area, the board has been discussing alternatives to its balance-sheet proposal, particularly since hearing so many complaints on that proposal at a five-day hearing last January.

One alternative would place a company's net unfunded, vested pension benefits on the balance sheet. That approach, unlike the board's initial views on pension accounting, wouldn't take salary increases in future years into account. "For most companies, this would reduce the liability on the balance sheet," said Melvin Penner, a partner with Arthur Young & Co., a Big Eight accounting firm.

Eugene H. Flegm, deputy assistant controller for General Motors Corp., said that this alternative treatment would have put only $100 million on the giant auto maker's balance sheet for 1983. "The pension-cost treatment initially proposed by the FASB would have created a liability much greater than that," he said.

Accounting Board Sets New Disclosure Rule for Certain Benefits

By a Wall Street Journal Staff Reporter

November 12, 1984

NEW YORK—The Financial Accounting Standards Board, as expected, approved a rule that requires companies to disclose in footnotes to financial statements the costs of post-employment health and life-insurance benefits.

The board last February decided to separate the question of disclosing health and life-insurance benefits from a broader pension-benefit study because it believed more research was needed on recognizing and measuring pension costs before deciding whether to place them on the balance sheet.

Under the new rule, the footnotes would describe the health and life-insurance benefits, spell out their costs for the period and describe accounting and funding policies for these benefits. The figures wouldn't appear in the balance sheet.

The disclosure rule, effective for financial statements issued for periods ending after December 15, is the same as a July proposal by the board except that it excludes health and life-insurance plans contributed to by more than one employer and administered by a union. "The availability of data for such multiemployer plans in the construction and trucking industries is questionable," according to the board.

If data on health and insurance benefits are unavailable for foreign operations, the new rule extends disclosure of them to June 15.

FASB Plan Would Make Firms Deduct Billions for Potential Retiree Benefits

By Lee Berton

August 17, 1988

NEW YORK—Accounting standard setters will soon propose a controversial rule that would require companies to deduct billions of dollars from earnings each year for potential medical and insurance benefits for retired employees.

Because the coming proposal by the Financial Accounting Standards Board could markedly reduce corporate earnings, a storm of protest is expected from industry, say accountants and corporate executives.

The proposal will probably be issued for public comment in September or October. A final rule would be promulgated in late 1989.

The proposal would require all U.S. companies to treat as a current expense each year a portion of the expected cost of post-retirement medical, insurance and certain other benefits for every employee, regardless of the employee's age or length of service. Currently, companies deduct such costs from profits only when benefits are actually paid to retired employees. The measure would take effect for fiscal years beginning after December 15, 1991.

The proposal would also require companies to create a reserve for benefits for retirees and active employees eligible for retirement under company plans. The reserve would be a liability on the balance sheet. That part of the proposal would take effect for fiscal years beginning after December 15, 1993.

The vast majority of companies don't set aside money for post-retirement medical, insurance and other benefits—as they do for pension funds—because such prefunding isn't deductible from taxable income. Pension fund contributions are deductible from a corporation's taxable income.

The FASB proposal would result in "a horror show for corporate earnings," says Lee Seidler, an accountant and senior managing director of Bear Stearns & Co., a major securities firm.

"If Congress doesn't act, which it likely won't because another deductible expense would only add to the [federal] deficit, companies may have to move quickly to gear down or eliminate such benefits," says Mr. Seidler. He adds that the FASB will be under enormous pressure to ease the impact of such a proposal.

Many companies say that reducing such benefits would infuriate unions and that unless they get relief from Congress, they may have to consider raising prices for their products. "There's no doubt that this FASB proposal leaves us between a rock and a hard place," says the benefits manager for a major manufacturing company.

While many companies aren't sure exactly how much the proposal would cost them because the FASB hasn't tied down all the criteria, such companies as Du Pont Co., Bethlehem Steel Corp., Ford Motor Co. and Aluminum Co. of America concede that it would raise their post-retirement benefit costs by tens of millions of dollars. The Labor Department estimates that the total size of the unfunded liability for such costs amounts to about $2 trillion.

The proposal is still being fine-tuned by the FASB staff, though, and it may be greatly changed after the FASB holds hearings on the measure next year.

Diana Scott, a project manager for the Norwalk, Connecticut–based FASB, says the proposal was made because "we reason that if a company makes a promise to pay certain benefits, it should begin accruing or reserving for such expenses." She says that the FASB recognizes the potential controversy and will test 25 companies later this year to see the economic impact of the proposal.

Earlier this year, the FASB staff eased some aspects of the proposal and delayed the target dates for implementation. Under the original plan, the entire proposal would have taken effect in 1991.

But even with the easing, which could reduce annual costs an average of 15%, the total impact will still be "very significant on corporate earnings," says Harold Dankner, a partner of

Coopers & Lybrand, the accounting firm that is conducting the 25-company test.

Mr. Dankner estimates that the proposal could raise post-retirement medical and insurance costs for most companies four to six times their current annual expenses for such benefits. "The final impact will depend on just how the rule comes out, and on the current costs and employee population of each company," he says. "We're already being flooded by inquiries from many major companies as to how [the board] can do this."

Towers, Perrin, Forster & Crosby, a New York benefits consultant, says that many companies are considering reducing dollar benefits, eliminating or paring down coverage for retirees' spouses and using more designated health providers such as health maintenance organizations.

Herbert Nehrling, assistant treasurer of Du Pont in Wilmington, Delaware, says the big chemical company is taking "a long, hard look at post-retirement medical benefits" as a result of the proposal. "While we have to keep down such costs for business reasons because they have been spiraling each year, this new accounting proposal gives us another reason to be more prudent," he says.

He adds that it will be difficult for Du Pont to reduce such benefits "because the issues are so big, expensive and emotional." He estimates that the proposal could double or triple Du Pont's annual $160 million bill for medical and other post-retirement benefits.

Lonnie Arnett, vice president and controller of Bethlehem Steel, Bethlehem, Pennsylvania, says that the reduction in profits resulting from the FASB proposal "would be a big number for us" and "in some bad years could completely wipe out reported earnings."

Robert D. Buchanan, a senior assistant controller for Alcoa in Pittsburgh, says the FASB proposal could raise Alcoa's annual costs for post-employment medical and other benefits by "tens of millions of dollars, depending on where it finally comes out next year."

In Detroit, Daniel Coulson, accounting director for Ford Motor, says the FASB proposal "could increase our existing post-employment medical benefit costs in the United States and Canada by multiples." In 1987 Ford paid $341 million for such expenses.

But few companies are willing to pinpoint such expected increased costs exactly. "We've done some figuring on the back of an envelope and we don't want to issue any figures right now because we don't want to alarm our investors or employees," says the controller of a major manufacturing company that prefers to remain anonymous.

CHAPTER 10

PENSION ACCOUNTING

As the United States economy has matured, an increasing portion of employee compensation has been allocated away from the paycheck and into what we loosely call "benefits." One of the key growth areas in employee benefits over the last 50 years is in pension plans. Once the province of top management, the pension plan is now a given element for the vast majority of employees in the United States. Pension liability, on a long-term basis, has increased to a point where it is material in relation to the net worth of the business. The accounting profession has tried to deal with the issue of pension accounting for over four decades. The primary difficulty was the treatment of pension costs as a pay-as-you-go expense with no long-term liability for the entity. In addition, many companies were reporting an asset in their balance sheet for pension funds that had accrued without reporting the related liability for pension funds that would be disbursed prospectively.

After 10 years of study, the FASB issued Statement No. 87, "Employers Accounting for Pensions." This was a landmark accounting standard affecting virtually all United States corporations. For the first time it created a consistent disclosure for this important balance sheet element. It should be noted that a new and related exposure draft on other post-employment benefits, disseminated on February 14, 1989, is the final segment of the original pension project involving benefits to the employee after the employee ceases work at the accepted retirement age. Many have commented that this cost, that was treated as an off-balance sheet liability for many years, will also materially affect corporate balance sheets, especially those of older, labor-intensive corporations.

FASB Proposal on Pension Accounting Seen under Fire at Hearings Next Week

By Lee Berton

January 5, 1984

NEW YORK—The Financial Accounting Standards Board is about to hear some loud griping about its proposal to change how companies account for pension plans.

For five days starting next Wednesday, more than 60 corporate financial executives and accountants will troop before FASB officials at hearings here. Most of those who appear will be complaining about the pension accounting proposal.

Never has the FASB, the accounting profession's rule-making body, encountered such opposition from its corporate constituency. Seven of the Big Eight accounting firms also disagree with the FASB on pension accounting; only Arthur Andersen & Co. goes along.

The problem for most companies is that although they currently deduct pension expenses from profit on their income statement, they don't have to label projected pension costs as a liability on their balance sheets. If the FASB adopts its current view, such projected costs would show up as debt on the balance sheet, eroding corporate debt-to-equity ratios.

That could hurt companies' standing with financial analysts and banks, and make it harder for them to borrow money.

The FASB hopes to put out a draft on pension accounting this year, with a final rule scheduled for 1985. "There are a range of views, and our minds aren't closed," says Donald Kirk, FASB chairman.

Plan's Supporters

Proponents of the change say future pension liabilities are a commitment that ought to be on balance sheets. David F. Hawkins, an accounting professor at Harvard Graduate School of Business and a member of the FASB's advisory council, said the

FASB's pension proposals would give investors a much clearer view of a company's commitments to its employees.

"The financial risk (connected with pension commitments) should be of great concern in assessing equity values," Mr. Hawkins explains.

But the ruling's opponents say these commitments aren't debt. "The FASB is wrong because that liability has no reality in fact," says Paul B. Lukens, vice president and controller of Cigna Corp., a Philadelphia-based financial-services concern. "It would be like recording next year's salaries as current debt."

The FASB proposal also limits the way companies can calculate the pension expenses deducted from profit. Currently, companies use one of several actuarial methods; the FASB rule allows only one method.

Rise in Costs Seen

"Ironically this could increase actuarial costs and create unnecessary work," says Harvey D. Moskowitz, national director of accounting and auditing for Seidman & Seidman, the 12th largest CPA firm. Some companies may use the required FASB method for reporting to their shareholders, but their old system for reporting to the Internal Revenue Service. This could double their actuarial fees, an actuary says.

Eugene H. Flegm, deputy assistant controller for General Motors Corp., says he opposes the FASB's proposal because it would cause gains and losses from the investment of pension assets to fluctuate more than they do now. That is because under the new system, companies would have to assess each gain or loss at market value rather than use an actuarial method that evens out the short-term fluctuations.

So far, says Harold Dankner, a partner in Coopers & Lybrand, a Big Eight accounting firm, none of his firm's clients has changed pension-investment strategies to blunt the possible adoption of the FASB proposal.

"Some companies may switch from stocks into bonds to assume a higher rate of return and smooth their earnings stream, and lose out in a bull stock market," he says. "And others may move into stocks and get clobbered when the market goes down and their portfolio is reassessed at its present value under the FASB proposal."

FASB Issues Second Proposal for Pensions

Plan Would Require Listing of Funds as a Liability by about 20% of Firms

By Lee Berton

March 22, 1985

NEW YORK—The Financial Accounting Standards Board issued a revised pension-fund accounting proposal that would require only about 20% of major U.S. corporations to put pension costs on their balance sheets as a liability.

Under the new rule, accountants note that labor-intensive companies, such as steel, auto and tire makers, would have to log the biggest balance-sheet liabilities.

Meanwhile, investment bankers predicted that the proposal, if adopted, could have a long-term healthful effect for the bond market.

Like the FASB's first proposal, issued in 1982, the current one would affect only those companies whose current pension liabilities aren't covered by assets such as individual and corporate contributions, and investment income. The chief difference between the two proposals is in the figuring of pension-fund costs.

The first proposal would have required almost all big companies to factor in employees' future salary increases as part of pension costs. That would have sharply boosted debt, eroded debt-to-equity ratios, and hurt companies' standing with financial analysts and banks, making it harder for them to borrow money, observers say.

As a result, it was strongly opposed by most companies and

by seven of the Big 8 accounting firms; only Arthur Andersen & Co., the biggest, went along.

But the latest proposal only includes current employees' salaries in the liability, and thus would reduce the size of the liability significantly, according to accountants.

"The FASB has backed off its views and this should make most companies quietly accept the latest proposal," says Pat McConnell, who writes an accounting newsletter for Bear Stearns & Co., a securities firm.

Currently, all companies deduct pension expenses from profit on their income statements, but don't have to record these costs as liabilities on their balance sheets.

'Smokestack' Industries Affected

Eugene Flegm, assistant controller for General Motors Corp. in Detroit, said in an interview that the latest FASB proposal would most affect companies in "smokestack industries."

FASB's Planned Rule Would Produce One-Time Profit Boosts at Many Firms

By Lee Berton

June 12, 1985

NEW YORK—The Financial Accounting Standards Board later this week will propose an accounting rule that would provide a big one-time boost to profits of many companies taking cash out of their employee pension funds.

That prospect has some corporate financial officials delighted. But others fear that the fat windfalls might cause distorted earnings perceptions among unsophisticated investors.

Under current accounting rules, in order for companies to get such one-time gains, they must switch from a defined-benefit to a defined-contribution pension plan. The new proposal would require taking the one-time gain regardless of whether the company stays with a defined-benefit plan.

In a defined-benefit plan, a company spells out exactly how much an employee will receive on retirement. In a defined-contribution plan, the company specifies only its annual contribution to the plan.

In recent years, as interest rates have climbed, pension plans have accumulated more money than they need to pay future benefits. Companies with such overfunded plans have withdrawn excess cash to use for other purposes, closed original plans and started new ones with just enough assets to meet future commitments.

Companies keeping defined-benefit plans under current accounting have had to amortize gains from cash overfunding over at least 10 years. Thus, for a $10 million gain, pre-tax profit would rise $1 million a year. The FASB proposal would require a company to take such a $10 million gain in the year in which the pension plan is switched, no matter which type of plan replaces it.

The Pension Benefit Guaranty Corp., the government agency that insures corporate defined-benefit pension plans, supports the FASB proposal because it feels the current rule induces companies to switch to defined-contribution pension plans.

If investments of defined-contribution plans do poorly, then a pensioner would receive less; a defined-benefit plan guarantees fixed pension benefits, no matter how the plan's investments fare.

Under current accounting rules, companies wishing to pump up earnings in one year were switching to defined-contribution from defined-benefit plans so they could take the gain from the plan's overfunding into pre-tax profits in one year. The current rule permits companies that switch to different plans to take the gain into pre-tax profits the first year.

Some companies like the new rule because they welcome the profit infusion. "We support the FASB's proposal because we feel the gain is real and immediate," says an official in the controller's department of Firestone Tire & Rubber Co. in Akron, Ohio. Last May 1, Firestone replaced an overfunded pension plan with another plan and recorded a $260 million gain.

Currently, Firestone would have to spread that gain over at least 10 years. If the FASB decides to adopt the proposal after receiving public comment, Firestone could recognize the gain in the first year.

But other companies oppose the proposal because they feel the one-time profit boost doesn't accurately reflect the company's real business. "We strongly oppose the new FASB proposal because an unsophisticated investor might think that the big jump in profit comes from selling products or services," says Richard A. Gulling, vice president, finance, and treasurer of Timken Co., a Canton, Ohio–based bearings maker.

Timken has asked Pension Benefit Guaranty for permission to terminate its old overfunded defined-benefit pension plan and switch to another defined-benefit plan. Mr. Gulling estimates that the gain to Timken would range from $90 million to $100 million. "We should have a decision within the next two weeks," Mr. Gulling says.

When companies switch from defined-benefit to defined-contribution plans to pump up profits, they are removed from the jurisdiction of Pension Benefit Guaranty and lose insurance protection. "About 350 companies with 300,000 pension plan participants moved out of PBGC jurisdiction since January 1, 1980," by shifting to defined-contribution plans, says David Walker, acting executive director, in Washington. Current insurance protection amounts to a maximum of $1,687.50 a month per pension-plan participant.

Tim Lucas, an FASB project manager, notes that under current accounting rules some companies that want the big one-time profit gain while keeping defined-benefit pension plans have temporarily switched to defined-contribution pension plans and then back to defined-benefit plans. Stroh Brewery Co., a closely held Detroit company, recently did that.

"We'd really like to keep this out of the newspaper because we don't want to get our unions all upset," says David V. Van Howe, a Stroh vice president and secretary. He declined to specify the one-time gain in cash taken from the previous overfunded plan.

Mr. Lucas says comments on the proposal are due by August

31. The FASB will hold hearings on several pension accounting changes, including this new proposal, from July 22 to 24 and on August 1 and 2.

FASB Is Expected to Issue New Rules Next Month on Pension Plan Accounting

By Lee Berton

November 27, 1985

The Financial Accounting Standards Board next month is expected to issue new rules on pension accounting. The rules have been eased in certain respects to meet objections of many companies.

The standard-setting body for accountants yesterday instructed the FASB staff to issue two important rules. "We are very hopeful that we can issue both these standards either just before or after Christmas," Timothy S. Lucas, an FASB project manager, said.

One rule would reduce the volatility of corporate earnings and would reduce some disclosures in current proposals. But it will continue to require about 20% of U.S. companies to post a bigger liability on their balance sheets for pension costs.

Earnings volatility would be reduced by the way the new rule would compute a company's return on assets from its pension plan. The current proposal values a plan's assets at their market price. The new plan would use a complex, market-related formula that would lessen the effects of any swings in market prices. Many companies had complained that the current rule made earnings unrealistically volatile.

A controversial aspect of the new rule that wasn't eased is a requirement that companies use one accepted actuarial method to measure pension costs, rather than a variety of methods. Corporations had complained that switching to a new method would be expensive, inflexible and confusing for stock analysts and investors.

An earlier draft of the rule would have required companies to place on the balance sheet pension cost liabilities based on future salary increases for employees. The final version bases the liability on current salaries of employees and therefore places, in most cases, a much smaller liability on the balance sheet.

However, many labor-intensive companies, such as makers of steel, autos and tires, still would have to log the biggest increases in liabilities under the final version.

The FASB also plans to issue a second rule that would require companies taking cash out of their pension plans to record a one-time gain.

Both rules would be effective for financial reports issued for calendar year 1987. The provision for placing the new liability on the balance sheet would be delayed until 1989.

Accounting Proposal Troubles Firms

Pension Rule Would Boost
Reported Liabilities

By Lee Berton

December 6, 1985

NEW YORK—Corporate financial executives are fuming about a controversial pension-accounting rule that the Financial Accounting Standards Board is expected to issue soon.

They say the proposed rule is vexing on two counts: It would burden corporate balance sheets by placing a hefty new liability on the books, and it would make bottom-line financial results more volatile. Thus, some companies would have a harder time raising capital, these executives argue.

"The FASB is wrong, it is moving too fast, and it should have left well enough alone in pension accounting," asserts Gary Millenbruch, a senior vice president of Bethlehem Steel Corp., which would be adversely affected by the rule.

"We concede that many companies would still prefer the status quo," says Timothy Lucas, a project manager for the FASB, the rule-making body for accountants. But he says the rule would better reflect "economic reality" by more accurately disclosing the real cost of current obligations.

Ruling Expected Soon
After three years of hearings and deliberation, the FASB expects to issue the rule later this month. "The board has given the staff a go-ahead, and we only have to iron out some minor points in the proposal," Mr. Lucas says.

Under the rule, companies with unfunded pension costs based on employees' current pay would have to put the liabilities on their balance sheets by the end of 1989. A pension fund is said to be underfunded when contributions and the fund's investment income aren't enough to cover expected benefit payments.

The FASB is encouraging companies to apply the rule earlier than 1989, but it's expected that those with large unfunded pension liabilities won't bite the bullet until the last moment.

The size of these reported liabilities would have been even greater under FASB's initial proposal, which would have based a company's pension obligations on expected future pay increases. But the initial proposal was relaxed after it generated more opposition from industry than any proposed accounting rule in the board's 13-year history. Seven of the eight biggest U.S. accounting firms opposed it; only Arthur Andersen & Co., the biggest U.S. accounting firm, supported it.

Some companies in heavy industries such as autos, steel and tires believe that despite the relaxation, the current proposal still spells trouble for them.

"It's poor accounting and assumes we're momentarily going to go out of business, which anyone knows couldn't be further from the truth," says Eugene H. Flegm, assistant controller of General Motors Corp., which had an unfunded pension liability of \$2.57 billion at the end of 1984. The figure wasn't reflected on GM's balance sheet but was disclosed in its annual report.

Mr. Flegm says the auto maker has more than \$18 billion in cash and securities in its pension fund and "could meet its pension obligations for the next 15 years if we didn't put another cent in the fund."

Why then, asks Mr. Flegm, should GM have to burden its balance sheet with the new pension liability?

Mr. Lucas says the FASB believes that "an unfunded accumulated liability" for pension costs is "a present obligation based on employees' past services." Just because GM can meet its pension payments to retirees over the next 15 years "doesn't change the fact that it has present pension obligations for such payments to all its employees that must be made after the year 2000," Mr. Lucas says.

The FASB set the four-year phase-in period to cushion the rule's effects. But some financial executives in depressed smokestack industries argue that boosting liabilities simply by a bookkeeping change is like kicking them when they're down.

The rule "will hit us at a most inopportune time," says Charles M. Hines, a vice president and controller of Kaiser Aluminum & Chemical Corp. The company has incurred sizable losses the past four years, and in the nine months ended September 30 it had a loss of \$50.4 million.

Kaiser "needs some breathing room over the next few years to restructure itself, and added debt on the balance sheet will simply make us look worse" to investors and lenders, says Mr. Hines.

Effect on Financial Ratios
Norman Weinger, a senior vice president of Oppenheimer & Co., a securities firm that has analyzed prospective effects of the proposed rule, agrees. "The added liability isn't happy news for heavy industrial companies with underfunded pension accounts," Mr. Weinger says. It will "impair several key financial ratios that analysts and bankers use to judge a company's potential for growth and leverage," he adds.

Wall Street analysts also say that market prices for these

companies' shares often don't reflect the huge unfunded pension liabilities that could undermine their financial structures. The stock market is often unaware of these liabilities, says Thornton O'glove, publisher of the *Quality of Earnings Report*.

The proposed rule also limits the period over which a company can charge off unfunded pension obligations. Such costs are typically incurred when a pension plan is initiated or improved. Currently, the costs can be deducted from profits over as much as 30 years. Under the proposed rule, the charge-off period is limited to the average remaining service period of employees or 15 years, whichever is greater. This part of the rule would take effect beginning with financial reports for calendar 1987.

For many heavily unionized companies, which typically have liberal pension plans, this change could cut profits or increase losses. Kaiser, for example, estimates that if the proposed rule were effective today, it would boost the company's expected pretax loss for 1985 by between 15% and 25%. As a result of the rule, pension costs of Reynolds Metals Co., a Richmond, Virginia-based aluminum producer, are expected to rise, reducing profits, says David Bilsing, controller.

Greater Volatility Seen
The other major complaint by companies is that the rule would increase the volatility of financial results. The latest proposal tries to ease such volatility by computing a return on pension assets under a complex formula that would lessen the effect of current changes in the assets' value.

But the rule still would have a yo-yo effect because it would require the pension benefit account to reflect current interest rates rather than an assumed constant interest rate, the current practice, say Wall Street stock analysts. Patricia McConnell, an associate director of Bear, Stearns & Co., estimates that under the proposed rule, a one-point decline in interest rates would boost pension expenses for some companies by more than 20%. "When the interest rate yield drops, under the new rule companies will have to fork up more money to meet required pension obligations," Ms. McConnell says.

"The FASB is trying to force us to put funny numbers on our

Unfunded Pension Liabilities

	Dollar Amount (in millions)[1]	Percent of Shared Value[2]
General Motors	$2,573	11.18%
Ford Motor	2,170	20.74
Chrysler	721	13.95
LTV Corp.	496	84.42
American Motors	469	148.33
Bethlehem Steel	209	24.78
Kaiser Aluminum	185	24.84
Reynolds Metals	181	24.31
Champion Spark Plug	77	23.25

[1]As of December 31, 1984
[2]As of market close December 4, 1985

Source: *Oppenheimer & Co.*

profit-and-loss statements and our balance sheets," asserts Paul E. Boehk, controller of Champion Spark Plug Co., Toledo, Ohio. "We'd be a lot happier if the rule makers went back to square one and reconsidered this rule."

The FASB's Mr. Lucas says that changes in significant accounting areas such as pension costs usually meet resistance from industry. "But we feel that under the new rule, financial statements will more accurately reflect the real economic costs of pension plans rather than the amount a company happens to have chosen to fund the plan during one year," he says.

FASB Issues Pension-Accounting Rule Despite Protests from Industrial Firms

By Lee Berton

December 27, 1985

NEW YORK—After three years of discussion, the Financial Accounting Standards Board issued its proposed rule on pension accounting that has been criticized by many companies in basic manufacturing industries.

The rule will require about 20% of public companies, mostly in heavily unionized industries, to increase the reported liabilities on their balance sheets, making raising additional financing more difficult. Companies in heavy industries such as steel and autos are particularly upset with the rule, which they say will harm their standing in the finance and banking community over the next three years while they are trying to emerge from their profit slump.

The major provisions of the rule, which were modified in response to some company objections, have been known for several weeks. The rule will require companies with unfunded pension costs, resulting in underfunded pension plans, to record liabilities representing such costs on their balance sheets by the end of 1989.

A pension plan is said to be underfunded when contributions and the funds' investment income aren't enough to cover expected benefit payments.

The rule also requires use of a uniform actuarial method to calculate pension costs, beginning with 1987 reports, and increased disclosure of some other pension-plan elements.

The proposal for the rule was issued in late 1982, bringing hostile reactions from many public companies. The FASB held three public hearings on the issue.

Donald J. Kirk, FASB chairman, said the final rule was passed this month by a 4-3 vote, reflecting its controversial nature. But despite the close vote on the rule, he said, the full seven-member board agreed that the current pension cost reporting system doesn't require adequate disclosure.

After the rule was proposed, the FASB received more than 400 protests from companies and from major accounting and actuarial firms. Their main argument was that the current method of accounting for pension costs, under which actual outlays are deducted from profits each year, already provides adequate disclosure.

Since then, the FASB has eased the rule by basing the required calculation of pension-cost liability on employees' current salaries rather than projected future salaries. In addition, the rule now permits companies to measure returns on pension-plan assets by using average annual yields. The initial plan was to require the returns to be calculated precisely each quarter, which would have increased the volatility of reported profits.

But major companies in heavy industry, which have far larger unfunded pension liabilities than companies in service and many other industries, are still unhappy with the final rule.

"Given all the opposition expressed about the new standard, we question whether this does constitute generally accepted accounting principles," a spokesman for Bethlehem Steel Corp. said yesterday. "The present accounting rules are not all that bad, and we feel that industry would be better served without the adoption of this new rule."

A Ford Motor Co. executive said yesterday that the auto maker had opposed the pension accounting rule and "still doesn't like the change." He said, "As a going concern, the liability (for unfunded pension costs) doesn't exist." Ford, like some other companies, has contended that the change will make financial statements more difficult to read.

Officials of General Motors Co. and Chrysler Corp. couldn't be reached for comment because of the holiday vacation taken by the auto industry.

Some critics also say adopting the required uniform actuarial method for measuring pension costs will cause unnecessary expense as companies change over from the current collection of perhaps a dozen methods used in various industries.

W. Bruce Thomas, chief financial officer at U.S. Steel Corp., said the company has objected to the plan several times because it is complicated as well as "restrictive in terms of how pension expense is calculated." However, he said the new rule won't result in U.S. Steel having to book a liability, "because our pension plan is so well-funded."

But FASB staff members say the new rule will permit measurement of the true economic costs of pensions and allow better comparisons of the impact of pension costs within and across industries.

Profit Volatility Rises after Rule Change

Some Earnings Said 'Created' by Bookkeeping

By Lee Berton

May 6, 1986

Last December, just before the Financial Accounting Standards Board issued new pension-accounting rules, financial executives warned that the regulations would make corporate earnings more volatile.

Initially that volatility often has meant increased rather than depressed earnings.

But critics of the new pension-accounting rules, which now also include many pension and other investment managers are fretting about a broader array of potential ramifications. In addition to earnings volatility, they are also warning that the new rules could:

• Spur more companies to reduce funding for pension plans, endangering employee benefits during economic downturns and times when pension fund investments do poorly.
• Eventually push some pension funds out of equities and into bonds to assure a safer and more predictable return on investments. By the end of the decade this could prove to be a stimulant for the bond market and a depressing factor for the stock market.

Among other things, the new rules permit many companies to pump up reported earnings. Companies can recognize gains from favorable investment performances of pension plans much sooner than under previous rules. Because the stock market had a healthy run-up late last year, many pension plans are currently bulging with money.

For example, at the end of 1985, Du Pont Co.'s pension fund had $3.6 billion more than it needed to meet pension obligations, and Manufacturers Hanover Corp.'s was overfunded by $240 million. Both companies converted those extra funds into profits.

But some investment specialists question the quality of such profits, compared with dollars earned from operations.

"The rules will make it difficult for investors to separate real earnings from created earnings," says Patricia McConnell, an associate director at Bear, Stearns & Co. "That's because these few 'pension-rule' profits result from new bookkeeping entries and aren't really money in the bank," says Ms. McConnell, an accountant.

Pump Up Annual Earnings

Most of the rules issued by the FASB, the chief rule-making body for accountants, must be applied by companies beginning in 1987. But because companies also can adopt them for 1985 and 1986 results, many with overfunded pension plans have decided to boost reported profits as soon as possible.

In 1985, for example, the new rules permitted a host of major companies, including Du Pont, Manufacturers Hanover, Marine Midland Banks Inc., Phillips Petroleum Co. and Morrison-Knudsen Co. to pump up annual earnings by whopping amounts. All five noted that money had been building up in their pension funds and that this was an appropriate time to recognize that in earnings.

If companies elect to adopt these rules in 1986, earnings gains have to be applied separately for each quarter. American Telephone & Telegraph Co., for example, boosted first-quarter per-share net income 24% to 47 cents a share by lowering pension expenses via adoption of the rules; without application of

1985 Profit Gains from FASB Accounting Rules			
	Total 1985 Earnings Per Share	*Portion from FASB Pension Accounting Rules*	*% Increase of Per-Share Net from Rules*
Morrison-Knudsen	$3.84	$1.49	63%
Marine Midland	6.06	1.50	33
Phillips Petroleum	1.44	0.29	25
Du Pont	4.61	0.65	16
Manufacturers Hanover	8.38	0.86	11

Source: *Bear, Stearns & Co.*

the rules, net would have been 38 cents a share. AT&T will have similar quarterly gains the rest of the year, says Rosemary McGovern, division manager for accounting policies.

But AT&T says its $100 million extra first-quarter profit shouldn't be considered cash earnings by regulators, who might want to offset the gain against phone-rate increases. AT&T's total earnings for the quarter was $530 million.

"The extra nine cents a share simply isn't cash in the house," concedes Ms. McGovern. "It just represents a difference in timing for recognizing pension expenses."

At Manufacturers Hanover, "The new pension rules simply permit us to take into earnings sooner money we already had gained from our pension plan," says Eugene McQuade, a senior vice president.

Bear Stearns's Ms. McConnell says the FASB should have left the former pension-accounting rules in place. She is particularly critical of a change that forces a company to switch its interest rate assumptions for pension earnings each year rather than use a hypothetical rate that smooths fund gains or losses over a long period of time.

"It'll only cause earnings to yo-yo all over the lot," she says.

Reflecting Reality

The FASB asserts that the rules are more reflective of economic reality. "If a company has significant delayed gains in its pension plans, we feel that those gains should be recognized sooner rather than stretched out over a long time," says Joan Amble, a FASB project manager. "We're trying to better reflect in today's financial results what's happening to pension fund assets right now."

Many pension benefits consultants worry that if companies eliminate their plans' "safety cushion" of overfunding, they will have less leeway in the future to boost fund benefits or to cover existing pension obligations. "An economic downturn and lower returns on pension fund assets could easily threaten the economic viability of many corporate pension funds without such cushions," cautions Lawrence Margel, the chief actuary for Towers, Perrin, Forster & Crosby, a benefits consulting firm.

Manufacturers Hanover, Marine Midland, Morrison-Knudsen, Du Pont and Phillips Petroleum say that the current health of their pension funds provides a sufficient buffer for future downturns.

Sealed Power Corp., a Muskegon, Michigan, auto parts maker, has reduced its funding for pensions by early adherence to the FASB rules. "Our plan for more than 6,000 employees is overfunded by $22 million, so we feel we have enough of a cushion to lower our funding," says Benjamin F. Cayce, Sealed Power's senior vice president, finance. "We feel our employees are well protected for the future as far as their pensions are concerned."

Liability on Balance Sheets

The new pension rules also require that, effective in 1989, companies with underfunded plans put a liability on their balance sheets. A plan is underfunded when its obligations exceed its assets. This will hurt heavy industries, such as automobile and steelmakers, most. That's because powerful unions there have obtained bigger pension fund benefits through collective bargaining over the years.

The liability provision also could eventually depress the

stock market, some experts say. "While most pension plans are overfunded today, that could easily change in the future with a stock market and interest rate downturn," warns Mr. Margel of Towers Perrin.

Sandy Lincoln, a vice president at A.S. Hansen Inc., a Deerfield, Illinois, benefits consulting firm, says that fear of having such a liability will convince some companies to drop common stock investments for bonds, which have an assured annual return.

"The new rules are encouraging the safe and sure path of fixed income rather than the risky but generally more lucrative investment of common stock," he adds.

Accounting Rule Seeking More Data on Pension Irks Public Retirement Plans

By Lee Berton

December 5, 1986

NEW YORK—Public-employee retirement systems are upset over a new Governmental Accounting Standards Board rule that requires states, cities and towns to disclose more pension data.

The retirement systems argue that the rule will be costly and confusing and will make their pension funding look better than it really is.

But the GASB maintains that the recently issued rule will make it easier for analysts to compare the pension data of diverse government entities at a "minimal cost." The GASB is the chief maker of accounting rules for governmental bodies.

New York state is "concerned about the rule because it could lead legislators, employee groups and unions to seek added employment benefits that we simply can't afford," said John Mauhs, a deputy state controller heading the state's retirement division.

The actuarial method mandated by the new GASB rule generally produces a smaller unfunded pension liability than the actuarial methods currently used by public pension funds. An unfunded liability is the amount by which a pension plan's obligations exceed its assets.

Two Reporting Forms

The new rule requires state and local government employers and public-employee retirement systems to disclose their unfunded pension liability a certain way—using one specific actuarial technique picked by the GASB. But, in addition, it allows the retirement systems to continue to use—and to also report— a different method to determine how much money they actually contribute to the pension plan.

Thus the new rule, in many cases, will require a government body to report its unfunded pension liability in two ways— reflecting how the plan is actually funded, and how the obligation would be measured under the new GASB rule's method.

"There's no question this rule is controversial," says Martin Ives, the vice chairman and director of research of the GASB in Stamford, Connecticut. "But public pension funds currently use up to a dozen different funding and reporting methods. And financial analysts find it impossible to compare them when considering which government securities to buy."

Significantly, even James F. Antonio, the current chairman of the GASB and former state auditor of Missouri, opposed the new rule. While he supports a single way of disclosing the pension obligation of government entities, he believes the disclosure should better reflect the actuarial measurement systems used by most of these entities.

Costs and Advantages

Vernon Strickland, president of the National Association of State Retirement Administrators, says that most states oppose the GASB rule because it "imposes another layer for their disclosure."

David Senn, executive secretary of the Montana Teacher's Retirement System in Helena, estimates that the added disclosure could cost the state "an extra $6,000 every other year, when we issue our reports." He added: "It will make us appear over-funded, which we aren't, and it just isn't worth it."

But the GASB's Mr. Ives said that despite current opposition, the rule will greatly improve the ability of financial analysts "to compare the relative pension funding status among all governmental employers and pension plans."

William W. Fish, senior vice president and manager of the public finance research group of Donaldson, Lufkin & Jenrette Securities Corp., a securities firm, agrees. "With all the current pension funding methods of government entities, it is like comparing apples and oranges right now," he said. "And comparing pension funding of government entities on a level playing field could be a factor in raising or lowering their debt ratings."

The new GASB rule on pension disclosure is effective for fiscal years beginning after December 15, 1986, with earlier use encouraged, Mr. Ives said.

CHAPTER 11

STATEMENT ON CASH FLOWS

Every business prepares an income statement and a balance sheet at the end of an accounting period. The income statement reports the results of its operations over a period of time, while the balance sheet is sort of a "snap-shot" of the business's financial position at the end of the period.

With the increased interest in cash flows, the FASB in 1987 issued Statement No. 95, entitled "Statement of Cash Flows," that requires a company to present a statement of cash flows for the accounting period along with its income statement and balance sheet. The two primary reasons for this statement are:

1. To provide information about a company's cash inflows and outflows during the period.
2. To provide information about the effects of cash on the company's operating, investing and financing activities during the accounting period.

This requirement replaces the existing requirement for a funds flow statement. This funds flow approach permitted definition of funds to include working capital or cash. Additionally, the structure of this funds flow statement permitted varying approaches to reporting and style presentation regarding the disclosure. As a result, the FASB no longer permits the use of the working capital basis in reporting funds flow, although there is some latitude with respect to the specific style and presentation of this important financial statement.

Creditors Want to Know Where and How Your Cash Flows

By Loyd C. Heath

August 12, 1985

> "Though my bottom line is black, I am flat upon
> my back,
> My cash flows out and customers pay slow.
> The growth of my receivables is almost
> unbelievable;
> The result is certain — unremitting woe!
> And I hear the banker utter an ominous low
> mutter,
> 'Watch cash flow.'"
>
> Herbert S. Bailey, Jr.
> ©Publishers Weekly
> Jan. 13, 1975

For years bankers have urged us to "watch cash flow," but it has never been clear just what cash flow is and where on a company's financial statements we can find the cash flow that we are supposed to watch.

The problem was highlighted in an article by David B. Hilder in this paper in 1983 that reported that "Several experts say [Charter Co.] had a negative cash flow of at least $10 million—and possibly as much as $70 million—in the first nine months of this year. But Charter insists that its cash flow is positive."

The financial statement that comes closest to reporting cash flow is formally referred to as a statement of changes in financial position. Informally it is called a "funds" statement. But whatever it is called, it is a mess. A number of years ago, the investment-management firm of Duff & Phelps dubbed it "not

---

Mr. Heath is professor of accounting at the University of Washington in Seattle and author of FINANCIAL REPORTING AND THE EVALUATION OF SOLVENCY *(American Institute of CPAs, 1978).*

much more than a miscellaneous collection of plus and minus changes in balance-sheet items."

Funds statements are deficient in several ways. First, there is little agreement on what is meant by funds. Currently, about half of the statements of large publicly held corporations are based on a working-capital concept of funds. The other half use cash, cash and "equivalents," cash and marketable securities or something similar. But the problem is worse than that.

Many companies combine two or more concepts of funds on the same statement. TRW, for example, reports $410 million of "Funds from Operations" for 1984, a figure that apparently is really working capital from operations. It then adjusts that figure with the changes in each of the working-capital accounts and labels the result: "Funds from Operations and Operating Working Capital"—whatever that means. I suppose it is really cash and marketable securities from operations. At least it is added to what appear to be other cash flows to get the bottom line on the statement that is labeled, "Decrease in cash and marketable securities."

Although generally accepted accounting principles require companies to report a figure called "funds from operations" on their funds statements, there is little agreement on what should be included in that figure. This makes intercompany comparisons difficult, if not impossible. Some companies deduct the amounts paid for plant and equipment, while others do not. Some include gains or losses from early retirement of debt, while others do not. And so forth.

Many of the transactions reported on a funds statement are reported in a confusing and misleading way. For example, if funds are defined as cash, the statement does not show how much cash was received from customers, how much was paid for goods and services, taxes, etc. Instead, the funds statement begins with net income that is then adjusted for depreciation and other accruals and deferrals that did not affect cash. Also, many transactions that did not affect either cash or income, such as the trading of company stock for real estate, are reported as if they were both sources and uses of cash, even though they were neither.

If bankers and other users of financial statements believe that cash flows are important, why are companies not required to provide that information in a clear, straightforward manner? Who is responsible for this gap in financial reporting, and what is being done about it?

In my opinion the blame lies squarely at the feet of the accounting profession. For years accountants have focused most of their attention on the problems of measuring income and have tried to convince financial-statement users that income should be based on an accrual, rather than a cash, basis—that expenses should be recorded in the year that they occur rather than in the year that they are paid.

Creditors certainly are interested in accrual-based income or profitability; in the long run, a company must be profitable to survive. But in the short run, a creditor's interest lies almost exclusively in cash flow. The question of overriding importance to a creditor is whether the borrower will generate enough cash to repay the debt. And if a creditor is interested in estimating future cash flows, a statement that shows where cash came from and how it was used in the past would be a good starting point. Nevertheless, accountants historically have not just ignored cash-flow information, they have been hostile to it. They seem to regard it as a challenge to the supremacy of the accrual-based income statement.

Seven years ago, the Financial Accounting Standards Board (FASB) initiated a project designed to provide the theoretical underpinning for financial reporting. Reporting on the project, the FASB took the position that information about earnings rather than information about cash flows is primary and that cash-flow statements "cannot adequately indicate whether or not an enterprise's performance is successful."

These words reflect the accounting profession's continuing bias against the very type of information users say they need. The FASB has not retreated from its position that cash-flow statements are inferior to income statements, but last December it finally took the position that "A full set of financial statements . . . should show cash flows during the period." That was a big step in the right direction and the board is to be commended for it, but much still remains to be done. The question now shifts to what cash flows are and how should they be reported. This past April an implementation project intended to address these questions was added to the FASB's agenda. However, even though I am a member of the task force that is supposed to guide the FASB in pursuing that project, I am not optimistic about its outcome.

When the board finally did put the cash-flow project on its agenda, it stressed that it is to be limited in scope. I am afraid that may mean that the board intends to do nothing more than patch up the old obfuscating funds statement.

If bankers and other financial-statement users really want to "watch cash flow," they need to make their concerns known to the FASB now. If they do not, the accounting profession, with its long-standing bias against cash-flow information, is likely to come up with another "funds" statement that focuses on reporting income statement accruals, deferrals and other transactions instead of a statement that reports real cash flows.

FASB Issues Proposal to Require Concerns to Report Cash Flow

By a Wall Street Journal Staff Reporter

August 1, 1986

NEW YORK—The Financial Accounting Standards Board proposed to require companies to include statements of cash flows in financial statements.

Financial analysts say that in many instances, cash flows tell more about a company's future than other financial data. "Cash flows can be a key indicator of a corporation's health and whether its earnings are of high quality," said Pat McConnell, an associate director of Bear, Stearns & Co., a brokerage firm.

The rule is likely to be unwelcome news for many companies, especially those wary of a possible takeover. Potential acquirers frequently focus on a target's cash flow to be sure it would be adequate to service the debt taken on to finance the acquisition. The rule would simplify this determination for would-be acquirers.

The FASB, the chief rule-making body for accountants, said that the cash flow statements would replace the statement of changes of financial position, which often are reported on the basis of working capital available.

Working capital accounts, which record current assets minus current liabilities, can include sales payments that haven't yet been received as cash. This occurs, for example, when a lease is agreed upon but isn't fully paid off.

In 1982, the Financial Executives Institute urged its 13,000 members to report financial information on a cash-flow basis; since then, a growing number of companies have done so, but in different formats. FASB officials say that debate about this proposal will center on developing one format.

The FASB proposal would require cash receipts and payments to be classified into operating, investing and financing categories. Comments are requested by October 31. If adopted, the rule would cover financial statements for fiscal periods ending after June 30, 1987.

FASB Rule Requires Public and Private Companies to Issue Annual Cash-Flow Statements

By Lee Berton

November 23, 1987

NEW YORK—The Financial Accounting Standards Board has mandated that every public and private company issue an annual cash-flow statement in addition to the usual financial report.

The rule received widespread support from accountants, industry and Wall Street. But some financial institutions and securities firms contend the data may distort the picture of their operations.

The cash-flow statement will be confined to receipts and disbursals of cash in operations, investments and financing. The statement is particularly important in the current economy as more companies go private, make acquisitions or restructure their operations, according to the FASB, the chief rule-making body for accountants.

Liquidity Measure

Cash flow is one of the best measures of corporate liquidity and "a good indicator of whether these transactions will succeed," says Diana Kahn, a project manager for the Stamford, Connecticut–based FASB.

For banks and brokerage firms, however, "such a cash-flow statement may not make sense," says Pat McConnell, associate director of Bear, Stearns & Co., a major securities firm. Ms. McConnell, an accountant, says the FASB's cash-flow approach understates the operating income and overemphasizes the expenses of banks and brokerages.

"However, the rule will generally be a boon for financial analysts who want to know more about the current cash position of companies they cover," Ms. McConnell said.

Some big commercial lenders believe the cash flows required to be disclosed by the rule "will be so large as to be meaningless," Ms. Kahn says. "Cash is their product rather than just a sign of their liquidity."

Higher Costs

The FASB rule forces many big corporations to issue statements based only on their cash transactions, which will likely raise their financial recordkeeping costs. Many smaller companies have long been issuing cash-based financial statements.

The rule is effective for financial statements with fiscal years ending after next July 15.

The cash-flow statement will replace the statement on changes in financial position currently included in the annual financial statements of all public companies.

CHAPTER 12

EARLY EXTINGUISHMENT OF LONG-TERM DEBT

As interest rates climbed and fell in the mid-1980s, companies were moved to create innovative transactions to reduce the amount of reported long-term debt on their balance sheets. Although most of these effects have run their course, we are in an excellent position to review the change in the economy, the flood of innovative financial arrangements, and the inevitable attempt by the accounting profession to "get their arms around" these complex transactions. Given that interest rate behavior tends to repeat over time, a good deal can be learned from the response of the accounting establishment to the changes that have occurred in the economy.

FASB Adopts, 4–3, Controversial Method that Critics Assert Allows 'Instant' Profit

By Lee Berton

November 30, 1983

NEW YORK—The Financial Accounting Standards Board approved a controversial accounting technique that critics say allows companies to create "instant" earnings.

The FASB, the rule-making body for the accounting profession, was itself sharply divided on the method, called "defeasance." It approved the rule by a 4–3 vote, with one of the negative votes being cast by Donald Kirk, FASB chairman. In August 1982 the Securities and Exchange Commission temporarily banned use of the technique, pending a ruling by the FASB.

Using "defeasance," companies can reduce debt on their balance sheets by selling the debt or creating a trust to service it. The device takes several forms, but in one variation a company buys government securities at a discount and places them in a trust, pledging the future income from the securities to pay off the interest and principal due on its own debt securities as they mature. The company scratches the debt from its balance sheet. Then, because the discounted government securities cost less than the potential cost of actually retiring the company's debt at face value, the company records a paper profit on its income statement.

Ruling Is Narrow

The FASB ruling permits defeasance only for a trust that purchases certain government or government-guaranteed securities at a discount. It doesn't include other types of transactions, such as selling the bonds to other companies rather than setting up a trust with government securities.

While the SEC is expected to lift its ban within a week or so, some commissioners still have reservations about defeasance. "I'm queasy about it because the debt is still legally debt, and the creation of earnings appears to be a charade," says John Evans, an SEC commissioner retiring on Friday.

But Lee Seidler, a professor of accounting at New York University's graduate school of business, said the FASB rule is "sensible" because it permits companies that can't economically retire their debt in the marketplace to obtain "financing relief."

Mr. Seidler, who is a general partner at Bear Stearns, a brokerage firm, said he expects "a large number of companies" to engage in defeasance as a result of the FASB's new rule.

Prior to the SEC's moratorium last year, a slew of companies, including Exxon Corp., New York, and Kellogg Co., Battle Creek, Michigan, used defeasance.

Two Cases Cited

Steven P. Johnson, an FASB project manager, said that under the new rule, Exxon would have been permitted to retire its debt while Kellogg wouldn't.

Last year, Exxon placed in trust six bond issues totaling $515 million; the trust purchased $313 million in government securities to service the bonds. The government securities generated sufficient interest to pay the principal and interest outstanding on the bonds. As a result, Exxon gained $132 million in profits for its 1982 second quarter.

Kellogg, on the other hand, sold $75 million in 8⅝% notes, due Oct. 1, 1985, to several "industrial companies" for more than $64 million, increasing its 1982 second-quarter earnings $5.7 million after taxes, according to Lou R. Somers, Kellogg's vice president, finance.

A. Clarence Sampson, the SEC's chief accountant, said that both Exxon and Kellogg would be permitted to retain their defeasance transactions because no accounting rules on the technique existed last year. "The SEC issued the moratorium because it felt that corporations shouldn't be permitted to create accounting rules before such rules exist," he added.

Morgan Guaranty Criticized on Method to Cut Firms' Debt

FASB Says Use of Foreign Securities Violates Intent of Defeasance Accounting

By Lee Berton

February 16, 1984

NEW YORK—The Financial Accounting Standards Board has raised questions about a new corporate financing tool set up by Morgan Guaranty Trust Co.

The financing tool involves a controversial accounting technique, called "defeasance," which critics say allows companies to create "instant" earnings.

Using defeasance, companies can reduce debt on their balance sheets by selling the debt or creating a trust to service it. Both the FASB and the Securities and Exchange Commission believe it is permissible if a U.S. company is retiring old debt, but only under limited conditions.

In November the FASB, the rule-making body for the accounting profession, permitted a limited form of defeasance. Since then, investment bankers have devised a variety of ways for companies to meet the new guidelines. "Defeasance is a hot idea on Wall Street right now and everybody is trying to exploit it," says one investment banker.

Public Comment

And that concerns the FASB. Robert C. Wilkins, a FASB project manager, said [is] that the Morgan Guaranty-type financing "violates the entire concept" of the FASB rule. He said that the FASB today will issue for public comment a technical bulletin that points out the problems with the transactions. That bulletin should become a rule within two months.

A. Clarence Sampson, the chief accountant for the SEC, said that while he doesn't believe the Morgan Guaranty-type transactions would stand up under the November FASB rule, "there's a possibility they might, and I'm glad the FASB is doing something about this potential problem."

Under the defeasance rules permitted by the FASB, a company may buy U.S. government securities at a discount and place them in an irrevocable trust. Future income from that trust would cover exactly the interest due on the debt. And because the government securities cost less than the potential cost of actually retiring the company's debt at face value, the company records a paper profit on its income statement.

The defeasance rule was intended for companies retiring old debt by using low-risk U.S. government securities. The FASB didn't contemplate the Morgan Guaranty–type transactions, in which companies set up "instant arbitage" transactions using new foreign bonds and securities paying different interest rates overseas. The government securities pay higher interest rates than the bonds, and because they cost less than the bonds, companies can record a paper profit.

Morgan Guaranty's Contention

Walter A. Gubert, a Morgan Guaranty senior vice president, said, "We've consulted legal and accounting advice and believe we follow the original FASB rule."

Morgan Guaranty has set up transactions for its U.S. corporate clients to issue 10-year, mark-denominated bonds that pay interest of about 7¼%. The companies then invest in West German government securities paying as much as 8.4% to pay off exactly the interest on the bonds. To comply with the FASB rule, the West German government securities are put into a trust.

PepsiCo., the Purchase, New York–based beverage and food company, two weeks ago did just that, issuing $91 million of mark bonds. It used the proceeds to buy West German government securities. Company officials weren't available for comment on how much profit will be booked because of the transaction.

In other transactions being considered by investment bankers, a U.S. company that has a subsidiary in the Netherlands Antilles would issue Eurobonds and buy U.S. government securities that pay higher interest. Such transactions are possible because the Antilles is a tax haven where withholding tax isn't paid under a tax treaty with the United States. Mr. Gubert of Morgan Guaranty said that his West German transactions result in a "locked-in immediate gain" and therefore have little, if any, risk.

But the FASB's Mr. Wilkins said the Morgan Guaranty–type transactions "contain sufficient risk" so that they violate the FASB rule. "We'll spell it out even more carefully in the technical bulletin," he said. In the case of the West German bonds, Mr. Wilkins noted, the government has the right to prepay the West German government securities, ending the trust before the bonds are retired. And he pointed out that the United States and the Netherlands are close to agreeing on a revised tax treaty regarding the Antilles, "presenting the risk that withholding taxes may have to be paid by the trust in the future."

FASB Mulls Ban on Defeasance Method in Which Firms Issue Debt to Post Gains

By Lee Berton and Ann Monroe

September 12, 1984

NEW YORK—A dispute between investment bankers and accounting rule-setters may be decided today when the Financial Accounting Standards Board considers whether to ban a controversial accounting technique known as "instantaneous defeasance."

Using defeasance, companies can reduce debt on their balance sheets by creating a trust to service it. Critics say the technique creates illusory profits.

The FASB, the chief rule-making body for accountants, last November approved defeasance if a company is retiring debt, but only under limited conditions. Since then, investment bankers have devised a variety of ways for companies to meet the FASB guidelines while using new instead of old debt in an instantaneous defeasance.

Under the FASB rules, a company may buy U.S. government securities at a discount and place them in an irrevocable trust. Future income from that trust would exactly cover the interest due on the old debt. And because the government securities cost less than the potential cost of actually retiring the company's debt at face value, the company records a paper profit.

But with instantaneous defeasance, companies raise debt

Ms. Monroe was a staff reporter of THE WALL STREET JOURNAL.

for the purpose of immediately taking the gain using the defeasance technique.

To make such a transaction attractive, the yield on the risk-free securities, which the company receives, must be at least equal to, and preferably higher than, the interest it is paying on its own debt. That's the case now in Europe, where highly rated U.S. companies can issue debt at a lower yield than they can get by buying U.S. Treasury securities.

The FASB has expressed a preference for banning instantaneous defeasance if its staff can develop a rule that meets accounting precepts. Alan Reese, an FASB project manager, said the FASB staff felt that instantaneous defeasance using new debt met the FASB's November guidelines.

But Mr. Reese said the board had instructed the staff to prepare a rule for today's vote that shows such instantaneous defeasance doesn't qualify. He said the staff was working on that rule yesterday.

The FASB last February began questioning instantaneous defeasance, which was first developed by Morgan Guaranty Trust Co. But the FASB's position against instantaneous defeasance has been opposed at one point or another by its own staff, seven of the Big Eight accounting firms, and the investment bankers that are collecting large fees by arranging such transactions and purchasing the securities involved.

At the Securities and Exchange Commission, the official position is that any decision is up to the FASB. But James C. Treadway, Jr., an SEC commissioner, said: "I am strongly opposed to instantaneous defeasance" and called it "a distortion of accounting principles."

The FASB's November ruling permits defeasance only for a trust that purchases certain government of government-guaranteed securities at a discount. The ruling doesn't allow other types of transactions, such as selling the bonds to other companies rather than setting up the trust, and it doesn't specify whether the debt must be old or new.

Meanwhile, some U.S. corporate issuers have been using the instantaneous defeasance technique, sources say, and others have been positioning themselves to do so if the accounting treatment is approved.

General Mills Inc. and American International Group Inc. have issued zero-coupon bonds in Europe within the last week, and sources said the proceeds of both issues were used to buy stripped U.S. Treasury securities that match the debt but pay a higher yield. American International officials declined to discuss the issue, and a General Mills spokesman said he didn't know the use of the proceeds of that company's offering.

Zero-coupon bonds don't pay any interest, and are sold at a deep discount. Investors make their profit from the difference between the discounted purchase price and the par value they receive at maturity. Stripped Treasury securities are issues that have been turned into zero-coupon bonds by separating their interest and principal parts.

According to figures prepared last spring for the FASB by Morgan Guaranty, a $400 million zero-coupon Eurobond might bring in proceeds of $41.5 million. Stripped Treasury securities to pay off such an issue, using instantaneous defeasance, could be purchased for $38.2 million. The $3.3 million difference is money the company wouldn't otherwise have.

Since any FASB decision could be retroactive, companies doing such transactions are risking that they mightn't be able to take the debt off their balance sheet using defeasance. Some investment bankers say that without defeasance treatment, such transactions aren't economically worthwhile.

For one thing, when done with zero-coupon bonds, such a transaction can balloon balance-sheet data over time, as the unpaid interest is added to the value of the securities. In addition, asks Thomas K. McCaughey, a vice president at Salomon Brothers, even if the transaction makes money, "is it worth using up (a company's) debt capacity?"

FASB Acts to Ban Use of Defeasance Applied to New Debt

By a Wall Street Journal Staff Reporter

September 13, 1984

NEW YORK—The Financial Accounting Standards Board told its staff to issue a rule banning a controversial accounting technique known as "instantaneous defeasance."

Companies using defeasance can reduce debt on their balance sheets by creating a trust to service it. Critics in the accounting profession say the technique creates illusory profits.

In November the FASB, the chief rule-making body for accountants, approved defeasance if the company is retiring debt, but only under very limited conditions. Since then, investment bankers have devised ways to meet the FASB guidelines while using new debt, which constitutes instantaneous defeasance.

The FASB asked its staff to curtail the type of defeasance using new debt. Some companies, awaiting the FASB rule, had been issuing debt, such as zero-coupon bonds in Europe, and also buying U.S. Treasury securities that pay a higher yield. If the FASB had approved instantaneous defeasance, these companies would have been able to enter on their books an immediate profit—the difference between the price of the two securities issues.

But the expected FASB rule, approved by a 5-2 vote and effective yesterday, prohibits taking the profit immediately. Under the rule, it must be taken as the securities mature.

"This new technical bulletin (rule) says that debt issued in contemplation of a defeasance doesn't qualify under the rule the FASB issued last November," Robert Wilkins, an FASB project manager, said. Mr. Wilkins said even if companies hold on to debt for a year after issuing it, it would be considered an instantaneous defeasance if they use it to book an immediate profit.

CHAPTER 13

EMERGING FINANCIAL DISCLOSURE ISSUES

Anticipation is the best defense against problems in the ever-changing world of financial and accounting disclosure. The complexity of new reporting requirements and the systems necessary to provide the required information both present real challenges and costs to the reporting community. The Financial Accounting Standards Board has therefore taken an interest in the asset impairment issue. This issue involves the current practice of precipitous "writing-off" of assets of a company. Why and when these write-offs or "big baths" are timed and how these write-offs are valued and disclosed are covered in this chapter.

Additionally, new accounting rules have been made that require consolidation of financial statements, and a new rule has been proposed that will require dramatic disclosures for financial instruments for all corporations. One accounting research manager for a Fortune 500 company estimated that if the exposure draft on financial instruments evolved as the final FASB statement, it would result in doubling the content in the financial section of his corporation's annual report.

Accountants Debate Tightening Rules for 'Big Bath' Write-Offs by Companies

By Lee Berton and Gay Sands Miller

February 11, 1986

NEW YORK—Accounting rule-makers are debating whether to turn down the spigot on a recent flood of corporate write-offs that have come to be known as "the big bath."

Write-offs of weak assets exploded in 1985, especially in the fourth quarter, and critics contend that some companies orchestrated the timing of such one-time charges to take advantage of the ebullient stock market.

In a stock market environment where investors seem eager to find the silver lining in every cloud, "write-offs have become fashionable," says a Wall Street executive. He adds that they are no longer viewed as embarrassing admissions of corporate weakness, but as bold moves to rid the books of obsolete assets and to set the stage for future earnings gains.

To be sure, the term "big bath" isn't new to accountants and there have been waves of big write-offs in past years. But accountants say that this year's write-offs are far larger and more widespread than ever before.

The profusion of write-offs is worrisome to a task force of the Financial Accounting Standards Board, the chief rule-making body for accountants. The size and scope of the current write-offs suggest to accountants that companies for some time have been quietly accumulating problems that they only now are ready to admit. The task force is urging the FASB to scrutinize whether companies should have less leeway in deciding when to take a bath.

The issue is timely for investors because write-offs, which once tended to slash stock prices, now often bolster them instead. "Wall Street applauds companies when they face up to the issues and take action to remedy their problems," says Richard

---

Ms. Sands Miller is a news editor of THE WALL STREET JOURNAL.

Harris, senior vice president of International Paper Co. The company charged off $118 million in the 1984 fourth quarter partly for idled lumber operations, and since has posted several smaller charges.

Only yesterday Western Union Corp. announced a $300 million write-off against its fourth-quarter earnings. Other recent charges against earnings include $1.2 billion by the big insurer Cigna Corp.; $725 million by Allied-Signal Inc., a maker of aerospace, electronics, chemicals and auto parts; $674 million by chemical maker Union Carbide Corp.; and $175 million by Aluminum Co. of America.

Under current accounting rules, companies have broad discretion to decide when to write off or reduce the book value of assets. Accountants generally go along with the company's view.

"When companies take a big bath in one quarter, they're generally addressing the sins of the past," says Thornton O'glove, publisher of *Quality of Earnings Report,* a newsletter. "The auditors should force them to take these write-downs earlier, when the trouble becomes evident, so they can't later hype the price of their stock" with a big bath.

Bullish Thing to Do

In the current bullish stock market environment, a major write-off is one of the most bullish things a company can do, says Norman Weinger, a senior vice president of Oppenheimer & Co., a securities firm. "The bigger the bath, the better," he says. "By cleaning up the balance sheet and reducing equity, a company can boost future profits and dramatically increase the future return." An example is CSX Corp., a railroad and energy company that slashed its annual depreciation expenses at least $25 million just by lowering the book value of the assets being depreciated.

Wall Street analysts generally favor the "big bath" in one quarter over a series of write-downs in several quarters. The bath allows a company "to wash away all of its past problems in one quarter and clear the way for a surge in profits," one analyst says, while a lingering series of write-downs "would probably erode the company's reputation and its stock price."

In many recent cases, the price of a company's stock has

Write-Offs Buoy Stocks

	Stock Price Day Before Announcement	Percentage Rise Three Days Later
Diamond Shamrock	$17.875 (July 8, '85)	7%
Schlumberger	33.00 (Dec. 11, '85)	7
CSX	29.125 (Dec. 10, '85)	6
Alcoa	36.375 (Dec. 6, '85)	4
Union Carbide	79.50 (Jan. 22, '86)	4

Source: Oppenheimer & Co.

risen sharply immediately after it announced plans to take a big bath (see accompanying table). For example, two trading days last July after Dallas-based Diamond Shamrock Co. announced it planned to take an $810 million second-quarter write-down, mainly for its Indonesian oil and natural gas properties, the price of its stock rose 7%.

"A strong case could easily have been made to take that write-down in 1984's fourth quarter," says Harry T. Hawks, an oil industry analyst with Schneider, Bernet & Hickman in Dallas. At that point, he adds, it was "highly evident" that Diamond Shamrock had spent too much in 1983 when it paid $1.27 billion in stock for Natomas Co., which owned the Indonesian properties.

But, Mr. Hawks notes, by timing the write-down and a corporate restructuring in the second quarter, Diamond Shamrock "cushioned the blow" of a reduction in its cash dividend in the quarter and "created positive news" that bolstered its stock price. The company paid part of the new dividend in partnership shares of the oil and gas properties.

Retorts Richard W. Arp, a corporate vice president and controller of Diamond Shamrock: "It's a very gray area in the accounting rules as to when a company should write down assets. We did it when we felt we had a good focus on the revenues those oil and gas assets could generate on a long-term basis."

Eager to put the company's best foot forward, Diamond Shamrock's house organ to 11,000 world-wide employees explained that the write-down may be good news. The article conceded that the company overpaid Natomas by $600 million, based on the mid-1985 outlook. But it said investors are "by and large receiving the news positively."

"Let's face it," says the public relations director of another major energy company that took a big bath in 1985's fourth quarter, "company officials take a write-down of assets when it's good for them."

Schlumberger Ltd., the giant oil-field services company, took a $250 million fourth-quarter charge against the assets of its Fairchild semiconductor operation. Company officials concede that the semiconductor business slumped sharply in 1985's first quarter, and a write-off might have been taken earlier in 1985. But Arthur Lindinaur, Schlumberger's executive vice president, finance, contends that "when to take a write-off is a very difficult judgment call. We thought the downturn early last year may only have been an inventory correction because of overstocking by our customers late in 1984."

Problems with Fairchild

Schlumberger has had problems with Fairchild "ever since it bought the semiconductor producer in 1979," says Russell Miller, an analyst with Alex, Brown & Sons Inc., a Baltimore-based securities firm. "You could make a good case for an earlier write-off last year, but Schlumberger was hoping for an upturn later in the year in the oil patch that would mask the Fairchild disaster. It just didn't happen."

The considerable leeway that companies have in deciding when to revalue assets is evident in the case of CSX. Formed in

1980 through the merger of two railroads, the Richmond, Virginia company deliberated for five years before scheduling a $560 million charge in the fourth quarter to shed unproductive railroad tracks and equipment and to dismiss 6,700 employees, or 12% of its railroad work force.

Analysts say the write-off came years too late and was forced by deregulation-inspired competition. But CSX contends that a "very measured" and "very reasoned" asset review was warranted to avoid the "internecine warfare (among managers) that had overwhelmed other mergers of this type."

Besides, a spokesman says, management was busy coping with the "dramatic change" in CSX's structure that came with its 1983 purchase of Texas Gas Resources Corp.

In the past two years, the Securities and Exchange Commission has filed enforcement actions against three banks for waiting until the fourth quarter to take write-downs of bad loan portfolios that should have been taken earlier in the year. Last September the SEC said one violator, Southwest Bancshares Inc., was waiting until the fourth quarter of 1984 to take the write-offs so they could be masked by a merger in October of that year.

In Dallas, a spokesman for MCorp, the merged holding company formed by Southwest and Mercantile Texas Corp., said, "This issue is past history and (officials here) would prefer not to participate in your article."

A. Clarence Sampson, the SEC's chief accountant, says the agency is "looking at all these big write-offs on an individual basis. While we haven't initiated any formal investigation, we can clearly see there's a lot more of them."

Adds another SEC accountant: "Every big company seems to be taking a hit and the stock market seems to like it. If we detect any that seem orchestrated to boost the stock price, we're certainly going to do something about it."

Neal McGrath, an FASB project manager, says that among questions the board may weigh later this year is whether a company should immediately set up a reserve, like an allowance for bad debt, as soon as it has evidence an asset is "impaired."

"The standards say that asset must be permanently impaired, and that leaves a wide range for judgment calls," says

Dennis Beresford, a partner of Ernst & Whinney, a major accounting firm.

Mr. Beresford, a member of the FASB task force that has asked the board to consider the "big bath" issue, believes that more definite guidelines should be laid down as to when a company can take the write-offs. "A more objective rule might require companies to take asset write-offs when it's probable future cash flows won't cover the carrying cost of the asset," he says.

But many stock market analysts believe that no matter how stringent the accounting rules, companies will continue to orchestrate asset write-offs to their advantage. Anantha Raman, a chemical industry analyst in Parsippany, N.J., says many chemical companies delay write-offs on some plants even after they have been idle several years. He adds: "They take advantage of the lack of definite accounting and auditing rules to play an economic guessing game."

Mounting Company Write-Offs Stir Calls for Uniform Accounting of Such Items

By Lee Berton

December 19, 1986

NEW YORK—As massive corporate write-offs mount during the fourth quarter, concern is growing among accounting rule-makers that disclosures, timing and measurements of such write-offs are too diverse.

"Accounting guidelines for taking such write-offs are all over the map," says Mark Malbon, a project manager for the Financial Accounting Standards Board, the chief rule-making body for accountants. "We're probably going to move in the direction of requiring companies to use more specific timing and measurement rules."

While he wouldn't cite specific companies, Mr. Malbon notes

that a recent survey by the FASB and the Financial Executives Institute showed that among the 55 major companies that responded to the survey, three different methods for measuring asset values after the write-down were used.

For example, the New York–based telecommunications giant American Telephone & Telegraph Co., which took a $3.2 billion write-down yesterday, uses one measurement system for its inventories, another for equipment on customers' premises and still a third for other equipment. "We're probably a bit more conservative in measuring our assets than other regulated competitors," concedes an AT&T spokeswoman.

"There's no question companies are measuring and timing write-downs differently, and it's difficult to compare results," concedes Mr. Malbon. He said the FASB staff plans to present a proposal to the board next year to eliminate such diversity.

The proposal likely would force companies to take these write-downs sooner and to readjust earnings upward in later quarters if the write-down has proven to be too big. "In other words, if current accounting issues papers are followed, companies would have to bite the bullet a lot sooner," says the FASB's Mr. Malbon.

A task force of the American Institute of Certified Public Accountants, which suggests rule changes to the FASB, plans to recommend that companies provide fuller disclosure about such write-downs. The task force, for example, would require companies to describe "risks and uncertainties" that lead to such write-downs earlier than they currently do.

"Such early disclosure would create a better early warning system for investors and creditors, and there would be fewer surprises for users of financial statements," says Arthur Siegel, task-force chairman and national director of accounting services for Price Waterhouse.

In recent years accounting rule-makers have wanted to increase disclosures about assets whose values seem impaired by increasing competition, obsolescence or damage. "We want the users of financial statements to be alerted sooner to problems companies are experiencing with their products, markets and services," says a partner for a major accounting firm.

FASB Issues Rule Making Firms Combine Data of All Their Majority-Owned Units

By Lee Berton

November 2, 1987

NEW YORK—The Financial Accounting Standards Board issued a controversial rule that forces all companies to consolidate in their financial statements the results of all majority-owned subsidiaries.

Many companies in the auto, retail and consumer-products businesses continue to oppose the rule because it will load a lot more debt on their balance sheets from finance, insurance and other subsidiaries.

Some of the companies affected by the ruling are General Motors Corp., Ford Motor Co., Chrysler Corp., General Electric Co., J. C. Penney Co., ITT Corp., Xerox Corp. and International Business Machines Corp.

"A lot of companies with nonconsolidated subsidiaries that are in far different businesses from the parent are going to be upset with this rule," said Pat McConnell, an accountant and an associate director of Bear, Stearns & Co., a securities firm.

"Looking at a retailer with an insurance subsidiary, for example, an investor will simply be more confused by the blending of such different debt levels," Miss McConnell asserted. Accountants note that finance and insurance companies are much more highly leveraged with debt than retail or manufacturing companies.

FASB Position

But the FASB said that a longtime accounting rule that permitted the nonconsolidating of certain subsidiaries allowed too many companies to keep significant debt off their balance sheets and made it difficult to compare companies in the same industries.

Eugene Flegm, assistant controller of GM in Detroit, said

that the new FASB rule "is unnecessary and will force us to lump our finance subsidiary—General Motors Acceptance Corp.—which is highly leveraged, with our auto manufacturing operations, which aren't."

Prior to the rule, GM's ratio of assets to all liabilities was 2 to 1; with the new rule, it would be about 1 to 1. And the rule would change GM's ratio of assets to long-term debt to 5 to 1 from 16 to 1, while its ratio of equity to long-term debt would change to 1 to 1 from the current 8 to 1.

Desegregating Data

"There's no question that our financial ratios would change sharply because of the FASB's action, but we feel the rating agencies for debt would simply desegregate the data and keep the current high rating on our debt," Mr. Flegm said.

The senior long-term debt of GM and its finance subsidiary continue to be rated double-A by Standard & Poor's Corp., said Mark E. Bachman, an S&P vice president, industrial ratings. "From a ratings standpoint, we see no change in the company," he added.

Mr. Flegm said that the new accounting rule "could cost GM up to $100,000 in new computer programming to produce our financial statements." He added: "On a cost-benefit basis, I still don't think it's worth it."

Bernard R. Doyle, manager of corporate accounting services for GE, Fairfield, Connecticut, said the new FASB rule will "produce information overload." He added: "GE's consolidated statements aren't really going to be intelligible because the FASB now requires that we add together nonhomogeneous operations."

Mr. Doyle noted that GE owns not only a finance subsidiary—General Electric Credit Corp.—but 80% of Kidder, Peabody & Co., the securities firm, and a reinsurance company, all of which aren't currently consolidated in the financial statements. "Consolidating them on our balance sheet as required by the FASB will be quite confusing," he said.

Larry Brooke, an FASB project manager, said the FASB doesn't believe that the GE financial statement after all subsidiaries are consolidated will be any more confusing than it is now. "We don't think that a balance sheet which combines a broadcasting company with a maker of light bulbs and jet engines is that monolithic or homogeneous," Mr. Brooke said.

Eli Akresh, manager of corporate planning and reporting for New York–based J. C. Penney, said the new FASB rule will force the retailer to consolidate the results of its insurance, banking and real estate operations. "We already consolidate our finance subsidiary," Mr. Akresh said.

"Combining insurance with retailing will junk up our financial statements more than it should," Mr. Akresh said. "We're not happy with the FASB's action. The FASB should have tackled the entire question of reporting about subsidiaries and joint ventures instead of just looking at this little piece of the problem."

Some companies already have begun to change their corporate structure to avoid having the new FASB rule force them to change their debt covenants. Early last month, Houston-based Tenneco Inc. created a holding company that will permit it under the new FASB rule to keep separate the debt of its pipeline business with heavy debt from its other businesses.

The FASB's Mr. Brooke said the FASB is aware of Tenneco's action to sidestep the new rule but doesn't know of any other company taking similar action.

Because of the deluge of complaints it received after the consolidation was proposed last December, the FASB has given companies another year to implement the new rule. It is effective for fiscal years ending after December 15, 1988, a year later than it would have been under the original proposal.

Accounting Board Proposes that Firms Disclose Risk of All Finance Instruments

By Lee Berton

December 1, 1987

NEW YORK—The Financial Accounting Standards Board proposed that companies disclose the credit risks of all financial instruments, including certain debt currently carried off balance sheets.

The controversial proposal to gather and record such data would be especially costly for financial institutions, such as banks and brokerage firms.

The proposal by the chief rule-making body for accountants would require all financial-statement issuers to disclose several items in footnotes. These would include the level of credit risk, interest rates and market values of all securities held by a company, and future cash payments and receipts for a much broader range of financial instruments.

The instruments covered would include some that aren't currently disclosed in financial statements, such as interest-rate swaps, letters of credit, options written for investment purposes and financial guarantees.

"It's questionable whether the cost of this proposal is worth the benefit," said James J. Latchford, senior vice president and controller of Chemical New York Corp., the holding company that owns Chemical Bank and Houston-based Texas Commerce Bank.

Mr. Latchford estimated that implementing the FASB proposal in its current form would cost his company "well in excess of $250,000" a year. He added, "We would virtually have to revamp all our financial reporting systems."

Bernard Doyle, manager of corporate accounting services for Fairfield, Connecticut–based General Electric Co., said, "The FASB may have gone too far." He estimated that the proposal would require GE to add at least two pages to its annual financial statement. "And we haven't even factored in our General

Electric Credit Corp. and Kidder, Peabody & Co. subsidiaries," Mr. Doyle said.

Arthur Siegel, national director of accounting services for Price Waterhouse, the nation's fifth-largest accounting firm, said he is "concerned about the cost of developing" the data that the FASB proposal would require. "And even if the costs are manageable, the proposal may produce so much data that the useful nuggets will be lost in the sand," he said.

Halsey Bullen, a project manager for the Stamford, Connecticut–based FASB, noted that the Securities and Exchange Commission in 1985 asked the FASB to initiate the financial-instruments project.

"Some companies aren't disclosing enough information about the new proliferation of financial instruments when it's important, and others may not be sure how to disclose such complex transactions," Mr. Bullen said. "We hope this new proposal can provide useful guidelines."

Comment on the FASB proposal was requested by March 20. The FASB said that several companies will be asked to experiment with the proposal to see how difficult it is to accumulate the data and whether financial-statement users really need it.

If approved by the FASB, the proposal would be effective for the financial period ending after December 15, 1988, Mr. Bullen said.

The proposal is part of a bigger FASB project on accounting for financial instruments. Other proposals, which aren't expected to be made until the end of the decade, would involve measuring the value of such instruments, and accounting for their transfer among subsidiaries and outside entities.

Investment bankers concede that new guidelines for financial instruments are needed because of the proliferation of new types of instruments such as collateralized mortgage obligations, repurchase agreements and securities with attached options.

"Accountants have a real problem trying to keep up with the ingenuity of Wall Street in tailoring these new products," said Lee Seidler, an accountant and managing director of Bear Stearns Cos., a major securities firm. "Some of these instruments are not only off-balance sheet but off-footnote, and need more explanation," he added.

PART 3

TAXES AND GOVERNMENT ACCOUNTING

CHAPTER 14

TAX "REFORM"

The Tax Reform Act of 1986 was marketed under the banner of "tax simplification." It is certainly not simple and presents many new challenges and opportunities to corporate taxpayers. Some perceive the TRA of 1986 as a vindictive act, a tax law to capture tax from those companies that historically, through ingenious tax avoidance strategies, paid little, or in some cases, no tax, in years when they reported robust profits and strong, positive cash flows, and paid out dividends to shareholders. Some aspects of the TRA of 1986 were designed to limit some of the benefits that manufacturing companies have traditionally enjoyed, and that have disproportionately affected the service industries negatively. Additionally, by extending useful lives for depreciable assets, the IRS has acted to limit the number of real estate transactions that were driven by tax avoidance considerations, as opposed to sound economic reasons.

Reagan's Rules on Accounting Will Harm Service Businesses

By Sanford L. Jacobs

July 8, 1985

Among the losers in President Reagan's income-tax plan are advertising agencies, architects, consulting firms, lawyers, accountants, personnel agencies—to name a few.

Mr. Jacobs was a staff reporter of THE WALL STREET JOURNAL.

Some 30 kinds of businesses would be subject to a provision limiting the use of the cash method of accounting for income tax purposes, says Donal E. Flannery, a partner of the accounting firm of Peat, Marwick, Mitchell & Co. "Almost any kind of professional service will be affected."

Most service businesses use the cash method of accounting, reporting income when money is collected and expenses when they are paid. Thus, cash-method businesses pay tax only on income they have pocketed. Accrual-method businesses, on the other hand, report income when they bill customers. So they pay tax on some income they haven't collected. (Of course, they also deduct some expenses before they are paid.)

A switch to the accrual method can cause a significant increase in income taxes the year the change takes place. Some businesses have two months or more of revenue billed but uncollected. "It can be fairly considerable," says James Power, a partner at Deloitte Haskins & Sells, accountants.

When the switch takes place, the tax code requires that an adjustment be made. A simple example, Mr. Flannery says, would involve $100,000 of accounts receivable at the beginning of the year of the change and $20,000 of accounts payable. The difference between these amounts—$80,000—must be added to income.

The Reagan proposal softens the impact by allowing the adjustment to be spread out over six years. So, in this example, $13,333 would count as income each year for six years. "It still will have a significant adverse effect," Mr. Flannery says.

A small-business exemption would allow companies with average gross sales of $5 million a year to continue on the cash method—if they are otherwise eligible. (Businesses with inventories would continue to be barred from using cash accounting.)

However, even small concerns would be forced off the cash method if they issue financial statements using the accrual method. That could snare many companies with less than $5 million of sales, says William Raby, a senior tax partner at the accounting firm of Touche Ross & Co., because bankers and other lenders usually demand accrual-basis statements. Satisfying them would bar a company from remaining on the cash method for tax purposes.

Mr. Raby says the Reagan proposal is inconsistent. One section imposes accrual accounting on more businesses, while another section bars the use of a basic accrual accounting device: the reserve for bad debts.

Generally accepted accounting procedures require businesses on the accrual method to set up a reserve for bad debts. Annual additions to the reserve are deductible under current tax law. But the Reagan proposal would end the deduction.

Accountants will collect more fees from small clients if the Reagan plan becomes law, CPAs say. It will take longer to compile business tax returns because entries that comply with generally accepted accounting procedures will have to be adjusted to comply with the tax code.

Before this, Mr. Raby says, the government was working to align the tax code more closely with generally accepted accounting procedures. "This proposal," he says, "is kind of the last step in emasculating whatever vitality that idea had."

New IRS Rule Could Curb Takeovers by Increasing Tax Bills for Acquirers

By Lee Berton

February 7, 1986

NEW YORK—The Internal Revenue Service issued a regulation late last month that, accountants say, could curtail the current brisk activity in corporate mergers and acquisitions.

The regulation could raise the tax bill of companies that acquire others. The IRS measure prohibits a company that paid more than fair market value for acquired assets from depreciating the excess amount.

As a result, for tax purposes, the value of acquired assets would be reduced, and so would depreciation charges that can be deducted from taxable profits, explains P. Michael Baldasaro, a partner of Arthur Andersen & Co., the biggest U.S. accounting firm.

For example, under previous IRS rules, if a company bought another for $20 million more than the fair market value, the acquirer could have increased the value of the acquired company's assets by $20 million. Under the new rule, that $20 million must be assigned to good will, which cannot be depreciated or deducted from taxable income.

Mr. Baldasaro estimates that, in the above example, the taxes paid by an acquirer would increase about $10 million over five years. "It's a big price to pay for overvalued assets, and will make many companies in the future think twice before they overpay for a marriage partner," he says.

To obtain the fair market value of assets, companies generally retain outside appraisers to judge what the assets would be worth in the current market. The fair market value generally far exceeds book value, or the amount at which assets are carried on financial statements.

Accountants say that acquisitions of companies in such industries as high technology, publishing, broadcasting and banking would be most affected by the IRS ruling. "That's because acquirers of companies in these industries generally have to pay a lot more than appraised values," says Arthur Siegel, a partner of Price Waterhouse, a major accounting firm.

Allan J. Edelson, controller of Capital Cities Communications Inc., which acquired ABC Corp. for $3.5 billion last month, said he was unaware of the new IRS rule, which is retroactive to August 1982. "The fair market value of ABC is subject to appraisal, and there are significant intangible assets to which we can assign value," he adds.

Accountants say that acquirers will have to find additional intangible assets at companies they buy; and use them to boost fair market value. "There will be pressure to assign higher values to contracts with authors and to mailing lists at publishing companies, and to patents and technology at high-tech companies," Mr. Siegel said.

Messrs. Baldasaro and Siegel say the retroactivity provision will surprise many companies. Any acquirers that increased the value of acquired assets beyond fair market value in the past 3½ years may be hit hard with increased taxes, they add. Companies engage in such "step-ups" to increase depreciation charges that lower taxes. But under the new IRS rule, companies must be careful that step-ups don't exceed fair market value, the two accountants say.

In an example of a conservative approach, General Motors Corp. paid $2.5 billion in cash and a new class of stock for Electronic Data Systems in 1984. Eugene Flegm, GM's assistant controller, says that "an appraisal showed that the fair market value of EDS was $2.2 billion." He says that GM assigned the excess to good will.

As a result, says Mr. Flegm, GM won't be affected by the latest IRS rule. "Had we assigned that (excess) to assets, we would have had to pay more taxes today," he adds. "We took the more conservative tax treatment."

A task force of the Financial Accounting Standards Board yesterday looked at the IRS rule to see if it must be applied to financial statements for 1985. The consensus was that acquirers that are affected by the rule may have to disclose the impact in footnotes to annual reports. Task force members also said they didn't expect the rule to be overturned by Congress or the courts.

Accountants Find Life Is Becoming Unusually Taxing

New Overhaul Plan Prompts a 4 A.M. Call from Paris amid Deluge of Queries

By Lee Berton

May 9, 1986

NEW YORK—At 4 o'clock yesterday morning, Mario Borini, national director of tax practice at Seidman & Seidman, got a frantic phone call from Paris.

A vacationing American investor wanted to know immediately how the latest tax-overhaul proposals would affect his income.

"Fortunately, I was able to tell him the good news that they would reduce his taxes to about $270,000 a year from his current annual tax bill of $400,000," says Mr. Borini. The overseas client told Mr. Borini he would toast him with a glass of champagne. "He was exuberant," the accountant says.

Mr. Borini's wakeup call illustrates how busy accountants are these days, trying to explain to clients the possible impact of the tax bills passed by the House and the Senate Finance Committee.

"We've got our best computer programmers eating lunch at their desks these days, developing a program to tell taxpayers how much they owe," says Gerald A. Leener, director of tax development and analysis for Coopers & Lybrand in Washington.

Byrle M. Abbin, managing director of the office of federal tax services for Arthur Andersen & Co., the biggest U.S. accounting firm, says clients in industries that are affected by the tax proposals are frantically phoning all six of Andersen's tax partners in Washington, trying to get "answers to tough questions."

The effects of the tax proposals on clients can surprise even their accountants. Mr. Abbin was scheduled to speak to a Washington real estate development group this week when the entire audience got up en masse and left the auditorium.

"They were so alarmed with aspects of the new tax proposals that they called for a bus and went directly to (Capitol) Hill to lobby against them," he says. "I was left standing with an empty room. It was quite shocking."

Mr. Leener of Coopers & Lybrand says partners have become busy again even though the April 15 income-tax filing deadline is past. "Nobody has canceled his or her vacation yet, but if these proposals heat up, it could happen," he says.

With the latest proposals stressing tax simplification, will taxpayers rely less on professional help? Most tax accountants don't think so, especially in the phase-in years of any new legislation.

"The new proposals may close up a lot of tax loopholes, but taxpayers will always worry how to keep their taxes down and will feel outside advice is good insurance," Mr. Borini says.

Companies with Big Inventories Face Tough Accounting Changes

By Lee Berton

May 14, 1986

Companies studying the impact of proposed tax-overhaul legislation might want to consider the fine print about accounting changes.

The Senate Finance Committee's tax bill is designed to increase the total business tax bill by $108 billion over five years. Within that sum, accountants estimate, are costs from often-obscure accounting changes that may reach $40 billion over the period.

"It isn't chicken feed," said William Raby, a tax partner for Touche Ross & Co., a major accounting firm. Most affected would be major industry groups, such as autos, steel, construction, retailing and most manufacturers that keep major inventories. They would have to give back to Uncle Sam big portions of their tax savings under accounting provisions included in the Senate Finance Committee's tax proposal.

Credit Accounting

One provision would deny use of the current installment method of accounting for sales under revolving credit plans. Under today's accounting, retailers pay taxes only on credit payments they receive.

But the Senate committee's proposal would force such retailers to pay taxes on a portion of installment payments to be received in the future, accountants note. "This provision would hurt retailers like Sears and Penney with high percentages of sales derived from credit," said Monroe Greenstein, a retail-industry analyst for Bear, Stearns & Co.

About 60% of sales at Sears, Roebuck & Co. and 57% at J. C. Penney Co. are made via credit cards, Mr. Greenstein said.

"The accounting provisions of the latest tax provisions are a partial if not a significant offset to the lower tax rates proposed for the retailers," the analyst added.

In Chicago, a spokeswoman for Sears said top officials of the big retailer were out of town prior to the annual meeting and unavailable for comment. "We just aren't commenting on the tax proposals, anyway," she added.

A spokeswoman for Penney said "it's premature to comment until specific language is developed" in the tax proposal.

Deferral of Costs

Another accounting provision would require major manufacturers and companies in heavy industry to capitalize, or defer, some of their inventory, construction and development costs, including interest, into future quarters or years. Those deferrals would increase federal taxes by reducing deductible costs.

Under current accounting, such costs are immediately deducted from taxable profits when incurred, lowering taxes.

James Conley, a tax specialist for Arthur Young & Co., noted that certain administrative, marketing and distribution costs for inventories would have to be capitalized under the latest tax proposal.

When a cost is capitalized, its deduction is stretched out. Thus, if a manufacturer spends $100 million for materials and labor to make products it keeps in a warehouse, the $100 million is immediately deductible under current tax law and the new proposal.

But, say, if an additional $20 million was spent for administrative, marketing and distribution overhead, it would have to be stretched out for as long as five years. Thus, the deduction would drop to as little as $4 million a year, or $16 million less than permitted under current tax law, Mr. Conley said.

Accountants say that most manufacturers that keep sizable inventories, such as auto and steel companies, would be hardest hit by the capitalization provision.

James Mogle, chief tax officer for General Motors Corp., said there are provisions in the tax proposal that will "help us while others will cost us money." He added that the accounting provisions could be a major offset to the proposed tax-rate reduction.

"But overall we favor the proposal because we feel that lowering the tax rate for individuals will benefit the economy and people will buy more cars," Mr. Mogle said. GM, he added, would "prefer to make money selling autos rather than through lower taxes."

Other Provisions Cited

Other accounting provisions in the tax proposal would boost business taxes in several ways. For example, one would prohibit companies other than financial institutions from deducting reserves for bad debts from taxable income.

Another would force owners of partnerships, "S" corporations and personal service corporations to pay more income taxes the first year they join their organizations. An "S" corporation is similar to a partnership in that taxes are levied on the organization's principals, and not on the business entity. Under law such a corporation must, among other things, be closely held.

"Once they find out about these accounting changes, a lot more of our business clients are unhappy," said Michael H. Frankel, director of KMG Main Hurdman's national tax office in Washington, D.C. "What they're learning is that what Congress may give them with one hand may be taken away with another."

State and Local Taxes Would Rise for Many People under Senate Bill

By Lee Berton

May 29, 1986

Benjamin Goliwas, a 42-year-old fund-raiser for handicapped children, has lived in New Orleans all his life and loves its Old World charm.

Mr. Goliwas is beginning to wonder, however, whether the charm would be worth the additional state taxes he would have to pay under the Senate Finance Committee's tax-overhaul proposal. By eliminating some key federal deductions, particularly for state and local sales tax, the proposal would raise Mr. Goliwas's state income taxes more than 20%.

"The state-tax boost may easily offset any proposed reduction in my federal taxes," says Mr. Goliwas. "It's unfair to be penalized just because I reside in New Orleans."

Fair or not, many people may be shocked to find themselves in Mr. Goliwas's shoes. Most taxpayers probably know by now that individuals in cities and states with high sales taxes would suffer under the Senate committee's proposal because they would no longer be able to deduct sales taxes on their federal income tax returns.

Feeling the Pinch
Residents of New Orleans would be some of the most heavily penalized because they pay a 4% state sales tax and a 5% local sales tax, the nation's highest among cities. Taxpayers in such other high-sales-tax cities as New York and Seattle would also feel the pinch.

But many people may not realize that, regardless of how their federal income taxes would be affected, enactment of the bill would swell their state and local income taxes. That's because in many instances the deductions allowed on state and local income-tax returns are the same as those allowed on federal returns. Unless states enact offsetting measures—such as following the federal government in lowering tax rates—loss of these deductions would increase state and local taxes.

At the same time, taxpayers in states where the tax rate is a fixed percentage of the federal rate would receive a windfall in the form of lower state taxes. Such states include Vermont, which levies taxes at 26.5% of the federal rate; Rhode Island (23.15%); Nebraska (19%) and North Dakota (10½% for short-form filings; from 2% to 9% for long-form filings).

Taxpayers in states with no or low income taxes, and low sales taxes, would benefit, says Eugene B. Fischer, a state tax specialist for Touche Ross & Co., a major accounting firm. Such states include Alaska, Vermont, Massachusetts and Maryland. In Delaware, Montana, New Hampshire and Oregon, which

The Hardest Hit		
	Deductions Lost on State and Local Forms[1]	Sales Tax Deductions[2]
Wyoming	52%	$624
Louisiana	50	678
Tennessee	48	585
Nevada	47	613
Washington	45	786
South Dakota	42	505
New Mexico	36	687
Texas	34	449
Mississippi	32	503
Alabama	31	550
Florida	29	371
Arizona	25	548
U.S. average	18	476

[1]Percentage of deductions on state and local income taxes that individuals would lose under Senate Finance bill.
[2]Average deduction per itemizing household for sales taxes, based on taxes paid in 1985.

Source: Coalition Against Double Taxation.

have no sales taxes, the effects of the Senate committee bill would be minimal.

"The impact varies a lot from state to state and city to city," notes Mr. Fischer. "And it isn't always easy to pinpoint because state and local taxes change so frequently."

Adds Robert Chlopak, executive director of the Coalition Against Double Taxation, a Washington-based, nonprofit organization of local union and civic groups: "The federal tax-reform proposals don't produce a level playing field in many respects, no matter what congressional tax reformers are claiming."

Because tax patterns differ widely in localities throughout the nation, it takes some hefty figuring to assess the effects of the Senate committee plan. But Mr. Chlopak's organization calculates that the elimination of the sales-tax deduction would, by itself, cut in half the total deductions taxpayers in Wyoming, Louisiana and Tennessee would be able to claim their state returns (see table).

Elimination of the sales-tax deduction would be especially tough for taxpayers in certain cities who pay high combined state-and-city sales taxes. These include residents of New York City, with an 8.25% total sales tax; Seattle, with 7.9%; Memphis and Nashville, Tennessee, with 7.75% each; and Buffalo, New York, and Baton Rouge, Louisiana, each with 7%.

The effects on state and local income taxes don't stop here, however, because the bill would also eliminate other key deductions. "This would penalize (residents of) those states that tie state-tax deductions directly to federal tax deductions," observes Gerald H. Miller, executive director of the National Association of State Budget Officers.

The bill, for example, wouldn't permit deductions for consumer-interest payments, for married couples who both work and for contributions to individual retirement accounts if the taxpayer is covered by a company pension plan. The bill would also eliminate the favorable treatment on capital gains.

As a result, Mr. Miller estimates, state taxes for individuals would rise at least 20% in the "deduction-coupling" states of Louisiana, Missouri, Utah and Oklahoma. In Colorado, Montana and Kansas, he figures, the state-tax take would rise about 15%. And the take would go up about 10% in Mississippi, Delaware, New York, Virginia, Maryland, Idaho, California, South Carolina and Hawaii, he says.

"After a new federal tax is passed, states may want to adjust their tax laws to give their taxpayers parity with previous state-tax rates," Mr. Miller says. But, he adds, "not all states will react quickly, and some can't afford to be too sympathetic to complaints about higher state taxes. They need the new money desperately."

Rate Cuts Unlikely

For example, in Louisiana and Oklahoma, where state taxes would rise sharply under the Senate committee proposal, the current loss of oil- and gas-tax revenues makes it unlikely that they will lower their tax rates.

On the other hand, in New York state, which has a 4% sales tax, there is talk of reducing state taxes. And in Connecticut, where the state sales tax for consumer purchases is 7.5%, a $78 million state-tax cut awaits legislative approval. It would, for example, remove the sales tax on meals costing less than $2.

Overall, there are so many factors involved in judging the likely effect of a federal tax-overhaul on residents of individual states that "it's a Gordian knot right now," says Mr. Fischer of Touche Ross. "But one thing is sure. In some states, taxpayers will get good news, in other states, bad news. But practically all of them will be surprised."

A Riverboat Gamble, Aided by Tax Break, Sails into Criticism

Special Rules Helped Work on St. Louis Party Ship; but It Still Could Founder

By Lee Berton

December 31, 1986

ST. LOUIS—Tonight, more than 400 local business and civic leaders and their spouses will board the S.S. Admiral docked here on the Mississippi for the fanciest floating New Year's Eve party in town.

In a lavish art-deco ballroom, they will dance to "In the Mood" and munch on Cajun-style chicken and poached salmon at a black-tie soiree thrown by William E. Maritz, a wealthy local businessman.

"This is my tribute to a great boat parked under the Gateway Arch," the 58-year-old Mr. Maritz says. Some 250 workmen have just finished a multimillion-dollar refurbishing of the five-

deck ship. They have converted it to a 160,000-square-foot entertainment center containing fancy restaurants and boutiques
and flanked by two dockside theaters.

"As youngsters, we used to smooch with our girlfriends on
the top deck," Mr. Maritz recalls. "The Admiral is a nostalgic trip
to the past."

A Business Coup
The party also will celebrate a present-day business coup scored
by 50 of the celebrators, including Mr. Maritz, with big assists
from the new tax law, the Department of Housing and Urban
Development and the city of St. Louis. By banding together in a
tax-shelter partnership and making the Admiral shipshape by
year-end, the limited partners can reduce their 1986 federal
taxes by about $50,000 each—with the tax reductions totaling
some $2.5 million.

Some legislators outside Missouri are less than thrilled. "It's
a disgrace for American taxpayers to have to pay more taxes
because some wealthy St. Louis businessmen want a lavish
playboat," Sen. Howard Metzenbaum says. The Ohio Democrat
has been scrutinizing transitional tax benefits ladled out by
Congress.

The boat—originally called the Albatross—is one of more
than 400 businesses benefiting from special tax exemptions during the transition to the new law. Retroactive to last January 1,
the law eliminates the 10% investment tax credit, except for special business projects. Most of the exemptions affect businesses
that either are troubled or will benefit the local economy.

But because of the rush to push through the tax bill, the list
of exemptions wasn't distributed to Congress before it was
passed. "As a result, some egregious exemptions were sneaked
through this year, and the Admiral is the worst of them," Sen.
Metzenbaum contends. "If St. Louis businessmen want a fancy
boat, let them pay for it themselves." However, he concedes that
with the law enacted, "there isn't much I can do about it." He
adds: "It's proof positive that good government programs so often
go awry when some folks have good friends in Congress."

The Missouri congressmen who gave the Admiral a bipartisan push by sponsoring the exemption were Republican Sen.

John C. Danforth and Democratic Rep. Richard A. Gephardt, whose district includes parts of St. Louis. "Transition exemptions are created to encourage capital investment and jobs, and the Admiral does just that," asserts Ronald Pearlman, a St. Louis tax attorney who helped set up the Admiral partnership and got the congressmen's staffs behind the project. The Admiral expects to hire up to 400 full-time and part-time employees, he says.

A Gephardt aide says refurbishing the Admiral has just as much merit as helping a troubled steel mill. And Sen. Danforth's press secretary calls the Admiral "economically important for downtown redevelopment of St. Louis, which has gone through hard times during the current economic turndown in the Midwest."

Sen. Metzenbaum also is upset that in 1983 St. Louis got a $5 million, 15-year low-cost HUD loan, which it re-lent to the Admiral partnership. "We have poor people living in slums and cuts in Medicare, so why should federal money go for this boondoggle boat?" he asks.

Retorts a HUD official: "When the Admiral repays St. Louis, the city is required to put the money plus the low-cost interest into housing and community development. A loan for a boat may seem unusual, but we lent $4 million to New York City to help set up the aircraft carrier Intrepid as a tourist attraction parked on the Hudson River."

Many Difficulties
The project to restore the Admiral has been marked by delays, huge cost overruns and unexpected problems.

The vessel—378 feet long and 95 feet abeam—was built in 1907 as a railroad ferry. In 1940, two river captains, Joseph and John Streckfus, installed a silver-painted sheet-metal superstructure and converted the Admiral to an excursion vessel that reminded some St. Louisans of the Confederate ironclad Merrimack. In 1979, the Coast Guard decided that the Admiral needed a new hull. But the Streckfus brothers couldn't afford the $1.5 million bill. So they sold the Admiral for $600,000 to a Pittsburgh businessman.

Two years later, Mr. Maritz and a few friends, upset at losing a local landmark, bought the Admiral, minus its diesel engines, for $1.6 million. "We surely overpaid, but we were driven by civic pride and felt this had to be done for St. Louis," Mr. Maritz says. "Little did we know what lay ahead."

More Money Needed

The group members expected to spend only a few million dollars. But after peeling away the sheet metal, they discovered that spiffing up the ship would cost about $25 million. To raise money, the limited partnership was formed. Chicago-based Bally Corp., which runs an amusement park here, agreed to be the general partner.

Each limited partner, including Mr. Maritz, forked over $160,000, with Bally's Six Flags unit contributing $1.7 million. HUD weighed in with its $5 million, and local banks lent $10 million at fairly low interest rates.

But the Pittsburgh man had towed the boat to Paducah, Ky., and the new owner—S.S. Admiral Partners—couldn't get it home quickly. "High Mississippi waters kept us from sailing under bridges, so we were delayed for several months," recalls William P. Haviluk Jr., the general partner's manager for the project.

A local contractor promised to finish sprucing up the Admiral by late 1985, but the superstructure needed more steel than anticipated, and such jobs as laying a dance floor turned into slippery propositions. "Putting a ballroom floor in a boat is like working with a potato chip," Mr. Haviluk says. "The floor curves all over the place."

Earlier this year, the contractor, after getting an extra $1 million from the city, was fired by the partnership. "We felt he was over his head, and so were we," Mr. Haviluk says.

A new contractor resumed work last June, but high water caused further delays. "Workmen had to be barged to the site. "We'll be touching up fixtures with a paint bucket in hand right up to the last moment," Mr. Haviluk says.

Messrs. Maritz and Haviluk concede that the success of the Admiral is questionable. "We'll have to gross about $15 million the first year, and that could be tough," Mr. Haviluk says.

When Mr. Maritz isn't fussing over the Admiral, he runs

Maritz Inc., a family business. "My company specializes in marketing studies, but I have to admit it's impossible to read the future on this project," he concedes. "The Admiral will either be the greatest thing since sliced bread or the world's biggest white elephant. Only time will tell."

Business as Usual:
Under New Tax Law, Corporations
Still Find Ways to Reduce Rates

Credits and Loopholes Permit Payments to Fall Behind Initial Hopes of Congress—Is More 'Reform' Coming?

By Lee Berton

June 2, 1988

Rewriting America's tax code two years ago, Congress tried to ease up on individuals and lay more of the burden on corporations. It eliminated many loopholes and special breaks in hopes of making companies pay more uniformly, and in exchange it cut the corporate rate.

Politically, the idea was a masterstroke. Practically, it's coming up somewhat short of the mark.

Not that the law's a flop. Business clearly is paying more. But lawmakers apparently underestimated the extent of the American corporation's desire—and finely honed ability—to avoid taxes.

"No matter how many loopholes Congress has tried to close, companies will continue to find ways to pay low tax rates," says Anthony Tinker, an accounting professor at City University of New York's Baruch College. "It's the easiest game in town."

Missing the Targets
It's also a game that's helping hold corporate tax collections stubbornly below original and even revised projections. The take

is up. But last fiscal year—in a low economy—it missed original Treasury goals by about $21 billion. This year the economy is better and so are payments, but they may still be $9 billion to $11 billion short of initial targets. So far, You-Know-Who has more than covered the shortfall because of unexpectedly strong personal incomes. But that won't last forever.

And in view of the gaping federal deficit, every corporate tax dollar that fails to materialize only adds to already strong pressure for higher rates or new taxes on both businesses and individuals not too far down the road.

A study commissioned by this newspaper of the 1987 financial statements of 60 major companies shows what is happening. On one hand, some legendary corporate low-payers and non-payers were corralled. General Electric Co., which paid at an average 2.4% rate from 1982 through 1985, paid at a 28.5% rate last year. General Dynamics Corp., which didn't pay any taxes from 1982 through 1985, paid $270 million in federal income taxes last year.

But the federal tax rate of 26 of the 60 companies actually dropped from the year before. And 51 of them paid at rates lower than the new 40% statutory corporate rate, the study shows. Though variations from the statutory rate always exist, a number managed rates way under it; a few paid microscopic rates: Transamerica Corp. paid 7%; International Business Machines Corp., 1.3%; and Merrill Lynch & Co., 0.1%, the study concludes (see table).

How They Did It
Corporate tax returns are private, so exact payments to the government aren't known. Rates in this article were computed by accounting experts using publicly available data. They differ from tax provisions in shareholder reports, which include current and deferred taxes.

The study indicates corporations fended off the tax man last year with skillful timing and application of a variety of allowable credits: by carrying forward losses from previous years, by using remaining benefits of the phased-out investment tax credit and by applying foreign tax credits on repatriated overseas earnings. Stock and bond losses cut taxes for some; others sold assets and used the 34% capital-gains rate to reduce total rates. Big banks generally paid at low rates because foreign loan-loss reserves and overseas branch losses hurt U.S. results.

Some of these devices will gradually disappear, but many won't. Some benefits from the old 10% investment tax credit may live on for a while. Equipment contracted for prior to March 1, 1986, and put into service before January 1, 1991, retains the credit, which can be spread three years back or 15 years forward.

A number of companies say the bulk of their accumulated benefits from past losses will expire in the early 1990s. But new ones, of course, would be generated by new losses. The 1986 law retains the old carry-back and carry-forward rules, so companies can use tax benefits generated by losses as they see fit to reduce their tax bills, going back three years and forward 15 years.

Minimum Tax Blunted
Companies queried for this story declined to say whether they were eligible to pay the alternative minimum tax last year; because their returns are confidential, there isn't any way of knowing. The minimum tax comes into play if it is higher than the standard tax bite.

Tax experts say, however, that in some cases the alternative minimum tax can, in effect, be reduced from its statutory rate of 20% to as little as 1% by offsetting it with previous tax-loss carry-forwards and carry-backs. Other tactics to duck it or lessen its bite are evolving, they say. They can include carefully selected mergers, controlling the timing of income reported on shareholder statements, the use of leased equipment and increasing deferred compensation for executives.

Such continued tax avoidance seems to be a factor keeping overall business-tax collections below their advance billing, though there is some debate about degree. For the fiscal year ended last September 30, the United States collected $84 billion in business income taxes, up from $63 billion the year before. But it had initially hoped for $105 billion. Luckily for Uncle Sam, individuals paid $29 billion more than expected, partly because of a one-time surge in capital gains taxes.

Treasury officials maintain the gap reflects an economy that grew more slowly than expected—which produced lower-than-expected taxable profits—rather than corporate tax-avoidance skills. Though they acknowledge that corporations still have plenty of ways to reduce their burden, they say they anticipated most of them.

Timing of Profits

But some tax experts argue that the economy alone doesn't determine corporate profits and tax bills for a given year. Corporations themselves have a lot to say about what profits—and thus what taxes—they will realize and when, regardless of how their businesses are going.

"Multinational companies have a high degree of flexibility in the timing and amount of their tax payments," says Lee Seidler, a Bear, Stearns & Co. senior managing director and writer of a well-known monthly tax newsletter. And, he says, "Every time Congress changes the law, it creates new, unintentional loopholes."

How Accountants Figured Tax Rates for WSJ Study

To gauge the impact of the new tax law on corporations, *The Wall Street Journal* commissioned two accounting professors to estimate federal tax payments of 60 large companies, based on the companies' annual reports for 1986 and 1987—the years preceding and following the overhaul.

The professors selected the biggest public companies in 10 categories and also included corporations that were listed in a past study as among the lowest federal income-tax payers from 1982 to 1985.

A company's profit and loss statement generally doesn't specify taxes actually paid to the federal government for any given year. Rather, the statement combines what taxes a company paid that year with taxes deferred to future years, and it reflects adjustments for various tax credits. The professors' study entailed computations to break out current taxes from such data.

The study was done by Paul R. Brown, an associate professor at New York University's Graduate School of Business, and Peter R. Wilson, an assistant professor at the school.

By a *Wall Street Journal* Staff Reporter.

This budget year, ending September 30, includes a full 12 months of the new tax law. The economy is stronger. And corporate tax collections are improving. Still, they aren't meeting rosy initial forecasts. The Treasury at first predicted it would collect $106 billion from business this budget year. The Congressional Budget Office last January scaled that down to $99 billion and now projects $95 billion to $97 billion.

At a time when the federal budget deficit looms so large, all of this has some key legislators furious. "The low federal tax rates that some corporations are still paying are a disgrace," says Rep. Fortney H. (Pete) Stark, a California Democrat on the Ways and Means Committee, which drafts tax legislation. "We wouldn't hesitate to introduce new legislation to correct these inequities," he says.

Raising Money

Some in Congress are already thinking about an increase in the alternative minimum tax for corporations and for individuals. "Don't rule out new excise taxes, value-added taxes and higher income taxes next year" either, warns a staff member for a key congressional tax committee.

The new tax law cut the old 46% corporate tax rate to 40% of taxable income for 1987 and to 34% from 1988 on. At the same time, the law tried to eliminate a lot of deductions that critics called "loopholes."

Among other things, it phases out by 1989 the 10% investment tax credit on new equipment and other production assets, and it stretches depreciation deductions over more years. It makes defense contractors pay taxes on revenues not yet received, and it cuts tax breaks on certain insurance-company and bank reserves.

Savings Aren't Wasted

Predictably, companies dislike any suggestion that they aren't pulling their weight, and argue that broad economic benefits flow from what they save on their tax bills. After all, they don't squander that cash, they say. They often use it to finance growth and expansion, which eventually creates more jobs—and more tax dollars. Thus, they argue, raising taxes to compensate for their money-saving skills would just hobble the economy.

"Even though we paid federal income taxes at only a 7% rate last year, we believe that business pays more than its fair share," says James Peirano, Transamerica's vice president for taxes. "If companies cannot take advantage of losses and credits, then the government will squeeze them out of business and cause many more bankruptcies."

Actually, the $20 million the San Francisco financial-services firm paid in federal taxes last year is more than usual. From 1982 through 1985 it didn't pay any, accumulating about $73 million in credits.

To hold down its bill last year, Transamerica used tax-loss carry-forwards generated in 1986 by its property and casualty insurance company. It took some remaining investment tax credits on airplanes, automobiles and shipping containers purchased in the past by its airline and car-rental units. And it got a credit for foreign taxes it paid that were at a higher rate than the 40% U.S. tax rate.

IBM's 1.3% federal tax rate last year translated into payments of only about $37 million. But some might excuse the giant computer maker. It had been far and away the nation's biggest taxpayer from 1982 through 1985, forking over a total of almost $5 billion.

John Akers, its chairman, recently told the annual meeting that the company benefited in 1987 from the lower statutory rate, plus investment tax credits from prior years and foreign tax credits. Michael Van Vranken, an assistant controller, indicates that the latter were significant: "We pay income taxes at the 50% rate in Australia, more than a 50% rate in West Germany and the United Kingdom, and 60% in Japan," he explains.

Merrill Lynch's tax rate was a meager 0.1% and its bill under a half-million dollars because of huge bond-trading losses early in the year, stock-trading losses during the market crash and the lower capital-gains tax rate on profits it made by selling real estate and leasing interests. A year earlier, it paid about $185 million, a rate of almost 24%.

Everyone's Different
There's some sensitivity about such comparisons. "The government should look at its entire corporate tax picture, not single

out companies that paid very low tax rates last year," maintains a Merrill Lynch tax specialist. "Each company has a unique tax situation that may help it pay less taxes."

That's not to say such spending wouldn't have occurred otherwise. Motives are hard to detect in the tax game, accountants note. And any cash invested in equipment or acquisitions is obviously indistinguishable from any other corporate dollars spent, such as for dividends or executive salaries.

Past Losses Helped

Many companies in 1987 used special accounting credits from previous business losses to cut their federal taxes. Philadelphia-based Cigna Corp. paid at only a 4.6% rate because of huge tax-loss carry-forward credits it accumulated from 1983 through 1985 in its property, casualty and liability insurance business.

"We used these credits last year and paid no tax on our non-life insurance profits, which rose because of rate boosts," notes Quincy Abbot, Cigna's senior vice president for taxes. Mr. Abbot says it was fortunate Cigna had the credits because "our life-insurance and group-health-insurance lines were hard hit by profit declines."

Mr. Abbot notes Cigna will pay significantly more federal income taxes in 1989 and 1990 as its tax-loss carry-forwards disappear. "The '86 law also forces us to discount our loss reserves by 20% as a deductible expense," he notes. "The higher taxable income left will catch up with us."

Other companies were able to duck higher taxes last year by adjusting their profit stream. H. F. Ahmanson & Co., a savings and loan holding company based in Los Angeles, reduced the amount of loans it resold to $2.6 billion from $5.9 billion in 1986. When loans are resold, they trigger tax payments on up-front loan fees that would be deferred if the loans were kept on the books.

Setting Up Reserves

By reducing such resales, Ahmanson cut its federal tax rate to 14.6% in 1987 from 29.2% the year before. But Gayle Sweetland, a vice president, says it isn't fair to look at only the federal taxes actually paid last year. "We set up a reserve for deferred taxes

Federal Income Tax Paid by U.S. Companies
Taxes paid in millions of dollars. Companies listed in boldface are among the lowest-paying corporate taxpayers from 1982 through 1985.

Company	Taxes Paid 1987	% Tax Rate 1987	Taxes Paid 1986	% Tax Rate 1986
Large industrial				
Amoco	378.0	30.7	(77.0)	*a*
AT&T	432.0	14.2	269.0	10.8
Boeing	**543.0**	**b82.5**	**66.0**	**6.4**
Chevron	239.0	39.6	(7.0)	*a*
Chrysler	216.0	11.8	64.0	3.4
Du Pont	850.0	b41.9	232.0	15.4
Exxon	514.0	23.8	124.0	5.8
Ford Motor	1068.0	24.3	809.0	28.4
Gen'l Dynamics	**270.0**	**b45.6**	**46.0**	**23.3**
Gen'l Electric	744.0	28.5	231.0	7.7
General Motors	(742.0)	*a*	(1928.0)	*a*
IBM	37.0	1.3	(168.0)	*a*
IC Industries	**122.3**	**39.4**	**108.0**	**b54.0**
Int'l Paper	**53.0**	**8.9**	**21.0**	**5.3**
Mobil	96.0	33.6	171.0	*a*
Philip Morris	844.0	30.9	811.0	36.4
Shell Oil	61.0	3.5	(17.0)	*a*
Texaco	227.0	*a*	(3.0)	*a*
United Tech.	151.0	24.6	107.5	*a*
Diversified service				
Cap. Cities/ABC	247.0	b48.0	206.0	b53.0
CBS	47.0	21.5	23.0	25.3
Fleming Cos.	30.0	39.6	31.0	41.6
Greyhound	**35.0**	**b50.7**	**54.0**	**b78.2**
Hospital Corp.	28.0	23.9	36.0	11.7
PepsiCo	**231.0**	**39.4**	**142.0**	**37.3**
Primerica	(0.2)	*a*	5.9	2.1
Retailing				
c Albertson's	82.0	b41.0	80.0	46.0
c J.C. Penney	413.0	b72.5	140.0	27.2
c K mart	371.0	36.7	320.0	35.8
Kroger	78.0	24.0	70.0	27.1
Sears Roebuck	447.0	27.5	271.0	16.7
Transportation				
Allegis (UAL Corp.)	6.9	*a*	(68.8)	*a*
Burlington North	74.0	11.2	18.0	3.6
CSX	24.0	3.7	20.0	2.7
Union Pacific	88.0	9.9	20.0	2.4
UPS of America	169.0	17.1	282.0	24.5

Federal Income Tax Paid by U.S. Companies (continued)

Company	Taxes Paid 1987	% Tax Rate 1987	Taxes Paid 1986	% Tax Rate 1986
Commercial banking				
BankAmerica	13.0	3.2	0.0	0.0
Chase Manhattan	10.0	1.6	(34.0)	a
Citicorp	56.0	2.9	33.0	5.2
J.P. Morgan	74.0	14.3	(26.0)	a
Mfrs Hanover	3.7	a	(87.0)	a
Diversified financial				
Aetna Life & Cas.	17.0	1.7	130.0	11.0
American Express	254.0	37.0	225.0	15.0
Cigna	33.0	4.6	85.0	13.6
Merrill Lynch	0.472	0.1	185.0	23.9
Salomon	(199.0)	a	184.0	42.6
Transamerica	**20.0**	**7.0**	**(4.7)**	**a**
Savings institutions				
CalFed	45.0	20.1	68.0	27.0
Gr. Amer. 1st Sav.	41.0	31.7	0.0	0.0
Gr. Western Finl	175.0	b41.9	100.0	20.7
H.F. Ahmanson	42.0	14.6	136.0	29.2
Meritor Financial	0.4	a	2.3	8.6
Life insurance				
Nationwide	23.0	28.1	25.0	31.7
Northwestern Natl.	21.0	38.2	16.0	24.1
Travelers	42.0	7.8	19.0	3.6
Utilities				
Bell Atlantic	568.0	30.2	737.0	37.0
BellSouth	893.0	35.0	792.0	28.7
GTE	140.0	9.7	30.0	1.8
Nynex	619.0	32.8	411.0	20.0
Pacific G&E	313.0	25.9	132.0	6.8

Figures within parentheses generally indicate tax credits for future years.
a—Tax rate not applicable because of pretax loss or accumulated tax credits.
b—Rate was above the statutory tax rates (40% in 1987 and 46% in 1986) because of income pushed forward from previous years, mostly under tax reform.
c—Fiscal years end Jan. 31, 1988 and Jan. 31, 1987. All other companies have years ending Dec. 31.

Source: Paul R. Brown and Peter R. Wilson, New York University.

that rose to $37 million last year from $17.7 million in 1986," she says.

Although the reserve is to pay future taxes, it did reduce Ahmanson's profits reported to shareholders last year, she adds. Ahmanson's pre-tax earnings dropped to $268.8 million last year from $465.8 million in 1986.

The tax law hit retailers hard because they have a lot less in depreciation deductions than big industrial companies. Nonetheless, the Cincinnati-based Kroger Co. supermarket chain reduced its tax rate to 24% in 1987 from 27.1% the year before. "We took a lot of special charges in 1987 for downsizing the company," notes Larry Peck, director of corporate taxes. Kroger permitted more than 6,200 employees to take early retirement, increasing pension and job-settlement costs.

The likelihood of more tax legislation frightens some companies. "We paid a federal tax rate of 36% last year, up from 15% the year before," observes Alan Lipner, senior vice president for corporate taxes of American Express Co. in New York.

"We couldn't compete abroad with foreign financial-services firms," many of which already pay lower taxes, he says.

CHAPTER 15

ALTERNATIVE MINIMUM TAX

The corporate alternative minimum tax (AMT) has been viewed as the most complex aspect of the Tax Reform Act of 1986. It is innovative in that it is not a simple "add-on" tax but a separate tax structure. For the first time, profit reported in published financial statements (prepared in accordance with generally accepted accounting principles) is linked to taxable income. The corporate alternative minimum tax also taxes items that are traditionally tax free, such as municipal bond interest. The alternative minimum tax has affected business organizations and a variety of operating decisions that they make, particularly in the leasing area. Certain foreign countries, including Japan and West Germany, report these profit numbers in their annual reports and in their tax returns, unlike current American practice. The advent of the corporate AMT, linking GAAP income and taxable income, may be the first step in this direction.

Tax Proposal Could Create Problem over Profit Reported to Shareholders

By Lee Berton

May 20, 1986

NEW YORK—The tax-overhaul proposal of the Senate Finance Committee has a provision that could create major problems for companies and their accountants.

The provision would for the first time make the net income a company reports to shareholders a major factor in determining the company's tax liability, accountants say. Traditionally, companies have reported much higher profit to shareholders than they report to the Treasury for tax purposes. That's because certain deductions allowable for tax purposes aren't recognized by accountants for public reporting.

The Senate committee's proposal is "a bad idea," asserts James Leisenring, research director of the Financial Accounting Standards Board, the chief rule-making organization for accountants. "Tax policies shouldn't interfere with external financial reporting, which has different aims and goals."

As part of the new corporate minimum tax proposal, the provision states that half the difference between the profit a company reports to shareholders and the profit on its tax returns would become taxable net income.

Figuring the new tax liability under this provision would be complex. That's because the new alternative minimum tax would be applied only if it is higher than the tax the company would have to pay. The Senate proposal provides for a lower corporate tax rate of 33%, down from 46% currently.

Assume a company's taxable profit is listed on its tax returns as $40 million. Under the Senate committee proposal, its income tax would be 33%, or $13.2 million. But if the company reported $100 million of profit to shareholders, the difference between $100 million and $40 million is $60 million. Half of $60 million is $30 million.

Under the Senate committee provision, the $30 million would have to be added to the $40 million taxable-income base, making a total of $70 million. This would represent the company's new tax base because of the higher profit reported to shareholders.

The Senate committee also has proposed an alternative minimum tax rate of 20%. That would amount to $14 million on the company's new $70 million tax base. Thus, the difference between the new $14 million liability and the $13.2 million in taxes that would have to be paid without a minimum tax is $800,000. This $800,000 is the added penalty imposed by the provision.

"This will create new tensions between 'book' or earnings reported to shareholders and the correct reporting of taxable income," says Stephen R. Corrick, a tax partner of Arthur Andersen & Co., the biggest U.S. accounting firm.

Janice M. Johnson, a senior manager in the national tax office of Seidman & Seidman, the 13th biggest U.S. accounting firm, says the new provision may force companies to pay taxes on profits that haven't yet been realized.

"If a company has recognized as income in financial reports to its shareholders fees billed to its customers that haven't yet been collected, there may not be cash available to pay these tax liabilities," Ms. Johnson declares.

Donald J. Kirk, chairman of the FASB, has written a letter to Sen. Robert Packwood, the Oregon Republican who is chairman of the Senate committee, expressing worries about the provision. "Our concern," says Mr. Kirk, "is solely that income tax determinations based on general-purpose financial reporting rather than on determinations within the tax law will create pressures that will be detrimental to the quality of financial reporting to investors and creditors."

The provision is also opposed by Alfred M. King, managing director of the National Association of Accountants, an organization of 95,000 management accountants. "The purpose of tax simplification should be to get away from a tax-driven economy filled with tax shelters," says Mr. King. "But this provision puts pressure on businessmen and accountants alike to make tax-driven decisions."

William Raby, a senior tax partner with Touche Ross & Co., says: "The fear of higher taxes shouldn't force businessmen to want to keep their reported profits lower. That's why 'book' and 'tax' income have always been kept in separate accounts."

Minimum Tax Proposal Touches Off Scramble

More Mergers, Increased Leasing of Gear Expected

By Lee Berton

September 10, 1986

NEW YORK—Many companies and their accounting firms are scrambling for strategies to avoid the alternative minimum tax on corporations proposed by congressional conferees.

Accountants and financial officers predict that corporate reaction to the proposal could produce widespread changes in the way companies do business. Among the likely changes:

• Companies that can't avoid the tax may seek mergers with those that can.
• There will be increased leasing of capital equipment.
• Companies will change the timing of income and deductions to avoid the tax, and will accelerate certain write-offs of plant and equipment.
• Companies will strive to reduce their income eligible for the alternative minimum tax by such measures as increased deferred compensation of executives.

The proposed minimum tax for corporations adds a slew of new income items to the current add-on minimum tax that some companies pay. And it eliminates a lot of current tax breaks that corporations have, accountants say.

Minimum Tax Proposal
The minimum tax proposal requires companies to compute their taxes under the regular system at a top rate of 34%, and again under the minimum tax rules at a 20% rate. The minimum tax would be paid if it is higher than the regular tax.

The proposal treats as taxable income the difference between book income, or that reported to shareholders, and tax income, which is reported to the Internal Revenue Service and generally is much lower. Specifically, half the difference between tax and book income becomes taxable under the proposal. The purpose is to force greater tax payments from companies such as General Electric Co. and W. R. Grace & Co. that have paid little or no taxes but report big profits to shareholders.

Accountants at major firms say that because the minimum tax would have such a wide impact, it's important that companies begin planning early to avoid it. Albert Ellentuck, national tax partner in Washington for Philadelphia-based Laventhol & Horwath, estimates that the proposal would boost federal taxes for at least one-third of Laventhol's 10,000 corporate clients.

But because of the alternative tax's complexity and broad sweep, accountants say that even companies with top tax strategists will find it tough to sidestep. "The alternative minimum tax will be one of the toughest to avoid because it forces companies that choose to put their best foot forward for investors to pay a tax penalty," says William Raby, a senior tax partner with Touche Ross & Co.

Merging of Companies

One strategy, accountants say, could be the merging of companies with potentially high minimum tax obligations with those that have none. That's because the total normal tax of the companies almost certainly will exceed the minimum tax potentially owed by one of them. "It would be a marriage made in the Internal Revenue Code," says Emil M. Sunley, director of tax analysis in the Washington office of Deloitte, Haskins & Sells.

Capital-intensive companies in the steel, utility, auto and industrial machinery businesses would be hard hit, while service companies in food, computer software and communications would generally avoid the new minimum tax, accountants say. That's because the proposal pushes into income the big differences in depreciation for book income and the more accelerated depreciation used for tax purposes.

Currently tax rules apply an added minimum tax to regular corporate taxes by treating as income the difference between the straight-line depreciation on buildings used for financial reporting and the accelerated depreciation calculated for tax accounting. The new proposal would extend such treatment to all properties, including machinery and equipment.

When a company leases, rather than buys, equipment, the

The Proposed Tax: A Hypothetical Case (figures in millions of dollars)		
	1987[1]	*1988*[2]
Income reported to shareholders	$ 8.0	$ 8.0
Taxable income	5.0	5.0
Tax	2.0	1.7
Minimum tax income	15.0	15.0
Alternative minimum tax (20% rate)	3.0	3.0
Excess of alternative minimum tax over regular tax	1.0	1.3

[1]Corporate tax rate combining current and new rate is 40% in 1987.
[2]Corporate tax rate is 34% beginning in 1988.

Source: Touche Ross & Co.

cost of leasing may be lower than the alternative minimum tax triggered if the property is owned and hence depreciated. Thus, leasing of equipment is another strategy being urged by accountants for capital-intensive companies that would lose a major portion of depreciation benefits. "The leasing price would be a lot more attractive, after the tax advantages of buying depreciable equipment diminish," says Peter Nevitt, chairman of a leasing subsidiary of BankAmerica Corp., San Francisco.

Adds William Rummler, president of Centron DPL Co., a Minneapolis-based computer leasing company: "Many of our customers say that because of the alternative minimum tax proposal they will be more inclined to lease equipment. The proposal may become one of our biggest marketing tools."

Other strategies to minimize the alternative tax would involve changes in timing of recording income, expenses, write-offs and reserves, notes Ralph J. Weiland, chairman of the federal tax committee of the Tax Executives Institute, a trade group based in Arlington, Virginia.

"It's important that companies try to minimize the difference" between book and tax income, says Mr. Weiland, who also is senior staff vice president, taxes, for Pittsburgh-based Alleghany International Inc., a maker of consumer and industrial products.

The proposed measure "will pressure companies and their accountants to keep book income low," asserts Laventhol's Mr. Ellentuck, who also is chairman of the tax division for the American Institute of Certified Public Accountants. "Accurate financial reporting shouldn't be influenced by tax considerations, or the tail wags the dog," he adds.

Because lowering book income would minimize the minimum tax, some companies may accelerate factory write-offs that are recognized only for book income purposes. Hewlett-Packard Corp., a Palo Alto, California-based computer, instruments and telecommunications company, is considering boosting plant write-offs to three a year from one or two yearly in the past, says Larry Langdon, director, tax and distribution. Hewlett-Packard has 53 U.S. plants.

Under both the current and proposed tax law, write-offs for factories and equipment can't be completely deducted from taxable income unless the buildings and machinery are disposed of. "We're in a high-tech business and are always considering idling obsolete lines, but we can't deduct the full costs of such lines from our taxable income until we sell or junk it," explains Mr. Langdon.

The company recently closed a precious-metal plating line for computer boards in California. "We took a more than $5 million write-off for book purposes and a much smaller deduction for tax purposes, based on the equipment's depreciable life," notes Mr. Langdon. By reducing book income more than tax income, Hewlett-Packard was able to lower the difference between the two. Similar action under the new tax proposal would lower the minimum tax.

Deferred Compensation Bonuses

Douglas M. Jerrold, federal tax manager for Reynolds Metals Co., Richmond, Virginia, says he will suggest to management that deferred compensation bonuses of executives be increased in the future. That's because accruals or reserves for such bonuses are deductible from book income but only reduce taxable income when they're actually paid out. "It's a timing difference that could reduce our minimum tax," Mr. Jerrold says.

Many companies are finding the minimum tax proposal so complex that they haven't yet figured out how to avoid it. "We want to see precisely where this bill comes out before we map any new income or expense moves," says Charles W. Rau, vice president, taxes, of MCI Communications Corp., a Washington-based producer of long-distance telephone equipment.

Mr. Rau says that tax administration costs of companies will rise sharply under the new minimum tax. He adds: "We don't need the extra work, and it won't be very productive for boosting the economy as tax incentives should."

Some accountants say that the proposed minimum tax will force some companies to set up as many as three more schedules to help figure their taxes. "The provision is certain to drive accountants close to insanity, but Congress seems to consider it a reasonable price to assure that all corporations pay some corporate tax," says Lee Seidler, an accountant and managing director of Bear, Stearns & Co., a large securities firm.

Companies that pay negligible federal taxes would be hardest hit by the proposal, accountants say. Legislators particularly point to GE and Grace. GE from 1981 through 1983 didn't pay any federal income tax, but it reported net income totaling $5.4 billion to its stockholders during that span. Grace, in the same period, paid at only a 5.3% tax rate on a total of $764.3 million in pre-tax income. For 1985, GE had an 11% federal tax rate, while Grace didn't pay any taxes because it had no U.S. income.

Asked whether any strategies to minimize the minimum tax proposal are planned, a GE spokesman said, "It's premature to talk about them." A Grace spokesman made the same comment.

Surprise Loophole: Firms Expect Leasing to Save Them Millions under New Tax Law

Lessors' Unexpected Bonanza May Face New Scrutiny by Congress and Treasury— Escaping the 'AMT' Trap

By Lee Berton

March 11, 1987

Alaska Air Group Inc. this year will lease as many as 10 commuter aircraft instead of buying them, thereby saving $4 million or more in 1987 taxes.

"If not for the new tax law, we would have purchased at least five of these planes," says J. Ray Vingo, the vice president for finance of the Seattle-based company.

Alaska Air is typical of companies discovering the leasing loophole in the new federal income-tax law. Collectively, they stand to save billions of dollars in taxes.

Congress expected that one of the law's provisions—a new alternative minimum tax [AMT] for corporations—would generate at least $22 billion of added revenue over the next five years. But some tax analysts say that skillful use of leasing could easily cut that in half.

Surprise, Surprise

Now that the law is on the books, congressional and Treasury tax experts are registering surprise at how sharply leasing may cut into expected tax revenues. They warn that Congress could decide to close the loophole.

"We don't know enough about it right now," a Treasury official concedes. "But based on what we are hearing, we'll watch the trend. If it opens too many tax leaks, we'll have to plug the holes."

Meanwhile, major corporations such as United Technologies Corp., CSX Corp., Goodyear Tire & Rubber Co. and Exxon Corp. are using or planning leasing arrangements to reduce taxes, although they prefer as little publicity as possible about the arrangements. "Such tax information is a private matter," says Oren G. Shaffer, Goodyear's vice president and treasurer. "Our tax attorneys tell us we really shouldn't talk about it."

But leasing brokers are rubbing their hands in glee. The new tax law is "a great marketing tool" for leasing, says Michael J. Fleming, the president of the American Association of Equipment Lessors, a trade group based in Arlington, Virginia. He says leasing volume may top $100 billion for the first time this year, up from $97 billion in 1986. Volume was only $15 billion as recently as 1975.

New Vistas

Corporations long have leased such assets as truck fleets and buildings. But because of the new tax law, leasing is spreading to other major assets like fiber-optics telephone lines, container ships, tire-making assembly lines, oil-drilling platforms and petroleum refineries.

Leasing can provide a tax loophole because of the new alternative minimum tax. Corporations have long been keeping two sets of books—one using accounting rules for reporting financial results to shareholders and the other, typically showing much lower profits, to report to the Internal Revenue Service. But alternative-minimum-tax rules now call for a 20% tax on half the difference between income reported to shareholders and income reported to the Treasury. The alternative tax must be paid if its total is more than the regular tax of 34% under the new law.

When a company buys equipment, it uses straight-line depreciation for income reported to shareholders and accelerated depreciation for tax reporting. Accelerated depreciation makes for higher expenses and lower taxable income during the early years of an asset's life. This widens the gap between book and tax income; under the new law, it makes for higher taxes under the alternative minimum tax.

Taxing the Gap

Leasing of equipment helps reduce the tax by preventing a gap between the two types of income. If a company buys $100 million in production equipment, it can deduct $20 million the first year under accelerated depreciation but only $10 million under straight-line depreciation. This creates a $10 million gap between income reported to shareholders and tax income. The bite from the alternative minimum tax, or AMT, on this $10 million gap is $1 million.

But if the company leases the equipment, it applies the same dollar deduction for rent on both sets of books; no gap is created.

"Buying equipment is a sure-fire way to trigger the AMT trap," says Peter K. Nevitt, the chairman of BankAmerilease, a unit of BankAmerica Corp. in San Francisco.

"Tax specialists have found ingenious techniques to get around the AMT through complex leasing arrangements," says William Raby, a senior tax partner with Touche Ross & Co., a major accounting firm. "Where there's a will, there's a way."

Because of the new tax law, Bank-Amerilease's Mr. Nevitt expects that assets leased by his company will rise more than 20% this year from the $1.5 billion in assets leased in 155 transactions last year.

Not surprisingly, critics of corporate tax avoidance are zeroing in on leasing. "It's simply a sham tax shelter for big assets," asserts Robert S. McIntyre, the director of Citizens for Tax Justice, a coalition of labor and public-interest groups that monitors how corporations avoid taxes. "Many of these new leasing deals have little economic substance."

BankAmerilease's Mr. Nevitt disagrees: "If Congress looks at the structures of these new leasing arrangements, they'll find that they're perfectly legal as far as the lessor's title and the lessee's rental payments go," he says. "Upsetting legitimate leasing will only undermine our economy and hurt the entire nation."

Still, the subject is sensitive with corporate America. This newspaper contacted dozens of companies and leasing brokers. Most companies took the advice of their tax attorneys and declined comment.

MCI Corp. is unhappy when it is asked about reports by leasing brokers that it plans to sell hundreds of miles of underground fiber-optic lines for $300 million to three other corporations and then lease back the lines to cut its income tax.

"This is a tax-oriented transaction that we'd rather not discuss," a leasing executive at the telecommunications company says. "It's not something we'll put in our annual report because we don't want the Internal Revenue Service jumping all over us. Don't mention it or we'll stop responding to your queries, since what we do with taxes is nobody's business unless we're required to disclose it in our financial statements."

Alaska Air Group's Horizon subsidiary is subleasing seven commuter planes from United Technologies of Hartford, Connecticut, which in turn is leasing the planes from a unit of Pacificorp Inc., a utility holding company in Portland, Oregon. Alaska Air confirms the leasing plan, but United Technologies prefers a low profile in the matter. Harry Gill, an associate general counsel, says, "It's not a good idea to talk about tax-oriented transactions."

Lawrence R. Appel, senior vice president of the Pacificorp unit, says that assets held by his company for "tax-sensitive" leasing will rise about 40% this year, to $200 million.

"The new tax law's AMT provisions have created a new industry with new players," Mr. Appel says. Pacificorp Inc., which owns Pacific Power & Light Corp., acquired the leasing division late in 1985 from Orbanco Financial Services Corp. in Portland.

"For every freight car we lease, we can save more than $1,000 in annual AMT taxes," says William H. Sparrow, the treasurer of CSX, which is getting back into leasing arrangements it used in the past.

"Many people thought that new tax act was the death knell of leasing because it kills the investment tax credit and reduces depreciation benefits for the lessor, providing less benefits to pass along to the lessee," says Mr. Sparrow. "But it hasn't turned out that way. If anything, the AMT will breathe new life into leasing."

CSX's Sea-Land Corp. subsidiary in Menlo Park, New Jersey, is negotiating the leasing of three huge container ships valued at $170 million from Argent Group Inc., a leasing firm based in New York City.

"We're structuring a lot of leases to avoid AMT that our clients would prefer to keep quiet," says Stephen Gottlieb, Argent's managing director. "Some of these deals will take a year or two to put together. I'd rather not alert tax authorities to how they're being done, or the deals will go up in smoke."

At Goodyear, Mr. Shaffer would only say that leasing is being looked at for various assets, including electronic engine analyzers for its 2,100 company-owned and franchised retail stores. He says Goodyear "wouldn't lease any equipment unless it was an economically sound business decision." He adds, "But there's no question we'd like to avoid the AMT trap."

Major international oil companies are considering certain leasing arrangements for the first time, to reduce taxes. The plans involve selling and leasing back refineries, pipelines and offshore-drilling rigs. Brokers say Exxon and Texaco Inc. are discussing such tactics with leasing brokers, but the companies won't comment.

Other new tax-law provisions besides the alternative minimum tax are influencing companies' buying and leasing decisions. Many multinational companies formerly bought equipment by borrowing in the United States, as the interest costs were a fully deductible U.S. expense. The new law requires all subsidiaries filing a consolidated return to prorate interest expense to their U.S. and foreign operations, even if all the interest is paid in the United States.

Rental expense, on the other hand, now can be allocated to the location of the rented property. Rental expense on equipment located in the United States, therefore, can be fully deducted.

"We can only say that we are beginning to look at sale-lease-backs for a wide range of U.S. assets" to reduce U.S. taxes, says Stephen Arbogast, the treasurer of Exxon Capital Corp., a leasing and financing unit of Exxon Corp.

A Texaco spokeswoman denies that the company is using such leasing techniques.

Some U.S. companies will avoid leasing if they can retain some of their past tax benefits from owning assets. ITT Corp. in New York expects to continue to buy most production equipment, says Kathleen McCreary, a senior tax attorney.

"We expect to be able to use the new tax law's depreciation schedules and investment tax credits still permitted us under transition tax rules for some years to come," Ms. McCreary says. "Leases are long, complicated and cumbersome and involve a big fee to investment bankers plus the loss of residual value of the property."

Ms. McCreary says ITT likes the idea of "owning a lot of our assets and thereby controlling their disposition."

Such preference for ownership, however, isn't putting much of a crimp in the business of leasing brokers. BankAmerilease is having the busiest first quarter in its history. Says Mr. Nevitt: "We're normally slack this time of the year, but because of leasing volume to avoid the new tax act, six of our leasing specialists have had to cancel ski vacations."

Treasury Is Asked to Probe Leasing Use as Tax Dodge

By a Wall Street Journal Staff Reporter

March 12, 1987

WASHINGTON—Sen. Bob Packwood, an architect of tax overhaul, asked the Treasury Department to investigate whether tax-oriented leasing is being used by companies to avoid the new alternative minimum tax.

The Oregon Republican cited an article in yesterday's *Wall Street Journal* that indicated certain leasing transactions are being used as a "loophole" to avoid the alternative minimum tax.

Sen. Packwood is the ranking GOP member of the Senate Finance Committee and is its former chairman.

"We can't allow profitable companies . . . to wiggle out of the minimum tax," Sen. Packwood said in a letter to Treasury Secretary James A. Baker. The minimum tax, Sen. Packwood said, was "the cornerstone of the tax reform bill."

Sen. Packwood said he would do "whatever is necessary to ensure that minimum tax is virtually inescapable." He asked Secretary Baker to provide him as soon as possible with data on the revenue loss from tax-oriented leasing and to suggest "whether corrective legislative action is needed."

A Treasury spokesman said that "if the senator has asked us to look at this, we certainly will, and we will respond to him."

Congressional tax officials said they realized some companies would use leasing deals to ease the bite of the alternative minimum tax. They said an estimate that the minimum tax would raise $22 billion from corporations over the next five years assumes that such leasing activity would occur. As a result, the revenue loss may be no greater than originally estimated, they said.

IRS Spells out Tax Computing for Companies

By Rose Gutfeld

April 27, 1987

WASHINGTON—The Internal Revenue Service issued temporary regulations on complying with the new tax law's tough *alternative minimum tax* for corporations.

The rules provide guidance on the law's book-income provisions. Under these provisions, corporations, in determining the income to which the minimum tax applies, must include a portion of their pre-tax book profits. They also deal with calculating the minimum tax and a new environmental tax for the purpose of figuring a company's liability for estimated taxes. The environmental tax was imposed by last year's Superfund waste-cleanup legislation.

The minimum tax was fashioned in response to disclosures that many profitable companies didn't pay any federal income taxes in recent years. It's expected to result in higher taxes for much of corporate America, striking hardest at capital-intensive concerns.

The measure essentially requires companies to compute their taxes twice, once under the regular system and once under the minimum tax provisions. They must pay whichever results in a higher tax.

The new regulations spell out how companies must calculate their adjusted book income. This calculation involves deciding which of several possible financial statements to use as well as making certain adjustments to that statement.

For most companies, that statement will be the one they supply the Securities and Exchange Commission. Others may use statements they have provided to shareholders or creditors. After that the IRS gives a list of other permissible statements in descending order of priority. If two statements are equally acceptable under the rules, a company is required to use the one that would result in a higher tax.

Required adjustments might involve the treatment of foreign affiliates or partly owned subsidiaries, according to Robert M. Brown, a partner in Peat Marwick's national tax practice here.

The regulations also spell out when a measure of current earnings and profits—rather than an estimate of book income—can be included in the calculation. They also explain how to deal with income that isn't included on a financial statement and how to prevent the omission or duplication of items.

Before putting the regulations into effect, the IRS is seeking comment on them for 60 days after they are published in the Federal Register. They will remain in force until final rules are issued.

CHAPTER 16

GOVERNMENT ACCOUNTING

The application of tough, consistent accounting rules to governmental units has been a controversial area for years. With an increasing number of state and local governmental units entering the capital markets for financial support, the pressure to provide reliable financial statements is mounting. Additionally, the increasing incidence of reported waste and fraud in government is creating a demand for more rigorous accountability, long applied to the corporate community.

Which accounting standards are most appropriate for this segment of the economy is a current dispute between the Government Accounting Standards Board and the Financial Accounting Standards Board. One of the key issues involves the case of two hospitals, one private and one public. Should they account for employee pension liability under the same rules or apply differential accounting practices that render analytical comparisons between the two similar entities very difficult, at best.

Crunched Numbers: Government's System of Accounting Comes under Rising Criticism

Its Emphasis on Cash Flows Favors Short-Term Ploys that Lift Eventual Costs— 'Capital Budget' Is Proposed

By Alan Murray

February 3, 1986

WASHINGTON—The problem with the federal government, Rep. Joseph J. DioGuardi says, is that it has too many lawyers and too few accountants.

Mr. DioGuardi is an accountant. Last year, after a career spent poring over the books of private corporations, he won a seat in Congress and began studying the books of the federal government. "I'm appalled at the way we account for government spending around here," he says, his voice rising with indignation. "We're using a Mickey Mouse, cash-basis accounting system."

The New York Republican is more emphatic than most of his fellow accountants, but he isn't alone in his critique. The government's top accountants, Comptroller General Charles A. Bowsher, agrees. So do various other accountants, budget officials and economists both inside and out of government. Federal budget-accounting procedures "would be illegal if they were practiced by publicly traded private corporations," says Michael Boskin, a Stanford University economist.

Policy Affected

Bad accounting methods, critics say, can produce bad government policy. Because Washington focuses primarily on the cash

---

Mr. Murray is a staff reporter of THE WALL STREET JOURNAL.

it spends and gets each year—and the difference, or deficit, between them—its drive to cut immediate outlays can lead to actions that turn out to be penny-wise and pound-foolish. For example, the federal government often leases buildings to avoid the big cash outlay of a purchase even though leasing costs more in the long run.

The Gramm-Rudman plan to balance the budget is creating new pressure to slash the deficit and is concentrating attention on the strengths and weaknesses of the government's accounting methods. "I think Gramm-Rudman may bring this whole accounting issue to the forefront," Mr. Bowsher says. "When people try to wrestle with this thing, I think there will be a lot of interest in getting a more streamlined, easier-to-understand accounting system."

Right now, White House officials say they are considering compilation of a "capital budget" in addition to the annual cash-based budget. The proposed budget would account separately for the government's long-term investments in real estate, computers, warships and other weapons and would attempt to estimate the rate at which such assets are wearing out. That's important, accountants say, because it helps the government keep track of the eventual costs of repairing or replacing those assets. The proposal, however, wouldn't exempt capital investments from the Gramm-Rudman deficit-cutting tax.

Budget Proposals
An example of the importance of accounting conventions will be evident in the Reagan administration's fiscal 1987 budget, to be unveiled Wednesday. That budget will include proposals to sell billions of dollars of federal assets, including the Naval Petroleum Reserve, the Bonneville Power Administration and part of the government's loan portfolio.

Under accounting methods used by private companies, such asset sales wouldn't necessarily increase net incomes. And if the assets were sold for less than the amount invested in them, they could result in a loss.

Under government accounting conventions, in contrast, the cash raised by those asset sales would help meet the new budget law's deficit target, regardless of the sale prices. "It's like selling your house to pay for your current spending," Mr. Boskin says.

The problem with that cash-in, cash-out accounting, critics say, is that it doesn't give sufficient attention to actual costs. For instance, the administration, as part of its budget proposal, is likely to lean more heavily on government loan guarantees rather than direct loans. But although loan guarantees might not require any cash outlays over the next few years, they could prove very costly in the long run if loans go bad.

Of course, the Generally Accepted Accounting Principles used by corporations have their own problems and often can be employed to cloud as well as to reveal a company's financial picture. What's more, sometimes the rules are bent. "When you're in Chapter 11, you manage for cash and to hell with all this other nice gobbledygook," says Donald Moran, a former Reagan administration budget official who currently is a vice president of ICF Incorporated, a Washington consulting firm. But accountants say the shortcomings of business accounting pale in comparison with the government's methods.

"Basically, the government is like someone who uses only a checkbook," says Morton Egol, a New York partner in Arthur Andersen & Co., a big accounting firm. "That's not a complete picture of its financial affairs. It doesn't reflect assets, liabilities, commitments in the future. How can you run a trillion-dollar business without knowing what its financial position is?"

Administration budget officials emphatically deny that they ignore the underlying costs of government programs. "Everybody here is very conscious of those things," says Edwin Dale, the spokesman for the Office of Management and Budget. He also notes that increasing emphasis on three-year and five-year budget projections helps lawmakers focus on longer-run costs. Along with framing the budget in terms of annual outlays, both Congress and the budget office also state spending in terms of budgetary "authority," which sometimes allows agencies to obligate funds over several years. And other defenders of the current accounting system contend that government accounts don't lend themselves to corporate-style ledgers.

Nevertheless, the combination of Gramm-Rudman's deficit-reduction goals and a simple cash accounting system may drive the administration and Congress to embrace proposals this year that will help raise cash or cut spending in the short run but increase costs over the long run.

Consider these examples:

• Faced with pressure to reduce spending, the Pentagon probably will try to stretch out weapons programs instead of cutting them outright. Under government accounting, that will slow spending and lower the deficit in the short run, but "the delays will make total program costs and total funding costs go up," says David Smith, a defense analyst at Sanford G. Bernstein & Co., a New York investment firm.

• As emphasis on the deficit increases, getting approval to buy or construct federal office space has become nearly impossible. "We haven't done any major construction since the Nixon years," says Raymond A. Fontaine, the comptroller for the General Services Administration. As a result, the government's rent bill runs about a billion dollars a year. Mr. Fontaine argues that because the government pays lower interest rates than private builders do and because it is almost certain to need the office space indefinitely, it would usually save money by owning rather than leasing. "The way it is now, at the end of 20 years you end up with nothing but a bunch of canceled rent checks," he complains.

• Getting approval to make new investments in computers and other equipment that might improve government productivity in the long run—but costs lots of money in the short run—is also increasingly difficult. "Anything that has a future payoff is really going to get hurt" under the new budget law, says Frederick Wolf, the director of the GAO's accounting and financial management division.

Such examples illustrate why Mr. Bowsher, Mr. DioGuardi and others believe that reforming government accounting is critical. "My colleagues tell me to take my green eyeshade off," Mr. DioGuardi says, "but I tell them I won't trade my green eyeshade for blinders."

Grimmer Picture

A comprehensive balance sheet listing all the government's assets and liabilities might help focus attention on true costs, the reformers believe. Such a system of accounting, Mr. DioGuardi contends, would also show that the government is much further in the red than commonly supposed.

"When you hear about $2 trillion in accumulated deficits, that's the good news," he says. "That's what's on the books. You wouldn't believe what is off the books."

Mr. Egol estimates that if accrued, but unfunded, Social Security liabilities are included, the government's liabilities exceed its assets by approximately $3.4 trillion, "more than the value of all stocks listed on the New York Stock Exchange." On this expanded basis, he argues, the fiscal 1984 deficit was more than $300 billion rather than the $185 billion commonly reported.

Stanford's Mr. Boskin is working on a similar calculation and, like Mr. Egol, has concluded that the government is "several trillion dollars" in the red. And a "prototype" financial statement prepared by the Treasury Department for fiscal 1984 found government liabilities of $4.74 trillion, offset by only $937.3 billion in assets.

Many Problems

Such calculations are fraught with problems, however. A key question, for instance, is how to treat Social Security. Mr. Boskin, Mr. Egol and the Treasury all choose to view it as a pension program. As a result, Social Security obligations stretching far into the future must be recorded on the liability side of the balance sheet. That decision alone adds $1.9 trillion to the government's liabilities in 1984. If the program is treated as a transfer-payment program financed annually and not a pension program, that huge liability disappears.

There are other problems as well. For instance, how do you calculate the annual depreciation of missiles, bombs or tanks? How do you account for investments in public education? And what about the federal government's one asset that no private company can match: the power to tax?

"At the high level of accounting theory, this all sounds intriguing," ICF's Mr. Moran says. "But it makes no sense because

government is different than any other form of enterprise."
Trying to put together a comprehensive financial statement for
the federal government, Mr. Moran adds, would be "fabulously
expensive."

No Bottom Line

David Nathan, a budget official at the Commerce Department,
comments: "The government deals in assets that are unlike anyone else's. There is no bottom line. How much is it worth, for
example, to be the only one in town allowed to print money?"

The proposal to establish a separate capital-expenditures
budget, long pushed by a variety of accountants and economists,

---

U.S.A. Inc. Financial Statement

Since 1976, the Treasury Department has drawn up an annual
consolidated statement for the U.S. government, on an experimental
basis. The following is from the most recent statement, for the fiscal year
ended September 30, 1984 (in billions of dollars).

Assets		Liabilities	
Cash (operating cash balance and international monetary reserves, including gold valued at $42.22 an ounce)	$ 72.8	Accounts payable	$ 161.5
		Unearned revenue (includes tax collections that must be refunded)	31.8
Receivables (delinquent taxes, accrued corporate taxes, outstanding loans and other government receivables)	301.4	Borrowing from the public (doesn't include intragovernmental holdings)	1,299.5
Inventories (goods for sale, work in process, and materials and supplies; excludes weapons stockpiles because such information is secret)	151.4	Accrued pension and disability plans (including Social Security)	3,181.8
Property and equipment (land, buildings, equipment and military hardware, valued at cost and adjusted for depreciation; excludes 670 million acres of public land)	312.1	Contingent liabilities for government guarantee and insurance programs	3.5
		Other liabilities	58.5
Other assets	99.6	Total Liabilities	$4,736.6
Total Assets	$937.3	**Accumulated Position**	**−$3,799.3**

contemplates a budget that would look at the cost of an investment over its entire life. By paying more attention to such a budget, proponents say, the government would be less likely to adopt
costly stretchouts of military purchases, to delay investments
that might save money in the long run or to sell capital assets
to reduce operating deficits.

"We equate a dollar going into salaries with a dollar going
into a building that will last 15 years," the GAO's Mr. Wolf says.
"That idea has been rejected by nearly everyone else." A capital
budget would help policy makers make such distinctions, he
adds.

Mr. Boskin says: "If you were a counsel to private industry,
you would advise that they know whether their money is in new
plant and R&D or whether it's going to pay their secretary. We
don't do that. There is a real potential for making ill-advised
long-term government decisions by not having a separate capital
account."

More Pork?

Despite the advantages of such a separate account, many OMB
officials argue that a capital budget would encourage "pork-
barrel" spending on federal buildings, highways and canals. Mr.
Bowsher says that he discussed the idea with David Stockman
last year and that the former budget director responded that a
capital budget would simply give big spenders in Congress an
opportunity "to rebuild every bridge in America." Capital bud-
geting, Mr. Moran agrees, creates "a serendipitous interaction
between the theoretical leanings of accountants and the practical leanings of politicians."

Whatever the merits of arguments for accounting reform,
they don't seem to be carrying the day in Washington. Mr.
DioGuardi is trying to rally the support of all the accountants in
Congress, but so far he has found only three others. "I can't identify more than a handful in the entire history of Congress!" he
exclaims.

And at any rate, says Mr. Nathan of the Commerce Department, accounting changes aren't likely to alter the way Washington works. "The budget is politics," he says, "and people want

to make new decisions every year. No one has ever been able to demonstrate to me that accounting methods are going to change the way decisions are made."

Activist Auditor: A Mississippi Official Shakes Up the System, Restores Bond Ratings

Raymond Mabus Also Attacks Misuse of State Assets, Drawing Some Animosity— Public Crews on Private Jobs

By Lee Berton

April 8, 1986

JACKSON, Miss.—When Raymond Mabus, Jr., took over as state auditor two years ago, Mississippi was buried under a mountain of unfinished audit work.

The state was four years behind on the audits. Overdue paper work covered desks and floors in the auditor's office. In one desk was a shoe box filled with $330,000 in uncashed checks, some a year old, for payments to the state from official agencies.

Most of Mississippi's 82 counties had accounting systems unique to themselves. One county didn't require any financial reporting by officials. It had "one drawer for receipts and another for canceled checks," Mr. Mabus says. Five counties couldn't raise money in the bond market because they had lost their credit ratings.

But through court action, firings, more stringent auditing and jawboning, Mr. Mabus has restored the bond ratings, recovered close to $2 million in misspent money and broken up an old-boy network that had made accountability a farce in Mississippi. Within 18 months, he brought state audits up to date.

With state and local governments habitually under fire for lack of fiscal responsibility, Mississippi has shown that with strong leadership, a state can get its act together. The result can be beneficial for taxpayers.

"A county with a bond rating can pay as much as one percentage point less (interest) to its bond buyers than a county without a rating," says S. E. Canaday, Jr., a vice president of John Nuveen & Co., a major municipal-bond underwriting firm. On a $5 million bond issue, a typical amount raised by big Mississippi counties, the saving could total about $750,000 over 20 years, Mr. Canaday estimates. Such savings help hold down property taxes.

Defenders and Critics

Some political observers believe that Mr. Mabus, a 37-year-old Harvard Law School graduate and a former Washington D.C. attorney, is providing the right tonic for the state. He is a "phenom in a pinstripe suit who has sent county officials scurrying for cover," says W. F. "Bill" Minor, a syndicated political columnist in Mississippi.

But critics call him a political opportunist and headline-grabber aiming for higher office. Mr. Mabus concedes he eventually would like to run for governor or even a loftier post. He says that if he were elected president, he would be the second from his state. "The first," he quips, "was Jefferson Davis."

Opponents aren't amused. "Ray Mabus has held a lot of press conferences in my area to cite local corruption, but so far there have been no indictments," says Frank A. Carlton, the district attorney for five counties in northwestern Mississippi. "He may be looking more for visibility than honesty."

So far, Mr. Mabus has achieved a bit of both. After closely scrutinizing the accounts of almost every agency in the state, he has recovered misused funds from 240 state and local officials, although only 13 of them have been indicted statewide.

Some Recoveries

In one instance, he pressed a hospital president to pay for supplies the hospital had purchased from his private business in violation of state law. In another case, Mr. Mabus got a university press director to reimburse the state because the director and his wife had used university facilities to print books they sold to stores. (The director admits he used the facilities but says they were a "trade-off" for free services and equipment his company supplied to the university; he says he hadn't been aware that the state had to be repaid.)

Mr. Mabus also retrieved funds from a bookkeeper for the State Board of Barber Examiners alleged to have issued duplicate payroll checks to herself. (The bookkeeper, who has left the job, says the money was "an overpayment for vacation and sick-leave time.")

Many top financial officials in other states shun the job of policeman. William R. Snodgrass, comptroller of Tennessee, in fact, criticizes Mr. Mabus's anti-corruption drive as unfitting for a state auditor.

"I'm an informer, not a reformer," says Mr. Snodgrass, who adds that a state financial officer shouldn't blow the whistle out loud but should quietly tell the legislature about misuse of state funds.

For decades, reporting standards for state, municipal and local governments in the United States have been a charade. "At most, only 10% of the nation's 80,000 state and local governments are conforming to current standards," says Robert N. Anthony, a Harvard University professor of accounting.

In 1984 a self-regulatory body called the Governmental Accounting Standards Board was organized to bring some order to the situation. But so far the GASB has moved slowly and hasn't tackled the types of problems that Mr. Mabus found when he was elected and began scrutinizing local government books in Mississippi.

"Following the GASB's new rules wouldn't have corrected very much in Mississippi," Mr. Mabus says. Stricter accounting and reporting rules alone, he notes, don't uncover fraud and misuse of public money at the local level. "It takes a tough auditor who's willing to put pressure on the law-enforcement authorities," he declares.

The first campaign promise Mr. Mabus fulfilled when he took office in January 1984 was to poke a hole in the bottom of a decades-old pork barrel. He put an immediate stop to the use of county work crews to dig graves and pave driveways free of charge for constituents favored by county supervisors.

"I told a state-wide meeting of the Mississippi Association of Supervisors that my office would no longer allow them to use public equipment, personnel and funds to do work on private property," Mr. Mabus recalls. The reaction was immediate and often vitriolic.

Within a few weeks, 16 bills were filed in the legislature to reverse Mr. Mabus's dictum. All failed to pass or were killed in committee. "I think the majority of the lawmakers realized the favors weren't being given out equally," says Mr. Mabus, who figures he saved the state $20 million a year in costs for labor and for gravel used in private driveways.

But he has received many menacing phone calls in the middle of the night suggesting what he could do with the gravel he was saving. "One fellow woke me up and, after cussing me out, said he'd built a new house and couldn't get his driveway graveled," recalls the state auditor. "He said he was going to get me for this."

Mr. Mabus taped some of the threats on his phone recording device and gave the tapes to the highway patrol. It wasn't able to track down the callers.

Past Practice

Mr. Mabus also has zeroed in on spending habits of county officials. "What I found was a hotbed of self-dealing and corruption that had taken place under my predecessor for two decades," he says.

His predecessor, W. Hampton "Hamp" King, says he wasn't at fault. "Mr. Mabus has a good publicity machine, but he thinks he's the only honest man in Mississippi," says Mr. King, who claims he also initiated a lot of enforcement actions during his 20 years on the job. "But I notified law-enforcement officials first before calling a press conference. A lot of the so-called embezzlements he's uncovered may simply be oversights by local officials. My approach was to be more understanding of local custom."

Mr. Mabus revamped the investigative unit in the auditor's office and hired 35-year-old Louisa Dixon, a former federal investigator of oil-price violations, as its director. He also brought in 31-year-old Jere Nash, the former executive director of Mississippi Common Cause, as deputy state auditor.

"The unit has been swamped with more than 1,600 com·
plaints from citizens, and more than 400 misuses of public
money have been discovered by our auditors," Mr. Mabus says.

County Cases

Over the past two years, for example, he recovered more than
$69,000 from a former Jackson County supervisor for unauthor-
ized appropriations and construction work done on private property. He collected more than $68,000 from a bonding company
for a former Forrest County tax collector for a shortage of funds
in the collector's account. And he recovered more than $37,000
from the Harrison County court clerk for health-insurance premium costs incorrectly billed to the county; court clerks, who are
paid on per diem basis, are supposed to pay such premiums from
their own pockets.

The Forrest County tax collector pleaded guilty to embezzle-
ment last year and received a three-year suspended sentence. In
the other two cases, the principals say that the incidents resulted from misunderstandings of the law but that they made
restitution.

Regarding the relatively few indictments obtained, Ms.
Dixon of the auditor's investigative unit says, "Prosecutors
elected by local voters in Mississippi generally aren't that interested in white-collar crime." She adds, "We sometimes announce
the bigger recoveries in a press conference, which can create
pressure on the prosecutors."

Mr. Mabus has set up eight committees to develop auditing
and purchasing guidelines for the state's 800 entities, including
hospitals, schools and courts, so they can issue uniform and in-
formative financial reports. "From now on," he says, "public officials can provide timely information so bond-rating agencies
can base their decisions on the latest and most accurate information."

The State's Rating

"We've never had anything like this from Mississippi before,"
says Benjamin F. Phillips, a vice president of Moody's Investors
Service, a bond rating agency. "It's a very positive step and a
dramatic turnaround."

Mr. Mabus's zeal has raised some hackles, however. Robert

Crook, a 22-year state senator from Ruleville, proposed a constitutional amendment that would require the state auditor to be a certified public accountant, which Mr. Mabus isn't. It died in committee.

A state personnel board forced Mr. Mabus to lower the starting annual salary of his deputy, Mr. Nash, to $32,000 from $40,000. Mr. Mabus contends that was because some key lawmakers had been targets of Mississippi Common Cause, the consumer-advocate group that Mr. Nash headed. Mr. Mabus had hired Mr. Nash at $32,000 and later raised him to $40,000.

"The old guard wanted me to run for cover, but I stuck to my guns," Mr. Mabus says.

Mr. Minor, the columnist, says of Mr. Mabus, "Many legislators see Ray as an upstart who doesn't know how to play the political game."

Decision to Run

Mr. Minor was indirectly responsible for Mr. Mabus's running for public office. Mr. Mabus became incensed when he read a 1982 column by Mr. Minor about a party thrown by Mr. King, then the state auditor, at an expensive Biloxi hotel. Mr. King, who was about to retire, had invited 125 aides to meet the man he favored as his successor.

"Ray was furious and called to ask what the auditor's job was all about," recalls Mr. Minor. "After I described the problems, he admitted he had no political experience but said, 'What the hell, I think I'll throw my hat in the ring.'"

In 1983, Mr. Mabus won by 21,568 votes over Mason Shelby, chief deputy auditor and the man favored by Mr. King, in a Democratic primary runoff. The victory surprised Mr. Mabus, who then ran unopposed in the general election. "Although I'd been an assistant to a previous governor, I'd never run for office myself," he says. "I promised to clean up political corruption in Mississippi, and that's what I'm trying to do."

Mr. Mabus was born in Ackerman, a town of 1,300 people in east-central Mississippi. After graduating from the University of Mississippi, he got a master's degree in American politics from Johns Hopkins University and then served in the Navy. After Harvard Law School, he worked for a Washington, D.C., law firm for two years. In 1980 he returned to Mississippi as counsel and legislative assistant to Gov. William Winter.

Bitten by Political Bug

"I helped draft an education reform act in 1982 and got bitten by the political bug," he says.

Mr. Mabus says that when he was campaigning he met a man who knew his father. The man shook his hand and said: "I'm going to vote for you because if you're half as cheap with the state's money as your father is with his, we'll be in good shape."

He lives in a three-bedroom Victorian home filled with modern and traditional paintings by local artists. A jogger and amateur photographer, he visits his parents, Raymond Sr., 84, and Lucille, 77, at least once a week.

The elder Mr. Mabus is a distinct penny pincher. On visits to his son at Harvard Law School, his son says, he would ask for separate restaurant checks because sales tax wasn't charged on bills below a dollar.

When Mr. Mabus was campaigning, he says, he met a man who knew his father. The man shook his hand and said: "I'm going to vote for you because if you're half as cheap with the state's money as your father is with his, we'll be in good shape."

Rule Requires States and Cities
to Make Specific Disclosures
on Investment Risks

By David B. Hilder

May 7, 1986

STAMFORD, Conn.—The Governmental Accounting Standards Board adopted a rule requiring state and local governments to make more specific disclosures about the riskiness of their investments and bank deposits.

Mr. Hilder is a staff reporter of THE WALL STREET JOURNAL.

The rule was prompted by the millions of dollars in losses that local governments incurred in recent years because they lent money or securities to government securities dealers that later failed.

The standards board determines generally accepted accounting principles for states, cities and other local government units. However, states and local governments decide for themselves whether to follow such principles in preparing their financial statements.

James F. Antonio, chairman of the standards board, estimated that 25 states currently follow its rules; he said an additional 14 are in the process of adopting them. About half of the nation's largest cities and counties follow the standards board's principles, Mr. Antonio said. He said the percentage is lower among smaller governments.

The new rules require governments to list on their balance sheets the market values of investments in three separate categories of increasing risk.

• Those that are insured, registered, or held by the state or local government or its agent in the government's name.
• Those that are neither insured nor registered, but held by the financial institution's or dealer's trust department in the government's name.
• Those that are both uninsured and unregistered, and held by the financial institution or dealer but not specifically in the government's name.

A similar three-category system also applies to bank deposits and securities held as collateral for bank deposits. Many state laws require governments to obtain collateral for any bank deposits that exceed the $100,000 amount covered by federal deposit insurance.

Currently, the standards board's rules don't require governments to specify what type of investments or deposits they have or where they are held.

Among the investments that are covered by the new rules are repurchase and reverse repurchase agreements of government securities. Governments routinely use such short-term transactions, known as "repos" and "reverse repos," to earn market interest rates on their idle cash.

A repurchase agreement occurs when one party, such as a broker-dealer, sells government securities to another, such as a local government, with the agreement that the broker will buy the securities back on a certain date for a higher price that includes interest. A reverse repo is the same transaction from the buyer's point of view.

Several local governments incurred losses last year when they engaged in repos with E.S.M. Government Securities Inc. of Fort Lauderdale, Florida, but didn't take possession of the securities that served as collateral for the transactions. When E.S.M. collapsed, it didn't have enough collateral to meet all of its obligations.

The new rules will take effect for reporting periods ending after December 15, and were adopted by a unanimous vote of the standards board.

The rules also require governments to make additional disclosures if their investment or deposit risks were significantly greater at any time during the reporting period than on the date for which the balance sheet was prepared. That decision on whether the additional risk existed, however, was left to the government and its outside auditors.

"The disclosures required (by the new rules) will help financial-report users assess the deposit and investment risks taken by government entities," Mr. Antonio said.

Accounting-Standards Boards' Rift Irks Many Colleges, May Hurt Private Ones

By Lee Berton
Staff Reporter of THE WALL STREET JOURNAL

NEW YORK—Colleges are learning a sad lesson: The existence of separate accounting standard-setting bodies can complicate their fund-raising, tangle their financial statements and confuse the investing public.

A disagreement has erupted between two such bodies that

is likely to give public colleges and universities an advantage over private ones in the financing arena, among others. It will affect investors in tax-exempt college securities, lenders, suppliers, donors and legislators who vote on education grants. And in the long haul, the dispute eventually could lead private colleges to boost tuition costs.

The flap, which concerns how colleges should handle depreciation of buildings and equipment, is between the Financial Accounting Standards Board, or FASB, and the Governmental Accounting Standards Board, or GASB.

The FASB, formed in 1973, sets accounting rules for all businesses and organizations with the informal blessing of federal regulators such as the Securities and Exchange Commission.

Formation in 1984
Over the FASB's opposition, the GASB was formed in 1984, under pressure from state and local governments, which wanted a separate body to set rules for them; government operations, the argument ran, require special accounting systems. Both boards are housed in the same building in Stamford, Conn., and share some staff. Under a mandate from the accounting profession, the GASB can overrule the FASB only in the government area.

The two bodies generally have kept peace—until now. Earlier this month, the FASB issued a rule requiring all colleges to depreciate buildings and equipment, effective for reporting periods beginning after May 15, 1988. Depreciation, or the deduction of annual costs to reflect wear and tear, reduces the value of assets and can lower profit.

Today, the GASB is slated to circulate a proposed rule that would exempt state-owned educational institutions from depreciation. The GASB's countermanding proposal has a comment deadline of Nov. 24, and is very likely to take effect before year's end, say GASB officials.

Private colleges fear the results of the proposed exemption. Private and public colleges compete briskly for financing by issuing tax-exempt bonds, and lower assets and profits tend to mean such bond issues must offer higher rates to attract investors.

In the past three years, more than $20 billion of such bonds has been sold publicly. Currently, there are about $60 billion of such bonds outstanding from private colleges and about $40 billion from public institution, estimates Leonard Wesolowski, comptroller of Yale University.

Most colleges and universities opposed the FASB rule when it was proposed last year. Many felt it would increase the cost of developing financial data without resultant benefits.

"Depreciating the university's 160 buildings and equipment worth over $1 billion could cost us up to $200,000 for new computer software to do the figuring each year," estimates William J. Hogan, comptroller of the University of Chicago, a private institution. "It really isn't worth it."

Complaints about the standards boards' clash also ring out from the public sector, despite the benefits from the proposed GASB exemption.

Hubert Parker, director of accounting for state-owned University of Georgia, maintains that depreciation of assets for any college is "nonsensical." He adds: "We're not public companies."

'A Dumb Idea'

And Stephen H. Terry, assistant vice president for finance at Michigan State University, says, "Two sets of rules on depreciation is a dumb idea that will only force us to keep two sets of books (so that financial statements can be compared by bond rating concerns, lenders and others) and even further increase bookkeeping costs."

Martin Ives, GASB vice chairman, disagrees. "The reason that the GASB and the FASB differ on some accounting issues is that we have different priorities as to who uses financial statements," says Mr. Ives. "We look at government accounting based on the needs of governmental officials, while the FASB looks at all accounting based on the needs of investors."

And the FASB stands firm. Ronald Bossio, an FASB project manager, maintains that all colleges and universities should depreciate assets. "Since buildings and equipment eventually need to be replaced, repaired and maintained, an organization should want to know how its assets are wearing out," Mr. Bossio says.

The FASB-GASB clash could be a key factor in determining

whether the GASB will continue to exist. The Financial Accounting Foundation, a body of business and professional members that oversees both boards, has begun a "survival" review of the GASB; this review was a concession won by the FASB when the newer organization, which is mostly made up of government officials, was created.

Accounting Plan Would Put Cities in Red

States Join Dispute over Handling of Costs

By Lee Berton

June 15, 1988

NEW YORK—The bottom lines of many major cities and states— particularly New York City—would quickly turn red under a measure proposed by the Governmental Accounting Standards Board, the chief accounting rule-making body for local and state governments.

After digesting public comment on the proposal, the GASB will vote on the proposal later this year. If approved, the measure would take effect in early 1989. An indication of the measure's controversial nature was reflected in the board's narrow, 3-to-2 approval of the draft proposal last winter.

As city and state financial officers begin to recognize the impact of the proposal made last December, opposition is mounting. If approved, the measure would force cities and states to deduct immediately from their surpluses a wide range of costs that the governments have deferred for as long as 40 years in the future.

Such costs include accrued vacation pay and earned sick leave for employees, court claims and judgments, certain pension liabilities and future lease obligations.

Taking an immediate hit for such costs in the general fund of cities and states could lower their debt ratings, force them to raise added funds in the bond market and eventually spur them to increase taxes, say accountants.

Effect on Big Cities

Many state and city officials agree that the costs should be given more current treatment, but argue that they should be phased in, over periods as long as 15 years, rather than absorbed all at once.

Under the proposal, New York City's current surplus of $51 million would be converted into a devastating deficit of $5.75 billion. Chicago would go from a $20 million surplus to a $50 million deficit. And Detroit would drop from a $14 million surplus to a $20 million deficit.

The GASB proposal "would mean immediate and severe fund-balance reductions or deficits for many governments," says Edward M. Klasny, national director of governmental accounting and auditing at Cleveland-based Ernst & Whinney, the third biggest U.S. accounting firm. A political entity's general-fund balance is the surplus or deficit remaining after general operating expenses are deducted from revenues.

Adds Mr. Klasny: "In some cases, this may create illegal def-

Surplus to Deficit:
How Cities Would Fare
Effect of GASB accounting proposal on selected municipalities

	Current Surplus	Deficit under GASB Proposal*
New York City	$51 million	$5.75 billion
Los Angeles	$138 million	$375 million
Chicago	$20 million	$50 million
Cleveland	$6 million	$20 million
Detroit	$14 million	$20 million
Pittsburgh	$10 million	$100,000**

*Pro-forma estimates.
**Surplus.

icits requiring short-term financing. In government units forced to quickly fund the resulting deficits, it could force them to raise taxes."

GASB staff members say the proposal would show more accurately the current obligations of government bodies, and whether the obligations require current or future payment. Even some opponents of the proposal, such as Mr. Klasny, concede it would "provide a more accurate picture of a government's overall financial conditions."

The GASB has held five public hearings on the proposal this year and has 172 written comments from government bodies and accountants.

A study by the GASB of 27 large cities, states, counties and school districts shows that 18 would have decreases in their general-fund balances under the accounting proposal. While the entities surveyed were assured anonymity, the survey does show that fund-balance declines ranged from 4.6% to 27.6% of the political bodies' annual revenue, the GASB says.

The political bodies requested anonymity because they fear both the political and economic consequences of the GASB proposal. "Without understanding that this proposal is simply an accounting change and isn't really money out of our pockets, all hell could break loose with our citizens and our councilmen," says William Van Note, first deputy comptroller of New York City.

GASB Members' Stance

Mr. Van Note says he is particularly distressed because three members of the five-member GASB, based in Norwalk, Connecticut, want the accrued costs deducted immediately from general-fund balances. James Antonio, GASB chairman, and Martin Ives, vice chairman, voted against the proposal last December.

"The majority of the board may wish to put (the change) into place all at once, but without phasing it in over a period of time, a lot of governments will go from a healthy surplus to a deficit overnight," says Mr. Antonio, former state auditor of Missouri.

"It would be a political disaster to impose the proposal without a phase-in period," says Ronald Picur, comptroller of the city of Chicago. "It would force our mayor to wear a red jacket that says 'deficit' and would confuse our city council, which believes in a balanced budget."

Charles Brown, director of finance for Cleveland, cautions the GASB to move slowly on the proposal. "It's taken the public a while to understand how government bodies are moving to generally accepted accounting principles," he says. "Rushing into accruing expenses we haven't yet paid will cause financial statements to take big swings to the deficit side and could create big confusion."

Rollin Henderson, chief accounting officer for Detroit, would prefer to continue to account for such costs as they are paid out. "They are more properly reflected in long-term obligations, since they aren't paid out in the current year," he says.

Negative Fund Balance

New York City's Mr. Van Note says that if the GASB forces governments to reflect such costs in the current general-fund balance, he would prefer to see the charge as a "separate line that can be amortized or accounted for by future revenues." He says he'd prefer to call the big one-time adjustment "a negative fund balance" rather than a deficit.

To prevent any economic and political hardships resulting from the GASB proposal, Ernst & Whinney's Mr. Klasny recommends phasing in the costs over a period of as long as 15 years. In this way, he adds, "governments and their constituents could avoid the shock and consequences of 'big-bang' implementation."

Mr. Klasny also suggests that the GASB delay the proposed rule's implementation for two years to enable governments "to begin planning for changes in their financial reporting."

PART 4

INDUSTRY-SPECIFIC REPORTING

CHAPTER 17

FINANCIAL SERVICES INDUSTRY REPORTING

This section covers the developments in the banking and insurance industries that impact the marketing of products and services.

The banking industry has gone through many changes in the last several years that have affected its accounting and reporting. Increased numbers of complex financial instruments, new competition from abroad, deregulation in some areas, yet increased regulation in others by the Federal Reserve Board, and the rise of bank failures, particularly S&L's throughout the United States have all contributed to creating a very challenging environment for banking and financial institutions.

The following collection addresses many of the problems in the banking industry, including those of money center banks and savings and loan associations. Lee Berton has been prophetic in his perceptions of the problems and resulting bank failures.

Fate of Banks with Problem Foreign Loans May Rest on Changes in Accounting Rules

By Lee Berton

November 2, 1983

At a recent meeting on the international debt crisis, federal bank regulators floated some proposals on how banks might account for troubled foreign loans. Some bankers didn't like what they heard.

"I don't mind disclosing more," one says. "But I don't want to have to give away the whole shop."

The debt crisis has moved into the domain of accountants and federal regulators, and what they decide during the next few months may determine the fate of some banks. If they don't change accounting rules or fudge existing rules, some banks may fail. But if they do change the rules, depositors may panic, fearing that some banks are a lot worse off than they seem.

"The stability of the entire financial system may be at stake," says Richard A. Hairsine, a director specializing in banking at the accounting firm of Main Hurdman.

Most people, of course, expect the accountants and regulators to find a solution that keeps the banks stable but also reassures depositors. But they say it will be difficult, and few predict what the solution will be. Some doubt that accounting changes alone will solve the problems.

"Unless the debtor countries quickly straighten out their economies or the banks quickly pay the piper for bad loans—both of which are unlikely if not impossible—the problem just won't go away," says an official of the American Institute of Certified Public Accountants.

The problem facing the accountants and the regulators—including the comptroller of the currency, the Federal Reserve Board and the Federal Deposit Insurance Corp.—involves how banks treat their overseas loans. Although the rules are hazy, some financial experts have argued for months that many loans to governments in developing countries—such as Brazil and Argentina—are of dubious value, and that banks ought to set aside some money to cover possible losses. They also insist that because new bank loans to many countries are simply being used to pay back interest, banks shouldn't record the current interest payments on the old loans as income.

While banks have done some of these things, they haven't done them to the extent that their critics seek, largely because the moves would substantially reduce profits. But several events in recent weeks have brought the issue to a critical point.

In particular, banks may soon be forced to classify some of the loans as "nonperforming." Banks have 90 days in which to collect overdue interest. If it takes longer than that, federal and state regulations require that the loan be called nonperforming and that the banks subtract as much as six months of interest payments that they have already counted as income, and no longer include interest as income.

If regulators don't change accounting rules for overseas loans, some banks may fail. But if they do change the rules, depositors may panic, fearing that some banks are a lot worse off than they seem.

Brazil, with some $70 billion owed to banks, may have many of its loans in that category when the banks report fourth-quarter earnings. Classifying those loans as nonperforming would sharply cut the bank's earnings.

Brazil's major lenders are trying to put together a new package of rescue loans for Brazil, which would permit payment of at least some of the overdue interest and ease the nonperformance problem. But the package would require that bankers make slight concessions on interest rates and fees, and some bankers fear that if they give such concessions, regulators will ask them to classify the loans as nonperforming. As the bankers see it, they lose either way.

"It's a serious problem and can get a lot more serious in a short time unless banks are given some direction," says Thomas H. Asson, a partner specializing in banking at Coopers & Lybrand, one of the eight largest U.S. accounting firms.

To avoid the Brazil problem, banks want regulators to change the rules, but they don't agree on what the changes should be. Bankers and regulators are discussing proposals to spread the losses over 10 years instead of accounting for them all in one year. On the other hand, they are also discussing a plan to convert such loans to "present value"—the reduced value they now have. Such a plan would involve huge write-offs over just one year.

Some regulators have talked about having banks set up a reserve for rescheduled foreign debts that would total 2% of the rescheduled loans. That would be in addition to the typical reserve of 1% of total loans that banks normally set aside for potential bad loans. And while the 2% is modest compared with what some legislators would like, it would reduce annual profits of the nine largest U.S. banks by as much as 14%, according to William Cline, an economist at the Washington-based Institute for International Economics.

The bankers are worried that Congress will preempt any regulatory action. Legislative proposals now before Congress would push bank regulators to force banks to set aside reserves for doubtful loans—with Congress deciding what is and isn't a doubtful loan. A House version would include all rescheduled loans—that is, all loans in which principal payments have been stretched out. A less stringent Senate version asks for reserves only if the borrower has repayment problems over a "protracted" period.

"Congress is asking what you guys are doing about this crisis," William A. Ryback, director of international banking activity for the comptroller of the currency, recently told a group of bankers meeting in New York City. Congress, Mr. Ryback told the bankers, "will accept complacency (only) so long before they enact legislative restrictions on banks."

The bankers argue that the economy will get hurt if the banks pay too high a price. At the New York meeting of bankers and regulators, for instance, a banker admitted that "Congress probably won't be very sympathetic if bank earnings suffer." But he warned that if bank earnings dry up, "the recovery may flop."

As it is, banks are being forced to disclose more about their foreign-debt exposure. Last August, the Securities and Exchange Commission recommended that annual reports of publicly traded banks, which represent the vast majority of U.S. bank assets, disclose the country, amount and type of loan that exceeds 1% of a bank's total assets. And starting next year, the FDIC will issue a report on banks' foreign-debt exposure every quarter instead of every six months, as it does now.

Such stepped-up disclosure should tell potential depositors and investors which banks have foreign-loan problems. "No more 'let the buyer beware,'" an accountant says.

Hard Numbers:
Bank Auditor's Job Gets Much Tougher; Some Firms Are Sued

Judging the Quality of Loans Becomes More Complex; CPA Insurance Costs Up
—Avoiding a 'Wheeler-Dealer'

By Lee Berton

May 9, 1984

NEW YORK—For years, the bank audit was the accountant's dream assignment. "Valuing the bank's loan portfolio was a breeze," one accountant recalls. "We usually took the bank directors' word for it. We made a lot of new business contacts through the bank, took a long lunch and went home early."

These days, however, the dream assignment has turned into a nightmare.

Bank auditors are being asked to judge the credit-worthiness of increasingly complex energy, agriculture, real-estate and international loans. As deregulation has pushed many banks into new areas such as venture capital and discount brokerage, auditors have to gauge the riskiness of the new businesses.

Bankruptcies Up

Moreover, bankruptcies of financial institutions have soared. A record 48 banks failed last year, 25 have collapsed so far this year, and many more are expected.

Meanwhile, auditors themselves are under attack. Some of their critics are raising conflict-of-interest questions about loans obtained by accounting-firm partners at banks that their firms subsequently audit. And outside auditors are facing more lawsuits by failed banks' disgruntled shareholders and creditors.

The Federal Deposit Insurance Corp. also is said to be considering court action against five accounting firms, including Peat, Marwick, Mitchell & Co. and Ernst & Whinney, involving audits of banks that later failed, were closed or were sold to other banks. The FDIC insures individual bank deposits for up to $100,000, and as its insurance losses mount, it is looking for reimbursement from the outside auditor for some of those losses.

"Based just on the 90 bank failures we had in 1983 and 1982, we've made out-of-court settlements of $6 million with six CPA firms over the past year," says Cecil Underwood, an FDIC attorney with a special section on accountants' liability set up late in 1980. "But the big settlements or suits . . . will come this year and in 1985," he adds.

Insurance Costly

Insurance-company officials say that partly because of such out-of-court settlements, liability insurance for CPA firms is becoming more expensive or disappearing altogether. "We dropped out of the business of insuring accounting firms for liability in January 1983," says Robert M. Liston, the executive vice president for underwriting for Shand, Morahan & Co., an insurance subsidiary of Alexander & Alexander Services Inc. "We couldn't get the premiums needed for the kinds of losses we were suffering." Shand Morahan continues to insure architects, engineers, attorneys, physicians and surgeons. "The risks aren't as great," Mr. Liston observes.

All this is making auditors nervous. "Our bank auditors have had a lot of sleepless nights," admits Martin Mertz, the national director of banking practice for Peat Marwick, which audits about 600 banks.

In view of the banking industry's mounting problems, however, C. Todd Conover, the U.S. Comptroller of the Currency, is pressuring banks with national charters to obtain audits from outside certified public accountants. He recently told a banking audience that an annual external audit "is not a luxury; it is an absolute necessity." Of 4,500 nationally chartered banks, about 2,000 are audited now; under the law, they don't have to be audited because they are regulated.

Under current audit procedures, an outside auditor should scrutinize a bank's credit-review procedures, its allowance for loan losses and the collateral for those loans. The bank's shareholders and depositors as well as its creditors and other banks that may buy its loans depend on the outside CPA's evaluations for assurance that their funds or business dealings are safe.

'A Guessing Game'

But auditors at major accounting firms admit that many of these tasks, particularly evaluating loans, are judgment calls that even the best auditor can miss. For one thing, there is no industry rule; the latest bank-audit guide, issued by the American Institute of CPAs, leaves decisions about the proper level of loan reserves to bank management and the outside auditor. "It's strictly a guessing game," says the managing partner of a medium-sized accounting firm. And auditors say that with mounting bankruptcies in energy, real estate and farming, old benchmarks no longer apply.

"The normal procedure has been to test 2% of the collateral for loans, but now if you suspect any problem at a bank, you may have to look at 50% of the loans," one accountant says. Such an audit is so expensive, he says, that it may not be worthwhile. He adds that his firm, for the first time, has turned down two bank audits. "One had a wheeler-dealer in management, and the other had a bunch of bad farm loans," he explains. "We don't need that kind of trouble."

Another accountant recalls that in checking the collateral on a $50,000 tractor loan to a farmer, it took the county recording office two weeks to tell the bank that the tractor had a prior lien against it. The bank was forced to set aside a $40,000 reserve for the loan, charging it against income. "Ten years ago, when farmers weren't so desperate and banking wasn't so competitive, the farmer wouldn't have been able to force the bank to grant the loan when he needed it—within three days," the accountant says.

Evaluating energy and real-estate loans can be even trickier; volatile prices make checking the collateral almost impossible. If oil prices plunge, for instance, an oil rig used as collateral could lose much of its value.

As to mounting international loans, "There's no way an outside auditor can tell whether countries that borrow to pay previous interest, like Brazil and Argentina, will eventually pay off," an accountant says. Repayment is only partly a financial matter; it is mixed in with a lot of politics and psychology.

But while auditors say their job is getting tougher, others blame the auditors. The House Subcommittee on Commerce, Consumer and Monetary Affairs plans to hold hearings late this year or early next year on whether bank regulators should be tougher with outside auditors of banks.

"The concept of the independent auditors is something of a myth," says Peter Barash, the subcommittee's staff director. "When brought in to do an audit, they become employees of the bank and are paid by the bank. Their professional standards don't seem to override this inherent conflict of interest." Too often, he says, "it seems the auditors are brought in to do a whitewash."

And, Mr. Barash adds, the feds don't help much. He notes, for instance, that bank regulators such as the Comptroller of the Currency and the FDIC, which can send armies of examiners into troubled banks at a moment's notice, haven't routinely informed outside auditors of the regulators' findings. Even if they do tell the auditors, he says, the auditors don't have to tell the public.

Since 1981, the FDIC has reported insurance-expense losses—amounts it expects to pay out over future years to troubled banks' depositors and creditors—of $2.6 billion. Before 1981, such losses ranged only from $30 million to $100 million a year.

Limited Role

For their part, accountants say that CPAs can only warn bank managements and press for changes, but that they haven't any responsibility to inform the public that a bank is in trouble. "Otherwise," Peat Marwick's Mr. Mertz says, "we might cause a run on the bank."

The accountants' dilemma, and shortcomings, are perhaps best illustrated by looking at two cases that have sparked lawsuits. In March 1982, Peat Marwick issued a clean audit opinion on the financial health of Penn Square Bank in Oklahoma City; four months later, federal regulators closed the bank, and they still are liquidating it.

Similarly, in January 1983, Ernst & Whinney, a Cleveland-based accounting firm with about 400 bank clients, issued a clean opinion on the financial statement of United American Bank, the Jake F. Butcher bank in Knoxville, Tenn.; 20 days later, the bank was closed by federal regulators and has since been merged with another bank.

The FDIC is said to be considering suing both Peat Marwick on Penn Square and Ernst & Whinney on United American Bank—alleging negligence in failing to follow generally accepted auditing standards when issuing the opinions. Both accounting firms already have been sued by private parties, who allege various failures and conflicts of interest.

Michigan National Bank of Detroit is suing Penn Square Bank management and Peat Marwick. It is asking $40 million of damages for energy loans that it brought from Penn Square and have been defaulted. The suit, filed in state circuit court in Kalamazoo, Michigan, last September, is still pending.

Lawrence Gladchun, the general counsel of Michigan National Bank, says: "We started purchasing participations in Penn Square loans in December 1980 and stopped late in June 1982, just before (Penn Square) was closed. Since we are bankers ourselves, I can assure you we would never have kept those loans if we weren't assured by the auditor's opinion."

Mr. Gladchun says Arthur Young & Co., another Big Eight accounting firm, had given Penn Square a qualified opinion—which securities analysts consider a red flag—on its 1980 financial statement, before Peat Marwick took over the audit in late 1981. Also, he observes, the Comptroller of the Currency in mid-1981 had issued a "cease-and-desist" order telling the bank's officials to stop making substandard loans that lacked proper documentation or sufficient collateral.

"If Peat Marwick knew about this order, it should have told other banks and customers of Penn Square," he says. Peat Marwick is being sued by five creditors of Penn Square; three of the plaintiffs are credit unions that sustained large losses.

Loans to CPAs

Peat Marwick officials also testified before the House subcommittee late in 1982 that a group of the CPA firm's partners borrowed $2.3 million from Penn Square before the bank became a Peat Marwick client in December 1981. Penn Square arranged to sell the loans to other banks that weren't Peat Marwick clients, but one $300,000 real-estate loan that was sold to another bank was later returned to Penn Square during the Peat Marwick audit.

Peat Marwick's Mr. Mertz contends that his firm acted ethically in the Penn Square audit. However, he admits that the $300,000 loan bounced back to Penn Square. "But it was paid immediately after that," he notes.

However, Mr. Gladchun says: "There was clear lack of independence on the part of Peat Marwick in relation to the propriety of the loans made by Penn Square to the CPA firm's partners."

As auditor for United American Bank, Ernst & Whinney was sued by a group of shareholders in federal district court in Knoxville in March 1983. Alleging securities fraud and misrepresentation of financial figures, the still-pending suit says that prior to Ernst & Whinney's opinion, the FDIC had warned United American officials that the bank was undercapitalized, required additional equity funds and needed to clean up its loan portfolio.

"Ernst & Whinney should have told the bank's shareholders and its customers of the FDIC warning," argues James McCollum, a Knoxville attorney representing the plaintiffs.

Regulators' Position

Magnus C. Nelson, Ernst & Whinney's senior partner in charge of banking, declines comment on the suit. Testifying before the House Subcommittee on Commerce, Consumer and Monetary Affairs last year, Mr. Nelson said: "At the time we issued our report, we knew nothing of the difference between the FDIC's findings and ours or of the possible closing of the bank."

Bank regulators concede that, despite meeting with accounting-firm representatives late last year on the issue of sharing bank audit data, they still won't give their examiners' reports directly to outside auditors. Instead, they rely on bank management to do it.

"It's like asking the fox to tell the farmer how he got into the henhouse," the subcommittee's Mr. Barash says. "It's outrageous that there isn't any automatic exchange of information between regulators and outside auditors."

Worried about the pending court cases, accounting firms have been increasing the training of their bank auditing staffs. Ernst & Whinney this summer will test up to 120 of its auditing supervisors with a computer model simulating a bank's operations. The supervisors will pretend that they are bank lending officers and have to decide, for example, whether their "bank" should accept deposits from a middleman.

Peat Marwick will expand its credit-review training course for 350 bank auditors next month to include details on how to make audit judgments about overdrafts, letters of credit, related borrowers, money transfers among banks and bank credit limits. "We've got to expand our banking horizons because the bank audit has become trickier," Mr. Mertz says.

FASB Is Expected to Determine Today Accounting of Freddie Mac Distribution

By Lee Berton

January 23, 1985

NEW YORK—The Financial Accounting Standards Board, the chief rule-making body for accountants, is expected to decide today on an accounting treatment that could hurt the financial health of 3,000 U.S. thrifts.

The FASB will consider whether the distribution of a special stock dividend valued at $600 million to $800 million by the Federal Home Loan Mortgage Corp., or Freddie Mac, can be counted as pre-tax earnings by the thrifts.

The staff of the FASB initially said that the distribution wasn't earnings because the thrifts indirectly own Freddie Mac through their control of the 12 regional Federal Home Loan Banks. "The big question that the FASB must decide is whether something of value has been transferred to the member institutions of the Federal Home Loan Bank Board that these institutions didn't have before," says Mark Pearson, an FASB project manager.

But during hearings last week in Stamford, Connecticut, where the FASB is based, spokesmen for the thrift industry voiced strong views that the Freddie Mac dividend is real earnings. "If the FASB doesn't recognize it as income, it could seriously hurt the thrift industry by lowering its net worth and reducing the value of stock of those thrifts that are publicly traded," says Brian Smith, associate director of research for the U.S. League of Savings Institutions, the industry's trade group.

Trading in Freddie Mac's preferred stock—permitted only among thrifts—is scheduled to begin today on the New York Stock Exchange. And some accountants believe that the thrifts shouldn't count the distribution as earnings before it begins trading. But the vast majority of the nation's thrifts had planned to declare the distribution as part of 1984 earnings.

"The distribution would account for 25% of our 1984 income, and I feel strongly that it's genuine income," asserts John B. Zellars, chairman of Georgia Federal Bank, a savings bank based in Atlanta. Mr. Zellars, chairman of U.S. League of Savings Institutions, estimated that about 50% of the nation's 3,000 thrifts need the Freddie Mac stock distribution as earnings to shore up their eroding net worth.

William M. Waller, chairman of State Federal Savings & Loan Association, Tulsa, Oklahoma, says that if the distribution is declared earnings by the FASB, it would provide the thrift with about $136,000 in added earnings for 1984. "This would certainly help us keep net worth at a respectable level," he adds. For 1983, the thrift had a net loss of about $2 million, mainly to maintain reserves for special subsidiaries' projects such as land development. Its net worth at the end of 1983 was $3.2 million.

Mr. Smith of the U.S. League of Savings Institutions estimates that the distribution could account for as much as 30% to 40% of U.S. thrifts' estimated 1984 total net income of $1.5 billion. "An adverse ruling by the FASB could have a devastating effect on the thrift industry," he adds.

Mr. Pearson said the FASB staff has prepared a memo on its latest views, after hearing the views of thrift industry representatives last week, and would present it to the FASB today. "It's expected that the FASB will make its decision" today, he added.

FASB to Let S&Ls List Freddie Mac's Stock as Earnings

By Lee Berton

January 24, 1985

NEW YORK—The Financial Accounting Standards Board voted to permit a special stock dividend given by the Federal Home Loan Mortgage Corp. to 3,000 U.S. thrifts to be counted as pre-tax earnings.

The chief rule-making body for accountants, based in Stamford, Connecticut, said it made its decision "based on representations of the Federal Home Loan Bank Board that an asset granting ownership rights not previously held has been transferred" to the thrifts.

The FASB's staff initially said the distribution wasn't earnings because the thrifts indirectly own the corporation, or Freddie Mac, through their control of the 12 regional Federal Home Loan Banks. But a later staff position, after testimony by thrift trade groups and the Bank Board last week, apparently changed to the thrifts' position.

The FASB said it will issue a proposal for the accounting treatment within a week, with a comment period of 15 days. Since the thrifts are pleased with the decision, it's unlikely the FASB will hear any opposition.

"We believe the distribution has enhanced the position of savings institutions and that this improved position should be reflected on their financial statements," said William B. Connel, president of the U.S. League of Savings Institutions, a thrift-industry trade group.

The accounting would permit the income imputed from the Freddie Mac shares to be booked as pre-tax earnings for 1984, which the majority of thrifts already had planned to do. Seven of the Big Eight accounting firms support this treatment, while only Touche Ross & Co. said the distribution wasn't pre-tax earnings.

Trading in the 15 million Freddie Mac shares—permitted only among thrifts—began yesterday on the New York Stock Exchange. Volume in composite trading was 233,100 shares, with the opening at $40.125 and the closing at $42.125.

Legerdemain:
Accounting at Thrifts Provokes
Controversy as Gimmickry Mounts

Inventive Techniques Mask Problems at Many S&Ls; Are Profits Overstated?
—Ill Will Toward Good Will

By Lee Berton

March 21, 1985

For many of the country's 3,000 savings and loan associations, accounting gimmickry has become a narcotic they can't deny themselves.

Financial legerdemain once viewed as a temporary evil to help save S&Ls in the early 1980s still mars the books of many thrifts, and its popularity is expanding. Among other things, S&Ls are shoring up their profits with an unusual stock dividend, they are still using a lot of "purchase accounting" gimmickry, and many are still doing fancy stunts with construction-loan accounting. But what a lot of them still aren't doing, according to critics on Wall Street and in the accounting profession, is making very much real money.

Last year, for example, $600 million of the industry's total profits of $2.1 billion came from a Federal Home Loan Mortgage Corp. stock dividend that some accountants don't think should be considered earnings at all. And half of the remaining $1.5 billion was generated by other "questionable accounting in the finest tradition of Lewis Carroll," asserts Jonathan Gray, a thrift analyst at Sanford C. Bernstein & Co., a New York securities concern.

Intractable Problem
Such gimmickry, according to critics, is masking a seemingly intractable problem. Much of the thrift industry hasn't recovered from the debacle of 1981-82, when heavy losses forced many S&Ls out of business. Fully one-third of all thrifts, for example,

wouldn't have any net worth if they had to strike intangible assets like good will from their balance sheets.

Defenders of thrift accounting, who include executives at some of the largest S&Ls and their auditors, counter that almost all thrifts still adhere to generally accepted accounting practice. They also note that nearly all thrifts are still financially sound in the sense that they take in more actual cash than they spend.

But even defenders concede that all isn't well in the thrift industry, which poses a dilemma for regulators and accountants. A crackdown on innovative accounting might seriously weaken public confidence in the thrift industry. Last August, a Securities and Exchange Commission move to curb alleged accounting abuses at Financial Corp. of America helped precipitate a liquidity crisis at the thrift concern, the country's largest. Last week's run on Ohio S&L deposits is an even more vivid illustration of the industry's dependence on public confidence. Yesterday, Ohio Governor Richard Celeste signed legislation providing for the reopening of 70 thrifts that have been closed since last Friday.

Embarrassing Questions

But regulators and accountants run the risk of being criticized for glossing over the industry's structural problems if they continue to sanction unusual accounting. The accounting profession is already facing embarrassing questions at recently begun congressional hearings on why auditors haven't fully informed the public about problems at financial institutions.

The controversy is pitting major accounting concerns, which generally support their S&L clients, against rule makers like the Financial Accounting Standards Board, which has tried to stop some controversial practices. Rule makers are "constantly scrambling to put out fires on the thrift accounting front," says Sandra K. Johnigan, the chairman of the savings and loan committee of the American Institute of Certified Public Accountants, another group that sets standards.

Nearly everyone agrees that many S&Ls won't get back on their feet until the country experiences a long period of stable or lower interest rates. But since that isn't likely to happen, the amount of gimmickry seems certain to increase. For example, a recent proposal to fortify the federal insurance fund for thrift deposits involves some complicated accounting but no increase in what laymen would consider hard cash.

Freddie Mac Controversy

The most recent accounting innovation is the stock dividend distributed last fall by the Federal Home Loan Mortgage Corp., or Freddie Mac, a quasi-governmental agency involved in the secondary mortgage market. The distribution was designed to bolster thrifts' earnings and net worth, but the FASB staff initially felt that the stock wasn't real earnings. S&Ls indirectly own Freddie Mac through their control of the 12 regional Federal Home Loan Banks, which helped set up Freddie Mac in 1970. At first, the FASB staff said thrifts couldn't receive something of value they already owned.

The thrift industry and its regulators launched an offensive. The U.S. League of Savings Institutions, the major trade group, got its members to ask their auditors for support. With the exception of Touche Ross & Co., all the Big Eight accounting firms advised the FASB to change its mind. Freddie Mac and the Federal Home Loan Bank Board, which regulates S&Ls, dispatched legal experts in a driving January snowstorm to FASB headquarters in Stamford, Connecticut. Regulators' arguments finally persuaded the rule makers to relent.

The stock dividend was a godsend to many thrifts. "We probably wouldn't have had any earnings last year without it," admits William M. Waller, the chairman of State Federal Savings & Loan Association in Tulsa, Oklahoma. Like other thrifts, State Federal also gets to count its Freddie Mac stock as an asset. That is another controversial issue among accountants.

Freddie Mac stock began trading last January on the New York Stock Exchange at $40.125 a share and has since fallen to $34.75. The only investors who are allowed to own and trade the stock, however, are S&Ls. Freddie Mac says public ownership "might change the fundamental character" of the agency. Hector Anton, an accounting professor at New York University's graduate school of business, asserts that "no private investor would want the shares."

At least one S&L doesn't think much of Freddie Mac stock, either. According to Big Board officials, one or more S&Ls sold

2,442 Freddie Mac shares short last month. (A short seller makes money when a stock drops.) The stock exchange won't disclose any names, and no thrift has owned up to shorting a stock that is supposed to be shoring up the industry's net worth. "It's like betting against your own bank account," notes Anthony M. Frank, the chairman of First Nationwide Financial Corp. in San Francisco.

Many thrifts are also increasing their profits with fees from mortgages sales that they haven't actually received. When an S&L sells a mortgage to another company, it often continues to service the mortgage by accepting delivery of the monthly payments. After deducting a servicing fee, it passes on the money to the new owner of the mortgage. Many thrifts immediately book all their expected fee income as profit when they sell a mortgage. Such income can be a significant portion of a thrift's profits.

At City Federal Savings & Loan Association in Elizabeth, New Jersey, $64.2 million of the thrift's $66.8 million in 1984 pre-tax earnings came from fee income associated with mortgage sales. Michael Rust, the director of corporate relations, concedes the profits aren't "money we can put our hands on, but since we don't make glass, pipe or computers, we don't need it right now."

Loans or Investments?

Accounting rule makers are also upset that some thrifts don't know the difference between a loan and an investment. Some S&Ls have been lending money to real-estate developers without asking for much of a down payment or any down payment at all. In exchange for this largess, the developer pays some hefty loan-organization fees and gives the thrift an equity interest in his project. The FASB thinks many such "loans" are actually investments since the thrift often assumes more risk than the developer. As a result, the rule makers don't think thrifts should book the loan fees as profit until the project has been successfully completed.

The FASB's advice is being loosely interpreted by thrifts, however. Alamo Savings Association of Texas, for example, books fee income even when it has as much as a 50% interest in a real-estate project. Its outside auditor, Arthur Young & Co., demanded a reduction in reported 1982 earnings because the thrift used to book income associated with projects in which it had as much as a 75% interest.

"I still think the 1982 loan fees should be booked as profit, but the rules seem to be changing daily," says C. R. Stahl, Alamo's president.

Purchase Accounting Mergers

Some of the most magical accounting of all involves thrift mergers. Back in 1981, S&Ls discovered they could acquire a failing competitor and turn its problems into profits because of certain quirks in the purchase method of accounting for thrift mergers. Purchase accounting mergers sprouted like electric-toaster giveaways, and some thrift executives joked that the industry's problems would be solved if they all merged into one institution.

The FASB subsequently stopped the most egregious excesses of purchase accounting, but the controversy continues. For one thing, many thrifts still have large amounts of good will on their books from those mergers. In many cases the good will, which is an intangible asset, is larger than their net worth.

Some analysts also charge that thrifts are creating phantom profits by selling loans acquired in mergers. The loans were generally acquired at a steep discount from their face value and then sold for more than original purchase price but still less than face value. Accounting practice says such transactions produce a profit. Ironically, the Internal Revenue Service says they produce a loss for tax purposes.

Basic Profitability

For example, Glendale Federal Savings & Loan Association in California reported $26 million in net income for its first half ended December 31. But David T. Hansen, a senior executive vice president, concedes that $15.5 million came from gains on mortgage sales that generated losses for tax purposes. "The accounting treatment for these mortgage-loan sales has helped us weather bad times," Mr. Hansen says.

Great Western Financial Corp. in Beverly Hills, California, is one of a few thrifts that avoided mergers with failing thrifts to protect the quality of their balance sheets and earnings. Of the thrift's $1 billion in net worth, only about $100 million consists of good will. Monroe Morgan, a senior vice president at Great Western, says the industry needs to make its basic business profitable rather than rely on accounting techniques to improve earnings.

Like many other thrifts, Great Western is trying to improve its basic profitability by emphasizing adjustable-rate mortgages. Such loans make thrifts less vulnerable to rising rates. But only about 30% of all mortgage loans outstanding are adjustable, according to Brian Smith, the senior vice president for research at the U.S. League. Mr. Smith thinks the only thing that will save many thrifts is six or seven years of stable or falling interest rates.

"If interest rates climb back to 18%, as they were in 1981-82, there would be significant hemorrhaging," Mr. Smith adds. "The viability of the industry and how to stop the bleeding would be squarely in the hands of Congress and the regulators."

Guidelines on Foreign Loan Swapping by Banks Are Set by Accountants' Panel

By S. Karene Witcher

May 2, 1985

NEW YORK—The accounting profession's standards-setting body has decided to issue guidelines on how U.S. banks should account for transactions involving certain foreign loans. The measures are controversial because they could cut earnings at some banks that swap foreign loans with other banks.

The guidelines, adopted yesterday by the accounting standards executive committee of the American Institute of Certified

---

Ms. Witcher is a staff reporter of THE WALL STREET JOURNAL.

Public Accountants, are intended to clarify existing accounting principles. They are aimed largely at banks that swap loans of financially troubled Third World countries, mainly in Latin America, and are expected to be issued by the end of this month to take effect immediately.

Banks swap foreign loans for a variety of reasons; some want to reduce loans to certain countries or pull out of them completely, while others want to diversify portfolios by adding more countries. And still others, especially Latin American banks, exchange loans for other loans and cash because they need liquidity.

The market for such loans has been growing the past two years, although it's unclear just how big it is. But U.S. bank regulators maintain that the amount of loans being swapped still is tiny compared with the $360 billion in foreign debt Latin America owes to banks and non-Latin American governments.

Some bankers maintain that the new guidelines won't dampen that market. But accountants believe the guidelines will cause some U.S. banks to shy away from exchanging certain loans because banks will have to prove to their auditors that the loans they swapped, and those they received, are valued at 100 cents on the dollar.

Otherwise, they must record a loss on the transaction that could reduce earnings. For bankers, it is a task that could prove difficult because many auditors believe those loans couldn't be sold to an investor for cash at face value.

"The burden of proof is on the bank" to show that the loans are worth what the bank says they are, says Thomas Macy, a partner at Price Waterhouse, who helped draft the new guidelines. Mr. Macy says that so far banks have usually argued the swapped loans were worth 100 cents on the dollar. But he adds: "We're saying that doesn't pass the smell test."

Banks argue that they use a swapped loan's face value because there isn't a sufficient market to establish a fair value for such loans. But Mr. Macy asserts that this is "self-serving" and that banks should find a better way to determine market values.

Although it isn't the accountant group's intention to dampen the swap market for U.S. banks, Mr. Macy says it "may well be that that is a side effect."

Moreover, some bankers fear the action may open the door for bank regulators and the Securities and Exchange Commission to require banks to write down entire loan portfolios on countries where a loan was discounted in a swap transaction. That could mean large write-offs against bank earnings. The accountants "aren't seeing the forest for the trees," frets a senior officer of a big U.S. bank that has done foreign loan swaps.

The guidelines state that a swap transaction that results in a loss won't necessarily affect the rest of a bank's loan portfolio to that debtor, or new loans to the borrower. But some bankers fear that regulators might not see the distinction as clearly as the accountants drew it.

Here's an example of how a swap transaction might result in losses for the banks involved:

Bank A trades a $10 million face value Argentine loan to Bank B for an $8 million Peruvian loan plus $2 million cash, or a total of $10 million. Under the new guidelines, the banks would have to record the loans at market value, say, $6 million for the Argentine loan and $4 million for the Peruvian loan. With the $2 million cash added by Bank B, the transaction is worth $6 million to each side and the implied loss for each bank is $4 million.

The banks could either charge the loss against earnings or dip into loan-loss reserves. Replacing the reserves would also result in lower earnings.

Community S&L's Accounting for 1984 Stirs Intense Debate within Profession

By Lee Berton

September 5, 1985

NEW YORK—Accounting practices that permitted Community Savings & Loan Association to shore up its profit and net worth for 1984 are the subject of intense debate in the accounting profession.

Community, the Bethesda, Maryland–based parent of Equity Programs Investment Corp., the troubled real estate syndicator that is delinquent on payments due on more than $1 billion in mortgages and mortgage-backed securities, reported that 1984 profit surged 45% to $16 million on a 70% revenue spurt to $140 million.

But a closer look at the 1984 annual report shows that almost 50% of the thrift's total revenue derived from fees related to the purchase of single-family houses by limited partnerships operated by Equity Programs.

And $78 million of its assets, or almost three times its net worth, assets minus liabilities, was accounted for by a receivable on loans Community made to the partnerships.

"Community S&L is using the most liberal accounting treatments available and playing the kind of games that have gotten many thrifts into trouble over the past few years," asserted John Shank, a professor of accounting at Dartmouth College's Amos Tuck School of Business Administration, Hanover, New Hampshire.

Officials at Equity Programs and at Alexander Grant & Co., auditor for Community and Equity Programs, defend the accounting methods they used. They said they are "comfortable" with Community's accounting treatments of the fees and the receivable from the partnerships. "We followed generally accepted accounting practices," said Larry Mathias, president of Equity Programs.

But Prof. Shank and other accountants believe that Equity Programs should have booked only as much as 25% of the $67 million in builders', loan origination and partnership organization fees that it credited totally to 1984 revenue. "Basic accounting principles say you can't take fees into profit until you have a bona fide arm's length buyer for the homes," Prof. Shank maintained.

Also, an accountant for a major accounting firm said that as collection of the receivable from the limited partnerships is "questionable," the quality of the receivable is "very dubious." He added, "Equity Programs' obligation as general partner is to keep these partnerships afloat and so the receivable probably isn't worth very much since it doesn't reflect an arm's length business transaction."

During the past few years, major accounting and auditing rule-making bodies have been debating how thrifts that make real estate loans or invest in real estate should book profit from such transactions. While many of the regulators concede that the quality of such earnings has been poor, they note that too conservative accounting treatments deferring such profit could sink many more thrifts.

A Required Charade

"The current accounting for thrifts may be a charade, but most of the rule makers and regulators seem to be convinced that the health of the nation and the economy requires such a charade," said Prof. Shank.

Several major accounting firms in the Washington, D.C. area said that Equity Programs, before its merger with Community in 1982, was seeking to change its auditor, suggesting that it was trying to gain more credibility with the financial community.

From 1974, when Equity Programs was started, until 1982, Equity Programs' auditor was James C. Jones & Co., a small local accounting firm in Annandale, Virginia. "Frankly, Equity Programs was auditor shopping for a CPA firm that would have a big name and also go along with its very liberal accounting policies," said a partner for a major accounting firm in Washington. The Securities and Exchange Commission frowns on companies that change auditors simply to obtain a firm that would permit more liberal accounting practices.

Declined to Comment

Mr. Jones declined to comment on Equity Programs' accounting, other than to say the firm is small. "I'd rather not say any more to the press," he said.

And Maurice J. Whalen, managing partner of Alexander Grant's Washington office, said "we feel we were right in issuing a clean opinion" on Community S&L's 1984 annual report. He declined to comment on the details of the accounting questions related to the fees.

Both he and Equity Programs' Mr. Mathias declined to comment on reports that Equity Programs was shopping for a friendly auditor with big-firm credentials in the late 1970s and the early 1980s.

In 1979, Equity Programs asked Arthur Andersen & Co., the biggest U.S. accounting firm, to be its auditor; after looking at Equity Programs' books and discussing the possible fee, Andersen declined to take the engagement.

"We were in there for a short period, possibly a week or more, considering whether to be the auditor," said Fred Brinkman, managing partner of Andersen's Washington office. But he declined to say why Andersen didn't take the job, citing "client confidentiality." Andersen continues to do "some tax work" for Equity Programs, he added.

Denver-based Fox & Co., an accounting firm that had problems with federal regulators over several of its audits, became Equity Programs' auditor in 1982. Last May, Alexander Grant acquired Fox, and so Grant is now the auditor for Community S&L and Equity Programs.

Double-Entry Doubletalk

By Lee Berton

September 17, 1985

A funny thing happened to almost $20 million of debt of the recently collapsed Beverly Hills Savings & Loan Association after it arrived at the Federal Home Loan Bank Board.

It was turned into an asset.

Board chairman Edwin Gray, several board officials and an accountant tried to explain that, under regulatory accounting principles, debt subordinated to the claims of the Federal Savings and Loan Insurance Corp. is considered an asset rather than a liability.

But they explained that their accounting approach only "analyzes risk for internal purposes." To the outside world, that debt is still a liability, they said.

Rep. John Dingell (D., Mich.) wasn't convinced. And he playfully remarked at a congressional hearing on the issue: "At one point in my career, I was a very wealthy man because I had a hell of a lot of debt. I must say that by those accounting principles, I am delighted to inform you I have become much poorer because I have little debt of late."

Mr. Dingell's joke highlights a serious problem that accountants are increasingly encountering with the public. Critics seriously wonder if in accountants' professional lives they so often resort to the mind-bending game of "double-think" that they have lost track of the truth.

Abraham Briloff, an accounting professor at Baruch College in New York and a frequent critic of CPAs, notes that accountants frequently wear blinders when it comes to the simple truth.

"Under so-called generally accepted accounting principles, companies are able to create an asset on the balance sheet called good will if they overpay for another company's assets," says Mr. Briloff. To his way of thinking, that excess payment should be immediately charged against income.

It isn't RAP (regulatory accounting principles) or GAAP (generally accepted accounting principles) but SAP (suckers are the public) when a liability is considered an asset, asserts Mr. Briloff. "And too often the average unwashed investor is taken in by this double talk," he adds.

My experience with accountants for the past 20 years shows that as CPAs get into more trouble, their reliance on double-think increases. Officials in a Big Eight accounting firm recently tried to tell me that when two people had shared the chief executive's job and a third person then replaced them as chief executive officer, the pair's role in the CPA firm wasn't diminished.

I asked the individual who was nominated as the new chief executive who would have the final word if there was a disagreement in the future. "I would," he said. Case closed.

In a recent Journal of Accountancy, the monthly publication of the 235,000-member American Institute of Certified Public Accountants, William Corbett, the AICPA's vice president for communications, tells CPAs how to improve their image problem.

A former director of public relations at Avon Products Inc. for 16 years, he urges them to promote the CPA license, to enhance a positive picture of CPAs, gain great awareness of CPAs' diverse services, publicize career opportunities in accounting, participate in the legislative and regulatory process and tell the public how CPAs police themselves.

He also says the public should know that audited financial statements are retrospective. "That is to say, they cannot guarantee the absence of all fraud, nor do they give assurance about the competence of management or the future viability or profitability of the entity," he states.

Mr. Corbett would be better advised to tell CPAs to try their hardest to avoid double-think and double talk. If CPAs weren't so involved in rethinking the truth, they might be straighter shooters.

Tighter Guidelines Weighed on Valuing Argentine Loans on Major Banks' Books

By S. Karene Witcher

November 14, 1985

NEW YORK—An accounting group is considering a tightening of its guidelines on how banks treat certain Argentine loans.

Some banks' earnings could be lowered, bankers say, if the banking committee of the American Institute of Certified Public Accountants decides on a strict interpretation of the auditing and accounting rules involved.

At issue are bonds and notes the Argentine government has issued to many U.S. banks in the continuing effort to restructure its $47 billion foreign debt. The securities were substituted for some loans the banks had made to private Argentine borrowers who were having repayment difficulties.

The institute, the accounting profession's 230,000-member trade group, is debating whether U.S. banks should recognize a

---

Ms. Witcher is a staff reporter of THE WALL STREET JOURNAL.

loss on the securities. The group issues guidelines, and it could be overruled by federal banking regulators. But its guidelines normally are observed in accounting-industry practice.

Although many banks carry the Argentine securities on their books at face value, similar bonds are trading in the market at discounts of about 25%. If banks were obliged to mark down the value of these securities on their books, their earnings would suffer.

Many bankers also fear that if the institute says the losses should be recognized, the same could apply to other loan restructurings, such as Brazil's.

"I couldn't predict" which way the accountants will decide, says Kenneth Cooper, a partner at Touche Ross & Co. But Mr. Cooper, who is a member of the trade group's banking committee, said he expects a decision before the end of the year, which would affect fourth quarter earnings.

Proponents of strict accounting argue that exchanging a loan to a private borrower for a government-issued security constitutes a swap.

In May, the accounting trade group issued guidelines on how banks should treat foreign loans they receive in loan swaps with other banks. It recommended that unless a bank could prove to its auditors that the loan it received was worth 100 cents on the dollar, it should be required to mark down the value of the loan and record a loss on the transaction.

However, accountants recognize that if they clamp down too hard on the banks, they could be overruled by the regulators. As one accountant says, "we are trapped" in the middle of a public-policy issue. Accountants have a responsibility to stockholders to accurately assess bank assets, he says; yet at the same time, accountants are inhibited from questioning the value of foreign loans, because doing so might discourage banks from lending more to the Third World and undermine the U.S. Treasury's effort to stave off defaults by those borrowers.

Banking sources say that two of the numerous banks potentially affected, Citibank and Morgan Guaranty Trust Co., have recently been marking down some of their Argentine securities. The move isn't expected to materially affect those banks' earnings, but disgruntled bankers at other institutions fear it could undermine the argument for continuing to carry the securities at face value. Some other banks could be more severely affected by such writedowns, they add.

Citibank declined to comment, but a source familiar with the transactions said the "numbers aren't huge." A Morgan Guaranty spokesman wouldn't comment on the bank's Argentine transactions. Most of Morgan's loans to Argentina were made to the national government or its agencies.

FASB Begins Project that Could Alter Accounting Rules on Some Borrowings

By Lee Berton

May 16, 1986

NEW YORK—The Financial Accounting Standards Board has begun a far-reaching project that eventually could stop companies and financial institutions from keeping certain types of borrowings off their balance sheets.

The project involves a study, just begun, focusing on how such instruments as repurchase agreements, interest rate swaps and collateralized mortgage obligations should be disclosed. Later, it will deal with how such financings should be labeled and measured. The project could take as long as five years and ultimately could result in accounting rules changes regarding off-balance-sheet figures.

Accountants say that how these items are treated by the FASB would affect reported profits and loan levels of many banks, which currently are under enormous pressure to minimize the effects of problem loans on their net worth.

"This project over the long haul could affect the bottom line and the assets and liabilities of every major U.S. financial institution," says John E. Stewart, a partner of Chicago-based Arthur Andersen & Co., the biggest U.S. accounting firm.

The FASB project is also aimed at ascertaining whether certain transactions constitute debt or sales. "At first glance, it isn't easy to tell whether some transactions are really borrowings," says Halsey Bullen, a project manager of the Stamford, Connecticut–based FASB, the chief rule-making body for accountants.

In a repurchase agreement, for example, a bank may sell government securities to a second party and agree to repurchase them later. In effect, the second party is making a loan to the bank with the securities as collateral. If the repurchase is completed overnight, accountants consider it a borrowing, even though a "sale" was made, Mr. Bullen notes.

But if the bank agrees to buy the securities back several years later, then opinions begin to differ as to whether it's a financing or a sale, Mr. Bullen says. "This is one type of question this project will address," he adds.

The project also will consider, among other things, whether a bank should be permitted to take loans off its balance sheet in its report to stockholders if it sells them to an outside entity created for that purpose.

In 1984, Citicorp, the nation's biggest bank holding company, began selling participations in loans from Citibank, its main banking subsidiary, to Chatsworth Funding Inc., an entity that hadn't any direct ownership by Citicorp. Chatsworth was backed by a financial guarantee from Travelers Corp., a major insurance company.

Last year the comptroller of the currency forced Citicorp to include such loans sold to Chatsworth on its balance sheet for regulatory reporting purposes. But the bank can continue to keep them off its balance sheet when reporting to stockholders, notes a bank spokesman. He notes that such loan sales, however, haven't been made for the past year.

Corporations and financial institutions long have been trying to keep certain types of debt off their balance sheets. A few years ago investment bankers perfected a financing tool called "defeasance" that removes debt and immediately creates earnings. Using defeasance, companies can reduce debt on their balance sheets by selling the debt or creating a trust to service it.

Both the FASB and the Securities and Exchange Commission believe such a tactic is permissible under limited conditions, such as when a company retires old debt.

"We're definitely going to take a closer look at all the ramifications of defeasance and how the investment bankers have been trying to create securities to skirt the more stringent accounting standards," says FASB project manager Mr. Bullen.

But some accountants are skeptical that the FASB can stop innovative financing techniques used to keep debt off the balance sheet. "The creative geniuses on Wall Street are just too smart for accounting standard setters," says Abraham Briloff, an accounting professor at Baruch College here and a well-known critic of the FASB.

David Fisher, a vice president for Salomon Brothers Inc., a major investment banker, says that firms such as his "don't develop new types of securities and transactions to get around accounting rules but to give companies the kind of products they need to remain competitive."

Accounting Change that Would Reduce Reported Loan-Fee Earnings Is Opposed

By Lee Berton

July 15, 1986

NEW YORK—A proposed accounting rule change that would sharply reduce reported earnings from loan fees for most thrifts and banks is drawing heavy opposition from financial institutions.

The proposal would force financial institutions to delay taking into income some of the loan fees they currently record as immediate profit. And it would require them to immediately record certain fee-origination expenses that they currently are allowed to defer for as many as a dozen years. The loan fees involved include nonrefundable points, front-end management fees to initiate a loan and other service charges for a loan.

The proposal is being made by the Financial Accounting Standards Board, the chief rule-making body for accountants.

The FASB will be holding three days of hearings on it in Washington, starting tomorrow.

Peter Horoszko, a project manager of the Stamford, Connecticut–based board, said that only three or four of 900 comment letters on the proposal "support it completely."

Meanwhile, some institutions are opposing the measure outright. Great Western Financial Corp., a Beverly Hills, California–based holding company, "vehemently opposes the proposal," said Ian Campbell, a senior vice president. Great Western operates 250 California thrifts and 400 loan offices in 30 other states.

"The FASB proposal would have a substantial negative effect on the thrift and banking industry and not contribute to more accurate financial reporting," Mr. Campbell said.

"This is an attempt by the FASB to correct past abuses, but we suspect it may be an overreaction," said Raymond Perry, a partner of Touche Ross & Co., a major accounting firm.

Some thrifts estimate that the FASB proposal could reduce their earnings from 10% to 40%, depending on how many real estate and home loans they sell to other lenders. Coral Gables Federal Savings & Loan Association, a mutual savings bank with 35 branches in Florida and Ohio, estimates that its first-half net of $12 million would be pared to $7.5 million by the proposal.

"The FASB is assuming that a portion of the 2½ points we charge for our residential loans are part of our loan yield, while we maintain it can be a pure fee that should be immediately considered as profit," says Kenneth J. MacNamee, a senior vice president at Coral Gables Federal.

The FASB, Mr. MacNamee maintained, is being pressured by federal regulators to "clean up past abuses that are no longer prevalent." Current loan fee accounting rules "need fine-tuning, not a complete overhaul," he added.

The FASB said the measure was proposed because too many financial institutions pumped up profits by too rapid recognition of income or by too lengthy deferral of loan origination costs. "While the average life of a home loan may be a dozen years, some thrifts were deferring these costs up to 30 years," said the FASB's Mr. Horoszko.

He said he has debated the proposal with more than 1,500 financial institutions, "and they admit there were reporting abuses but no one in the room will own up to them."

He said thrifts and banks say it's difficult to pinpoint costs, "particularly internal costs such as administration and salaries for employees connected with the loan process, such as appraisers."

The FASB proposal would permit thrifts to defer such costs if billed to the thrift by an outside appraisal firm. But it would require internal costs to be immediately deducted from profits. "It's amazing how quickly the thrifts and banks are pinpointing exact costs now that they feel they may have to deduct them immediately from profits," Mr. Horoszko said.

D. Garfield Searfoos, a Touche Ross partner, said he is "puzzled why the FASB won't allow financial institutions to defer such costs when it allows manufacturing companies to defer a lot of the costs for keeping inventories." The penalty to earnings for the financial institutions "therefore isn't fair and the accounting treatment isn't uniform," Mr. Searfoos added.

Pending any change in plans, the proposal would become a rule by the end of this year and would affect financial statements for fiscal years beginning after Dec. 15. Many thrifts have asked for a year's delay in implementing the proposal because it would be retroactive to previous years for all loans currently on their books.

Implementation of the proposal could be costly for many financial institutions, said Touche Ross's Mr. Perry.

Failed S&L Accounted for an Investment as Loan to Hide Loss, Bank Board Says

By John E. Yang and Lee Berton

September 15, 1986

The Federal Home Loan Bank Board said the managers of a failed California thrift improperly accounted for a $190 million real estate investment in order to hide losses.

The Bank Board said Beverly Hills Savings & Loan Association in Beverly Hills recorded its investment in apartment complexes throughout the United States as loans. By doing that, the thrift's management was able to conceal resulting "considerable" operating losses, according to the board's report.

Touche Ross & Co., which had been the S&L's auditor, defended the accounting, saying it was permissible under generally accepted principles. In Los Angeles, the thrift's former president and chief executive officer, Dennis M. Fitzpatrick, didn't return telephone calls for comment.

Accountants say it's unusual for federal regulators to interpose themselves in the accounting standard-setting process. In the past, they add, regulators tended to be lax and wink at more liberal accounting treatments in order to help the ailing thrift industry. But under pressure from Congress in recent months, regulators have decided to opt for more conservative accounting treatment, recognizing that the public was losing faith in the health of the nation's financial institutions.

New Management

The board closed state-chartered Beverly Hills Savings in April 1985 and reopened it with new management as a federally chartered thrift, Beverly Hills Federal Savings & Loan. The board is continuing its probe into the thrift's operation.

In 1982 Beverly Hills Savings bought the properties with

Mr. Yang is a staff reporter of THE WALL STREET JOURNAL.

J. D. Stout Co., a California real estate developer, manager and syndicator, the report said. Stout was a general partner with 40% equity; Beverly Hills Savings was a limited partner with 60%.

Under its accord with Stout, Beverly Hills provided all the capital to buy, refurbish and operate the apartments. The thrift's ultimate investment of $190 million represented about 7.3% of total assets.

In early 1983 Beverly Hills Savings' share of the interest expense, depreciation, management fees and operating losses of the apartments threatened to bring the thrift's net worth below the level required by regulators, the Bank Board said. After discussing the matter with its independent auditor and legal counsel, Beverly Hills Savings began accounting for all of its participation in the apartment projects as loans rather than as investments, the report said.

Transactions' Substance

To do this, BH Mortgage Corp., a wholly owned subsidiary of Beverly Hills Savings, lent the partnership formed by Stout and the thrift enough money to buy the thrift's interest in the apartment projects. Thus, operating losses on the apartments were no longer recorded on Beverly Hills' books, and interest income and loan fee income were earned.

But, the Bank Board concluded, "the change in the legal form of the apartment program did not change the substance of the transactions, and therefore, the change in the accounting treatment was inappropriate."

The report criticized the thrift's management and its auditors—who weren't mentioned by name—for failing "to meet their duty to ensure that (Beverly Hills') financial statements accounted for the apartments in compliance with generally accepted accounting principles."

Accounting Principles

Touche Ross was dismissed as auditor by Beverly Hills in the fall of 1984. Richard Murray, general counsel of Touche Ross, said the firm was dismissed because it asked the thrift to modify its 1983 financial results. He declined to elaborate.

Mr. Murray said the Bank Board seems to be seeking to set or influence "the interpretation of generally accepted accounting principles by financial institutions under the board's authority."

In a prepared statement, Touche Ross said the Bank Board's resolution on Beverly Hills "suggests that regulated financial institutions, and perhaps others, may no longer be entitled to the latitude exercised by" Beverly Hills.

Touche Ross Position

In an interview, Mr. Murray said Touche believes the accounting treatment accorded Beverly Hills' switch of the transaction to a loan from an equity position for the apartment project "while not conservative, was within the boundaries of choices" available to Beverly Hills under generally accepted accounting principles.

Under equity accounting rules, to retain its percentage of ownership, Beverly Hills would have been required to increase its investment in the apartments when the real estate market soured in Southern California in 1983. Booking the transaction as a loan permitted Beverly Hills to avoid writing down the properties and recognize some interest income at the same time.

Accounting rules prohibit recognizing profits from an equity position in real estate until the property is sold. Beverly Hills originally owned 60% of the apartment project but converted its joint venture position to a loan in the early 1980s. This switch was permitted by its auditor, Touche Ross.

In recent hearings before a House subcommittee investigating the accounting profession, Touche Ross was criticized by federal regulators and others for selecting too liberal accounting treatments for Beverly Hills.

Philippines' Creditor Banks Accept Plan to Be Paid Interest in the Form of Notes

By Peter Truell and Lee Berton

March 23, 1987

The Philippines' major creditor banks have accepted a proposal under which they may choose to receive some interest payments in the form of notes, sources close to the country's debt talks said.

Their acceptance establishes an important precedent for future settlements with other debtor countries. It also raises the accounting question of how banks will value such notes.

Philippine Finance Minister Jaime Ongpin and his country's main creditor banks still are working to reach agreement on other issues in rescheduling more than $13 billion of debt, including $10.3 billion of medium-term and long-term debt owed to foreign banks and $3 billion of trade financing. Talks on those issues will resume later this week.

Banks Have Option

The note proposal, which has drawn approving comments from U.S. Treasury officials, gives creditor banks the option to take payments covering the interest-rate margin on Philippine debt in so-called Philippine Investment Notes. These notes, denominated in U.S. dollars and not paying interest, could be exchanged for local currency for investment in the Philippines' debt-for-equity swap program. Banks will be offered a slightly higher interest-rate margin if they accept the notes than if they take a cash payment.

The Philippines has proposed that the interest-rate margin for cash payments be ⅝ percentage point over the banks' cost of funds, while the notes would have a face value equal to a one-

---

Mr. Truell is a staff reporter of THE WALL STREET JOURNAL.

point margin over the cost of funds. But the margins have yet to be resolved.

Other debtor countries, eager to encourage debt-for-equity swaps and to limit cash payments on their debt in foreign currencies, probably will want to take advantage of an option such as the Philippines' note proposal.

Accounting Treatment Uncertain

Meanwhile, because accounting principles haven't been established yet for the notes, banks that choose to take the notes likely will be on their own in either accepting them at par value or discounting them because they're only exchangeable into Philippine pesos, a restricted foreign currency.

Major U.S. accounting firms are split on how to value the notes. At the conservative end is Price Waterhouse, which audits major U.S. banks and would have them sharply discount the notes. The more liberal view, opposing such a discount, is taken by the accounting firm of Arthur Young & Co., which is a consultant to investment bankers advising the Philippines.

A spokesman for the Federal Reserve Bank of New York said: "We hope the Philippine debt talks move toward a smooth conclusion." But he declined to comment on the issue of the notes.

The Philippines and its bankers still have to resolve the question of interest-rate margins, and also have to agree who will monitor the Philippine economy once the country's present International Monetary Fund program expires in the middle of next year.

Talks on these issues were adjourned over the weekend to allow some bankers to attend the Inter-American Development Bank's annual meeting in Miami. The talks will resume later this week, with the more optimistic negotiators expecting an agreement before the weekend.

Auditors Press Banks to Bite Bullet on Foreign Loans

Firms Cite Recent Reserve-Taking, Despite Fuzzy Accounting Rules

By Lee Berton

June 8, 1987

NEW YORK—Outside auditors of the major U.S. banking companies will be stepping up pressure on the companies to sharply boost their loan-loss reserves in the second quarter for shaky foreign loans, accountants say.

Partners at big accounting firms that audit banks are reluctant to discuss such reserves for specific clients. But they admit that the recent move by Citicorp, followed by four others, to boost such reserves is a big incentive for them to get tougher with their other bank clients.

Accounting firms are in somewhat of a no-win situation. One problem is that auditors are hobbled by a lack of specific professional rules for treating such reserves. They can insist that the banks either take more adequate reserves or face a qualified opinion of financial statements, at the risk of friction with bank management and loss of lucrative business. Or they can accept the banks' more favorable valuation of the loans, and risk lawsuits by shareholders for failing to adequately represent the financial condition of the banks in their audits.

John Shank, professor of accounting at Dartmouth College, Hanover, New Hampshire, says the measurement of loan-loss reserves is a "black hole" in both accounting and auditing literature. "Because it is so wishy-washy, when a crisis arises such as Brazil or Mexico failing to pay back or stopping interest payments, the auditors just don't know what to do."

Nonetheless, because of the decisions of the five banks to create these reserves, the auditors are expected to plow ahead and recognize "the urgencies in the international debt market that make such reserves more of a reality," one auditor says.

"We'll likely see more increases in reserves against loans to less-developed countries in this quarter," says William J. Dolan, Jr., managing partner who is in charge of bank clients of Chicago-based Arthur Andersen & Co., a major accounting firm.

"We're going to have to consider the recent action of the major players in banking as new input to our auditing decisions," says Mr. Dolan, who also is chairman of the banking committee of the American Institute of Certified Public Accountants.

Inconsistent Treatment

Some accountants question how outside auditors have so far permitted some banks to initiate whopping reserve increases while not forcing other client banks with similar loan exposure to boost reserves.

"There isn't anything in the good book of GAAP (generally accepted accounting principles) that spells out exactly what loan-loss reserves should be," says Loyd Heath, a professor of accounting at the University of Washington in Seattle. "The banks seem to have the upper hand in setting these reserves and the differences in their policies have the auditors' heads spinning."

Citicorp, for example, which has $11.7 billion in Latin American loans, has boosted its reserves by $3 billion, citing suspended interest payments by Brazil and Ecuador and sharply limited payments of principal and interest by Peru. Citicorp says its current financial strength allowed it to more realistically value its Third World debt, particularly in Latin America.

In the wake of Citicorp's action, Chase Manhattan Corp., Security Pacific Corp., Norwest Corp. and Bank of Boston Corp. followed suit. But Manufacturers Hanover Corp., with $7.6 billion in such loans, hasn't taken similar action. Citicorp and Manufacturers Hanover are clients of Peat Marwick, the biggest world-wide accounting firm.

Asked whether Manufacturers will create such a reserve, a company spokesman said "it is a matter for the board of directors and will be reviewed by the board at its regular monthly meeting on June 16." He declined further comment.

Banks with Largest Latin American Loan Exposure and Their Auditors (in billions of dollars)

Bank	Latin American Loan Exposure	Reserve Increase Required to Cover 25% of Latin Loans and 100% of Non-Performing Loans	Auditor
Citicorp	$11.7	$0.00*	Peat Marwick
Manufacturers Hanover Corp.	7.6	2.76	Peat Marwick
BankAmerica Corp.	7.3	3.06	Ernst & Whinney
Chase Manhattan Corp.	7.0	1.17*	Price Waterhouse
Chemical New York Corp.	5.3	2.33	Price Waterhouse
J.P. Morgan & Co.	4.6	0.74	Price Waterhouse
Bankers Trust New York Corp.	3.2	0.96	Arthur Young
First Chicago Corp.	2.6	0.47	Arthur Andersen
Continental Illinois Corp.	1.8	0.47	Price Waterhouse
Security Pacific Corp.	1.8	0.38*	Peat Marwick
Marine Midland Corp.	1.8	0.52	Price Waterhouse
Wells Fargo & Co.	1.6	0.53	Peat Marwick
Irving Trust Co.	1.5	0.37	Peat Marwick
First Interstate Bancorp.	1.5	0.84	Ernst & Whinney
Mellon Bank Corp.	1.4	0.77	Peat Marwick

*This reserve increase reflects recent boosts in Latin American loan-loss reserves to 25% by Citicorp and Chase Manhattan and to 36% by Security Pacific. (Bank of Boston Corp., which had Latin American loan exposure of $1 billion at March 31, recently boosted such reserves to 36%; its auditor is Coopers & Lybrand. Norwest Corp., with Latin American loan exposure of $592 million at March 31, boosted such reserves to 25%; its auditor is Peat Marwick.)

Source: Keefe, Bruyette & Woods, Inc.

'Judgment Call' on Reserves

Thomas F. Keaveney, Peat Marwick's national director of banking, says Citicorp and Manufacturers may decide differently on foreign loan-loss reserves, since the decision is a "judgment call by management." He adds: "Within broad parameters, auditors can and do challenge bank managements' estimates of loan-loss reserves. But the judgment must first be made by management and then reviewed for reasonableness by the auditor."

Even a recent study issued by the accountants institute, called "Auditing the Allowances for Credit Losses of Banks," doesn't give any specific advice on how to reserve for troubled foreign loans; it simply advises the auditor to consult an outside specialist who knows a debtor country's economic, political and social climate. An institute official says the study is aimed at small accounting firms rather than the bigger firms, "which have developed their own guidance for such loans."

Douglas R. Carmichael, an accounting professor at the City University of New York's Baruch College, says that "how tough a stand auditors are willing to take (on loan-loss reserves) remains to be seen." He concedes that "it looks funny to the public that some banks recognize losses on foreign debt while others don't, while the auditors stand idly by."

Big Effect on Capital

Banks currently are allowed to include loan-loss reserves in their primary capital, which regulators require them to keep at a certain minimum ratio to assets. But Mr. Carmichael notes that if regulators change their minds about including such reserves in capital, it "could put outside auditors in a double squeeze" over the financial condition of their bank clients. Major banks would then be forced to raise more money to meet capital requirements, even as boosts in loan-loss reserves are eating into profits.

In a proposal made last February by the Federal Reserve Bank, the Comptroller of the Currency and the Federal Deposit Insurance Corp., the question was raised about including loan-loss reserves in primary capital. Five years ago regulators boosted the primary capital requirement to 5½% of bank assets from 5%. Up to now, primary capital has included stockholders' equity, certain permanent debt and preferred issues and the allowance for loan losses, which the regulators would prefer to keep. But a Fed official concedes that if sentiment grows for excluding loan-loss reserves, as is done in other nations, "we'd have to take a serious look at the move."

James J. McDermott, Jr., a senior analyst at Keefe, Bruyette & Woods Inc., a securities firm that specializes in bank stocks, points out that eliminating the reserves would consume major portions of the primary capital of many major banks with foreign loan exposure and limit their ability to make more loans. For example, it would reduce the primary capital of BankAmerica by about 30%, Manufacturers Hanover by about 19%, Mellon Bank by about 20% and Irving Trust by 14%.

"Increasing loan-loss reserves at BankAmerica, together with the effect of this proposal, could eat into the core business of the bank's branches and its Seafirst bank unit in Seattle," says Mr. McDermott.

Clausen Resists Major Reserve

A. W. Clausen, BankAmerica's chairman, at a recent news conference after the company's annual meeting in San Francisco, indicated that despite mounting pressure, he won't boost reserves against troubled foreign sovereign debt by anything close to the steps taken by Citicorp and Chase.

A spokesman for Cleveland-based Ernst & Whinney, the auditor for BankAmerica, declines comment on any action planned for BankAmerica or the subject of loan losses for foreign debt in general. "It's too complicated a subject so we'd rather not discuss it," he says.

Some auditors maintain that the reason banks' judgments are so diverse on foreign-loan reserves is that nations, unlike companies, don't issue financial reports. An accounting rule issued in 1975 "tells us that if the loan loss is known and can be estimated, we would require our client banks to accrue an allowance or reserve for it," says Kenneth F. Cooper, national director of banking for Touche Ross & Co., a major accounting firm. Touche Ross has 300 banking clients, but none with big Latin American debt exposure.

"But it's difficult for us to separate nationalistic rhetoric from reality when countries in debt speak with so many voices," says Mr. Cooper, who is a member of the CPA institute's banking committee. Since banks set up a reserve for a "market basket of debt" rather than for specific loans, it's difficult to compare loan exposure from one bank to another, partners at other accounting firms say.

"It will be difficult, if not impossible, to get comparability for these reserves among accounting firms and even among each firm's clients," says Mr. Carmichael. Accounting firms don't audit quarterly financial statements, but "judgment day" may come when 1987 annual reports of the banks are issued, he says.

"If auditors don't qualify their opinions, rather than give a clean bill of health to banks with big troubled foreign-loan exposure that refuse to set up reserves, then there'll be big reasons for the public to question whether auditors are properly doing their job," says Mr. Carmichael.

Insurers Oppose Proposal on Rule Mulled by FASB

Accounting Change to Cut Profits of Firms Selling Universal Life Policies

By Lee Berton

June 19, 1987

NEW YORK—Controversy is mounting over a proposed accounting rule that would sharply cut profits of insurance companies that sell universal-life policies.

Insurance companies, which are fighting the measure, say it is possible that universal-life premiums could rise if the proposal by the Financial Accounting Standards Board goes through. The FASB is the chief rule-making body for accountants.

For the industry, the stakes are enormous. Last year universal-life premiums totaled about $3.25 billion, or 25% of all life insurance premiums. There is more than $600 billion in universal-life policies currently in force, about 10% of all life insurance policies in force.

As interest rates have risen in recent years, the popularity of universal-life policies has increased. The policies differ from traditional whole-life policies in that they generally offer significantly higher interest or stock-market returns and can be linked to a specific portfolio of investments. Also, premiums paid on universal life can be changed each year by the policyholder or insurer, whereas traditional life policies charge a fixed premium each year of the policyholder's life.

The FASB says that because the universal-life premiums can vary based on interest rates and market performance, such premium income can't be recorded the same way as fixed, regular income from traditional life premiums.

The FASB proposal would reduce the reported profits from these policies as much as 80% in each of the first five years of their contract life, estimates Stephen D. Bickel, executive vice president of American General Corp. The Houston-based holding company has 23 life insurance subsidiaries, 17 of which sell universal-life policies.

The proposal would reduce policy profits in two major ways. It would force insurance companies to deduct bigger portions of universal-life policy costs, such as agents' commissions, and medical examination and administrative costs, in earlier years of the policy term. And it would limit in early years the recording of income from certain fees that policyholders pay for early termination of universal-life policies.

The proposal wouldn't limit or reduce such income from traditional life policies. "Universal life-type policies lack the fixed and guaranteed terms in most traditional insurance contracts; therefore, recognition of income from such policies should be different," said Wayne Upton, an FASB project manager.

"The FASB is wrong," countered Selwyn Flournoy, senior vice president of the Life Insurance Co. of Virginia, a Richmond-based unit of AON Corp., Chicago. "Universal life-type policies may be different from regular life in form, but the two types of policies are the same in substance. The proposal will confuse investors by setting up two accounting systems—one for whole life and one for universal life-type products."

Insurance companies assert that unless they can redesign

universal-life policies to sidestep the FASB proposal, the accounting change may force them to raise the premiums for future policies.

"The FASB proposal would make such policies a less attractive product for insurers, and premiums could go up," says Richard S. Robertson, executive vice president of Lincoln National
Corp. The Fort Wayne, Ind., company has more than $1 billion
of its reserves in universal-life products, making it one of the
biggest sellers of such insurance.

The FASB has scheduled hearings here Monday and Tuesday on the proposal, which was made last December. Insurance
companies are expected to pack the meeting. "The FASB has
chosen some bad options and we're going to strongly oppose the
proposal," said William Schreiner, an actuary for the American
Council of Life Insurance, a Washington-based trade organization representing 630 life insurance companies.

Mr. Schreiner said he will ask the FASB to reconsider the
proposal because insurance companies are concerned it could seriously reduce their reported earnings.

Mr. Upton said that after the hearings, the FASB is scheduled to issue a final rule by the fourth quarter. "If approved late
this year, the rule would be effective for financial statements of
insurers issued after December 15, 1988," he added. Of 60 letters
of comment received by the FASB from the insurance industry,
30 opposed the proposal entirely, while the other 30 opposed
parts of it, Mr. Upton said.

The proposal would affect only stockholder-owned insurance companies, who sell the bulk of universal-life policies. Mutual insurance companies, which are owned by their policyholders, aren't guided by FASB rules.

Two Major Thrifts Balk at Writing Off Stakes in FSLIC as FASB Rules Require

By David B. Hilder

July 17, 1987

Two major thrift concerns said they didn't write off their investment in the secondary reserve of the insolvent Federal Savings and Loan Insurance Corp. in the second quarter, contrary to current accounting rules.

However, the two companies, Los Angeles–based CalFed Inc. and San Diego–based Great American First Savings Bank, said that they will write off their FSLIC investments if pending legislation that would reestablish the reserve fund isn't enacted.

Great Western Financial Corp., based in Beverly Hills, California, the nation's second-largest thrift holding company, also doesn't plan to write off its investment in the FSLIC fund, although many other thrifts already have written off their FSLIC investments or announced their intent to do so.

Widening Rift over Reserve

The actions indicate a widening split within both the savings and loan industry and the accounting profession over how to treat the $824 million FSLIC secondary reserve, which was wiped out when federal auditors declared earlier this year that the FSLIC is insolvent by about $6.3 billion.

A House-Senate conference committee has agreed to reestablish the reserve as part of a pending bill that would recapitalize FSLIC with $8.5 billion in new borrowing authority. But neither chamber has voted on the conference committee version of the bill, and the White House has threatened a veto because it believes that the borrowing authority is too small and that other parts of the bill would stall financial deregulation efforts.

On May 21, the Emerging Issues Task Force of the Financial

Mr. Hilder is a staff reporter of THE WALL STREET JOURNAL.

Accounting Standards Board, which sets rules for publicly held companies, agreed that thrift concerns should write off their share of the secondary reserve in the second quarter. That was based partly on a directive on May 13 from the Federal Home Loan Bank Board that thrifts should write off the reserve for regulatory accounting purposes.

The FASB task force met again last week—after the conference committee agreed to reestablish the reserve—but didn't change its position on the write-off, largely because a bill hasn't been enacted, according to minutes of the meeting.

The task force is likely to take up the issue again at its meeting August 20. Thrift executives and accountants are expected to argue that the FASB isn't required to follow regulatory accounting decisions and that it often handles issues differently.

In addition, thrift executives argue that it would distort financial statements to write off an asset in one quarter and reestablish it in the next.

"I would have to reinstate it in the third quarter having written it off in the second quarter," said George P. Rutland, CalFed's president and chief executive officer.

'Today's Facts'

Currently, however, the FASB and the Securities and Exchange Commission haven't changed their position. Clarence Sampson, chief accountant of the SEC, said yesterday that if thrift concerns file quarterly reports without writing off the reserve, he would ask them to revise the filing. "When you have to file you have to base it on today's facts and today's facts are that you have to write it off," he said.

Mr. Rutland of CalFed said he will decide by August 19, the latest date the 10Q report can be filed, whether to change it to reflect a write-off if the bill isn't enacted by then. Great American indicated it would amend its SEC filing if the bill isn't passed.

CalFed said its second-quarter net income of $48.2 million, or $1.74 a fully diluted share, would have been reduced by $8.9 million, or 31 cents a share, if the write-off had been taken. Year-earlier net was $44.5 million, or 1.61 cents a fully diluted share. CalFed has a $16.1 million investment in the FSLIC reserve.

Great American said its second-quarter net of $25.6 million, or 95 cents a fully diluted share, would have been cut by $4 million, or 15 cents a fully diluted share, if it took the write-off. Year-earlier net was $23.2 million, or 91 cents a fully diluted share. Its FSLIC investment totaled $7.9 million.

Great Western Financial has a $49 million investment in the FSLIC secondary reserve, which would result in an after-tax charge of about $27 million, or 22 cents a share, if written off according to an estimate by analyst Robert G. Hottensen, Jr., of Goldman, Sachs & Co.

Two other big thrift companies, Financial Corp. of America, Irvine, California; and H. F. Ahmanson & Co., Los Angeles, said they haven't changed their plans to write off their FSLIC investments. The outside auditor for both companies is Peat Marwick Main & Co., which also is CalFed's auditor.

CalFed's Mr. Rutland said Peat Marwick agreed that the decision on whether to take the write-off was within the discretion of CalFed's management.

Accountants Drop Proposals to Alter Rules

By Karen Slater

October 22, 1987

NEW YORK—The Financial Accounting Standards Board has dropped two proposed accounting rule changes that would have hurt life-insurance company earnings.

The proposals, which were strongly opposed by insurers, involved accounting treatment for certain expenses paid and fees received on sales of universal-life policies. These popular policies feature flexible premium payments and returns tied to fluctuating interest rates or mutual-fund performance.

Ms. Slater is a staff reporter of THE WALL STREET JOURNAL.

Implementation of the two provisions would have immediately cut reported earnings of some life insurance companies by 2% to 17%, according to estimates by Ronald McIntosh, an accountant and life-insurance stock analyst with the New York securities firm of Fox-Pitt, Kelton Inc. But with the removal of the provisions, he said, the FASB's continuing rewriting of universal-life accounting "is basically a nonevent from an earnings standpoint."

At its weekly meeting in Stamford, Connecticut, the rule-making body for accountants voted 5-to-2 yesterday to allow insurers to continue to record as immediate revenue certain surrender charges that policyholders pay for early termination of policies. The proposal issued by the FASB last December would have limited the recording of that income.

In addition, the FASB last week dropped a proposal that would have forced the insurers to deduct a bigger portion of universal-life policy costs, including agent commissions, in earlier years of the policy term.

Wayne Upton, an FASB project manager, said the decisions aren't final. The accounting board still has to review the amended universal-life policy in its entirety and decide whether to seek public comment on it again, a discussion expected at a meeting November 11. However, Mr. Upton said he doubts the board will change its position on these two issues.

The FASB was divided on the two issues when it made its original proposal, and its reversals follow the recommendation of the FASB staff. Mr. Upton said the FASB wasn't motivated by any potential impact on insurers' earnings, but was persuaded by some of the industry's arguments. Insurers had argued in part that the universal-life products shouldn't be subject to a radically different accounting treatment than other life insurance policies.

The treatment of acquisition costs is the more significant of the two issues for Lincoln National Corp., of Fort Wayne, Indiana, where executive vice president Richard S. Robertson said the FASB's reversal on that subject "is a big step in the right direction."

Mr. Robertson explained that under the FASB's December proposal, the insurer's reported income would have looked worse the more new business the company wrote.

CHAPTER 18

THE OIL AND GAS INDUSTRY REVENUE RECOGNITION PROBLEM

The oil and gas industry has a basic revenue recognition problem. It takes many years to explore, find, and extract natural resources from beneath the earth's surface. As a result, expenses are not regularly matched with revenues in the same accounting period. The accounting rules for this industry have increased in complexity during a time of decline in natural resource prices.

The following section illustrates how accounting rules play a major role—frequently the deciding role—in profit determination for an entire industry. There is also insight into some of the political play involved when accounting rules collide with a very powerful industry.

Slippery Figures: Oil Firms' Reserves, Treated as Vital Data, May Be Just a Guess

Estimates Can Vary Wildly, and Some Concerns Shop for One that Suits Them— Three Views of North Slope

By Steve Frazier and Lee Berton

August 28, 1986

In biblical times, it took a miracle to turn a few loaves and fishes into a feast. But nowadays petroleum companies can multiply their oil and gas reserves with a stroke of the pen.

Consider the overnight growth of two oil fields Chevron Corp. sold recently to affiliates of Pennzoil Co. and Goodyear Tire & Rubber Co. On Chevron's books, the fields totaled less than 23 million barrels of oil. But Pennzoil calculates that the one it bought holds 80 million barrels all by itself, and Goodyear claims more than 100 million for its field.

The sudden eightfold increase stems chiefly from the new owners' decision to include in their estimates wells that haven't been drilled yet. Unfortunately, it won't be known for years which of the estimates—if any—are accurate.

The reserves that oil and gas companies report to shareholders carry great weight. Stock-market investors use the numbers to help evaluate the companies. So do current and prospective lenders. The estimates can alter net income, and managers' performances are measured partly by them. These days, with so many energy companies hurting, the estimates loom especially large; lower oil and gas prices can force reserve write-downs that weaken large oil companies and drive smaller ones out of business.

Mr. Frazier was a staff reporter of THE WALL STREET JOURNAL.

Taking a Hit

Yet few investors appreciate how much of a guessing game reserve estimating is, unless properties touted as gushers yield only trickles and the value of their holdings plunges. Bankers who have lent money on reserve values can suffer similar shocks.

Derrick Luksch and his father, Karl, of Sacramento, California, lost more than $500,000 in a Louisiana drilling fund that had valued its reserves at $24.5 million. Within months, independent appraisals chopped that value by 92%. "It took every bit of cash I had," says the younger Mr. Luksch. "This will restrict my life style from now on."

The program's operator, James A. Latham, says he is sorry that the reserves didn't measure up. "You have to be very cautious of reserve estimates," he admits. "They are very close to a guess, even by the best experts." His Latham Exploration Co. now faces a lawsuit by the Luksches.

Although reserve reports can profoundly affect an energy company's balance sheet, they have escaped the detailed regulation applied to other financial data. Outside audits don't cover them, largely because reserves are so hard to measure. Securities and Exchange Commission guidelines are so broad that an engineering trade group once counted no fewer than 50 sets of definitions in use in the industry—all supposedly following SEC guides.

Multiplying Guesses

It isn't unusual to have half a dozen oil companies drilling in the same field and publishing reserve figures differing by as much as 300%. The wild variations can result from slightly differing assumptions about rock characteristics, the thickness of the deposit, the amount of area a discovery well will drain and other such factors.

"It's pretty frightening," says William Strevig, an investment banker who specializes in oil properties. "You take a guess, multiply it by another guess, and try to put a value on it."

Reserve estimates also can vary because of the temperament or biases of engineers—or because of outright manipulation. Industry critics say energy companies or lenders can shop for the result they want by selecting outside petroleum engineers by their reputations. For their part, outside engineers complain of pressure from their employers to produce attractive estimates.

In general, oil and gas reserves may be "proven developed" or "proven undeveloped." The latter—not tested by a well but "reasonably certain" of commercially successful exploitation—are especially hard to estimate and bring the most disagreement among engineers. Then there are so-called probable reserves and possible reserves, sometimes little more than wishful thinking.

Slippery Slope

Those who try to measure reserves are guided as much by rules of thumb as by science. For instance, they generally raise estimates when oil and gas prices rise, figuring more can profitably be recovered from a pool, and lower them when prices fall. But even when prices are falling, some producers order their engineers to assume rising prices in the future, thus lengthening the projected economic lives of wells and inflating production volume. Others average low-cost and high-cost production to get a figure that makes more of a field appear economical to recover.

From company to company, there is little consistency. Atlantic Richfield Co. recently wrote off 8.3 trillion cubic feet of gas—enough to keep every gas stove and furnace in the United States lit for six months—after deciding that plunging prices had killed chances to build a pipeline to transport gas under Alaska's North Slope. But Standard Oil Co. merely demoted its share to "undeveloped." And Exxon Corp. didn't change the status of its North Slope reserves at all; half of Exxon's proven domestic gas reserves consist of the same sort of gas that disappeared from Arco's books.

"It might be confusing to some investors," concedes A. L. Monroe, Exxon's controller, "but they can make adjustment by reading the annual reports of the three companies." Exxon's latest report did discuss the issue, but investors are hard put to spot and keep track of these distinctions.

Some engineers say estimates are so subjective that a reserve report may reveal as much about the engineer as about the property. "Whether you are talking about religion, politics, sex or petroleum engineering, you have your liberals, your conservatives and those that try to walk right down the middle," says Clarence Netherland of the Dallas engineering firm of Netherland, Sewell & Associates.

A few years ago, engineers looking at a tricky new gas field in Colorado variously estimated total production, in oil equivalents, from 7,000 to 150,000 barrels per well. Each engineer had reasons, and each found receptive clients, recalls Roland Blauer, a Denver engineer. "People with high estimates found themselves working for drilling-fund promoters," he says. "People with lower estimates ended up working for banks or private companies who wanted a more conservative view."

Critics contend many outside engineers are ready to bend results to woo potential clients. Melvyn I. Weiss, a lawyer active in several shareholder suits, says that for independent engineers, "the key motivation seems to be M.A.I.—made as instructed."

Some engineers acknowledge the problem and are pushing for tougher rules that they say would keep employers off their backs. "There is a great deal of pressure brought on reserve engineers to paint the rosiest picture possible, and we need new guidelines to help them resist some of the pressures," says Chapman Cronquist, the head of a task force working on this. He says tighter definitions might curb "charlatans" involved in "all the abuses that cropped up in the last five years."

Keplinger & Associates

Some disgruntled investors seek relief in court. William Porter, a Houston lawyer, recently counted 23 suits filed against the top 15 petroleum-engineering consultants, most dating from the first crack in energy prices several years ago. He expects another flurry of suits growing out of the recent collapse in prices.

One target of several suits is Keplinger & Associates Inc., a big Houston consulting firm. "During the oil boom, the oil patch said that Keplinger was a seller's engineer," says Richard Dole, who heads energy accounting for Coopers & Lybrand. "In the long run, this isn't the best thing to be known as."

In June, Keplinger agreed to pay $4.5 million to settle

charges that it overstated the reserves of Houston Oil Trust, a royalty trust spun off to shareholders when Tenneco Inc. acquired Houston Oil & Minerals in 1981. Tenneco paid $20 million to settle claims in the same case.

Houston Oil Trust has been plagued by sharp revisions in reserves and payouts to its owners since it was established; one lawyer estimates that losses exceed $1 billion. One offshore field that had been projected to yield gas until 1996 was abandoned this spring; others have been plagued with technical snafus and curtailments of gas-sale contracts.

Deep Gas

Another Keplinger client, Amarex Inc., also had problems. Drilling-program investors who sank more than $140 million into the company assert that Keplinger used liberal guidelines to evaluate a deep-gas prospect that represented 44% of Amarex's total reserves. Keplinger's estimates exceeded those of another engineer, Ryder Scott & Associates, by 2½ times, according to a suit and SEC filings. Later, after Amarex had filed for bankruptcy protection in late 1982, Keplinger wrote down 87% of its undeveloped reserves. The company's assets have been sold, and the buyer won't discuss Amarex decisions.

H. F. Keplinger, Jr., the chairman of the consulting firm, denies that it is consistently more liberal than others. He says much of the blame lies with oil companies that didn't fully explain to investors the uncertainties of such estimates. "Everything got so superheated that people didn't really take the time to look carefully at the reports," Mr. Keplinger says, adding that "95%" of the drop in reserve values was due to price declines.

Whatever the case, Keplinger's troubles illustrate the hazards in estimating reserves "reasonably certain" of commercial success. Many times, these vanish without a trace. "One man's reasonable certainty is another man's grave doubts," says William Donovan, a Denver engineer. "The only true test is the drill bit."

And small shifts in definitions can have big effects. Until this year, British Petroleum Co. counted undeveloped reserves if its directors had approved funds to develop them. Then BP adopted the U.S. "reasonably certain" rule—instantly raising its undeveloped reserves of oil by 37% and of gas by 93%.

Such reserves also are especially susceptible to changing economics. If a company runs out of money to drill on unexplored acreage, it may never earn a dime from undeveloped reserves listed on the books as major assets.

But even familiar, developed fields can yield nasty surprises. In the late 1970s and early 1980s, Texaco Inc. had to break long-standing gas-supply contracts after slashing its reserve estimates on Louisiana gas. In one case alone, it agreed to pay a utility well over $1 billion in cash and fuel-supply guarantees to settle a contract dispute.

"We're more conservative now," says James Kinnear, vice chairman.

SEC officials say they rarely charge anyone with misstating reserves because the calculations involve so much interpretation. However, in 1984 the Houston SEC office accused a former consultant for Mariah Oil & Gas Corp., William H. Cook, of taking a proper estimate on certain gas reserves and multiplying it by 1,000. The tract amounted to more than three-quarters of Mariah's reserves, and the company later filed for bankruptcy-law protection. The consultant consented to an order barring such manipulation without admitting or denying he had done it.

SEC Accounting Staff Proposes Change that Oil Firms Say Would Hurt Industry

By Steve Frazier and Bruce Ingersoll

October 23, 1986

The Securities and Exchange Commission's accounting staff is proposing a mandatory change for oil companies that many independent producers said would further depress the struggling industry.

Mr. Frazier was a staff reporter of THE WALL STREET JOURNAL.

At an SEC meeting set for next Thursday, Clarence Sampson, the SEC's chief accountant, is expected to recommend that the agency abolish the "full-cost" accounting method and require all oil and gas companies to use the "successful-efforts" method. The petroleum industry is the only one where the SEC allows two different accounting methods, but heavy lobbying by independent producers has thwarted efforts to enforce a common standard.

Independent oil concerns have enlisted oil state politicians in efforts to derail the proposed rule change. They contend the accounting switch, which would require many companies to restate financial results and write down stockholder equity, could force some companies into technical default on lending accords.

"I think it would hurt exploration and development, and acquisition of investment capital at a time when you need everything you can get to survive," said George Mitchell, chairman of Mitchell Energy & Development Corp. "This industry is already in a state of shock."

Under the full-cost method, which is most heavily used by mid-sized and small oil companies with aggressive exploration programs, oil producers can capitalize their drilling costs, even money spent on dry holes. Under the successful-efforts method, companies charge off their dry holes against current earnings, capitalizing only their successful wells. According to an Arthur Andersen & Co. survey of 348 public oil and gas companies, more than 60% use the full-cost method, but all the international oil giants use successful-efforts.

The different treatments of exploration costs can produce sharply different versions of a company's profit and net worth, or assets minus liabilities. During drilling booms, full-cost companies have higher earnings and net worth statements because they aren't writing off their dry holes. They argue the accounting method allows them to undertake risky exploration projects without having sharp swings in their reported earnings.

But critics argue that the full-cost method inflates earnings and hides the cost of inefficient exploration efforts. "I don't think an oil company should be permitted to carry a dry hole as an asset," said David O'Glove, publisher of the *Quality of Earnings Report*. "It's like a mirage."

Debate over the accounting method has produced some extraordinary conflicts among accountants, oil companies and regulators over the past 10 years. The accounting profession's rule-making body, the Financial Accounting Standards Board, recommended in 1977 that all companies follow successful-efforts accounting. The SEC instead invented a third accounting method, but finally decided to let companies choose between full-cost and successful-efforts. The agency, though, required more detailed disclosure of oil and gas reserves owned by oil companies.

The issue was reopened earlier this year when the sharp drop in energy prices further confused the financial statements of smaller oil and gas companies.

The debate has divided the SEC staff. Mr. Sampson contends that requiring a single accounting method would make producers' financial statements more comparable, to the benefit of investors.

But Gregg Jarrell, chief economist of the SEC, argues that full-cost accounting more accurately depicts the "economic reality" of what is happening in smaller companies. He noted that charging off dry holes immediately, as required by successful-efforts, produces a "boom or bust" picture of the earnings of smaller companies. Such an approach overlooks the fact that dry holes help smaller producers zero in on gushers, Mr. Jarrell said. "Just because you missed finding oil doesn't mean you have been unproductive," he said.

Others in the field oppose reopening the issue because the industry and investors have learned to look past which accounting method is used and instead judge oil companies by their overall performance in building up oil and gas reserves. Richard Adkerson, lead energy partner at Arthur Andersen, said reopening the issue wastes valuable effort at a time when struggling companies need guidance from the SEC on other issues related to oil and gas disclosures. He said, "The real focus these days in understanding what is going on at oil companies is what's going on with oil and gas reserves."

SEC Rejects Plan for Accounting Change at Oil Firms, Citing Producers' Problems

By Bruce Ingersoll

October 31, 1986

WASHINGTON—The Securities and Exchange Commission decided against proposing an accounting change for the oil and natural gas industry, concluding that the harm to struggling producers would outweigh any benefits to investors.

The SEC rejected a staff recommendation that the agency sound out the public on whether to abolish the full-cost accounting method, used by more than 60% of the nation's oil and gas companies, and to require that all of the companies use the successful-efforts method.

The 4-1 vote against the SEC chief accountant's proposal was a triumph for a coalition of independent producers, which was able to get Energy Secretary John Herrington, Interior Secretary Donald Hodel and numerous oil-state lawmakers to lobby for the preservation of both accounting methods.

They contended that mandating successful-efforts accounting would retard domestic oil and gas exploration and further depress an industry reeling from the oil-price collapse.

Companies using the full-cost method argue that it enables them to undertake risky exploration projects without having sharp swings in their reported earnings. Critics argue that the method inflates earnings and hides the cost of inefficient exploration efforts.

"What we're talking about is adding one more problem to the already very difficult life of an independent oil producer," said Gregg Jarrell, the SEC chief economist. He lined up against Clarence Sampson, the chief accountant, arguing that there isn't any evidence that companies are abusing the full-cost method to puff up their financial results or that investors are being misled.

Mr. Ingersoll is a staff reporter of THE WALL STREET JOURNAL.

"I can't conclude investor protection requires elimination of full-cost accounting," said SEC Commissioner Charles Cox.

The petroleum industry is the only one in which the SEC gives publicly held companies a choice of accounting methods. Under the full-cost method, used mostly by small and midsized producers with aggressive exploration programs, companies can capitalize their drilling costs, even money poured into dry holes, up to the value of their reserves.

Under the successful-efforts method, companies charge off their dry holes and other exploration costs against current earnings, capitalizing only their successful wells.

According to an Arthur Andersen & Co. survey of 348 public companies in the petroleum industry, 210 use full-cost accounting. All the so-called majors use the successful-efforts approach.

The full-cost companies feared that a mandatory switch would force producers to restate their financial results at considerable cost and to write down billions of dollars in stockholder equity. Even the threat of an accounting change, some said, was depressing stock prices.

"Everybody has been looking for a way to help the industry," said Robert Odle, lobbyist for several independent producers. "Today a federal agency found a way: The SEC removed the uncertainty about what the rules are going to be."

Commissioner Aulana Peters voted to seek public comment on the idea. But the other commissioners weren't persuaded that the advantages of a single accounting method, such as more-comparable financial statements, justified a "very disruptive" change, as one staffer put it.

According to SEC Chairman John Shad, even if the agency had sought public comment, it probably would have decided to preserve the status quo.

At the Interior Department, Mr. Hodel lauded the SEC decision, saying that it "prevents the creation of another obstacle to domestic production of oil."

In Amarillo, Texas, David Batchelder of Mesa Limited Partnership, said, "I think they (the SEC) made the right decision." He added, "For certain independents, it would have had a material effect" on earnings that could have put the companies in default of their debt agreements.

The partnership, which is one of the nation's largest natural gas producers, Wednesday said it switched to the successful-efforts method. Mr. Batchelder said the change didn't affect the company's current-year results because it isn't drilling wells right now, but Mesa showed large losses restated for the previous year under the new accounting method.

CHAPTER 19

UTILITY INDUSTRY REPORTING

The utility industry is generally a regulated industry. Yet it always seeks funds from the same financial markets as corporate America. The demand for sound accounting and reporting practices for this industry is growing. However, there are problems, successes and failures with nuclear energy; uncertain rates and need for approvals by local government agencies; and increased incidences of major law suits involving public utilities. These have made the accounting for this industry far more challenging than in the past.

Utilities Face Rule Changes on Profits

By Lee Berton

November 20, 1984

Electric utilities, already mired in nuclear-power problems, face the possibility of more bad news: proposed accounting rules that could reduce the earnings they can report and alter important financial ratios.

That could "strike at the utilities' ability to maintain dividends on common, and could produce an instant dramatic effect on the prices of their stock," says Edward Oelsner, managing director, investment banking, at Dean Witter Reynolds Inc., the brokerage subsidiary of Sears Roebuck & Co.

It could also lead to higher electric rates, as the utilities' increased costs of raising money in the stock and bond markets are passed on to consumers.

The proposed rules were drafted by the staff of the Financial Accounting Standards Board, the chief rule-making body for accountants. The seven-member board, based in Stamford, Connecticut, has asked its staff to take another look at the proposals, which will be taken up at a board meeting today.

If adopted, the proposed rules would limit utilities' ability to defer costs and claim profits that haven't been realized.

For decades accountants have permitted utilities to defer borrowing and other costs while constructing power-generating units. They have also let utilities include so-called noncash profits in current reported income. These noncash profits consist of allowances for funds used during construction that are expected to be recovered from future rate increases.

Now the accounting standards board is under pressure from big accounting firms to set more rigid rules, in part because shareholders of troubled utilities are suing CPA firms for losses they incurred after buying the utilities' stock. The plaintiffs say their investments were based on faith in the noncash earnings. But they say these earnings turned out to be of such poor quality that outside auditors shouldn't have let the utilities include them.

Since late 1983 such shareholder suits have been filed against Arthur Andersen & Co., the big Chicago-based CPA firm that audits the financial reports of Public Service Co. of Indiana; Peat, Marwick, Mitchell & Co., involving its auditing of Public Service Co. of New Hampshire, and Price Waterhouse & Co. as auditor for Long Island Lighting Co. The suits include the CPA firms in a long list of defendants.

Deferral periods generally used to range from two to four years. But in recent years construction delays at nuclear power plants have stretched them to 10 years or longer. At the same time, the amount of expenses utilities defer has grown, thanks largely to the $3 billion to $5 billion being spent on building nuclear plants.

For example, noncash profits of Long Island Lighting Co., the Mineola, New York utility that has been plagued by delays with its Shoreham nuclear plant, rose to 99% of reported profit available for common dividends in 1983 from only 13% in 1970.

Public Service Co. of New Hampshire, which has experienced long delays with its Seabrook nuclear plant, had noncash earnings of 110% of reported profit for common dividends in the 12 months ended last July 31.

Meanwhile, state regulators are becoming increasingly hesitant to allow utilities to recover their deferred costs within five to 10 years. Indeed, with the prospect of nuclear plant abandonments, regulators have raised doubts about whether some utilities will ever be able to recover deferred expenses.

These doubts worry many accountants. "Some utilities, which apparently aren't being permitted to make their rates high enough to recover their costs, are keeping their accounting as though they could," says Paul LePage, a project manager for the accounting standards board.

About 40 electric utilities have nuclear projects under construction, and some are encountering increasing resistance from state regulators to quickly raising rates to cover the costs. The California Public Utilities Commission, for example, is weighing a proposal that would delay the recovery of costs for nuclear plants for as long as 19 years. And the New Mexico Public Service Commission is considering keeping electric utilities from raising rates until consumer demand for the power can be shown.

"Rate-making is a new ball game with mega-dollar plant costs, and we just can't guarantee return of costs and coverage of dividends and interest to the utilities," says Marilyn O'Leary, executive director of the New Mexico Public Service Commission. Accounting standard-setters, she says, are "just going to have to be a lot more flexible."

If standard-setters tighten the rules, says Kevern Joyce, financial and general accounting manager for Public Service Co. of New Hampshire, "we may be unable to earn an adequate return on our investment."

But critics of the current accounting method say the increasing proportion of earnings derived from noncash profits casts doubts on all utility accounting rules.

If cost recovery isn't likely, some accountants say, expenditures should be written off. When cost-deferral periods stretch out, they add, the likelihood of recovering those costs becomes more remote.

"Today's regulators can't always make commitments for their successors," says Stephen A. Duree, a partner at Fox & Co., a Denver-based CPA firm.

Decision Is Put Off on Accounting Rule that Would Cut Many Utilities' Profits

By Lee Berton and Bill Paul

July 17, 1985

NEW YORK—An accounting rule that would have reduced earnings and dividends of utilities with big nuclear projects is hung up on technicalities and probably won't be issued this year.

The Financial Accounting Standards Board, the chief rule-making body for accountants, has been considering since last year a rule that would limit utilities' ability to defer costs and claim profits that haven't been realized. It also would force utilities to take an immediate loss if a state regulatory disallowed recovery of certain new-plant construction costs.

Currently, utilities are permitted to book profit long before they've been granted rate increases that would account for such earnings. They call the profit "allowances for funds used during construction." In certain cases the allowances have enabled utilities to report earnings instead of losses. This has led some at the FASB to question the quality of all utility profits.

For example, in the 12 months ended last July 31, Public Service Co. of New Hampshire, which has had long delays with its Seabrook nuclear plant, had a noncash profit that was 110% of the net income applicable to common stock dividends.

The seven-member FASB tentatively agrees that such noncash profits can be booked "only if recovery by future rate increases is probable." But the FASB is split on the disallowance question. Three members support recognizing a loss for any dis-

---

Mr. Paul is a staff reporter of THE WALL STREET JOURNAL.

allowance by state regulators of construction costs, while the other four have disparate views. "There's a lack of consensus, and it's unlikely there will be any new rule until next year; it probably won't be effective until 1987," says Paul LePage, an FASB project manager.

Wall Street analysts say the delay bodes well for utilities completing nuclear plants this year, particularly utilities subject to significant disallowances by regulators.

Mark D. Luftig, a utility analyst with Salomon Brothers, says that had the FASB acted promptly on the disallowance question, a number of utilities might have been forced immediately to write down the value of new nuclear plants by hundreds of millions of dollars per plant. Mr. Luftig says that such write-downs might have wiped out some utilities' retained earnings and legally prevented them from paying dividends.

Utilities that were facing such a prospect this year include Gulf States Utilities, Kansas City Power & Light, Kansas Gas & Electric and Middle South Utilities.

In New Orleans, R. Drake Keith, Middle South treasurer, said that FASB's indecision "demonstrates the complexities" of the disallowance question, and shows how difficult it is for a utility to negotiate new rate schedules with state commissions. The other three utilities declined comment.

In the first quarter of 1985, about 44% of electric utility earnings were attributable to allowances for funds used during construction, according to Edison Electric Institute, a trade group.

Utilities Will Fight Accounting Proposal

Plan Could Require Nuclear-Cost Write-Offs

By Lee Berton and Bill Paul

May 28, 1986

NEW YORK—Utilities with big nuclear projects are preparing to take on accounting standard-setters next week over a proposal that utilities say could sharply limit growth of profit and assets.

Among other things, the proposal would force utilities to write off any nuclear plant costs that they can't recover within 10 years through rate increases granted by regulators.

The utilities have been steaming since last December, when the Financial Accounting Standards Board issued the proposal. And from June 4 through June 7, the chief rule-making body for accountants will hold public hearings on it at its headquarters in Stamford, Connecticut.

"We'll be there with our verbal guns blazing," says one utility executive who calls the proposal a "survival issue" for the utility industry.

Cutoff Called Arbitrary

"We feel the 10-year cutoff is very arbitrary and could do immense damage to all utilities with major power plants on their drawing boards," says Robert J. Harrison, president and chief executive officer of Public Service Co. of New Hampshire, Manchester.

The cutoff would apply to all types of power plants, but utilities building nuclear plants would be hit particularly hard because of costly and lengthy construction times. Many of the 27 nuclear plants now under construction in the United States were begun more than a decade ago. Moreover, state regulators usually don't allow utilities to charge customers for construction

---

Mr. Paul is a staff reporter of THE WALL STREET JOURNAL.

costs until a plant is in operation, and they increasingly require that such costs then be phased into rates over several years.

The FASB won't decide on the proposal before fall, says Paul LePage, a project manager for the rule makers. "There's no question we're going to have to take a hard look at all the pertinent comment that comes out of these hearings," he adds.

Mr. LePage says the choice of 10 years was discretionary. "We could have set a seven, eight or even nine-year cutoff," he says, "but if we seem arbitrary as all get-out, it's because we haven't been very comfortable in the past with accounting judgments made by utilities and their auditors."

Cost Deferrals

For many years accountants have permitted utilities to defer borrowing and other costs connected with construction of power-generating units. Utilities also have had free rein to include so-called non-cash profit in current reported earnings.

Non-cash profit consists of allowances for funds used during construction that the utilities expect to recover from future rate increases. But as the percentage of such non-cash earnings has risen, standard-setters are beginning to doubt the quality of those earnings.

Also, as regulators have stretched out recovery periods for nuclear plant costs, the probability of recovering such costs has lessened, according to Mr. LePage.

PS of New Hampshire, for example, reported net income of $113.7 million last year. But without non-cash earnings and allowances for funds used during construction, the utility says it would have reported a loss of $62.3 million.

If the FASB proposal is adopted, it could force the company to write off major portions of its $1.8 billion investment in the troubled Seabrook nuclear plant, and it would sharply limit the utility's non-cash earnings. "The FASB proposal could easily wipe out our entire net worth of $1.38 billion," says the utility's Mr. Harrison.

The FASB proposal also would force utilities to write down costs for certain abandoned nuclear plants. Currently, as regulators permit rate boosts, utilities can phase in recoveries of costs for such plants into income. But because of enormous outlays for nuclear plants, write-downs could add up to hundreds of millions of dollars if the FASB proposal is approved.

Mobilized Opposition
That's why the utilities plan to pack the hearings next week with foes of the proposed rule changes. Mr. LePage says that 72 witnesses, mostly opposed to the proposal, will attend the four-day hearings—the largest number ever to speak out on an FASB proposal.

After the FASB issued its proposal late last year, Mr. Harrison got 20 other utilities to join PS of New Hampshire to build a $500,000 war chest to fight the FASB's proposal. He named the lobbying group the Committee for Consistent Accounting Practices.

The committee hired a Washington public relations firm that has enlisted big banks, brokerage houses, law firms and manufacturing companies dependent on electric power to write a barrage of letters to the FASB. The rule-making body received at least 1,600, more than it has ever received on any issue. But the effort has produced a backlash at the FASB.

"Frankly, we just got a lot of form letters, all saying the same thing, but few giving us useful information to consider in looking at our exposure draft" of the utilities-accounting proposal, says Mr. LePage. He concedes that few in the industry support the proposal.

FASB Response
Donald Kirk, FASB chairman, was so upset by the flood of form letters that he sent back his own form response to many of the complainers. In his reply, Mr. Kirk took issue with critics' contention that the proposal would sour investors on utilities and give regulators ammunition to delay rate boosts. Rather, he asserted, the FASB is seeking to improve disclosure of utilities' financial results.

"We doubt that relevant, reliable financial information will evoke irrational reactions on the part of investors or regulators," Mr. Kirk said.

The utilities sharply disagree. "The FASB shouldn't require us to write down productive facilities," says Richard Bushey, vice president and controller of Southern California Edison Co. Mr. Bushey is particularly upset by a section of the FASB proposal that would force utilities to write down a plant's book value by the amount state regulators determine was spent in cost overruns.

At the hearing, General Public Utilities Corp., Parsippany, New Jersey, which owns the Three Mile Island nuclear facility near Harrisburg, Pennsylvania, plans to criticize the FASB for proposing that a utility immediately write down a nuclear plant "to its lesser value when state regulators determine it's an abandoned facility."

This change "could seriously impair a utility's net worth and damage its bond ratings and dividend payouts," says Verner H. Condon, GPU chief financial officer and a vice president.

Mr. Condon also strongly objects to a section of the proposed rule that would require a utility to write down the value of a new plant if regulators feel it creates unneeded or excess capacity. Capacity that is currently considered excessive could be sorely needed within five years because of rapid industrial and residential growth, he says.

The utilities accuse the FASB of failing to recognize that rate discussions with regulators can drag on for years because of nuclear plants' immense costs and the emotional opposition they generate from certain public groups. "The FASB board and staff doesn't fully appreciate the complexities" of trying to recover such big costs, says Southern California Edison's Mr. Bushey. "We're going to have to show them in Stamford" next week, he adds.

New Accounting Board Rule Is Expected to Cut Some Electric Utilities' Earnings

By Lee Berton

December 30, 1986

NEW YORK—The Financial Accounting Standards Board issued a rule that is expected to cut earnings of some electric utilities that have abandoned nuclear plants or been denied rate increases.

But the chief rule-making body for accountants didn't act on a proposed rule that would have required utilities to write off any nuclear plant costs they can't recover within 10 years. Thus, utilities can continue to amortize or defer such losses for as long as 40 years.

The earnings rule limits the amount of noncash profit that utilities may recover from expected rate increases. Noncash earnings—called allowances for funds used during construction—have contributed increasing portions of utility earnings in recent years. Some financial analysts have criticized certain utilities for reporting such earnings even though rate increases may be doubtful.

The rule also forces some utilities to record losses for an abandoned nuclear plant under certain conditions, and for a completed plant if certain costs for the plant are disallowed by regulators. Under current accounting practice, these costs can be deferred as long as 40 years.

Electric utilities with huge nuclear projects have bombarded the Stamford, Connecticut–based board with letters opposing any stiffening of accounting rules regarding costs connected with plant abandonments or rate disallowances. While they are happy that the FASB backed off the 10-year lid on cost recovery, they still would have preferred the status quo on profit recognition.

"We're glad the FASB has recognized that phasing in of cost recoveries through rate allowances is a more complex problem than the board originally thought," said Robert J. Harrison, president and chief executive officer of Public Service Co. of New Hampshire. The Manchester-based utility recently wrote off sizable portions of its investment in two nuclear plant units.

"But we can't say we're pleased that the FASB is making more rules that threaten the survival of the essential electrical utility industry," added Mr. Harrison, who got 20 other utilities to help Public Service of New Hampshire build a $500,000 war chest to fight the FASB's original proposal.

Paul LePage, FASB project manager, said the seven members of the FASB couldn't agree on the 10-year lid on cost recovery and may have to issue a second proposal on the matter. "What we do know is that electric utilities have been phasing in such recoveries in periods varying from five to 40 years," he said.

The new rule is effective for financial reports with fiscal years beginning after Dec. 15, 1987. The FASB said utilities under certain circumstances may delay applying the rule for another year if application would cause them to violate a loan agreement. To be eligible for the delay, a utility must be actively seeking to change its loan agreement.

Many Utilities '88 Profits Will Top Forecasts but Only Because of an Accounting Change

By Bill Paul and Lee Berton

February 1, 1988

Look for a bunch of electric utilities to report better-than-expected profit this year. But don't be fooled, caution analysts and utility executives. The companies are just taking advantage of a little-known accounting rule change.

CMS Energy in Jackson, Michigan, kicked things off Tuesday, announcing that its Consumers Power subsidiary will get a

---

Mr. Paul is a staff reporter of THE WALL STREET JOURNAL.

$60 million boost to 1988 earnings, courtesy of the changed rules. In all, says Paul Bjorn, head of Price Waterhouse's public utilities service group, some 25 utilities likely will derive earnings gains this year from the accounting changes, though few will add as much as CMS.

Dominion Resources in Richmond, Virginia, for instance, will add about $15 million to $16 million this year, or 15 cents to 16 cents a share. Northeast Utilities in Berlin, Connecticut, says it qualifies under the accounting changes, but adds that their effect on 1988 profit will be nil.

Whatever a utility adds, "there won't be any more money in the till," says Bill D. Johnson, vice president and controller of Dominion Resources. "Investors," Mr. Johnson adds, "have a tendency to forget that."

The amount of each utility's profit boost will depend on how much it had to write off on an abandoned power plant or some other asset. In most cases, the abandoned asset in question is a star-crossed nuclear power plant.

The Financial Accounting Standards Board in December 1986 changed the way utilities should treat these abandoned assets. The new rules permit some utilities to upgrade earnings several years back. They remained optional for 1987 and will be mandatory for 1988.

Under FASB Standard No. 90, a power company writes off, up front, all the interest that it would have earned on its plant investment over the life of the facility if it had gone into operation. A company either can take the entire hit in one year or restate prior-year earnings back to the date of the actual abandonment.

Previously, the utility took that charge in chunks, spread out over future years. The amount of each year's write-off generally offset the amount per year that the utility could recoup from rate payers on its plant expenditures. In short, the two amounts balanced. Now the charge will be up front, but the amount recouped will still be recorded over time. So in subsequent years, profits will look better.

In some instances, says Paul R. LePage, a project manager for Stamford, Connecticut–based FASB, a utility's annual profit could be 10% higher as a result.

Individual utilities report varying impacts. For instance, because of its canceled three-unit Cherokee nuclear facility, Duke Power will get a boost of $15 million, or 15 cents a share, this year and a total of $58 million over six years, a spokesman says. Carolina Power & Light, which was involved in four plant cancellations, including one coal-fired unit, will get a boost of $9 million, or 11 cents a share, to 1988 earnings.

Meanwhile, United Illuminating, New Haven, Connecticut, which is affected by the canceled Seabrook 2 nuclear plant, says FASB 90 will contribute only a couple pennies a share at most to earnings—"nothing significant," according to a spokesman. It's the same story at Central Vermont Public Service.

Analysts advise paying close attention to utilities' annual reports because all this restating of earnings can get complicated. Take Orange & Rockland Utilities, Pearl River, New York. It will shortly inform readers of its 1987 annual report that because it had a stake in the canceled Sterling nuclear power plant, it will be restating earnings for each of the past five years, and getting a modest boost in future earnings until the year 2000.

This all stems from New Jersey regulators' decision not to permit the utility to earn any interest on that portion of its plant investment, $14 million, that would have resulted in power for New Jersey rate payers. (By contrast, New York regulators permitted interest to be earned on the $36 million that would have provided power to New York rate payers, and thus FASB 90 doesn't apply.)

As a result of its ill-fated $14 million, Orange & Rockland says it will trim 1982 profit $2.8 million, or 23 cents a share, and 1983 profit $1.3 million, or 10 cents a share.

The boosts to profit will be reflected first in 1984 earnings, which will be restated upward roughly $480,000, or four cents a share. Same with 1985. Profits for 1986 through 1992 will get an annual boost of three cents a share, while 1993 through 2000 will enjoy an annual increase of two cents a share.

PART 5

HUMOR IN ACCOUNTING

CHAPTER 20

THE LIGHTER SIDE
OF ACCOUNTING

One of the signs of a self-confident and mature profession is a self-effacing sense of humor. This collection of articles captures the lighter side of the profession. It roasts independent and corporate accountant alike, without mercy, but with a good deal of refreshing wit. One is reminded of a chief internal auditor in California who mentioned that his high school guidance counselor told him to pursue a career in accounting because he didn't have the charisma to become an actuary!

Why You Never Saw Charles Bronson Cast as Hero Accountant

Accounting Called Too Dull for the Screen; Profession Is Plagued by Poor Image

By Lee Berton

April 26, 1984

Chances are you haven't seen the TV series "Frontier Accountant." You probably never will. It is a figment of comedian Bob Newhart's imagination.

A former accountant, Mr. Newhart says accountants are considered so dull that even "Space Actuary" and "Northwest Notary" would have a better chance of making it on TV.

"Accountants are thought of as being precise but unimaginative," says the comedian, who spent a year and a half totting up petty-cash vouchers and doing the books for two Chicago companies in the mid-1950s. "CEOs don't like to hear a lot of laughter coming from their accounting departments. That might spell trouble."

Every profession is plagued by unflattering stereotypes. Lawyers are ambulance chasers; doctors are seven-day-a-week golfers. But accountants complain that their stigma is particularly cruel—and more widely accepted. Ask people what accountants are like, accountants say, and more often than not the respondents will come up with words such as "boring," "unimaginative" and "plodding."

"Accountants are perpetually fighting their shiny-pants, green-eyeshade and number-cruncher image," says Albert Newgarden, a communications consultant with Arthur Young & Co., a major accounting firm. "It may never go away."

Funny Thing Happened

Consider what happened to Brian Garfield's 1973 novel, "Death Wish." The book portrays an accountant who becomes a vigilante, hunting down young hoods and murdering them.

But in the movie based on the Garfield novel, actor Charles Bronson portrays the vigilante—and the character is an architect. Says Mindy Album, secretary to Dino De Laurentiis, one of the movie's producers: "Mr. D thinks accountants are dull and dippy. An architect belongs to a more virile profession. Anyway, would you believe Bronson playing an accountant?"

The Monty Python group of comedians clearly couldn't imagine it. In their "Big Red Book," the British movie and TV entertainers write about an accountant describing why his work is "exciting." An excerpt: "In the next office to mine is a Mr. Manners, who is a chartered accountant, and, incidentally, a keen Rotarian. However, Mr. Edgeworth and I get on extremely well with Mr. Manners, despite the slight prestige superiority of his position. Mr. Edgeworth, in fact, gets on with Mr. Manners extremely well, and if there are two spaces at lunch it is more than likely he will sit with Mr. Manners. So far, as you can see, accountancy is not boring."

Accountants also charge that newspapers help perpetuate their image of dullness. The Washington Post, for instance, called a meeting of the nation's governors a few years back "almost as exciting as a convention of certified public accountants." A November 1982 article in the Financial Times of London stated that bureaucrats in business, unions and government are "dinosaurs . . . about as imaginative as the average company accountant."

Countless Jokes

Then there are the countless accounting jokes, which often picture the profession as being one-dimensional, overprecise and— you guessed it—boring. For example, did you hear the one about the accountant who is asked the color of a particular horse? His answer: "Brown on this side." Or the one about the man in a hot-air balloon who gets lost and lands in a field? "Where am I?" he asks a passerby. "In a basket in a field," is the reply. "You must be an accountant," the balloonist says, "because your information is perfectly accurate, but it's of absolutely no help."

Then there is Mr. Newhart's recollection that as an accountant he had a "strange theory" that if he got within two or three bucks when doing a debit-and-credit reconciliation, it was OK. But, he says, "This never caught on."

There are more accounting jokes, but they are too dull to repeat.

True, all the jokes and stereotypes aren't completely unfair. Look at the Dull Men's Club, whose motto is "we're out of it and proud of it." Some 20% of its 580 members are accountants, making them the club's largest occupational group; lawyers and dentists each make up only 5% of the club. "For accountants, dullness is enhancing," says Joseph Troise, a Sausalito, California, writer and the club's president. Club seminars focus on such topics as "Dressing to Break Even" and "You Can't, Even If You Want To."

Moreover, it could be that after all these years, the stereotype has become a self-fulfilled prophecy. After all, a dull profession attracts dull people.

"The TV heroes Perry Mason and Dr. Ben Casey have helped attract youngsters to the law and medicine," says Stuart

Kessler, the incoming president of the New York State Society of Certified Public Accountants. "But television and the movies ignore accountants because creative people think they're dull and deadly."

To raise the public's consciousness, Mr. Kessler plans to tell anyone who will listen about accountants who hang-glide, sky-dive and travel to the Amazon and Antarctica. "Why, there's even a rock music group in Rochester, New York, called the Audit Brothers, and they're all CPAs," he says.

At the state society's annual meeting in June at Lake Tahoe, Nevada, Mr. Kessler plans to play a folk song entitled "The Ballad of Henry the Accountant," sung to the tune of "John Henry." "It'll show we can be folk heroes," he says.

Still, even the slightest deviation from drabness can be a professional risk. Charles Kaiser, Jr., the managing partner of Pannell Kerr Forster, an accounting firm based in Houston, says his partners think he is flaky because he is "so out front." Mr. Kaiser's latest daring escapade: He approved putting a picture of King Kong on the firm's 1982 publication, Panorama, and had the cover this year done by cartoonist Charles Addams.

"My partners are happy that I no longer deal with clients," Mr. Kaiser says. "I'm too irreverent."

Yet even the most ardent believers in the "accountants are dull" theory agree that it isn't fair when the profession must suffer for another's sins. The February 1968 issue of the *Journal of Accountancy,* for example, quoted a diatribe of Elbert Hubbard, the American author who died in 1915, supposedly directed against accountants. According to the publication, Mr. Hubbard referred to accountants as "cold, passive, noncommittal, with eyes like a codfish, polite in contact but at the same time unresponsive, cool, calm, and as damnably composed as a concrete post or a plaster-of-paris cat, a human petrifaction with a heart of feldspar. . . ."

The quote has been often repeated in accounting texts and articles, and accountants cite it as an indication of their image problems. But Mr. Newgarden of Arthur Young researched the quote and discovered it was actually said more than half a century ago about a company purchasing agent.

Fortunately for accountants, Mr. Hubbard never wrote anything about them.

You Think Accountants Are Dull?
This Won't Change Your Mind

By Lee Berton

April 10, 1985

In your most terrifying nightmare, have you ever imagined getting caught in a stampede of accountants pushing their way into a small room? Does anyone out there have a subconscious that vicious?

Maybe not, but last week such a stampede actually took place in Washington, D.C. Fortunately, if you're not an accountant, you probably weren't there.

The occasion was House subcommittee hearings on the role of auditors in the collapse of E.S.M. Government Securities Inc. For the first time ever, a partner in a major accounting firm, Alexander Grant & Co., was being accused of taking a payoff to certify false financial statements.

Sold Out

"It was like the World Series," says Robert Berliner, a partner at Arthur Young & Co., an accounting firm. "We couldn't even buy tickets."

Accountants started lining up outside the Rayburn House Office Building at 5:30 A.M. for hearings that began at 10. "I would have given my eye teeth to be admitted," says Sandra Johnigan, a partner at Arthur Young.

Only three of the 50 or more accountants who waited in line for up to four hours got into the hearing room. Dozens of them had to watch the hearing on TV network monitors in the hall. Most of the 80 seats inside the hearing room were taken by the press and witnesses.

A Wild Bunch

The organizers of the event didn't have any idea that accountants could be so, well, excitable. "We never thought so many accountants would want to get in," says Michael Barrett, chief counsel and staff director of the subcommittee. The last time there were major hearings on accountants—in the late 1970s—there were, to no one's surprise, some empty seats.

With so many thrill-seeking accountants around, Mr. Barrett of the subcommittee says he may have to move the next hearing to a caucus room with more than 500 seats. "We apparently goofed this time," he says.

Samuel Hudgins, a managing partner at Arthur Andersen & Co., acknowledges that the stampede was quite a spectacle. "I'd never seen accountants trying to shove their way into a hearing room before," he says. "It's not like us."

And Now, Live from Costa Mesa, Sinatra Sings: 'I Debit It My Way'

By Lee Berton

August 8, 1986

Some accounting firms like to hire new CPAs from the best business schools. Other firms are partial to tax experts who have worked in the government.

And then there's Arthur Young & Co.'s Costa Mesa, California office. It appears to go for accountants whose names regularly appear in Variety.

Yes, this is the firm that sends Frank Sinatra to meetings of potential clients so it can draw big crowds. It assigns Tom Jones to audits, and women swoon. And it pages Jimmy Stewart on its office intercom while clients are around.

Are You Sitting Down?

The gag (and who says accountants aren't funny?) is that these aren't the *real* stars; they just have the same names. Still, says Richard Swintek, managing partner of the office, business is booming. And, he adds, the firm doesn't purposely hire show-business personalities. "It's a coincidence," he says.

Although Dean Martin and Peter Finch left the firm several years ago, famous names continue to win the firm some strange clients. Mr. Sinatra, 30, a principal in the tax department, says a client, a reputed barfly, told him that attending the client's Christmas party was part of Mr. Sinatra's job.

"He'd invited dozens of cocktail waitresses, who all showed up, but their jaws dropped when they saw me," adds Mr. Sinatra, who people say bears a slight resemblance to his namesake.

Mr. Jones, a 31-year-old audit manager, says his name is a great icebreaker for getting past secretaries. "They never forget my name and some even ask me to get up on a desk and sing. I'm still waiting for them to toss flowers and underwear as viewers do at singer Jones."

It's a Wonderful Life

Mr. Stewart, a 32-year-old audit partner, says he can always get his car out of a restaurant parking lot first if he's in a rush to get to a client. "The valets hear my name and push me up front," he adds.

Mr. Sinatra (the accountant, that is) recently attracted 110 top executives of high-tech companies to a seminar where he spoke on accelerating business growth. "We usually get only about 30 of our members but Sinatra's name and his outgoing style filled the hotel auditorium," notes an American Electronics Association official.

"Sinatra's been our biggest attention-grabber," says Peggy Krieger, manager of the association's Orange County office. "We're thinking of billing him as 'Ole Brown Eyes Is Back.'"

Wanted: Aloof, Sober Individuals to Act as Corporate Wet Blankets

By Lee Berton

February 5, 1987

After a long day of poring over the company's books and accounts, the average corporate controller is apt to be ready to unwind a bit with colleagues. Some may even feel like downing a few fingers of scotch, neat.

They had better steer clear of Daniel Ferguson. The vice chairman and chief executive officer of Naples, Florida–based Newell Co., a maker of household hardware and other items, warns that "cocktails and controllers don't mix."

'Mr. Stable'
In an article in the latest issue of Management Accounting, a monthly magazine for controllers and other financial officers, Mr. Ferguson writes that at Newell business functions "it's OK for sales guys to party, we expect that. But the controller is the guy we know is minding the till. He is Mr. Stable and can't afford to lose control. He has to be the minister, the chaplain, the respectable man."

Officials at the National Association of Accountants, which publishes *Management Accounting,* generally concur with this philosophy. "If you have a good sense of humor," says an NAA spokesman, "you don't make a good controller."

Some controllers, not surprisingly, don't agree. "The controller shouldn't be holier-than-thou," maintains Robert G. Weiss, vice president and controller of Shering-Plough Corp. in Madison, New Jersey. "A controller shouldn't get stiff," he adds, "but he shouldn't act stiffly, either."

Charles Stracuzzi, controller of a Blount Inc. grain-storage handling subsidiary in Grand Island, Nebraska, admits to drinking occasionally at company parties. "I can remember one Tucson, Arizona, outing last January where I had up to six drinks," he recalls. "But I try to clock myself so I don't take more than one drink per hour."

Mr. Ferguson notes that in his 21 years as Newell's CEO, the company has had five controllers—and none of them drank very much if at all. "A controller can't be the party guy," he explains.

Risking Trollhood
On the contrary, argues Leo J. Heile, controller for two ITT Corp. units. Today, he says, controllers are more involved in big transactions and "must be able to relate to everyone in the company on business and social levels." He worries that too little fun turns controllers into "trolls."

While Mr. Heile acknowledges that he "can't afford to play the buffoon," he doesn't think that means acting the cold fish. "I take a drink every now and then," he confesses, "and even get a bit silly."

Take Heart, CPAs: Finally a Story that Doesn't Attack You as Boring

By Lee Berton

May 13, 1987

Requesting entrance to Dartmouth College's business school, an honors student from a Midwest university wrote, "I chose an emphasize in accounting . . . because I intend on becoming a top executive."

Now that may not surprise people who have read a lot of financial statements. But John Shank, a Dartmouth business professor, was horrified. "Unfortunately too many accounting students are already Neanderthals as far as writing goes," he says. "What the American Institute of Certified Public Accountants wants to do will make them even worse."

Why Is Prof. Shank Mad?
And just what is the leading membership body for accountants doing to get Prof. Shank's dander up? It is proposing to make all the questions on the national CPA Exam multiple choice; now, essay questions account for 40% of the exam.

"Taking essays out of the exam will give accounting students even less incentive to improve their writing skills," says Prof. Shank.

Accounting organizations in New York, Texas and Florida also oppose getting rid of the essay questions. "It would deliver a message to students that writing is not important," says Robert Gray, executive director of the New York State Society of Certified Public Accountants.

The American Institute says that making the exam multiple choice would make it more objective, ease marking and shave a half-day off the 2½-day test. The institute will vote on the proposal later this year. About 140,000 accountants take the test each year—with passage mandatory for becoming a CPA.

"We're not so much interested in whether accountants can write well but whether they know the disciplines of accounting," says Jim Blum, the institute's director of exams.

Debitts and Creddits
But some accounting firms disagree, insisting that the lack of writing skills by new hires is a major problem.

"One of my big problems is to copyread the footnotes written by these graduates," says E. M. Campbell, managing partner of Campell & Wiggins in Winter Haven, Florida. "One recently wrote a footnote without any capitals, quotes, commas, colons and semicolons," he says. "It was just one long run-on sentence. Fortunately, I was able to correct it before my client saw it."

Not surprisingly, some students are happy to see the essays go. "They're too tricky, anyway," says a Texas graduate who just took the exam. "Without essays, I could guess the answers more easily."

Talk of CPAs: Rules, Image and Numbers

By Lee Berton

September 25, 1987

NEW YORK—This city was host to an unusual—some might say frightening—sight over the past week: 2,000 celebrating accountants.

The accountants were members of the American Institute of Certified Public Accountants, which turns 100 years old this year. Spending money they've earned from scrutinizing the books of business, government and nonprofit organizations, the CPAs snapped up theater tickets, sampled hors d'oeuvres in the Metropolitan Museum of Art and watched the Rockettes dance at Radio City Music Hall.

But hard issues such as rising liability exposure and the need to spot more management fraud in audits also took up a lot of time. "Public opinion polls say we're held in very high esteem by most people," says Philip B. Chenok, president of the institute, the leading membership group of 255,000 CPAs. "But we know that any slip (will mean) a big fall in confidence."

For close to a decade, certified public accountants, who serve as public watchdogs in auditing corporate books, have been regulating themselves.

But accountants are alarmed by the increasing number of malpractice lawsuits filed by disgruntled shareholders, lenders and suppliers of companies whose books were given clean opinions by accountants shortly before the companies had severe business problems.

So the American Institute of Certified Public Accountants is seeking new rules to require accounting firms that audit public companies to have mandatory "quality reviews" of their audit practices every three years by outside accountants. Such reviews currently are voluntary.

The institute also wants mandatory continuing professional education for all accountants. And it wants to raise education levels for CPAs to five years from the current four by the year 2000 and to strengthen its code of ethics.

Ballots go out in November to members, with two-thirds approval of those who vote needed for passage.

The accounting profession has a long way to go in hiring minorities for high positions, some accountants assert.

Bert N. Mitchell, managing partner of New York-based Mitchell/Titus & Co., a big black-run accounting firm in the United States, says there are "a lot more black lawyers and doctors than black CPAs."

Mr. Mitchell, the first black president of the New York State Society of CPAs, estimates that there are only about 3,000 black accountants in the United States—less than 1% of all CPAs in the nation.

"Blacks are almost invisible as Big Eight firm partners," says Mr. Mitchell. But that may be changing. Last year, Mitchell/Titus, which has eight black partners and one white partner, lost five black senior managers to personnel raids by Big Eight firms. "Five years ago, the big white-oriented firms wouldn't have touched our people with a 10-foot pole," he says.

Accountants often carp about numbers, so it's no surprise that some are nitpicking about their centennial. Eli Mason, a New York City accountant, says this year is really only the 91st anniversary of U.S. CPAs. He notes that New York passed the first state law licensing CPAs in 1896.

But Gary Previts, a Cleveland accounting professor and former president of the Academy of Accounting Historians, says the first U.S. accounting professional group, a predecessor of the institute, was formed in 1887. "They may not have been certified, but they were there a century ago," says Mr. Previts.

The institute asked the Postal Service to design a stamp to celebrate its centennial. The stamp has just been issued and shows a pen point on a ledger book—an image that many accountants want to avoid these days. Some accountants at the annual meeting say they would have preferred a more up-to-date image, like a computer, to show what accountants do. "The Post Office should have emphasized the profession's future rather than its past," says Ralph Rehmet, a New York accountant. "Thank heaven the stamp doesn't show a green eyeshade."

Accountants get picked on so much, that they really enjoy a joke at another profession's expense. That, anyway, explains why they are hysterical when humorist Art Buchwald tells them what a CPA does after messing up an audit and losing his license to practice. "He becomes a financial planner," Mr. Buchwald says.

There but for a Few Voice Lessons Might Have Gone All the Osmonds

By Lee Berton

June 7, 1988

Cherie Curtis's memories of her teen years might not be everyone's idea of a happy adolescence.

"I recall posting invoices, deposit slips or checks in accounting journals or ledgers with other kids in my family," says Mrs. Curtis, a 24-year-old resident of Farmer City, Illinois. "Accounting really got under our skin."

It Makes One Shudder

How did it get there? Home life is largely to blame. Mrs. Curtis's parents, George and Mary Monical of Pontiac, Illinois, are both certified public accountants—as are six of their 17 children. Mrs. Curtis, an accountant who works part-time for her parents, is now studying to make it seven.

"Sure, we take a lot of kidding," says Mrs. Monical, a former Fulbright scholar who passed her CPA exam last November. "People ask us if we're just in the business of raising tax deductions who will then help other people get tax deductions. I guess you can say that's true."

Mrs. Monical remembers the time, several years ago, when the Illinois Department of Revenue questioned the number of dependent deductions listed on the family's tax return. "'Can you believe that?' I asked my husband," she says. "Here we are with a house full of CPAs, and they doubt we can count our own children. They must be out of their minds."

Mr. Monical wrote the department a letter citing the family's numerical expertise—and joking that, nevertheless, some of the neighbor's kids might have mistakenly turned up in the count. They haven't been bothered since.

A Guy after Our Own Heart

Being around so many CPAs isn't always fun for those in the family who aren't caught up in the thrill of accountancy. Mrs.

Curtis says that her husband, Guy, who manages a restaurant, "got really irritated a while back when I was chatting with one of my CPA sisters about schedule C sole proprietorships, Sub S corporations and regulations about filing with the SEC." She adds: "Can you believe he found it dull and thought we were trying to keep him out of the conversation?"

Mrs. Monical, who says she "fell in love" with accounting after a single course, concedes that there are drawbacks to having such a large family. One is that, in phone calls, she often doesn't have a chance to gab about her favorite topic: "I would love to chat more about our professional problems. But with so many children and their families, by the time we get through talking about the family and the logistics of getting together, there's not enough time. Too bad."

Accountants as Heroes: It Doesn't Add Up

By Lee Berton

August 31, 1988

"Magnum, CPA"; Dr. Ruth "Westerner" discussing that dirty three-letter word, "tax"; Mr. Rogers telling kids whether it is better to own or lease their tricycles. An accountant's wildest fantasies?

Could be. But they also are listed as "possible new TV pilots" for the fall season in an academic paper recently published by educator William D. Samson.

Mr. Samson, an associate professor of accounting at the University of Alabama, wants very much to upgrade the image of the hapless accountant, who has been taking it in the neck for centuries.

You want examples of hapless? Try this: As the Roman Empire disintegrated, for many political, military and economic reasons, it naturally lost great swatches of territory, including Egypt. So who got blamed for losing Egypt? Accountants, naturally—for miscounting tax revenues and not informing the emperors that business was going badly in the provinces.

A modern example is Rep. John Dingell (D., Mich.) blaming accountants for failing to inform the nation years ago that banks and savings and loan associations had stretched their capital so thin that there would be rough times ahead.

It's bad enough accountants are scapegoats for imperial or corporate insolvency—they also are perceived as boring. Maybe that's because people catch them reading things like "Predictive Achievement and Simulated Decision Makers as an Extension of the Predictive Ability Criterion." Definitely not a heavy-breather.

In his paper, Mr. Samson concedes the accountant is often thought of as "a wimp, a humorless clod [and] a dull, hard-working, passionless android." Perhaps if accountants could see themselves as TV heroes they might have more self-confidence and be popular at cocktail parties, he says. Then "people will strain to hear their latest exploits of ticking, testing, tying, tracing, reconciling and footing."

No way, CPA. Even the managing partner of a fairly big accounting firm concedes that one of his best managers was "so dull we used to slip his lunch in under a closed door to his office. Thank heaven he liked pizza."

Gary Previts, past president of the Academy of Accounting Historians and an accounting professor at Case Western Reserve University in Cleveland, puts the problem in historical perspective. "Even in the early 1800s, most educators thought that outside of law, medicine and the clergy, the business professions didn't employ the higher powers of the mind."

The problem that accountants encounter with their public persona, says Mr. Previts, is that "we have a perception as opposed to an identity, and the two get co-mingled unfairly. We generally suffer from a certain stuffiness and lack the ability to enjoy ourselves and our limitations." In other words, except for a few like Mr. Samson, most accountants don't like to joke about themselves.

Mr. Samson believes accountants should loosen up. In his paper, he imagines them writing mysteries about intrigue in CPA firms, struggling for power as partners of a family firm (sound familiar?) and searching in outer space for "perfect tax systems which all citizens perceive as fair." In his sitcom, the perfect system is one that doesn't tax at all.

Because accountants tend to take themselves so very seriously, it took Mr. Samson a while to get his paper published: The July issue of *Management Accounting,* a monthly magazine of the National Association of Accounting in Montvale, New Jersey, carried it. But this was after four other accounting journals and two academic journals rejected the piece as unsuitable for their audiences, Mr. Samson says.

Now that it's been published, Mr. Samson says he hasn't received any hate mail from accountants, no one has tried to bar him from practice as a CPA, and all five of his dogs remain healthy. "Therefore," he concludes, either "accountants weren't offended or accountants don't read."

Actually, Mr. Samson may be on the leading edge. In the movie "Midnight Run," Charles Grodin is a mild-mannered CPA with a sense of humor who steals from the mob to give to charity. And the Comic Strip, a New York nightclub for comedians, has slotted an amateur night for "funny CPAs" only. Watch out, Bob Newhart! Here come more wisecracking accountants. Mr. Newhart gave up accountancy for comedy decades ago.

As in Accounting, Timing Is Crucial in Stand-Up Comedy

Delivery Is Key in Both, Too; the Bottom Line on Jokes Accountants Tell on Stage

By Lee Berton

October 18, 1988

NEW YORK—Children play doctor, nurse, fireman and policeman. "But why don't they play accountant?" wonders Howard Bookbinder, a 49-year-old accountant from Fair Lawn, New Jersey.

Mr. Bookbinder knows that the very thought is preposterous, and he is playing it for laughs. But the audience here at a club called the Comic Strip is merely polite, rewarding him with just a few chuckles. Mr. Bookbinder, who is sharp with a tax-man's pencil, is learning a thing or two about timing and delivery in stand-up comedy.

Accountancy's keenest wits are working the room tonight, vying for the title "Funniest Accountant in America." Contestants are office wags who often convulse their colleagues—other accountants—but then, they may be easily amused. Tonight's program features 13 finalists in a contest dreamed up by a Manhattan executive-recruiter, Mitchell Berger. It is probably the only talent search for comics ever to have been announced in *Accounting Today,* a weekly newspaper for you know who.

Funny Down Deep

Mr. Berger, of Howard-Sloan Associates, aims to change popular conceptions of the profession. "I want to prove to the world," he says, "that not only are accountants not boring, but underneath their cool, calculating and meticulous exteriors, they are wild and crazy guys." But then Mr. Berger isn't an accountant.

Some real comedians doubt the proposition. Comic-turned-TV sitcom director David Steinberg says that accountants are more often the butt of other people's jokes than the creators of their own. "A 'funny accountant' is an oxymoron, a contradiction in terms like 'business ethics,'" Mr. Steinberg says. "Accountants may want to be funny, but they're everybody's grownups, telling us what we can and cannot do. Let's face it. Only people who don't mind acting like children are funny. And people want their accountants to be levelheaded and deadly earnest. No giggles, please, when you look at my tax return."

Comedian Jackie Mason is aghast that accountants would even want to be funny. A big laugh-getter in his own act, Mr. Mason says, is the one about a Jewish family's greatest accomplishment: to have a son become a doctor. "But if he's a little retarded, a lawyer. And if his mind doesn't work at all, an accountant."

What, No Stage Fright?

Mr. Mason has trouble envisioning accountants seeking the limelight. "When you say hello to accountants," he says, "they usually hide behind a pole or under a desk, they're so shy."

But tonight at the Comic Strip, there is nowhere to hide. Mike Sweeney, a comedy-club veteran acting as master of ceremonies, warms up the audience of 235, most of them friends and relatives of contestants. He says: "Accountants invented actuaries so they could laugh at someone else."

Then Mr. Sweeney holds up two fingers behind his head. "That's the Big Eight symbol for 'I'm a nerd,'" he says. The audience roars.

Gary Press, a 26-year-old manager at Siegel, Sacks & Co., a small New York accounting firm, bounds on stage. His shtick: how tough it is to get laughs on the job. "I don't think my clients would be thrilled if I asked them, 'Guess what has two arms and two legs and owes the IRS $2 million?'" he says.

Moments later, he brings down the house by remarking: "An accountant trying to be a comedian makes as much sense as the Mormon Tabernacle Choir performing at Woodstock."

Some members of the audience hold up big photos of Mr. Press. "Do you work for him?" Mr. Sweeney asks these accounting groupies.

One woman nods, prompting the emcee to observe: "What a coincidence that you're here tonight."

Though many of the contestants wear open shirts, jeans and other standard comedy-club attire, Michael Mondaruli has chosen a jacket, tie—and hat—for his moment in the spotlight. The 35-year-old accountant with Schachter & Co. tries a joke about the fictitious CPA firm of Schachter & Corleone: "Corleone only does contracts." No reaction. He doggedly presses on, with the one about the eye doctor who tells the accountant to "cover one eye and read the bottom line." The accountant asks, "Before or after taxes?" More silence.

Then Mr. Mondaruli suggests some new TV shows: "Arthur Young & the Restless," "The Price is Right Waterhouse" and "Ernst & Whinney the Pooh." Glasses clink, chairs scrape, people cough.

As Mr. Mondaruli exits, Mr. Sweeney suggests brightly: "You can depreciate that last act on your Schedule C next year." He then bursts into a song based on "It's a Small World," spoofing a Walt Disney World exhibit he calls the "Hall of Accountants." "It's a world of tax fraud," he chirps, "it's a world of jail. . . ." This time laughter explodes.

Long Form

From a ringside table, Sam Hoyt, a media-relations manager for the American Institute of Certified Public Accountants, urges that the master of ceremonies pick up the pace. Each accountant is supposed to limit his bit to five minutes, and most are running long.

"It's hard for accountants to be funny," Mr. Hoyt says. "Most of them maintain their professional demeanor almost unconsciously, no matter where they are." Maybe so. But many of the written and videotaped entries from which these finalists were culled were so obscene as to be eliminated out of hand. So much for decorum.

The next act is Martin Edelstein, the 32-year-old director of taxes at M. Bernstein & Co. He announces that "attendance here tonight qualifies for two units of CPE credit." CPE stands for continuing professional education, and every accountant does have to spend about 40 hours in the classroom each year. Mr. Edelstein is kidding, of course.

"People are walking out in protest," Mr. Sweeney observes, to no one in particular. The crowd is indeed thinning out, even as Frank Dodge, a 52-year-old San Francisco accountant, flashes the license plate from his car, "TAX DODG." Wayne Deering, a 37-year-old accountant from Kalamazoo, Michigan, steps up and surveys what's left of the crowd. "I haven't seen so many people since my trial," he says.

Emptying the House

By the time the last act appears, nearly a third of the audience has fled. Nonetheless, Irwin Mittleman, a 35-year-old CPA from Maplewood, New Jersey, proceeds gamely. "Accountants," he ventures, "are so boring that if they were drowning and their whole life [flashed] before them, they'd probably fall asleep."

Out in the audience, Mr. Mittleman's wife, Penny, confides that it's hard to have a lot of fun with so many accountants around. "Except for my husband, I try not to associate with them," she says.

As the evening comes to an end, Mr. Press walks away with the title and the grand prize, a videocassette recorder. He is the unanimous choice of three judges—the publisher of *Accounting Today,* the club's manager, and Scott Blakeman, the former co-host of "Funny People," an amateur comedy show televised on NBC last summer.

Mr. Blakeman, 33, who teaches a course in stand-up comedy at the New School for Social Research here, says it's a lot easier for salesmen and housewives to be hilarious than for accountants. "It doesn't seem to be in their nature," he says, adding: "My aunt used to do my tax return, but she got out of accounting because she was too funny."

Picture the Marlboro Man Sporting Horn-Rims and a Pocket Protector

By Lee Berton

October 31, 1988

Those who saw the decline of the West in TV commercials for lawyers might want to avoid downtown Los Angeles. For, sitting on the side of Olympia Boulevard, there's now a billboard ad for a certified public accounting firm.

Stonefield & Josephson, which had the sign put up in early September, realizes that courting recognition in this way is bound to raise some eyebrows.

To Boldly Go ...
"We know that not another accounting firm would be caught dead advertising on a billboard," says Joel Stonefield, the firm's managing partner. "Other accountants may call us unprofessional and ungentlemanly, but we think it works."

It used to be that professional-ethics rules prohibited advertising of any kind by accounting firms. But in the late 1970s, federal regulators, citing antitrust laws, forced accountants and other professionals to drop such bans. Since then, most CPA firms have stuck to such media as newspapers and trade publications.

"It's beyond my understanding that any CPA firm would use a billboard," says Jerrold Hunt, the partner in charge of Price

Waterhouse's Sacramento, California office and president of the 28,000-member California Society of Certified Public Accountants. "You don't sell professional services with jazzy advertising."

The 14 foot by 48 foot billboard shows a chart with sales climbing and profits dropping. "There are a million stories like this . . ." the copy warns. Then—"For the select few"—the ad gives the firm's name and phone number. The one-year campaign, during which the billboard will be moved among six sites within Los Angeles, is costing the firm $42,000.

'What Next?'

Gerald McClosky, president of Ad Management Services, the Los Angeles creative firm that designed the ad, says he pushes clients to try new approaches. At first, he suggested a client newsletter to Stonefield & Josephson's eight partners, who felt it wasn't their cup of tea. "One even asked, 'What next, billboards?'" Mr. McClosky recalls. "And another partner asked, 'Why not?'"

Mr. Stonefield concedes that he at first thought the billboard idea was "stupid." Now, however, he says that with the first promotional frontier crossed, "there may be no limit to where this can take us—blimps, skywriting, baseball scoreboards—as long as we get proper recognition."